Linguistische
Arbeiten 386

Herausgegeben von Hans Altmann, Peter Blumenthal, Herbert E. Brekle,
Gerhard Helbig, Hans Jürgen Heringer, Heinz Vater und Richard Wiese

Phonology and Morphology of the Germanic Languages

Edited by
Wolfgang Kehrein and Richard Wiese

Max Niemeyer Verlag
Tübingen 1998

Die Deutsche Bibliothek – CIP-Einheitsaufnahme

Phonology and morphology of the Germanic languages / ed. by Wolfgang Kehrein and Richard Wiese. – Tübingen : Niemeyer, 1998
(Linguistische Arbeiten ; 386)

ISBN 3-484-30386-7 ISSN 0344-6727

Gedruckt auf alterungsbeständigem Papier.
Druck: Weihert-Druck GmbH, Darmstadt
Buchbinder: Industriebuchbinderei Nädele, Nehren

Table of contents

Section III: Morphology

Wolfgang Kehrein and Richard Wiese

Preface

Phonology and morphology are those subdisciplines of linguistics which both deal with the properties that give words their shapes, and which help to define the relationships between words. The contributions collected in the present volume apply principles of phonology and morphology to the Germanic languages. In other words, this volume deals with the formal structure of words in the Germanic languages. The Germanic languages belong to the best-studied languages of the world; yet, many descriptive and theoretical questions are still open to debate. This may be surprising at first blush, but is the result of new theoretical perspectives and of a more and of more stringent approach to the study of word structures. Furthermore, even for well-studied languages new facts come to light with surprising frequency, and often under the guidance of those new theoretical perspectives.

On the level of descriptive phenomena, the interplay between phonological, in particular prosodic, structures and morphological principles or even idiosyncratic information is of particular importance in present-day research. We have labelled the middle section of this book "Prosodic Morphology", but this aspect of current work plays a role in other contributions as well. All of the contributions in the "Morphology" section, in fact, postulate some amount of prosodic structure to be relevant for morphology. Conversely, most of the papers in the section labelled "Phonology" address prosodic issues and have something to say on the shape of words. After all, the phoneme has almost always been defined as the minimal unit distinguishing words (or morphemes).

On the level of theoretical frameworks, it is some variant of a constraint-based approach which is in the focus of present work and of the papers in this volume. Constraints, in their simplest version, say what an item should look like, and are either violable (as in Optimality Theory) or inviolable (as in most versions of Computational Phonology.) Constraints, at present most notably in Optimality Theory, are therefore suitable tools for linguistic analysis and are readily applied to the problem of describing the gestalts of words. Interface problems, such as those between phonological and morphological structures, can also be addressed by constraints.

The study of a typologically (or otherwise) related set of languages is particularly revealing in establishing how languages vary. In this connection, we note that the papers in this volume address phonological and morphological isssues from the whole (European) range of Germanic languages, from Icelandic in the North-West to Alemannic German in the South. However, the languages spoken by larger populations, namely English, German, and Dutch, receive more attention here than the "smaller" languages. Furthermore, the reader will find comparative analyses of phenomena across the Germanic languages. The phonological phenomena studied within these languages range from subsegmental units in phonology over the classical problems of phonemic contrast versus redundancy to prosodic properties, such as syllables, pitch accents, stress patterns, etc. Topics on the morphological side include aspects of the whole hierarchy of units, starting with roots and other morphemes, but also addressing problems of derivational and inflectional nature up to larger units such as words (versus phrases). But prosodic properties, such as syllables and feet, tones, stress patterns, etc., are in the focus of many discussions.

The present papers result from a workshop by the same name at the Philipps-Universität Marburg, Germany, in August 1997, organized by the editors of this volume. Financial and other support for this conference (and thereby for the present volume) from the Philipps-Universität, the Institut für Germanistische Sprachwissenschaft and the Marburger Universitätsbund is greatly appreciated.

Most contributors to this volume (and Curt Rice, University of Tromsø) have served as reviewers of papers, thereby increasing the quality of the papers and the cross-fertilizing between ideas and proposals; Hanna Christiansen and Carmen Scherer deserve special thanks for their help with the production of the volume.

Marburg, April 1998

Section I: Phonology

Kristján Árnason

Vowel shortness in Icelandic

1. Introduction[1]

1.1. The traditional analysis, and some problems

There is general agreement that a distinction between long and short segments is phonologically significant in both consonants and vowels in Icelandic. And it is also not a matter of dispute that the distribution of long and short segments follows some relatively clear rules. Vowel length is (indirectly) dependent on consonantal structure, and vice versa. According to the most widely accepted view, vowel length is not phonemic in the traditional sense, but governed by a rule, which lengthens or shortens vowels according to the environment. The most prosaic statement of the rule is that vowels are long before one or no consonant within the same word, as in *man* [ma:n] 'remember', *mana* [ma:na], 'to egg on', but short before two or more consonants (barring an exception which will be described later): *land* [land] 'land (nom.sg.)' *landa* [landa] 'land (gen.pl.)'. In this spirit, pairs like *man* [ma:n] 'remember' and *mann* [man:] 'man', where there is a non-minimal distinction, since neither [man] nor [ma:n:] occurs, have been analysed on the phonemic level as respectively /man/ and /mann/ with underlying distinctions in consonantal structure. According to the traditional statements, vowel length (and consonant length) is only relevant in stressed syllables, and all unstressed vowels are short.

Although this picture looks relatively clear, and many of the arguments that have been used in analyses like that of Benediktsson (1963) and Árnason (1980) seem to carry considerable force, there are certain aspects of the structure that have not been dealt with properly. One of these is the so-called half-length of consonants, a phenomenon, which has been noted for a long time, but never properly analysed. Consonants after short vowels and before other consonants, as in *hestur* [hɛsˑtʏr̥] 'horse' and *vindur* [vɪnˑtʏr̥] 'wind' are described as half long by phoneticians such as Guðfinnsson (1946:69), Ófeigsson (1921:XIX), and Einarsson (1927:77). It has never been clear how this phenomenon should fit into the simple model assumed in Benediktsson's analysis in 1963. The only place where this is dealt with in the phonological literature is in Haugen's analysis (1958), and Thráinsson's treatment of preaspiration (1978). Another part of the structure, which needs clarification, is the relation between stress and vowel length. The usual statement that vowel length is only relevant under stress, and that all unstresssed vowels are short, is worthy of reconsideration. It will be shown that vowel shortness is not of one kind.

---

[1] I am grateful to Janet Grijzenhout, Wolfgang Kehrein and Richard Wiese for comments on an earlier version of this paper.

1.2. Some terms

Before going further, clarification is in order concerning some of the terms that will be used in the discussion.

I will use the term *Duration* to mean actual duration of chunks of speech, segments, syllables, and feet.

Phonological length of segments refers to phonological structure in segments, having an effect on duration, and this will be used to refer to length of segments, irrespective of whether that length is underlying or distinctive in traditional terms.

Syllable structure means phonological structure of syllables having an effect on duration and rhythm.

A distinction will be made in the following discussion between what may be called *accidental length/shortness* and *structural length/shortness*. As shown in (1), the tradition is that vowels are transcribed phonetically as long only in stressed (initial) syllables:

(1)	*kvistir*	[kfɪsˑtɪr̥]	'branches'
	kvikindi	[kfɪːcʰɪntɪ]	'creature'
	suður	[sʏːðʏr]	'south'
	skurður	[skʏrˑðʏr]	'ditch'
	spurull	[spʏːrʏtl̥]	'inquisitive'

In words like *kvistir* and *skurður* in (1), the transcription indicates that [ɪ] and [ʏ] are short in both syllables of each word. But the shortness of the first and second vowel of each word is not of one kind, as I will illustrate.

The initial syllables of all the words in (1) have word stress, and having word stress means being assigned the intonational accent, when the word is rhythmically strong in an utterance. This involves increased duration of what here will be called the *nucleus* of the syllable, and the nucleus is that portion of the syllable where stress is realized. (Allen (1973) uses the term *stress matrix* to refer to the portion of the word where stress is realized. In that context we can say that the nucleus of the syllable forms the stress matrix in Icelandic, but other languages may have disyllabic stress matrices according to Allen.) The effect of stress that is relevant to the discussion in this paper is lengthening or increased duration of the nucleus. In a form like *skurður*, the vowel is *structurally short*. Being structurally short means that the vowel cannot form the nucleus by itself, instead, the consonant is lengthened. This lengthening of the consonant is the traditionally termed "half length" as indicated in the transcription of *kvistir* and *skurður*. If the vowel is *structurally long*, as in *suður*, the stress is realized on the vowel, which is lengthened in proportion to the amount of stress.

The shortness of the vowels in the second syllables as transcribed in (1) is different from the shortness in the initial syllables. Since these syllables do not have the word accent, under normal conditions their duration is likely to be less than that of vowels in (word) stressed syllables; they are less prominent and not as likely to be lengthened by intonation or sentence stress. But in spite of this, these vowels can in fact be said to be structurally long, and may be lengthened under certain conditions, for example when they are in focus and get "contrastive" stress. This is exemplified in utterances like (2), where the endings are emphasised in order to make clear the appropriate inflectional form:

(2) Fleirtalan af *kvistur* er *kvistIR* [kfɪstɪːr̥], ekki *kvistAR* [kfɪstaːr̥]
The plural of *kvistur* ('branch') is *kvistIR*, not *kvistAR*

In words like *kvikindi* and *spurull*, however, the vowels are not lengthened, even if they get a contrastive accent, and this is because they are what we call structurally short (and the consonants may become "half long" if the stress is strong). The second vowels of *kvistir* and *suður*, are, then, structurally long (because only one consonant follows), but their accidental length varies.

We note that accidental length/shortness is not the same as actual duration. The accidental length/shortness of a segment is only one of the factors that have an effect on duration.

1.3. Long and short vowels

Assuming that there is a phonologically significant distinction between structurally long and short vowels, there are several ways that can be thought of, pre-theoretically, as to how they should be analysed. Some of these are listed below:

(3)
a. There is a fundamental or phonemic distinction between two sets of vowels that has an effect on duration and rhythm.
b. A distinction between long and short vowels is not fundamental or phonemic; rather phonological length is derived indirectly, from syllable structure or from structure on the skeletal tier.
c. Some sort of combination of both. It is possible to say that there is a phonemic distinction in vowel length and that there are also rules for their distribution, stated in terms of syllabic structure, or on a skeletal or moraic tier. Thus, the short/long vowels fit into different syllable trees or skeletal templates, not unlike nouns and verbs attach to different nodes in syntactic trees. This sort of arrangement can either be pictured with the trees or skeletal templates as the primary structure, or with the segmental structure as primary and the skeletal structure as secondary, as if built up on the basis of the structure of the segments. But it is also possible that the question of which comes first, segmental or skeletal/syllabic structure is not significant.

It will be argued here that vowel length is phonologically distinctive in Icelandic in the sense that phonological relations refer to a "phonemic" distinction between long and short vowels, and that such a distinction has an effect on rhythmical structure, such as syllabification; and this in turn has an effect on the surface duration of chunks of speech. Basically, it will be argued that the Icelandic system is the same as the Norwegian and Swedish one, where vowel length is distinctive even if the distribution is predictable to a certain degree (cf. Eliasson 1985, Lorenz 1996, Kristoffersen 1997).

1.4. The structure of this paper

Section 2 describes the Icelandic vowel system, arguing that vowel length is distinctive, and showing that there is complementarity of vowel length and consonant length. Section 3 describes the relation between vowel length and syllabification, showing that there is an interesting difference between lexical and postlexical structure. The different constraints concerning syllabification are described. Section 4 considers the problem of how to represent vowel shortness, concluding with a suggestion that the short vowels be characterised as "nonmoraic". Section 5 proposes to analyse consonant length in terms of gemination, and section 6 present a brief comparison with languages like English, German and Latin, which have short vowels, but differ from Icelandic in allowing disyllabic stress matrices.

2. Long and short vowels in Icelandic

2.1. The vowel system

The vowel system of Modern Standard Icelandic has the following eight monophthongal vowel qualities, which according to standard analysis have long or short allophones depending on the environment:

(4)	High	i			u
	Hig-mid	ɪ	ʏ		
	Low-mid	ɛ	œ		ɔ
	Low			a	

In addition to this, there are five diphthongal phonemes, all of them falling:

(5) /ai/, /ei/, /œi/, /au/, /ou/

These also occur both as long and short, according to the same rule as for monophthongs.

The rule of thumb, the "length rule", is that a vowel is structurally short if it is in a closed syllable and structurally long if it is in an open syllable. Accordingly, *vo.rið* [vɔːrɪθ] 'the spring' has a long vowel in an open first syllable, whereas *hes.tur* [hɛsˑtʏr̥] 'horse' has a short vowel in a closed first syllable. Certain clusters, such as *pj*, *sv* and *kr*, as in *nepja* [nɛːpʰja] 'cold weather', tvisvar [tʰvɪːsvar̥] 'twice' and sykra [sɪːkʰra] 'to sugar', have long vowels before them and this can be attributed to the fact that the clusters in question form onsets to the following syllables. Word final consonants are extrametrical, giving a long environment in forms like *vor* [vɔːr̥] 'spring'.

The most common formulation of the length rule in processual metaphors is that vowels are lengthened in open syllables (Árnason 1980, Kiparsky 1984), i.e. the syllabification is part of the input, and the output gives the segmental length. A slightly more complicated analysis, involving two rules, is presented in Anderson (1984). Anderson assumes that first a consonant is included in the nucleus if another consonant follows, and the vowel, as a consequence becomes short, and after that a complementary rule lengthens vowels in lengthening environments. Whatever the details, the general view is that vowel length and syllabification go hand in hand but that the conditioning factor is the syllabification. But this formulation contains a chicken and egg problem: Are the vowels structurally short because they are in closed syllables or are they in closed syllables because they are structurally short?

2.2. Arguments for distinctive segmental length

In this section we will look at some arguments that, in spite of the predictability of the distribution of long and short vowels, support the idea that the distinction between structurally long and short vowels is in fact distinctive or phonemic in some sense.

2.2.1. A historical argument: diphthongization and merger (*flámæli*)

The structurally long low-mid vowels, /ɛ/, /œ/ and /ɔ/, as represented in (4), tend to diphthongize by forming high onglides. This diphthongization is most evident when the vowels are lengthened by stress, as shown in (6):

(6)	*fögur*	[fʏœːɣʏr̥]	'pretty'
	tekur	[tʰɪɛːkʰʏr̥]	'comes'
	sofa	[sʊɔːva]	'sleep'

The diphthongization happens only in structurally long vowels, but not in structurally short vowels, such as in *þröstur* 'thrush', *hestur* 'horse', *kostur* 'option'. Pronunciations like [θrʏœstʏr̥], [hɪɛstʏr̥] and [kʰʊɔstʏr̥] are abnormal. Even if the vowels in these forms have a relatively long duration under extra heavy stress, they stay monophthongal. This shows that what is relevant is the structural length, and not the accidental length or actual duration.

The diphthongal character of the structurally long vowels is not always as clear in pronunciation, and it varies with duration as a function of stress. When the vowels are less stressed and shorter, the diphthongal quality is less clear. This variation might be seen as due to a diphthongization of underlying monophthongs, due to increased duration or the addition of morae under stress. But it could equally well be looked on the other way, so that the normal pronunciation is diphthongal, and the monophthongal allophones are then due to less clear articulation of diphthongal vowels when unstressed or short. Actually, the fact that the vowels in *þröstur*, *hestur* and *kostur* do not diphthongize when lengthened supports the latter. In that case, historically speaking, the diphthongization applies to a well-defined set of vowels, namely structurally long low-mid vowels.

But although it can be argued that there is such a category as "structurally long low-mid vowels", this obviously does not prove that vowel length is phonemic, since it could be said that the openness of the syllable is the relevant factor, or it might be maintained that contextually defined (but still relatively abstract) bimoricness of the long vowels (by a rule which states that vowels are bimoraic in open syllables) was responsible for the diphthongization, so that we are dealing with a sort of split of the vowel colour between the two morae. But this contextually defined bimoricness would then of course have to be reverted to monomoricness in unstressed positions.

New light is shed on the facts of diphthongization when they are compared with the facts of another innovation in Modern Icelandic. This is the so-called *flámæli* (slack jawed speech), which is a merger of the respectively rounded and unrounded high mid vowels /ɪ/ and /ʏ/ with the corresponding low mid vowels /ɛ/ and /œ/. This merger is confined to the structurally long vowels. Thus, long /ɪ/ in *skyr* ([scɪ:r] in the standard dialect) 'a kind of yoghurt' lowers and merges with long /ɛ/, as in *sker* ([scɪɛ:r̥] in the standard) 'reef'. And similarly long /ʏ/, as in *flug* ([flʏ:x] in the standard) 'flight' lowers and merges with long /œ/ as in *flög* ([flʏœ:x] in the standard) 'piece of ground without vegetation (pl.)'. This dialect feature, which started to emerge in the 19th century, had its heyday in the first half of the 20th century. It became subjected to heavy stigmatisation and is now almost extinct and only occurs in the speech of older people. This variant is thus about to be ousted by the more conservative "correct" dialect. As an example of the *flámæli* dialect, I use the speech of speaker ÓÞ, who was born in 1908. (The recording was made in 1986).

A detailed analysis of ÓÞ's speech shows that he has a clear merger in the structurally long system, and no merger in the structurally short system. Thus he can be said to have the two systems pictured in (7) and (8):

(7) Structurally long vowels:

High	i			u
Mid	ɛ [ɪɛ]	œ [ʏœ]		ɔ [ʊɔ]
Low			a	

(8) Structurally short vowels:

High	i			u
Hig-mid	ɪ	ʏ		
Low-mid	ɛ	œ		ɔ
Low			a	

A simple way of looking at the *flámæli* as a phonological and a historical phenomenon is as a spontaneous change, basically involving a lowering of the long high-mid vowels, so that they merge with the corresponding low-mid ones. This basically involves the abolition of structurally long /ɪ/ and /ʏ/. And since the merger does not affect the structurally short vowels, we need some means of identifying the vowels that participate in the merger, or conversely the ones that do not.

An example which shows the interplay of diphthongization and merger is the form *árið* 'the year', when pronounced by speaker ÓÞ with a distinct contrastive or emphatic stress on the second syllable, and appropriate lengthening of the second vowel. The form that emerges has a lowered and diphthongized second vowel: [au:rɪɛ:θ], (actually, the form has stress on both syllables, as is indicated by the length marks). The relation to the "correct speech" form [au:rɪθ] thus shows first that the structurally long /ɪ/ of the second syllable is affected by the *flámæli*-merger, and secondly that the vowel is diphthongal, at least when lengthened. The second vowel of *árið* is a structurally long vowel, even if it is "accidentally short" most of the time, being an unstressed vowel by principles of word stress. The traditional descriptions of *flámæli* state that it is most likely to occur in long vowels, but less likely to affect short vowels (Guðfinnsson 1964:81-2). What [au:rɪɛ:θ] shows is that we are dealing with structural length, irrespective of accidental length. Structurally short vowels are unaffected by *flámæli* in ÓÞ's speech.

Thus again, structural length or shortness is something which must be identified independently of surface duration or moraicity, and this identification is needed for two processes, which are manifested in the speech of ÓÞ. The "slack-jawed speech" affects structurally long high-mid vowels and makes them low-mid, and the diphthongization affects low-mid structurally long vowels; the structurally short vowels are unaffected in both cases. It is as if they are "protected" against these processes.

But we may again ask whether the mid vowels in the final syllables of words like *árið* and *gestur* 'guest' in ÓÞ's dialect are „underlying" monophthongs, which become diphthongs when they are long, or whether they are monophthongs that become diphthongs when short. A detailed phonetic investigation of the flámæli dialect is needed to determine the exact pronunciation of the accidentally short, but structurally long, vowels of forms like these, but it seems that they are simply reduced vèrsions of the underlying diphthongs, although they sound monophthongal when especially weak. Similarly, in the "correct speech"-dialect, the accidentally short occurrences of /ɛ/, /œ/ and /ɔ/ in contexts like in (9) quite often sound indistinct and could be transcribed as monophthongal.

(9)	Hann *er* asni	[hanɛrastnɪ]	'He's an idiot'
	Einst*ök* heppni	[einstœkhɛhpnɪ]	'Special luck'
	Jón *og* Gunna	[jounɔkʏna]	'John and Gunna'

A similar tendency for reduction of short diphthongs toward monophthongs takes place in (accidentally or structurally) short diphthongs in forms like *frábær* 'excellent' and *hæstur* 'highest'. In elaborate speech these are pronounced as [frau:bair̥] and [haistʏr̥], but in less careful pronunciation, the diphthong /ai/ starts to sound like [æ], or even [a]: [frau:bær̥]/ [frau:bar̥], [hæstʏr̥]/[hastʏr̥]. Here the historical background is clearly that the diphthongs are the basic forms. And in view of this, the simplest assumption is that the vowels /ɛ/, /œ/ and /ɔ/ are in fact phonologically diphthongal, and the monophthongal character of the reduced forms is phonetic. (It may be noted that the „new" diphthongs are rising, but the old ones are falling, and the monophthongization affects the less syllabic parts of the diphthongs.)

It was mentioned above that a possible interpretation of the diphthongization of the low-mid vowels /ɛ/, /œ/ and /ɔ/ would be to identify them as (structurally) bimoraic and to see the diphthongization as due to bimoricness. Such an interpretation of the merger involved in the *flámæli* is far less plausible, however. There is no obvious reason why the merger should affect bimoraic vowels. If anything, a merger should be more likely to occur in short or monomoraic vowels, where the quality of the vowels is likely to be less distinctly realized. Instead, the merger occurs in those vowels that have the greatest chance of being realized in full. A more plausible interpretation is to assume that the merger is a spontaneous, systematic, merger of the structurally long vowels. Spontaneous change is of course a somewhat mysterious concept, but such changes are known to occur, i.e. changes that cannot be related directly to any environment or take place unless otherwise stated. We can say that *flámæli* occurs, unless restricted by some special environment, and the restricting environment is structural shortness. And in fact we could treat diphthongization in the same way. There is no fundamental contradiction in assuming that diphthongization is a spontaneous change, checked by whatever feature or structural property it is that distinguishes the short vowels. (Aspiration and preaspiration of hard stops is a case of what would seem like spontaneous diphthongisation withour moraicity being involved. And in fact, as shown by Hayes 1990, autosegmental theory is not very well fit anyway to account for diphthongization.)

What the facts of diphthongization and *flámæli* show is that structural length, or shortness is relevant in the phonological structure of Icelandic, and it is here suggested that both processes are general, unconditioned changes that affect the vowel system, unless checked by structural shortness.

This argument is based on the neogrammarian hypothesis; namely that all and only the members of a category undergo the same change, barring some constraining environments. Thus the fact that the /ɪ/ in the first syllable of *vinur* 'friend', and in the second syllable of *árið* participate in the same way in both merger and diphthongization, show that they are in some sense the same, and distinct from the short /ɪ/ in *vindur*. This is exactly similar to the Grimm's law correspondence between Indo-European /p/ and Germanic /f/, except in special surroundings like after /s/. I.e. something happens to all occurrences of a phoneme, barring some special circumstance.

2.2.2. A morphophonemic argument: Output-Output correspondence

As discussed by Árnason (1980), Kiparsky (1984) and Benua (1995), action nouns can be derived from verbs like *sötra* 'to sip' *grenja* 'to cry' and *klifra* 'to climb', by simple truncation of the final vowel, forming nouns like *sötr* 'the act of sipping', *grenj* 'the act of crying' and *klifr* (beside *klifur*) 'the act of climbing'. In this paradigm, the vowel length of the base forms is preserved in the truncated forms, i.e. a long vowel in *sötr* and short vowels in *grenj* and *klifr*, as shown in (10).

(10)	*sötra*	[sʏœːtʰra]	'to sip'	-	*sötr*	[sʏœːtʰr̥]	'the act of sipping'
	grenja	[krɛnja]	'to cry'	-	*grenj*	[krɛnj]	'the act of crying'
	klifra	[kʰlɪvra]	'to climb'	-	*klifr*	[kʰlɪvr]	'the act of climbing'

The structural length or shortness of the vowels is thus preserved through what in terms of Correspondence Theory is classified as Output-Output correspondence. This is an indication that structural length is a systematic distinction that is relevant in paradigm like the ones in (10). And if we can decide exactly which part of the structure is relevant (e.g. vowel length or syllabification), we may use that as evidence in trying to isolate the relevant characteristic.

According to Benua (1995), the syllabification in a truncated form like *sötr* is different from the syllabification of a base form like *sötra*, and what is copied from the base form to the truncated form is vowel length, and not syllabification. If this is correct, we could take it directly as an argument that some sort of phonemic vowel length is independent of syllabification. But this argument is conclusive only to the extent that we can exclude the possibility that the syllable structure is preserved, or that /tr/ in *sötr* is somehow extrametrical and forms an onset to some empty nucleus.

Similar effects occur in the forms in (11):

(11) *vit* [vɪ:t^{h}] 'intelligence', *vits* [vɪts] or [vɪ:ts] 'id. genitive'

Here, there is optionality, as to whether the vowel length of the nominative form (call it the Base form) is copied in the genitive. By all normal standards, we would assume that the final /t/, which is extrametrical in *vit* [vɪ:t] should become part of a closed syllable in the genitive *vits*. The only way to keep the syllable in [vɪ:ts] open is to assume either that /t/ governs an empty nucleus before the /s/ or that /ts/ forms an onset to a following empty nucleus. So, assuming empty nuclei creates an escape hatch for those who want to maintain that it is syllable structure, which is relevant, but this would require stretching these tools quite far.

2.2.3. "Diphthongal" vs. "monophthongal" pronunciation

Once vowel length is established as a distinctive property, a dialect difference that can be analysed in terms of vowel length is demonstrated in (12). Many of the traditional descriptions regard the dialect difference in terms of diphthongal vs. monophthongal pronunciation of forms like *bogi*, and these are the terms used in the table in (12).

(12)

	"Diphthongal"	"Monophthongal"	
stiginn	[stɪijɪn] / [stij:ɪn]	[stɪ:jɪn]	'the staircase'
veginn	[vɛijɪn] / [vɛj:ɪn]	[vɛ:jɪn]	'the road'
huginn	[hʏijɪn] / [hʏj:ɪn]	[hʏ:jɪn]	'the mind'
lögin	[lœijɪn] / [lœj:ɪn]	[lœ:jɪn]	'the law'
daginn	[taijɪn] / [taj:ɪn]	[ta:jɪn]	'the day'
bogi	[pɔijɪ] / [pɔj:ɪ]	[pɔ:jɪ]	'bow'

As shown by the phonetic transcriptions, and as noted by Einarsson (1932:44), it is possible to analyse the difference between the dialects as a difference in vowel length (or syllabification). In the "monophthongal" pronunciation the vowels are long, and the second syllable begins with a glide, and in the "diphthongal" dialect, the vowel is short, and ends in a glide, which also forms an onset to the following syllable and is thus a sort of geminate.

It has been noted (Árnason 1987:87-88) that in dialects that do not traditionally have monophthongal pronunciation, analogical levelling may have the effect that in paradigms like that of *bogi*, shown in (13), the long vowel of the oblique forms *boga* is copied into the nominative, so that the pronunciation becomes [pɔ:jɪ].

(13)

Nom.sg.	*bogi*	[poijɪ] / [pɔ:jɪ]
Oblique sg.	*boga*	[pɔ:ɣa]
Nom.pl.	*bogar*	[pɔ:ɣar̥]

An analogical form like [pɔːjɪ] for *bogi* can be attributed to output-output correspondence or a simple copying of the vowel length into the nominative singular form.

2.2.4. Short diphthongs

As stated earlier, the traditional phonemic diphthongs listed in (5) are subjected to the length rule in the same way as other vowels. This means that whatever means there are used for the representation of short monophthongs, the same should be used for the structurally short diphthongs in (14).

(14)	/ai/	*græn*	[kraiːn]	'green',	*Grænland*	[krain·land]	'Greenland'
	/ei/	*leysa*	[leiːsa]	'to solve',	*leysti*	[leis·tɪ]	'solved'
	/œi/	*haus*	[hœyːs]	'head',	*hausnum*	[hœys·tnʏm]	'the head-DAT'
	/au/	*blása*	[plauːsa]	'to blow',	*blástu*	[plaus·tʏ]	'blow-IMP'
	/u/	*kjósa*	[cʰjouːsa]	'to select',	*kjóstu*	[cʰous·tʏ]	'select-IMP'

The fact that the diphthongs occur as short means that the diphthongal characteristic cannot be handled in terms of moraic structure, as is the most natural way to treat diphthongs (cf. Hayes 1990:61-62). Rather, the short diphthongs must be taken to be monomoraic, but with a complex or moving melody. Both parts of the melody of a diphthong like /ai/ must belong to the "root node", which can occur in a long or short environment, or alternatively with some sort of phonemic marking of length.

This can be taken as indirect evidence against a strict moraic analysis of vowel length in general, and that languages can have phonological length distinctions, which cannot be derived from concatenation of segments, nor from morae or slots on a separate timing tier. So this once more argues for a distinction in terms of structural length/shortness as independent of the timing tier. But syllabification is still a candidate.

2.3. Complementarity of vowel length and consonant length

An old problem within structuralist linguistics is whether consonant length or vowel length is phonemic in pairs like the ones in (15):

(15)	*man*	[maːn]	'remember (1. or 3. pers. sg. pres.)'	(long V + short C)
	mann	[manː]	'man (acc. sg.)	(short V + long C)
		*[man]		(short V + short C)
		*[maːnː]		(long V + long C)

As shown, there is complementary distribution between vowel length and consonant length, but no forms occur with a short vowel followed by a short consonant, nor with a long vowel followed by a long consonant. As described by Benediktsson (1963) and Árnason (1980:14-23), four types of analysis have been proposed of this structure. One is that length is distinctive in both vowels and consonants; another is that vowel length is distinctive and consonant length predictable, and the third is that consonant length is distinctive (cf. above p.

1). In the fourth solution, suggested by Haugen (1958), length is abstracted away from the individual segments and made a part of what Haugen calls the 'accent' of the syllable, the place of length being the distinguishing mark between *man* and *mann*.

If vowel length is distinctive, as argued here, the problem is solved, of course. But some discussion of the arguments for each of the other solutions is in order. If distinctive length (or geminate structure) is assumed for both vowels and consonants, there is no way of explaining why there are no forms with long vowels followed by long consonants, and no forms with short vowels before short consonants. This is therefore not an attractive solution. The solution using accents is reminiscent of the syllable cut parameter proposed by Vennemann, which will be discussed in section 4.2, and we will have a closer look at that option in that context. The solution adopted by both Benediktsson (1963) and Árnason (1980) is to assume that consonant length, or rather underlying gemination, is the primary distinction, so that a form like *mann* is phonemically /mann/, and that the length rule applies in the regular manner giving a short vowel before two consonants. The arguments for this solution are partly phonological, namely that this way the length rule can be stated in its general form, giving short V's in closed syllables, i.e. before two or more consonants, and partly morphophonemic. Referring to alternations like *hús* [hu:s] 'house (nom.)' – *húss* [hus:] 'house (gen.)', compared to e.g. *vor* [vɔ:r] 'spring (nom.)' – *vors* [vɔr̥s] 'spring (gen.)', the suggestion is to take the genitival marker to be an /s/ which is added to the forms in both *húss* and *vors*, creating short environments. Those forms where there is no such morphological motivation, as in *hissa* 'surprised', then get a free ride.

But as we have seen, the morphophonemic argument is not conclusive, since vowel length may be retained before shortening clusters in forms like *skips* and *sötr*. Although these examples are not very common, their importance should not be underestimated, and indeed they show that morphophonemic arguments can go either way.

A similar problem has long been a matter of discussion in Norwegian and Swedish (cf. e.g. Eliasson 1985, Lorenz 1996, Kristoffersen 1997). As shown in (16) the same sort of complementarity as in (15) prevails in Norwegian and Swedish.

(16)	Norwegian:			(cf. Kristoffersen 1997)
	hat	[hɑ:t]	'hate'	
	hatt	[hɑt]	'hat'	
	hake	[hɑ:kə]	'chin'	
	hakke	[hɑk.kə]	'pick axe'	
	Swedish:			(cf. Eliasson 1985)
	vis	[vi:s]	'wise'	
	viss	[vis]	'certain'	
	breda	[bre:da]	'wide (pl.)'	
	bredda	[brɛd.da]	'to widen'	

The morphophonemic argument for assuming underlying consonant gemination (with predictable vowel length) carries less weight in Norwegian and Swedish than in Icelandic, because there are much more examples where vowel length is independent of following consonantal structure, as e.g. shown in inflectional paradigms like the ones in (17):

(17) Norwegian:

gu:l	'yellow'	-	*gu:lt*	'id. neuter'

Swedish:

vi:se	'to show'	-	*han har vi:st*	'he has shown'

Furthermore, examples like the ones in (18) suggest that vowel length is the more persistent quality than consonant length in Swedish and Norwegian; it is the shortness of the vowel and not the length of the consonant which is preserved between corresponding forms.

(18) Norwegian: (Kristoffersen 1997:3)

terrasse	[tæ'rɑs.sə]	'terrace'
terrassere	[tærɑ'se:rə]	'to make a terrace'

Swedish: (Eliasson 1985:112):

kokett	[kɔ'kɛt:]	'coquettish'
kokettera	[kɔkɛ'te:ra]	'to coquet'

This shows that consonant length in Swedish and Norwegian is only realized if the syllable is stressed and the preceding vowel short.

3. Short vowels and syllabification: the "length rule"

We will now look in more detail at the length rule, which is responsible for the distribution of long and short vowels.

3.1. Two versions of the length rule

There are two versions of the length rule, depending on morphosyntactic level. The main generalisation is, as we have seen, that long vowels occur in open syllables, but short vowels in closed syllables. Although the basic generalisation is the same throughout, there is a slight difference between on the one hand underived words and forms derived through inflection and first level affixation, and on the other hand compounds and second level derivatives. We will refer to these levels as Level I and Level II. And furthermore, post-lexical cohesion produces forms, which behave in the same way with respect to the length rule as Level II forms. (See e.g. Kiparsky 1984 and Indriðason 1994 for different suggestions about levels in Icelandic morphology and phonology).

To exemplify, the forms in (19a) with one or no following consonant have long vowels, and the forms in (19b) (all Level I) have short vowels before two or more consonants:

(19)	a. *frí*	[friː]	'holiday'
	vona	[vɔːna]	'to hope'
	fríða	[friːða]	'pretty (fem. nom. sg.)'
	tala	[tʰaːla]	'talk'
	vita	[vɪːtʰa]	'know'
	b. *fríðs*	[friðs]	'pretty (gen. sg., masc. or neut.)'
	hestur	[hɛstʏr]	'horse'
	hundur	[hʏntʏr]	'a dog'
	sats	[sats]	'galley' (in printing)
	ætla	[aihtla]	'to intend'
	vitsins	[vɪtsɪns]	'the wisdom (gen.)'
	lax	[laxs]	'salmon'
	veisla	[veistla]	'party'

Final consonants are extrametrical, so that vowels are long before one final consonant, as in (20).

(20)	*fríð*	[friːθ]	'pretty (fem. nom. sg.)'
	von	[vɔːn]	'hope (noun)'
	skip	[scɪːpʰ]	'ship'

Contrasting with the forms in (19b), vowels are long before consonant clusters consisting of *p,t,k,s* followed by *v,j,r*, as in the examples in (21):

(21)	*nepja*	[nɪɛːpʰja]	'cold weather'
	vökva	[vʏœːkʰva]	'to water'
	titra	[tʰɪːtʰra]	'to vibrate'
	tvisvar	[tʰvɪːsvar]	'twice'

This can be accounted for by assuming that the clusters *pj*, *kv*, *tr* etc. form onsets to the following syllables, making the preceding syllables open. We refer to the consonants in the set *p,t,k,s* as *strong consonants*, and the consonants in the set *v,j,r* as *weak consonants.*

The application of the length rule in compounds is shown in (22) and (23). The forms in (22) show short vowels in front of two consonants:

(22)	*rauð#vín*	[ˈrœyðvin]	'red wine'
	við#kvæmur	[ˈvɪðkhvaimʏr]	'sensitive' to#touchable
	al#góður	[ˈalkouðʏr]	'all-good'
	her#maður	[ˈhɛrmaðʏr]	'soldier' (army#man)
	vin#margur	[ˈvɪnmarkʏr]	'popular' (friend#many)

But as pointed out by Gussmann (1985), the rule for compounds is not quite the same as for noncompounds. Forms like *hvítvín* 'white wine' and *útvalinn* conform to the pattern shown in (21) in having long vowels before a *t* followed by *v* and *r*. But as shown by the other forms in (23) vowels are structurally long before the strong consonants, *p*, *t*, *k* and *s*, regardless of which consonant follows.

(23)	*hvít#vín*	[ˈkfiːtʰvin]	'white wine'
	út#valinn	[ˈuːtʰvalɪn]	'specially selected' (out#chosen)
	út#syni	[ˈuːtʰsinɪ]	'view' (out#sight)
	vit#grannur	[ˈvɪːtkranʏr̥]	'stupid' (wit#skinny)
	hvít#leitur	[ˈkfiːtleitʏr̥]	'white-looking'
	út#saumur	[ˈuːtsœymʏr̥]	'embroidery' (literally 'out-knitting')
	haus#tak	[ˈhœyːstak]	'head-lock (in wrestling)'
	bak#svipur	[ˈpaːksvɪpʏr̥]	'look from the back'
	haus#laus	[ˈhœyːslœys]	'headless'

And the same applies postlexically. The structural length of the vowels in (24) depends on whether a consonant follows or not:

(24)	*Ég kom HEIM*	[heiːm]	'I came home'
	Ég fer HEIM á morgun	[heiːmaumɔrkʏn]	'I'm going home tomorrow'
	Ég kom HEIM til hans	[heimˑtɪlans]	'I came to his house' (literally: 'home to him')

But if the consonant following the vowel is a strong consonant, the vowels are always long:

(25)	a. *Ég sendi DÓS til hans*	[d̥ouːstɪlans]	'I sent him a tin (... a tin to him)'
	b. *Ég át LAUK með því*	[lœyːkmeðvi]	'I ate onion with it'

3.2. A strength hierarchy in consonants

There is no doubt that the length rule is (historically at least) closely connected to syllabification, involving a hierarchy of sonority or strength of consonants. As discussed in Árnason (1980:38-43), the phonetic naturalness of *v*, *j* and *r* as a class in the modern language is questionable, *v* and *j* normally being classified as fricatives, and *r* as a sonorant. But there is still no reason to deny them the status of some sort of structural class on the grounds of their behaviour with respect to the length rule. The group *v,j,r* may be placed as "weak" on a scale of strength, below nasals and the lateral /l/, simply because they can follow strong consonants within onsets. (A possible phonological interpretaiton of the weakness of *v* and *j* is that they should be classified, along with *r*, as approximants.)

weak					strong →
v, j, r	l	n, m	fricatives	b, d, g	p, t, k, s

Fig. 1: Strength scale for consonants[2]

The strength scale shown in Fig. 1 can be related to constraints, which rank the strong consonants higher than other consonants as onsets (wanting to be as far away from the nucleus as possible). The strong consonants' "independence" of the nucleus is enough to suppress the "ambition" of the weak *v,j,r* for onsethood. This has the effect that in long vowel forms like *ne.pja*, *vö.kva*, *ti.tra* and *tvi.svar* in (21), the second syllables have complex onsets. In other forms the first consonants do not have enough strength to form onsets over the following consonants, so that the initial syllables of e.g. *bið.ja* 'to ask', *hes.tur*, 'horse', *vin.da* 'wind' *van.ta* 'need' etc. are closed, and the vowels short. And this overrides the general tendency that syllables should not end in consonants or have codas.

This "balance of power" is different on the two levels of the phonology, as we have seen. On the lexical level, the strong consonants are part of the coda when other consonants than the weakest ones follow, but on the postlexical level they are altogether excluded from the coda, or equivalently, can form onsets in front of any consonant.

3.3. Lexical and postlexical constraints

It was suggested in section 2 that structural shortness of vowels should be taken as a primitive in the phonological system of Modern Icelandic. Since the normal case is for vowels to be structurally long it seems natural to look at vowel shortness as a special property, a sort of privative feature which expresses the characteristic that a vowel is incomplete as a carrier of stress. And if this is done we can derive the syllabification from segmental structure. What the shortness entails is that the short vowels cannot alone carry the lengthening that comes with stress. The normal case is for vowels to be able to cope with stress, but the short ones are abnormal in this respect. Normal vowels are classified as V, but the short vowels are marked with a special characteristic, which we may represent with an asterisk *V. The normal vowels are moraic in the sense that they can carry a syllabic beat, but the short vowels may be characterised as nonmoraic, since they cannot carry a regular stress beat by themselves.

Interacting with this feature of the vowels is a constraint, which demands that each syllable have a nucleus, which can serve as a stress matrix. The constraint, which we may call FillNucleus, informally stated in (26a), interacts with NoCoda, stated in (26b).

---

[2] The scale in Fig. 1 represents a very rough classification of the Icelandic consonant system. Icelandic obstruents may be classified into fricatives, (f,θ,x) and stops, and the stops again into 'soft' stops (b,d,g) and 'hard' stops (p,t,k). Both 'hard' and 'soft' stops are voiceless, but the hard stops can be characterised as having (pre- or post-) aspiration.

(26) a. FillNucleus:
Short vowels (*V) take consonants as complements in the nucleus
b. NoCoda
There is no consonant in the coda

For each particular short vowel, the *V constraint is ranked very high, so that a vowel that has this feature may not be lengthened (except at a very "surfacy" stage, depending on phonetic circumstances.) The effect of the constraints in (26) is that short vowels cannot occur in open syllables and conversely open syllables cannot have short vowels (FillNucleus). NoCoda acts against a consonant in the nucleus, which secures that syllables, other than short vowel ones, are open.

Also active in this context is a family of constraints that all consonants want to be onsets, i.e. start a syllable, and least of all they want to be a complement to a short vowel. There is competition between consonants, and in certain cases consonants can form onsets "across" other consonants. Thus, in the lexical phonology, *p,t,k,s* can form onsets across *v,j,r,* but not across other consonants, whereas in the postlexical phonology, *p,t,k,s* refuse to enter the nucleus, and form onsets, whatever the consequences. No other consonants can form onsets across other consonants.

We will simply refer to these constraints as Onset, and here there is a difference between the two levels in the phonology of Icelandic, informally stated in (27):

(27) Onset:
A consonant is an onset
Ranking:
Lexical:
p,t,k,s beats v,j,r
Postlexical:
p,t,k,s beats all
Otherwise no complex onsets word internally

The constraints give different outputs on different levels. The results on the lexical level are shown in (28), and on the postlexical level, the results are the ones shown in (29).

(28) a.

nepja	Onset (lexical) p,t,k,s beat v,j,r	NoCoda	FillNucleus
nep.ja	*!	*	
n*ep.ja	*!		
n*e.pja			*!
☞ ne.pja			

b.

venja	Onset (lexical) p,t,k,s beat v,j,r	NoCoda	FillNucleus
v*e.nja	*!		*
ven.ja		*!	
ve.nja	*!		
☞ v*en.ja			

c.

satsinn	Onset (lexical) p,t,k,s beat v,j,r	NoCoda	FillNucleus
s*a.tsinn	*!		*
sat.sinn		*!	
sa.tsinn	*!		
☞ s*at.sinn			

In (28a) the first form, *nep.ja* fails because it violates Onset and NoCoda, and the second form, *n*ep.ja* violates onset, since *p* is not in the onset. The third form, *n*e.pja* violates FillNucleus, since a short vowel does not have a complement, so the only form that survives is *ne.pja*. In (28b) *v*e.nja* is ill formed because of Onset and FillNucleus, *ven.ja* violates NoCoda, and *ve.nja* violates Onset, since it does not allow *n* to form an onset across another consonant. The only form that satisfies all constraints is *v*en.ja*. In (28c) a similar situation holds.

(29)

	Onset (postlexical) p,t,k,s beat all	NoCoda	FillNucleus
út.syni	*!	*	
*út.syni	*!		
*ú.tsyni			*!
☞ ú.tsyni			

In (29) the form of Onset is different, and the outcome for the compound *útsyni* is different from (28c) (the noncompound *satsinn*); the well-formed structure for the compound has a long vowel.

4. How to represent vowel shortness?

We will now consider more closely how structural shortness of vowels is to be represented.

4.1 Moraic theory

According to moraic theory, long vowels are "lengthened" short vowels, i.e. vowels that occur in bimoraic environments. Short vowels should then be the normal case, where one segment corresponds to one timing unit, as represented in (30):

(30)
```
μ      μ  μ
|       \/
I       I
```

By this logic, length is not a part of the segment and does not belong to the root node. The actual prediction thus seems to be that, other things being equal, there is no such thing as distinctive vowel length or lexical marking of prosodic characteristics in the root node of segments. In spite of this, moraic theory might (and must in some instances) be willing to assign moraic structure to segments, some vowels being characterised as bimoraic and others as monomoraic. This distinction can then have an effect on syllabification, and is in fact an essential part of analyses which assume that stress is attracted by heavy syllables, and syllable weight in turn derived from vowel length.

The account that has been given above seems to suggest that in Icelandic the short vowel is the special case, and the long vowel the normal one. But if this is true, then the naturalness or "iconicity" of the phonological labelling becomes less attractive; the normal case (the long V) is the one that needs more information (two morae), but the special case is representationally simpler (one mora).[3]

4.2. Syllable cuts

Building on insights by Sievers and Trubetzkoy, Vennemann (1991, 1992) treats length and related phenomena in German and some other languages with the help of a distinction be-

[3] Although it is argued that moraic analysis of vowel length, where long vowels are bimoraic, and short vowels monomoraic, is awkward in the languages studied here, it is still possible that in other languages this sort of analysis is appropriate. Thus the tonal structure of Japanese, where tonal contours occur on segments so that different values may be assigned to different parts of one and the same segment (cf. Pierrehumbert and Beckman 1988), may well justify assuming the mora as a unit in the structure of Japanese vowels. Similarly, Andersen (1993) maintains that vowel length is involved in the morphophonemics of Dinka (a Western Nilotic language) in a way that justifies analysing vowel length in terms of skeletal positions or morae. If subsyllabic beats can be shown to have clear phonological effects, then so be it, but languages where this can be clearly related to moraic structure of segments are, by the logic applied here, typologically different from Icelandic.

tween two values of a syllable prosody which he calls *syllable cut* (Ger. Silbenschnitt). The two values allowed in this parameter are *smooth cut* and *abrupt cut*. Abrupt cut, which is the marked value, is "defined by an energy contour with a sharp drop at the very end of the syllable nucleus", whereas smooth cut is defined by a "slow drop of the energy contour extending over a large portion of the syllable nucleus" (Vennemann 1992:1-2). In abruptly cut syllables, consonants take part in the "decrescendo" of the syllable, and such syllables are always closed and heavy. Smoothly cut syllables on the other hand can be open. The conception that consonants take part in the "decrescendo" of the syllable reminds of the suggestion made here that consonants form part of the nucleus of the syllable, which is where stress is realized. According to Vennemann, vowels in abruptly cut syllables tend to be monophthongal, centralised, lax and short, and the parameter distinguishes between forms like German *Beet,* 'turnip' with a smooth cut and a long vowel, and *Bett* 'bed' with an abrupt cut, and a short vowel. Final syllables with abrupt cut are necessarily closed, whereas abrupt cut in open syllables is only possible if another syllable follows within the same word, as in German *Komma* 'comma'.

It might be an option to apply this to Icelandic and say that the shortness of the short vowels is due to an abrupt cut on these syllables, so that the first syllable of *hes.tur* has an abrupt cut. According to Vennemann, under abrupt cut connection lines to the peak of the syllable connect to two segments, the vowel and the following consonant, and this is reminiscent of Haugen's consonantal nucleus, which in our terms corresponds to vowels which take consonants as complements in the nucleus. We are not in a position to evaluate fully the relative merits of the syllable cut theory and the proposal made here, and indeed they may be "notational variants" of the same idea. In both accounts, Icelandic is analysed so that a close contact is made between a vowel and a consonant in one case (short vowel, abrupt cut) and not in the other case (long vowel, smooth cut). The results for Icelandic may seem to be the same either way, since we have the complementarity of short vowel and closed syllable and long vowel and open syllable.

But there seem to be some differences in the prediction of the two approaches. For example if vowel shortness is seen as some sort of distinctive characteristic of vowels, it should be theoretically possible to have short vowels without a consonant following, i.e. when the demand for a coda is not satisfied for some reason. In the syllable cut theory, abruptly cut syllables have to have a following consonant in order for the cut parameter to operate. But if a system were to be found where short vowels occur without a following consonant, that would seem to favour the vowel shortness analysis. And a comparison with Italian, which in many respects has a similar structure to Icelandic (cf. e.g. Chierchia 1986), is interesting here. Italian shows similarities to Icelandic with respect to vowel length; it has a distinction between long and short vowels, but with predictable distribution, long vowels occurring in open syllables and short vowels in closed syllables. Thus e.g. *ca.pra* 'goat' has a long vowel (cf. Icelandic *da.pra* 'sad (fem.sg. acc.)'), and *cam.bio* 'change' has a short vowel in a closed syllable (cf. Icelandic *lam.ba* 'lamb (gen. pl.)'). But one interesting difference between Icelandic and Italian is that word final vowels are short in Italian, even if no consonant follows. It would seem that the shortness of the word final vowels in Italian cannot be deduced directly from the choice of syllable cut; the final short vowel in *città* cannot have an abrupt cut, since such syllables have to be closed. Assigning the property of shortness to the segments themselves seems to do the job, however. We may note that Vennemann's definitions are indeed stated solely in terms of the characteristics of the vowels. We will therefore continue exploring the possibility of looking at vowel shortness as a primitive constraint in the system.

4.3. "Nonmoraic" vowels

The simplest and most down to earth way of encoding the prosodic properties of the short vowels is to represent them by some sort of privative feature, called simply *short*. This could be interpreted as a property of vowels that has the effect that they cannot be stretched or lengthened under stress. Another term that comes to mind is *defective*. Basically, this means that a short vowel cannot serve as a stress matrix by itself or create a beat in the rhythm of the utterance without some sort of assistance, consonantal or otherwise. It has this negative property of not being able to form a full stress matrix. If this lexical distinction between two kinds of vowels is to be expressed in terms of morae, the most appropriate representation would seem to be to designate the vowels as "*nonmoraic*", since they are incomplete as carriers of the syllabic beat or as matrices for stress. They need additional material before they can carry stress or a syllabic beat.

The implication is that, generally, vowel shortness, i.e. the specification of some vowels as short, or "nonmoraic", is an option open to languages, and among the languages that use that option are (all?) the modern Germanic languages and Italian.

5. Consonant length: gemination

We have so far had little to say about consonant length, except that "half long consonants" are consonants that are in the nucleus and are stretched according to stress. Without entering on an elaborate justification, we assume that there are no phonologically long or short consonants, rather there are single consonants and geminates, i.e. ambisyllabic consonants. Ambisyllabic consonants belong simultaneously to two syllables, in other words, they close the preceding syllable and form an onset to the following one at the same time, as in (31).

(31)	*man.ni*	[man:i]	'man dative'
	krab.bi	[kʰrab̥:ɪ]	'cancer'

The shortness of the vowel of *manni* demands a consonant in the coda, but that same consonant also forms an onset to the following syllable.

In monosyllables and word finally, the same holds, only the consonant forms a potential onset to a following empty nucleus, due to catalexis, or is extrametrical.

(32)	*ma.n*	[ma:n]	'(I) remember'
	man.n	[man:]	'man-ACC'

6. Disyllabic vs. monosyllabic stress matrices

Icelandic, Norwegian and Swedish have in common that stressed syllables follow what is sometimes referred to as Prokosch's Law (cf. e.g.Vennemann 1988:30), i.e. they are heavy by stress (weight to stress). The effect is that stressed syllables are lengthened in proportion to the amount of stress, and the lengthening occurs on the vowel if it is long, but on the consonant if the vowel is short, as we have seen. But there are other systems, like German, English and Latin, where a distinction between long and short (alternatively tense and lax) vowels is generally assumed to be significant or phonemic. Similarly, Old Icelandic had a distinction between short and long vowels. And it is reasonable to ask whether the sort of analysis that we have proposed for Modern Icelandic can also be used in these systems.

What all of these systems seem to have in common is that the short vowels create complications when it comes to realising stress. Long vowels serve as normal carriers of stress or phrasal prominence, whereas special measures are called for when vowels are short. But the problem of short vowels is solved in different ways in e.g. Old Icelandic and Latin on the one hand, and modern Icelandic (and Italian) on the other. In Old Icelandic and Latin the problem of realising stress on short vowels is solved either by making a following tautosyllabic consonant (if available) form part of the stress matrix, as in Latin *re'fectus* 're-made' or else by forming *disyllabic stress matrices*, as described by Allen (1973) for Latin, and by Árnason (1991) for Old Icelandic. Thus, the first two syllables of Latin *brevitas* 'shortness' form a disyllabic stress matrix, and similarly the two syllables of Old Icelandic *talaða* 'talked':

```
(33)      /  \                      /  \
     b  r  e  v  i  t  a  s        t  a  l  a  ð  a
```

In Allen's terms, one heavy or two light syllables form stress matrices, disyllabic ones in the latter case. And this disyllabic stress is the basis for metrical resolution, which occurs in both Old Icelandic and Latin poetry.

A similar phenomenon, what Riad (1992:269-347) calls "balance", is found in some Scandinavian dialects. This is a special effect by which a "unipositional stress foot" is realized on two syllables and which gives rise to the stress pattern known as level stress (Riad 1992:189). The term "level stress" derives from the fact that the two syllables are felt to be equally strong in some sense. The crucial difference between this system and that of the modern standards is that this option of disyllabic stress is not available in the latter, since they follow Prokosch's Law, which is basically that stress matrices are monosyllabic. In Modern Icelandic the length rule (which has its historical origin in special historical changes of vowel length) secures that a short vowel is always followed by a tautosyllabic consonant. In Italian, the situation is similar. Normally, a consonant is available following a short vowel, but in the case of word final short vowels a problem arises. What happens here is that so-called "raddoppiamento sintattico" comes into play. In raddoppiamento, a consonant is "borrowed" from a following word within the syntagm, in order to create a sufficient stress matrix when the vowel is short, and this gives forms like *città triste* [tʃitat.triste] 'sad city' (cf. Chierchia 1986:6).

The modern Scandinavian languages (and Italian) thus follow Prokosch's Law, by, if the vowel is short, including following consonants in the stress matrix. Thus a heavy or branching rhyme is formed:

(34) h [e s] t u r 'horse' m [a n] t o 'coat'

The difference between Icelandic and the modern Scandinavian standards on one hand and English, German, Latin and the so called "Balance dialects" of Scandinavian on the other is that the latter allow disyllabic feet or stress matrices (cf. Allen 1973, Mester 1994, Bye 1996, Riad 1992).

7. Conclusion.

What I have tried to show in this paper is that in spite of the fact that the distribution of long and short vowels is to a large extent predictable in Icelandic on the basis of some sort of syllabification, there is good reason to assume that an independent distinction between long and short vowels is phonologically significant in Icelandic. From the prosodic point of view at least, the marked member of the long-short pair is the short vowel, and it would seem that this should be somehow encoded into the representation.

References

Allen, W.Sidney (1973): *Accent and Rhythm.* Cambridge: Cambridge University Press.

Andersen, Torben (1993): Vowel Quality Alternation in Dinka Verb Inflection. *Phonology* 10, 1-42.

Anderson, Stephen (1984): A Metrical Interpretation of some Traditional Claims about Quantity and Stress. In: Mark Aronoff, R. Oerle (eds.): *Language Sound Structure: Studies in Phonology Presented to Morris Halle by his Teacher and Students,* 83-105. Cambridge, MA: The MIT Press.

Árnason, Kristján (1980): *Quantity in Historical Phonology*. Cambridge: Cambridge University Press.

— (1985): Icelandic Word Stress and Metrical Phonology. *Studia Linguistica* 39, 93 -129.

— (1987): Icelandic Dialects Forty years Later: the (Non)survival of some Northern and South-eastern Features. In: Pirkko Lilius, Mirja Saari (eds.): *The Nordic Languages and Modern Linguistics 6*, 79-92. Helsinki. Helsnki University Press.

— (1991): *The Rhythms of Dróttkvætt and other Old Icelandic Metres.* Reykjavík: University of Iceland, Institute of Linguistics.

Benediktsson, Hreinn (1963): The Non-Uniqueness of Phonemic Solutions: Quantity and Stress in Icelandic. *Phonetica* 10, 133-53.

Benua, Laura (1995): Identity Effects in Morphological Truncation. In: Jill Beckman et.al. (eds.): *University of Massachusetts Occasional Papers in Linguistics* 18: *Papers in Optimality Theory,* 77-136. Amherst: Department of Linguistics, University of Massachusetts.

Bye, Patrik (1996): Scandinavian 'Level Stress' and the Theory of Prosodic Overlay. *Nordlyd. Tromsø University Working Papers on Language and Linguistics*. 24, 23-62.

Chierchia, Gennaro (1986): Length, Syllabification and the Phonological Cycle in Italian. *Journal of Italian Linguistics* 8, 5-34.

Einarsson, Stefán (1927): *Beiträge zur Phonetik der isländischen Sprache*. Oslo: A.W. Brøggers boktrykkeri A/S.
— (1932): Um mál á Fljótsdalshéraði og Austfjörðum 1930. *Skírnir* 106, 33-54.
Eliasson, Stig (1985): Stress Alternation and Vowel Length: New Evidence for an Underlying Nine-Vowel System in Swedish. *Nordic Journal of Linguistics* 8, 101-129.
Guðfinnsson, Björn (1946): *Mállyzkur I*, Reykjavík: Ísafoldarprentsmiðja h.f.
— (1964): *Mállyzkur II*. Ólafur M. Ólafsson og Óskar Ó. Halldórsson unnu úr gögnum höfundar og bjuggu til prentunar. Reykjavík: Heimspekideild Háskóla Íslands & Bókaútgáfa Menningarsjóðs.
Gussmann, Edmund (1985): The Morphology of a Phonological Rule: Icelandic Vowel Length. In: Edmund Gussmann (ed.): *Phono-Morphology. Studies in the interaction of Phonology and Morphology*, 75-94. Lublin: Redakcja Wydawnictw Katolickiego Uniwersytetu Lubelskiego.
Haugen, Einar (1958): The Phonemics of Modern Icelandic. *Language* 34, 55-88.
Hayes, Bruce (1990): Diphthongisation and Coindexing. *Phonology* 7, 31-71
Indriðason, Þorsteinn G. (1994): *Regluvirkni í orðasafni og utan þess. Um lexíkalska hljóðkerfisfræði íslensku*. Reykjavík: Cand. mag.-thesis, University of Iceland.
Kiparsky, Paul (1984): On the Lexical Phonology of Icelandic. In: C.C. Elert, I. Johansson, E. Strangert (eds.): *Nordic Prosody III*, 135-64. Stockholm: Almqvist & Wiksell.
Kristoffersen, Gert (1997): Quantity in Norwegian Syllable Structure. Bergen: Ms. University of Bergen.
Lorenz, Ove (1996): Length and Correspondence in Scandinavian. *Nordlyd. Tromsø Working Papers in Linguistics*. 24:111-28.
Mester, Armin. (1994): The Quantitative Trochee in Latin. *Natural Language and Linguistic Theory* 12, 1-61.
Ófeigsson, Jón (1920-1924): Træk af moderne islandsk Lydlære. Blöndal, Sigfús: *Islandsk-dansk ordbog (Íslensk-dönsk orðabók)*, XIV-XXVII. Reykjavík: Verslun Þórarins B. Þorlákssonar; Copenhagen: H. Aschehoug (W. Nygaard).
Pierrehumbert, Janet, and Mary Beckman (1988): *Japanese Tone Structure*. Cambridge, MA: The MIT Press.
Riad, Tomas (1992): *Structures in Germanic Prosody*. Stockholm: Stockholm University, Department of Scandinavian Languages.
Thráinsson, Höskuldur (1978): On the Phonology of Icelandic Preaspiration. *Nordic Journal of Linguistics*. 1, 3-54
Vennemann, Theo (1988): *Preference Laws for Syllable Structure*. Berlin: Mouton de Gruyter.
— (1991): Syllable Structure and Syllable Cut Prosodies in Modern Standard German. In: Pier Marco Bertinetto et al. (eds.): *Certamen Phonologicum II: Papers from the 1990 Cortona Phonology Meeting*. Torino: Rosenberg & Seiller, 211-243.
— (1992): From Quantity to Syllable Cuts: On So-called Lengthenings in the Germanic Languages, paper presented at the Phonology Meeting, Krems, 4-7 July 1992.

Janet Grijzenhout

The role of coronal specification in German and Dutch phonology and morphology

1. Introduction

This paper discusses the distribution and behaviour of consonants in different morphological environments in German and Dutch. To account for the asymmetric behaviour of coronal consonants in different languages, it has been proposed that coronals are unspecified for place in underlying representations (e.g., Avery & Rice 1989, Paradis & Prunet 1989, 1991). Hall (1995) shows that this may also be the case for German. As pointed out by him, there is, however, also convincing evidence that at a certain stage of the derivation, the place feature Coronal must be specified in German. McCarthy & Taub (1992, and references cited there) make the same point for English: there is evidence that supports coronal underspecification throughout the derivation of English, but there is also contrasting evidence that shows that Coronal must be specified quite early in the derivation of English. Hence, coronal underspecification is problematic.

In this study, I will attempt to account for the distribution of consonants by imposing restrictions on the position of consonantal place features within syllables. In particular, I will argue that (i) the occurrence of the feature Labial is restricted to syllable edges, (ii) the feature Coronal should be specified because it plays a role in phonotactic restrictions and in morphological processes, and (iii) velars lack a consonantal place of articulation (cf. Rice 1996).

The structure of this paper is as follows. Section 2 discusses German phonotactic restrictions and lexical processes that refer to coronals. Section 3 concentrates on Dutch phonotactic restrictions and the absence of Schwa-insertion across the morpheme boundary when coronals are involved. Section 4 is concerned with place assimilation and section 5 deals with the phonological representation of velar consonants. Section 6 concludes.

2. The distribution of German consonants

The German consonant system includes the phonemes in Figure 1 (based on Hall 1992, Ramers & Vater 1995, and Wiese 1996):

	labial	alveolar	palato-alveolar	palatal	velar	uvular	glottal
-son	p, b, p^f, f, v	t, d, t^s, s, z	ʃ, ʒ	ç[1]	k, g		h
+son	m	n, l				ʀ[2]	

Figure 1: The German consonant system

All the phonemes presented in Figure 1 may occur in word-initial position, but word-initial /s/ and /ʒ/ are rare: they occur in certain loan words such as *Sphäre* [sfɛːʀə] "sphere", *Slalom* [slaːlɔm], and *Genie* [ʒeniː] "genius", and /s/ occurs before /k/ in sequences like *Skandal* "scandal".

In word-initial position, stops (1a-c), the affricate /p^f/ (2a-c), and the fricatives /f/ and /ʃ/ (3a-c) may be followed by sonorant consonants. Except for /ç/, all non-coronal obstruents may be followed by uvular /ʀ/ or a coronal sonorant, but not by a labial sonorant. In the examples below, brackets indicate that words of this type are rare and an asterisk denotes that the cluster in question is unattested word-initially. The data are from Hall (1992, 1995), Vater (1992), and Wiese (1996):

(1)	a.	(pneumatisch)	*pmie	*tnie	*tmie	Knie	*kmie
	b.	Platz		*tlie		klug	
	c.	Prinz		Trend		Kranz	
(2)	a.	*pfnie	*pfmie	*tsnie	*tsmie		
	b.	Pflege			*tslie		
	c.	Pfropf			*tsrie		
(3)	a.	*fneu	*fmeu	[ʃ]nee	[ʃ]mied	*[ç]nie	*[ç]mie
	b.	Fleisch		[ʃ]leim			*[ç]leim
	c.	frank		[ʃ]rank			*[ç]rank

Strident fricatives are the only obstruents that may precede /m/ word-initially:[3]

(4)	a.	*pmal	*tmal	*kmal
	b.	*fmal	[ʃ]mal "narrow"	*[ç]mal

Initial clusters of three consonants consist of a voiceless strident fricative plus a stop and a liquid:

1 The fricative /ç/ has three allophones: it is realised as velar [x] after non-low back tense vowels, as uvular [χ] after low vowels, and as palatal [ç] otherwise (Trubetzkoy 1939, Kohler 1990, Wiese 1996: 209-218). For a discussion of these alternations I refer to 5.1.

2 There is a considerable variation in the pronunciation of /ʀ/ in German (Trubetzkoy 1939). In most dialects it is a uvular vibrant prevocalically, and it is vocalised postvocalically.

3 Initial /sm/ clusters are rare, but they do occur. Some examples are: *Smaragd, Smog*.

(5) a. [ʃ]pleißen "to split" *[ʃ]tlave [s]klave "slave"
b. [ʃ]prache "speech" [ʃ]traße "street" [s]krupel "scruple"

To account for the exceptional occurrence of [ʃ] and [s] before [m] and obstruent-sonorant clusters, I follow Vennemann (1982, 1988) who proposes that there is a word-initial appendix at the left edge of the core syllable for voiceless strident fricatives which precede one or two consonants:[4]

(6) appendix onset

s/ʃ C C

With respect to the distribution of consonants in onset positions, three generalisations can be made. First, as pointed out by Hall (1992:71), among others, the first position in an onset cluster must be filled by an obstruent (7a). Second, homorganic obstruent-sonorant sequences such as /pm/, /bm/, /fm/, /tn/, /dn/, /tl/, and /dl/ are not allowed word-initially. Word-internally, they sometimes occur in onsets (e.g., *Han.dlung* "plot"). The generalisation that in onset position two consonants may not have the same place of articulation (7b) is therefore not absolute and may be violated under certain conditions (e.g., to maximise word-internal onsets).

In recent literature (e.g., Hall 1995, Wiese 1996), it is usually assumed that /n, l/ and /ʀ/ are unspecified for features under the Place node. Together with a ban on distinct place features in the onset, coronal underspecification and underspecification of /ʀ/ is used to rule out initial sequences like /km/, while allowing sequences like /kn/, /kl/, and /kʀ/. Instead of these two assumptions (and additional rules which assign the feature Coronal to /n,l/ and Dorsal or [+low] to /ʀ/ at a later stage in the derivation), I here propose only one restriction, to wit, in onset clusters the second member may not be specified for the consonantal place feature Labial (7c):[5]

(7) if appendix onset

$_{PrWd}$(s/ʃ C_1 C_2

---

[4] Contrary to Wiese (1991), I do not assume that strident fricative + obstruent clusters form a single segment word-initially. Wiese proposes that, e.g., /sk/ is a kind of 'reversed affricate' in words like *Skandal* and *Sklave*, but not word-internally in words like *Fran.zis.kus*. In contrast, I propose that /sk/ clusters consist of two segmental positions both word-initially and word-internally.

[5] In 5.1 it will be argued that the palatal fricative does not occur in an onset cluster for independent reasons. With Wiese (1996:238-242), I assume that initial clusters in words like *Twist* and *zwei* "two" obey conditions (7a) and (7b), and escape condition (7c), because the second member of these clusters is a desonorised vowel /ʊ/ which is not characterised by a C-Place feature.

a. then C_1 = [-sonorant] ∧ C_2 =[+sonorant]

b. and

```
*C1      C2
 |        |
Placei   Placei
```

c. and the C-Place feature Labial can only appear in the left-most position of an onset.

Statement (7c) may be unusual and daring, but it is observationally adequate and it helps to explain the distribution of labial consonants in different languages (e.g., Dutch, see section 3).

The proposed onset structure in (7) and the generalisations in (7a-c) account for the distribution of initial consonants in German without the aid of coronal underspecification. The next subsection considers the distribution of final consonants in German.

2.1. Syllable-final consonant clusters

In syllable-final position, obstruents are voiceless, but this is not indicated in the spelling. Nasals may precede homorganic stops (8a) and affricates (9a), and [n] may precede fricatives (10a). The liquids [l] and [ʀ] may precede syllable-final stops (8a-b), affricates (9b-c), and fricatives (10b-c). Orthographic <pf> and <z> represent the affricates $[p^f]$ and $[t^s]$, respectively. There is no velar affricate in Standard German. Examples of clusters with final alveolar [s] are *Gans* "goose" and *Hals* "neck". Orthographic <sch> stands for postalveolar [ʃ], and <ch> is pronounced [ç] in the examples below:

(8)	a. plu[mp]	"awkward"	bu[nt]	"colourful"	kra[ŋk]	"sick"
	b. Kalb	"calf"	kalt	"cold"	Kalk	"lime"
	c. Korb	"basket"	Bord	"brim"	karg	"scanty"

(9)	a. Kampf	"fight"	Tanz	"dance"
	b. *Kalpf		Salz	"salt"
	c. *Karpf		Herz	"heart"

(10)	a. Senf	"mustard"	Mensch	"person"	manch	"many"
	b. Schilf	"reed"	falsch	"false"	solch	"such"
	c. Nerv	"nerve"	Marsch	"march"	durch	"through"

Syllable-finally, liquids may precede [m] and [n], and [ʀ] may precede [l]:

(11)	a. Salm	"salmon"	Köln	"Cologne"
	b. Schirm	"screen"	Gehirn	"brain"

(12) Kerl "fellow, chap"

The data presented in (8-12) are compatible with the so-called "sonority sequencing principle" which requires post-vocalic consonants to fall in sonority (e.g., Jespersen 1904, Selkirk 1984). Words with final *-lm*, *-rm*, *-ln*, and *-rn* in (11a-b) suggest that liquids are higher in the sonority hierarchy in German than the labial nasal /m/ and the alveolar nasal /n/ and the final cluster in (12) shows that /ʀ/ is higher in the hierarchy than /l/. Hall (1992:64) proposes the following sonority hierarchy for German. The direction of the arrow indicates increasing sonority:

(13) Sonority hierarchy for German (based on Hall 1992)

obstruents — n, m — l — ʀ — vowels →

The following consonant sequences are excluded syllable-finally, because they violate the sonority sequencing principle. The members of the obstruent clusters in (14a-b) have an equal level of sonority according to Hall (1992), and in the obstruent-sonorant clusters of (14c-d) sonority increases, rather than decreases:

(14) a. *..pk, ..bk, ..fk, ..kp, ..kb, ..kf, ..pç, ..kç, ..çp, ..çb, ..fç, ..çf,
b. *...tk, ..dk, ..tp, ..tb, ..tf, ..tç,
c. *..pm, ..tm, ..km, ..pn, ..pl, ..pr, ..tn, ..tl, ..tr, ..kn, ..kl, ..kr,
d. *..fm, ..sm, ..çm, ..fn, ..fl, ..fr, ..sl, ..sr, ..çn, ..çl, ..çr.

Some post-vocalic sequences not mentioned in (14a-b) are attested, even though they have an equal level of sonority. In these clusters, the second member is always an alveolar obstruent:

(15)	a. Abt	/apt/	"abbot"	Akt	/akt/	"act"
	b. oft	/ɔft/	"often"	Recht	/ʀɛçt/	"law"
	c. Gips	/gɪps/	"plaster"	Keks	/ke:ks/	"biscuit"

If we want to maintain that decreasing sonority in the rhyme is a valid condition for syllable-wellformedness in German, the examples in (15a-c) with final alveolar obstruents pose a potential problem. Moreover, we have to account for the fact that alveolar obstruents are also special in that in words with more than two final consonants, the consonants following a VXC sequence are alveolar obstruents. Following earlier proposals by, e.g., Vennemann (1982, 1988), I assume that word-final alveolars after a consonant (16a-b) and after a VXC-sequence (16c-d) are accommodated in an appendix at the right edge of the core syllable:[6]

[6] The "core syllable" that Vennemann (1988) refers to is that part of the syllable which is put between brackets in examples (16a-c).

(16)

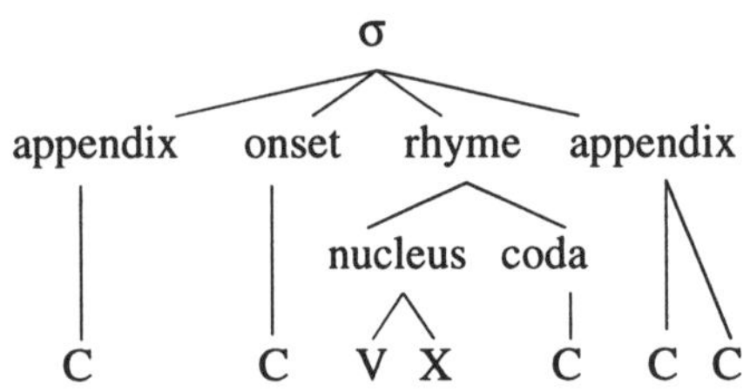

	C		C	V	X	C		C	C	
a.		(	ɔ	f			)	t		"often"
b.	ʃ	(	p	ɛ	ç		)	t		"woodpecker"
c.		(	h	ɛ	ʀ	p	)	s	t	"autumn"
d.		(	k	e	e	k	)	s		"biscuit"

When a nasal or a liquid follows an obstruent at the right word-edge, it is syllabic, i.e., the head of its own syllable. The examples below can therefore not be used to argue against the claim of a decreasing sonority-level in the rhyme of a syllable:

(17) a. Atm /tm̩/ "breath" Ofen /fn̩/ "oven" Rechen /çn̩/ "rake"
b. Büffel /fl̩/ "buffalo" Kessel /sl̩/ "kettle" Kachel /çl̩/ "tile"

Contrary to consonants in onset position, two adjacent consonants in rhyme position may have the same place of articulation (see e.g., 8a, 9a). To exclude syllable-final labial-dorsal sequences like /mk/ and /mç/, I here propose that if there is a labial consonant in the rhyme, the feature Labial is the rightmost C-Place feature in that rhyme.[7] This implies that the first consonant in a rhyme can only be a labial consonant when it is the only consonant in that rhyme, or when it is followed by another labial consonant as in *plump* "awkward". In final labial-coronal sequences like /pt/, /ft/, /mt/, and /ms/, the labial segment is rightmost in the rhyme and the coronal obstruent is in the appendix (see 16a). With respect to place of articulation, we can thus account for permissible syllable-final clusters when we assume that labial obstruents and nasals are restricted to the rightmost position of a rhyme (18b).

In summary, the following restrictions with respect to post-vocalic consonant clusters apply in German: (i) sonority decreases in the rhyme (18a), and (ii) if the feature Labial occurs, it is the rightmost C-Place feature in the core syllable (18b).

(18) if

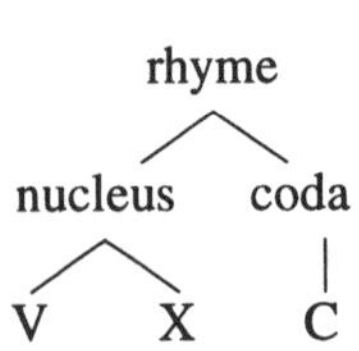

[7] Hall (1992:122) accounts for the lack of these sequences by the following filter: *[+nasal, Labial] [+cons, +high].

a. then X = [+sonorant] and sonority-level X > sonority-level C

b. and the C-Place feature Labial can only appear in the right-most position of a rhyme.

The proposals in (7) and (18) account for the distribution of German consonants without the use of coronal underspecification. As will be discussed next, the main advantage of these proposals is that phonological rules such as Schwa-insertion can refer to the feature Coronal.

2.2. German Schwa-insertion

In German, Schwa is obligatorily inserted between an alveolar stop and an alveolar obstruent in verbs which do not show umlaut or ablaut (19a,b) and between a coronal obstruent and a coronal fricative in certain adjectives (20a,b).[8]

(19)	a.	arbeit + t	arbeit[ə]t	"work-3 sg. pres."
	b.	arbeit + st	arbeit[ə]st	"work-2 sg. pres."

(20)	a.	kalt + ste	kält[ə]st[ə]	"coldest"
	b.	heiss + ste	heiss[ə]st[ə]	"hottest"

Hall (1995) points out that a condition which accounts for the alternations in (19a-b) and (20a-b) makes specific reference to the place feature Coronal. Especially, the following environments are necessary:

(21) a. [-son, -cont, Coronal] _______ ....
b. [-son, Coronal] _______ ....

The rule of Schwa-epenthesis at the morpheme boundary is sensitive to the environment in (21a-b), i.e., an environment in which the feature Coronal is specified. Hall (1995) points out, that this is an argument against coronal underspecification, at least at the level where the suffixes *-t*, *-st*, and *-ste* are added to the stem. I already showed in 2 and 2.1 that coronal underspecification is not required to account for phonotactic restrictions either. On the basis of these considerations, I conclude that coronal underspecification does not play a role in German. I hope to have shown that most of the data which have been used to support the opposite position can be handled in a different way.[9] The implication of my proposal is that alveolars and palatoalveolars are specified for the feature Coronal at *all* phonological and morphological levels.

---

[8] Wolfgang Kehrein pointed out to me that *end*-final adjectives do not show Schwa-insertion in this environment: *wütend + ste* → *wütendste* **wütend[ə]ste* "most angry".

[9] For an account of nasal assimilation I refer to section 4.

3. The distribution of Dutch consonants

The Dutch consonant system includes the segments presented in Figure 2 below:

	labial	alveolar	palatal	velar	glottal
-son	p, b, f, v	t, d, s, z		k, x	h
+son	m, w	n, l, r	j	ŋ	

Figure 2: The Dutch consonant system

The segment /s/ is the only segment that can precede obstruent-sonorant clusters or /m/ in word-initial position and this is used as an argument in favour of an extra position for the strident fricative at the left edge of a word by van der Hulst (1985:57):

(22) appendix onset
s C C

Consonants in Dutch have more or less the same distribution in word-initial position as in German, i.e., stops and fricatives may be followed by nasals and liquids. Dutch does not have a voiced velar stop (written <g> represents the voiceless velar fricative /x/). The labial continuant represented by orthographic <w> is exceptional in that it may follow the stops /t/, /d/, and /k/ and the voiced strident fricative /z/.

(23)	a.	(pneu)	*pmie	*tnie	*tmie	knie	*kmie
	b.	plank		*tlank		klank	
	c.	pruik		trui		kruik	
	d.	*pwaad		dwaas		kwaad	

(24)	a.	(fnuiken)	*fmie	snoek	smoel	(gnoe)	*gmie
	b.	flank		slank		glans	
	c.	fruit		*sruit[10]		gruis	
	d.	*fwaad		zwaard		*gwaad	

To account for the distribution of obstruents and sonorants in Dutch, I propose here - as in section 2 for German - that the first member of a bipositional onset cluster must be an obstruent (25a). Unattested initial **tn-*, **tl-*, **pw-*, and, at least for most speakers, **sr-*

[10] As far as I am aware, the only word in Dutch which starts with an /sr-/ cluster is *Sranang* (English based Creole spoken in Surinam). It should also be pointed out that some speakers of Dutch pronounce initial /sxr-/ clusters as [sr-].

sequences suggest that - as in German - homorganic obstruent-sonorant sequences are not allowed, i.e., there is a ban on two identical places of articulation syllable-initially (25b).

Unattested clusters with /m/ as the second member in (23a) and (24a) imply that - as in German - the second consonantal place feature in an onset cannot be Labial (25c).[11] Clusters involving /s/ and the labial nasal are not subject to (25c), because the strident fricative belongs to the appendix and the labial nasal is thus the only member of the onset in words like *smoel* "mug".

(25) if appendix onset

$_{\text{PrWd}}($ s C_1 C_2

a. then $C_1 = [\text{-sonorant}] \wedge C_2 = [\text{+sonorant}]$

b. and $*C_1$ C_2
Place_i Place_i

c. and the C-Place feature Labial can only appear in the left-most position of an onset.

The sound represented by orthographic <w> is a labial continuant which differs from the labial fricative [v] and the labial approximant [w]. Its status is ambiguous; on the one hand, it has distributional properties which characterise it as an obstruent, e.g., just like fricatives (see 24c), this segment appears before /r/ in onset clusters (*wraak* "revenge"). On the other hand, this segment also behaves as a sonorant in that it may appear after stops and fricatives in onset clusters (see 23d, 24d). From a phonological point of view, we may say that this segment is somewhere in-between an obstruent and a sonorant. With respect to its articulation, this segment also falls in-between fricatives and approximants. In onset positions, the labial continuant spelled <w> involves a movement of the lower lip which is less tense - or more relaxed - than the movement one makes to articulate the labial fricative represented by orthographic <v>, but it involves more turbulence than the labial approximant in words like *boa* [bo:wa]. I here propose to represent the difference between the labial continuant spelled <w> and the one spelled <v> as a difference in anchoring of the feature Labial: the sound in words like *vies* "dirty", *veeg* "sweep", and *lava* is an obstruent which bears the C-Place feature Labial (see 26a), whereas the sound in words like *wieg* "cradle", *weeg* "weigh" and*lawaai* "noise" is an obstruent which bears the V-Place feature Labial (26b).[12] The labial approximant which is used as the hiatus consonant after a back vowel in, e.g., *boa* [bo:wa], which is part of a diphthong in, e.g., *goud* [xawt] "gold", or which occurs

[11] In 5.1, it will be argued that the second consonant in the onset cannot be a velar nasal for independent reasons.

[12] In this paper, I will employ a feature geometric model as proposed by, for instance, Clements (1989), Hume (1992), and Ní Chiosáin & Padgett (1993) with consonantal and vocalic place features for consonants. C-Place implies a consonantal constriction. This renders the use of a feature [+/-consonantal] superfluous.

word-finally in, e.g., *meeuw* [me:w] "seagull" differs from the two labial fricatives in that it is a sonorant:

(26) a. labial fricative
[-son]
|
C-Place
|
Labial

b. labial fricative
[-son]
|
C-Place
\
V-Place
|
Labial

c. labial approximant
[+son]
|
C-Place
\
V-Place
|
Labial

Due to the fact that identical place features in the onset are ruled out (see 25b), we predict that the segment represented in (26b) is found with coronals and velars only. It does indeed occur after a coronal or a velar stop in onsets (see 23d), but not with a velar fricative. Before I suggest an explanation for the gap in the distribution of this fricative, consider first that the fricative spelled <v> (represented in 26a) can co-occur with /l/, but the fricative spelled <w> (represented in 26b) cannot:

(27) a. vla "custard" c. vroom "pious"
b.*wla d. wraak "revenge"

Ní Chiosáin & Padgett (1993:23), among others, point out that a C-Place feature means a large degree of consonantal constriction and a V-Place feature means less constriction. C-Place and V-Place thus correlate with, respectively, a lesser and a greater degree of sonority. Under this assumption, the fricative spelled <v> and represented without a V-Place node in (26a) is less sonorous than the corresponding fricative which is spelled <w> and which is represented without C-Place features, but with a V-Place node in (26b).

The sonority scale below was originally proposed by van der Hulst (1985:59). I have modified it slightly by adding the labial fricative in (26b), represented below as $v_{V\text{-Place}}$:

(28) Sonority hierarchy for Dutch (based on van der Hulst 1985:59)

stops — frics — $v_{V\text{-Place}}$ — m — n — l — r — j/w — vowels →

Initial clusters containing two stops or two fricatives, and initial clusters involving a stop and a fricative other than the one spelled <w> (i.e., $v_{V\text{-Place}}$) are not attested, except in loans such as *psalm* or *xylofoon* (where x = /ks/). This is presumably due to the fact that the rise in sonority is not strong enough. In other words, in word-initial clusters, segments may not be of the same sonority level and they may not be adjacent on the scale in (28). The distance on the scale in (28) between stops and $v_{V\text{-Place}}$ (the fricative spelled <w>) is enough to allow the onset clusters *tw-*, *dw-*, and *kw-*, while clusters of stops and other fricatives like **tf-*, **dv-*, or **kz-* are prohibited.

If I am right in the assumption that the sonority distance of the fricative spelled <w> and /l/ is closer than the sonority distance between other fricatives and /l/, the following account may be provided for the fact that words like **wla* and **wlieg* are not attested; the sonority distance is not large enough to allow onset formation of this fricative and /l/.

To formalise the observations made immediately above, I follow Selkirk (1984) and assign sonority-values to the segments in question. The sonority-values in (29) are merely a means to refer to the fact that there should be a minimal sonority distance between two segments in onset position. Assuming the values below, the minimum sonority distance between two consonants in onset position should be 1.25:[13]

(29) Sonority hierarchy for Dutch:

1	2	2.5	3	3.25	3.5	3.75	4	5
p,t,k,b,d	f,s,x,v,z	$v_{V\text{-Place}}$	m	n	l	r	ŋ/j/w	vowels

The proposal in (25a) can be revised as follows to give a more faithful account of possible onsets in Dutch:

(30) if

	appendix	onset	
$_{PrWd}$ (	s/z	C_1	C_2

then C_1 = [-sonorant] and the sonority-distance of C_1 and C_2 is minimally 1.25 on the scale in (29)

This condition excludes any onset cluster containing two stops or two fricatives, but it allows a sequence of, for instance, a voiceless stop and the voiced fricative in *kwaad* ”angry“ or a voiced stop and the voiced fricative in *dwerg* ”dwarf“. If we assume an extra-syllabic position for strident fricatives at the left word-edge, condition (30) is not violated in initial <zw> clusters, because /z/ does not belong to the onset.

3.1. Syllable-final consonant clusters

In word-final position, obstruents are voiceless. Nasals may precede homorganic stops (31a), or the strident fricative (32a). Liquids may precede voiceless stops (31b-c) and voiceless fricatives (32b-c, where written <g> represents the sound /x/):

(31)							
a.	plomp	”clumsy“	bont	”colourful“	ra[ŋ]k	”tendril“
b.	tulp	”tulip“	halt	”stop“	kalk	”lime“
c.	harp	id.	hart	”heart“	kerk	”church“

[13] I here propose that the high sonority level of the segments /ŋ/, /j/, and /w/ makes them unsuitable to occupy typical consonantal positions such as syllable codas. On the other hand, they are too consonant-like to occupy the first nucleus position. These segments thus favour the second nucleus position.

(32)	a.	*me[nf]		mens	”person“	*ma[nx]	
	b.	kalf	”calf“	mals	”tender“	velg	”rim“
	c.	korf	”basket“	mars	”march“	merg	”marrow“

Both liquids may precede /m/ (33a), and /r/ may precede /n/ (33b). Liquids may not precede /ŋ/ (33c) and they may not cooccur in word-final position (33d):

(33)	a.	kalm	”calm“	arm	”arm“
	b.	*kaln		kern	”kernel“
	c.	*kalŋ		*kerŋ	
	d.	*kalr		*kerl	

With respect to syllable structure, van der Hulst (1985) observes that one of the most prominent constraints in Dutch grammar is that the syllabic nucleus has two positions which must be filled either by a long vowel, or a diphthong, or by a short vowel and a consonant. Van der Hulst (1985) furthermore proposes that segments associated to the second nucleus position and the coda, respectively, may not be adjacent on the sonority scale in (28). This not only explains why /lm/ and /rm/ are possible syllable-final clusters, whereas /ln/ and /rl/ are not; it also explains why the diphthongs /ej/, /ow/, and /yj/ cannot be followed by /r/.

Adjacent nasals and fricatives are not acceptable syllable-final clusters in Dutch. Exceptions are clusters with nasals followed by /s/, but these clusters escape the prohibition on syllable-final nasal-fricative clusters, because /s/ is in the appendix, not in the rhyme (see 34b). The appendix also accommodates final alveolar obstruents after -VXC sequences (e.g., 34c):

(34)

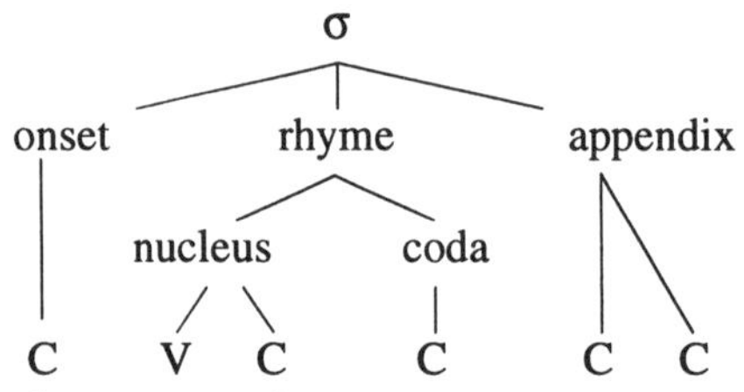

a.	(k	a	f		)	t		”cover“
b.	(m	ɛ	n		)	s		”person“
c.	(h	ɛ	r	f	)	s	t	”autumn“

A final /-mk/ sequence can be excluded when we assume - as in section 2.1 for German - that the C-Place feature Labial is restricted to the rightmost position in the rhyme (35b).

(35) if

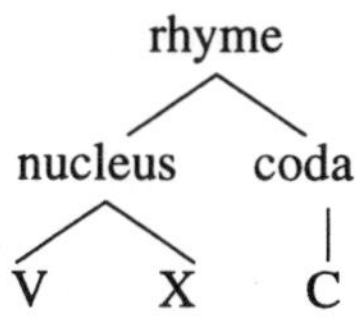

a. then X = [+sonorant] and the sonority levels of segments X and C are not adjacent on the sonority hierarchy

b. and the C-Place feature Labial can only appear in the right-most position of a rhyme.

Phonotactic restrictions in the onset and the rhyme in Dutch do not require coronal underspecification. Rather, the fact that alveolar obstruents are found preceding an onset and following a rhyme at the edge of a prosodic word (see 22 and 34, respectively) suggests to me that a statement which accounts for these facts - e.g., the use of an appendix - requires specific reference to the feature Coronal. This is, however, not the only reason to assume coronal specification. In 3.2 I will further motivate the use of an appendix after the core syllable for alveolar obstruents and in 3.3 I will present arguments in favour of coronal specification for alveolar sonorants.

3.2. Dutch word-internal Schwa-insertion

In syllable-final clusters, Schwa-insertion is optional between a liquid and a following labial or velar consonant in most dialects of Dutch (see leftmost columns below). Schwa is never inserted between a liquid and an alveolar obstruent (see rightmost columns):

(36)	a.	hulp	- hul[ə]p	"help"	halt	- *hal[ə]t	"stop"
		valk	- val[ə]k	"falcon"			
	b.	harp	- har[ə]p	"harp"	hart	- *har[ə]t	"heart"
		hark	- har[ə]k	"rake"			
(37)	a.	half	- hal[ə]f	"half"	hals	- *hal[ə]s	"neck"
		velg	- vel[ə]g	"rim"			
	b.	herfst	- her[ə]fst	"autumn"	hars	- *har[ə]s	"resin"
		erg	- er[ə]g	"bad"			
(38)	a.	helm	- hel[ə]m	"helmet"	*heln		
	b.	arm	- ar[ə]m	"arm"	kern	- ker[ə]n	"kernel"

At first sight, it may seem that we need to refer specifically to the feature Coronal to account for these data, e.g., in a statement like the following:

```
(39)      *C      ə      C          coronal consonants may not be separated by Schwa
           |             |
         Place         Place
           |             |
        Coronal       Coronal
```

However, (39) makes the wrong prediction for words like *kern*, where Schwa can be inserted between /r/ and /n/. Now consider that word-internal Schwa does not occur between two consonants which are not tautosyllabic:

(40) a. harpoen - *har[ə]poen "harpoon"
b. valkuil - *val[ə]kuil "pitfall"
c. ergo - *er[ə]go "therefore"

Geert Booij (1995:127f.) points out that we may conclude that in monomorphemic words, optional Schwa is found exclusively between two consonants in the rhyme. If the syllable structure proposed in (34) is correct, the fact that Schwa is not inserted in word-final clusters of a liquid and a following alveolar obstruent may be attributed to the fact that the alveolar obstruent is in the appendix and, hence, not part of the rhyme. An alveolar sonorant, on the other hand, is part of the rhyme and for this reason we find Schwa-insertion between final /r/ and /n/, but not between final /r/ and /t/ or /s/:

```
(41)                        σ
                 ___________|___________
                /           |           \
            onset         rhyme        appendix
              |           /   \            |
              |      nucleus   coda        |
              |       /  \       |         |
              C      V    C      C         C
          (   k      ε    r      n  )                "kernel, nucleus""
          (   h      ε    r         )      t         "deer, stag"
```

The fact that alveolar obstruents are special in the sense that they may occur outside the core syllable requires specific reference to the place of articulation of these consonants. In my view, this is an argument against coronal underspecification and in favour of coronal specification.

Independent evidence that alveolar obstruents are specified for place of articulation in Dutch comes from the phenomenon of *d-weakening* (Zonneveld 1978). In most dialects of Dutch, the voiced stop /d/ is weakened and realised as the glide [j] between a full vowel and suffixal Schwa in the examples below.[14] Unlike the hiatus-glide (43a-c), the place of

[14] *D-weakening* is not a general rule of Dutch and there are many exceptions. The rule applies in *rijd + en* [rejə] "to drive", but *spreid + en* [sprejdə] "to spread" does not become *[sprejə].

articulation of the glide that results from d-weakening is not determined by the preceding vowel, but is always realised as [j]:[15]

(42)	a.	goed + e	[xuj̲ə]	"good one"
	b.	rood + e	[ro:j̲ə]	"red one"
	c.	raad + en	[ra:j̲ə]	"to guess"

(43)	a.	hiaat	[hij̲a:t]	"hiatus"
	b.	boa	[bo:w̲a]	id.
	c.	chaos	[xa:ɔs]	id.

The question now is whether we can support the claim that alveolar sonorants are also specified for a C-Place feature. This issue will be considered next.

3.3. Dutch Schwa-insertion across the morpheme boundary

The suffix -(ə)lijk usually involves Schwa after a long vowel plus a morpheme final stop (44a-c), fricative (45a-c), or sonorant (46a) except when the morpheme final consonant is /n/ or /r/ (46b-c). In the latter case, Schwa does not appear: [16, 17]

(44)	a.	hoop + elijk	hopələk	"hopefully"
	b.	haat + elijk	hatələk	"spiteful, hateful"
	c.	smaak + elijk	smakələk	"tasty"

(45)	a.	lief + elijk	liefələk	"sweet"
	b.	vrees + elijk	vresələk	"dreadful"
	c.	behaag + elijk	behagələk	"cosy"

(46)	a.	lichaam + elijk	lichamələk	"bodily"
	b.	gewoon + elijk	*gewonələk/gewoonlək	"usually"
	c.	gevaar + elijk	*gevarələk/gevaarlək	"dangerous"

I here propose to attribute the fact that Schwa is not found between /n/ and /l/ or between /r/ and /l/ after long vowels to an inalterability effect. Across morpheme boundaries, sonorant coronals are "fused" and form a linked structure which may not be separated by Schwa (+ is a morpheme boundary):

---

15 *D-weakening* may be analysed as a change from [-son] to [+son] with simultaneous degradation of the feature Coronal from a C-Place dependent to a V-Place dependent.

16 A coronal sonorant in the nucleus followed by a coronal sonorant in the onset of a following syllable is not subject to the same condition, e.g., /n/ after a lax vowel in *bemin* "love" is followed by Schwa in *bemin[ə]lijk* "loveable".

17 The examples give the spelling of Dutch, with the exception of [ə] for <e> and <ij>. Dutch has "open syllable lengthening", e.g., <haat> with a double vowel symbol and <hatelijk> with a single vowel symbol in the first syllable both have a tense long /a:/ sound.

(47)

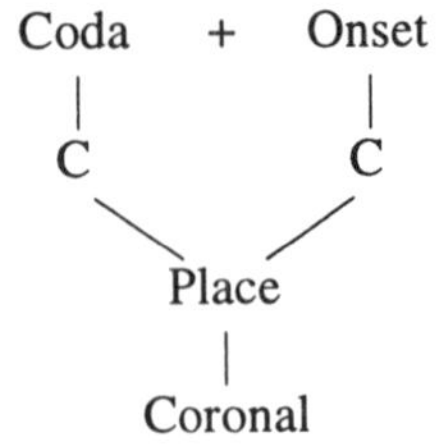

A similar proposal has been made by Ní Chiosáin (1991) for Modern Irish. In Irish, initial consonants lenite in compound-formation and prefixation (48a,b), i.e., initial stops and /m/ are realised as continuants, and initial /f/ is deleted in that environment. Lenition does not take place when both consonants at either morpheme boundary are coronals (49a,b). Lenition is indicated in the orthography by insertion of <h> after the lenitable consonant:

(48)	a.	sean ”old“	+	máthair ”mother“	→	seanmháthair ”a grandmother“
	b.	ró ”very“	+	te ”hot“	→	ró the ”very hot“
(49)	a.	sean ”old“	+	duine ”person“	→	seanduine / *seandhuine ”an old person“
	b.	an ”very“	+	deas ”nice“	→	an deas / *an dheas ”very nice“

To account for the fact that Lenition of coronals is blocked across certain morpheme boundaries, Ní Chiosáin (1991:34 ff.) proposes that: ”coronal fusion applies to derived coronal clusters which occur at formative junctures following prefixation or compounding and when certain proclitics precede nominal forms“. I suggest a similar condition for Dutch: coronal fusion applies to derived coronal clusters which occur at formative junctures following suffixation of, for instance, *-(e)lijk* and *-(e)ling*.

The facts of Dutch and Irish are not totally equivalent, since coronal fusion in Irish applies to all coronal consonants, whereas it is restricted to coronal sonorants in Dutch. To account for the fact that Schwa-insertion is blocked in (46b-c), I propose that morpheme final /n/ or /r/ and suffix initial /l/ are fused in Dutch and form a linked structure which may not be broken by Schwa. This account relies on the fact that /n/, /l/, and /r/ are specified for place of articulation at the stage where coronal fusion applies.

4. On place assimilation

A further issue is why /n/ - rather than /m/ - is prone to place assimilation in German and Dutch. The traditional analysis is that /n/ is unspecified for a place feature at the stage in the derivation where assimilation applies. Since I have argued above that it is not necessary to assume coronal underspecification in the phonology and morphology of German and Dutch, I will have to account for this phenomenon in a different way.

Consider first that a nasal may be followed by a homorganic stop (50a-c) and /m/ may be followed by /k/ in underived words in Dutch:

(50)	a.	amper	"barely"
	b.	ander	"other"
	c.	a[ŋk]er	"anchor"
	d.	imker	"bee-keeper"

In derived words, underlying /m/ does not change its place of articulation when a non-labial stop follows (51a-b), whereas underlying /n/ may be optionally realised as a labial or velar nasal under the same conditions (52a-b). There are no prefixes with a final velar nasal. A nasal does not assimilate when it follows a stop (53).

(51)	a. om	+ draaien	omdraaien	*ondraaien	"to turn around"
	b. om	+ kleden	omkleden	*oŋkleden	"to change clothes"
(52)	a. in	+ pakken	inpakken / i[m]pakken		"to pack up"
	b. in	+ kijken	inkijken / i[ŋ]kijken		"to look into"
(53)	op	+ nemen	opnemen	* opmemen	"to pick up"

The following examples from Hall (1995) illustrate that labial nasals do not change their place of articulation in German when a non-labial stop follows (54a-b), while assimilation of alveolars is optional (55):

(54)	a. um	+ drehen	umdrehen	*undrehen	"to turn around"
	b. um	+ kleiden	umkleiden	*uŋkleiden	"to clothe"
(55)	un	+ klar	unklar / u[ŋ]klar		"unclear"

I tentatively conclude from the examples above that the nucleus position does not favour a nasal consonant with a C-Place feature, whereas, in contrast, the onset position requires a C-Place feature. The first onset of the stem *nemen* "to pick" in (53), for example, is perfectly happy to accommodate an alveolar nasal consonant.

We can reformulate the notion that the nucleus does not favour a specification for consonantal place of articulation as a constraint: the nucleus may not contain a nasal segment with an independent place feature under the C-Place node.[18] When a stop follows a nasal consonant in nucleus position (see 52, 55), the stop provides a C-Place feature and the nasal consonant shares its place of articulation with that stop:

(56)

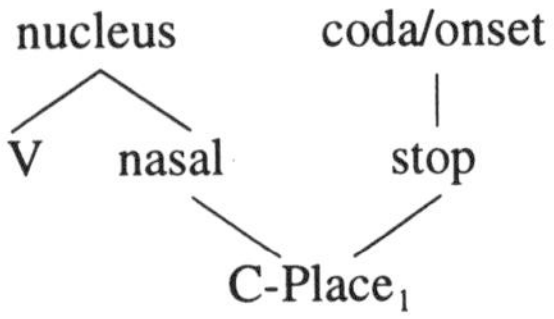

To explain the data in (51) and (54) with a labial nasal in nucleus position and a following non-labial stop in onset position, I assume that it is more important to preserve the input feature Labial than it is to satisfy the ban on an independent consonantal place feature for nasals in the nucleus. In a correspondence theoretic framework (e.g., McCarthy & Prince 1995, McCarthy 1996) this would mean that the constraint "Identity (C-Place Labial)" is ranked higher than the constraint which says that a nasal stop in nucleus position may not have independent place features (this would be a constraint which forces place assimilation):

(57) Input Dutch *om* + *kleden*, or German *um* + *kleiden*

Input: Labial nasal + non-labial stop	Identity (C-Place Labial)	*Nucleus (V Nasal$_{C\text{-}Place}$)
☞ o[m]kleden		*
o[ŋ]kleden	*!	

The observed variation between alveolar /n/ and the assimilated nasal in (52a-b) and (55) can be explained if we assume that the constraint "Identity (C-Place Coronal)" is not ranked with respect to the constraint requiring assimilation in Dutch and German. In Dutch *inkijken* and German *unklar*, the constraint which forces place assimilation is violated and "Identity (C-Place Coronal)" is satisfied, because /n/ preserves its consonantal place of articulation. In Dutch *i[ŋ]kijken* and German *u[ŋ]klar*, the constraint requiring place assimilation is satisfied, but the underlying C-place feature - Coronal - is not preserved:

[18] Words with a short vowel and a following coronal or labial nasal (like Dutch *pan* "pan" and *lam* "lamb") show that the constraint in question is violable. In a constraint-based approach such as Correspondence Theory (see McCarthy & Prince 1995), this constraint should be ranked lower than MAX - otherwise the optimal output for *pan* would be *pa* - and it should be ranked lower than DEP - otherwise the input form *pan* would surface as, e.g., *pant*.

(58) Input Dutch *in* + kijken, or German *un* + *klar*

Input: Coronal nasal + non-coronal stop	Identity (C-Place Labial)	*Nucleus (V Nasal$_{C\text{-}Place}$)	Identity (C-Place Coronal)
☞ i[n]kijken		*	
☞ i[ŋ]kijken			*

The examples in (51) and (54) show that prefixes that end in labial /m/ in German and Dutch preserve their consonantal place of articulation and examples (52) and (55) illustrate that prefixes that end in alveolar /n/ may optionally assimilate. As there are no prefixes that end in /ŋ/, nothing can be said about the behaviour of velar nasals in potential assimilation contexts. Little attention has been given in previous literature on velars and the status of the feature Dorsal. I will briefly point out some issues concerning velar consonants in German and Dutch in the next section.

5. On velars

It is striking that in many languages dorsal consonants exhibit a defective distribution. For example, Standard German has labial and coronal affricates, but no velar affricate (see Figure 1). Standard Dutch has voiced labial and coronal obstruents, but lacks voiced velar obstruents (see Figure 2). English has labial and coronals fricatives, but no velar fricative. Furthermore, velars have a restricted distribution. Dorsal fricatives cannot precede sonorants in syllable-onset position in German and the velar nasal does not occur in onset position or after long vowels or diphthongs in German, Dutch, and English.

Whereas autosegmental rules may single out the features Labial and Coronal, delinking and spreading of the feature Dorsal seems to be unattested. Furthermore, we find OCP-effects on the feature Labial, e.g., in Arabic roots (McCarthy 1988) and in Belauan verbal morphology (Altjohann 1997). There are also OCP-effects on the feature Coronal. Schwa insertion between two alveolar obstruents across a morpheme boundary in German (section 2.2), for example, may be attributed to an OCP-effect. OCP-effects on the feature Dorsal are rare. Thus, velars are exceptional in that (i) they do not exhibit certain manners of articulation in a language's sound system, (ii) they are excluded from certain syllable positions, and (iii) no autosegmental process refers to the feature Dorsal. I suspect that this is a universal tendency and in what follows, I pursue the idea - based on Rice 1996 - that palatals, velars, and uvulars lack a feature for consonantal place of articulation.

5.1. On palatals and velars

For Dutch, I argued in section 3 that the voiced fricative spelled <w> is the only fricative which is sonorant enough to occur after stops in onset position. This property was attributed to the fact that the segment has a C-Place node, but lacks a consonantal place of articulation (see 26b). Now consider that the palatal fricative is exceptional in German in that it may not precede sonorants in onset position. The sound [ç] occurs in absolute syllable initial position (e.g., *Chemie* "chemistry" and *Ar.chi.tekt* "Architect", where ch = [ç]), but, in contrast to other fricatives, it does not occur in an initial consonant cluster.

The condition that the first consonant in onset position is [-sonorant] and the second one is [+sonorant] in German (see 7a) does not exclude prohibited onset clusters like *[çn-], *[çl-], or *[çr-]. The condition has to be revised to a condition which prescribes a minimal sonority distance in onsets. The figures presented in (59) below are tentative and are used merely to enable us to refer to a number to express the notion of "sonority-distance". Assuming the values below, the minimal sonority distance in German onsets is 2. This condition allows for initial stop + nasal sequences, stop + liquid sequences, and fricative + liquid sequences, and excludes onset clusters with [ç] as a first or second member:

(59) Revised sonority hierarchy for German

1	1.5	2	3	3.5	3.75	5
|	|	|	|	|	|	|
stops	frics	ç	nasals	l	ʀ	vowels

As for /$v_{V\text{-Place}}$/ in Dutch, I propose for /ç/ in German that the sonority level of this segment is higher than the sonority level of other fricatives, because it lacks a consonantal place of articulation. It is similar to other fricatives in that it is [-sonorant] and [+continuant] (see 61a below).

The fricative [ç] is in complementary distribution with [x] and [χ]. According to Kohler (1990), the palatal fricative occurs word-initially, word-finally after consonants, and after front vowels (60a). The velar fricative occurs after non-low back tense vowels (60b), and the uvular fricative is found after low vowels (60c):

(60) a. dich ch=[ç] "you (acc.)"
b. Buch ch=[x] "book"
c. Dach ch=[χ] "roof"

The data in (60b-c) suggest that vocalic place features are provided by preceding vowels in the case of [x] and [χ]. To distinguish the three fricatives, I suggest the following place specifications:

(61)

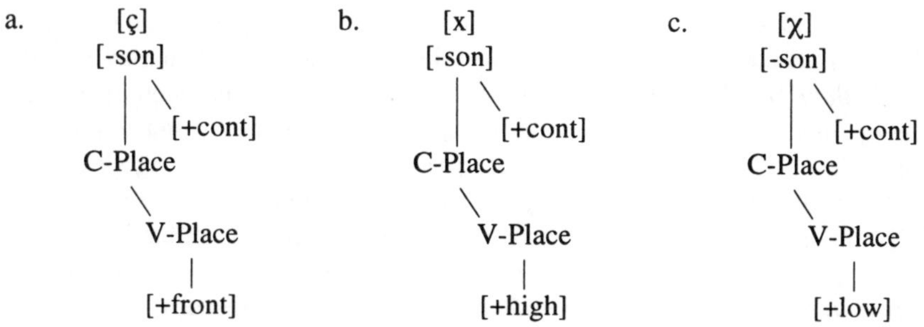

One of the consequences of this approach is that velars other than [x] are also expected to lack a C-Place feature and to bear the V-Place feature [+high]. Consider in this respect that [s] usually precedes velar [k], while [ʃ] precedes [p] and [t] (see 5a-b). With Hall (1992), I assume that [ʃ] and [k] share the feature-specification [+high]. Under this view, the strident fricative is realised without the feature [+high] in sk-clusters (62b) to avoid an OCP-violation:

(62)

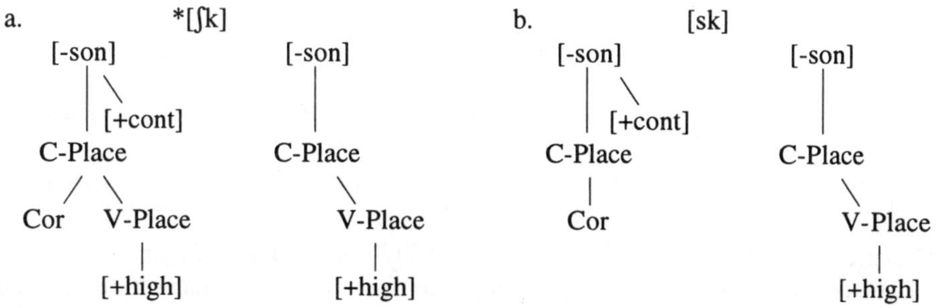

The representation of /ʃ/ above is further motivated by the following correlation between German and Dutch. In many cases, initial clusters with /ʃ/ in German correspond to initial clusters with /sx/ in Dutch:

(63)	a. German:	Schirm	"screen"	schreiben	"to write"	sch=/ʃ/
	b. Dutch:	scherm	"screen"	schrijven	"to write"	sch=/sx/

I here propose that German /ʃ/ (64a) has the two place components which characterise the fricatives /s/ and /x/, respectively, in Dutch (64b):

(64)

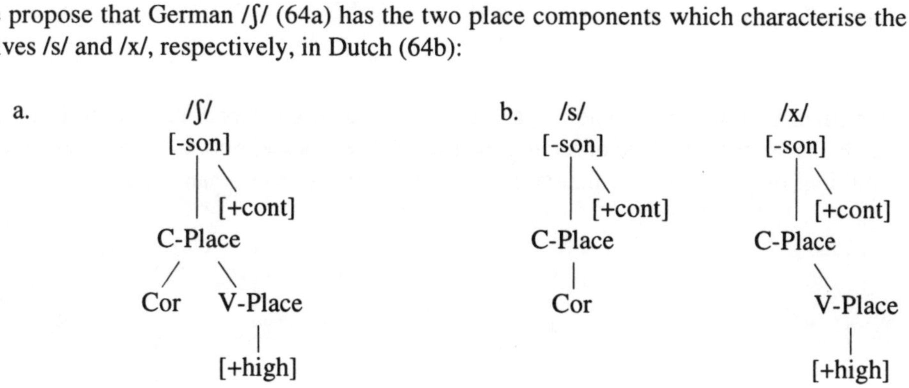

The velar nasal does not occur in onset position of syllables, nor after long vowels in German. It is only attested after short vowels and the only consonants that may follow [ŋ] are [k] and [g] (*Bank* [baŋk], *Tango* [taŋgo]). It is usually assumed that there is no underlying phoneme /ŋ/ in German, rather, the velar nasal only emerges as a result of nasal assimilation (e.g., Wiese 1996: 219). To account for [ŋ] in words like *lang* 'long', it is assumed in the literature that the nasal inherits its place features from syllable-final /g/ which is realised as [k] in Northern dialects of German ([laŋk]) and which is deleted in syllable-final positions in Standard German ([laŋ]). This analysis is supported by alternations such as *Diphthong* (without final [g]) and *diphthongieren* (with [g] realised in onset position). In accordance with the proposal above for the representation of velar stop [k] in German (see 62b) and the velar fricative [x] in German and Dutch (see 61b and 64b, respectively), I assume that the velar nasal is also represented by V-Place features, rather than by a C-Place feature such as Dorsal (see 65c):

(65)

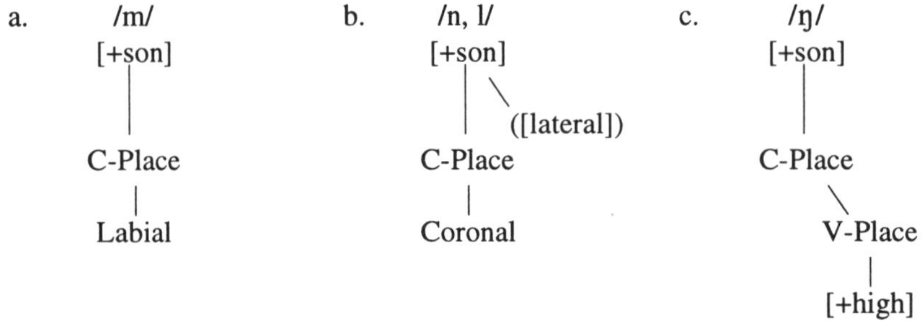

In German, Dutch, and English, [ŋ] may only fill the second nucleus position. If velars lack a C-Place feature, we may attribute this phenomenon to the fact that onsets and codas are typically consonantal slots, i.e., slots which require a consonantal specification. The phonological representation of velar nasals without any specific consonantal features such as [-sonorant] or a feature for consonantal place of articulation may account for the fact that they are not found in typical consonantal positions such as the coda position of a syllable. I leave further consequences of this proposal for future research.

6. Conclusion

This paper focuses on syllable-initial and syllable-final consonant clusters in German and Dutch. The structure of the onset and the rhyme (see 66a and 66b, respectively), as well as conditions on places of articulation (see 67), are identical in German and Dutch:

(66) a. Maximal onset: C_1 C_2

b. Maximal rhyme: nucleus coda

V X C where X = [+sonorant] and sonority level X > sonority level C

(67) a. consonants in the onset do not have the same place of articulation
b. the C-Place feature Labial is leftmost in the onset and rightmost in the rhyme

The marginal differences in the distribution of consonants that exist between the two languages are attributed to different sonority-requirements:

(68) a. German onset condition:
C_1 = [-sonorant] and the sonority-distance of C_1 and C_2 is minimally 2 on the scale in (59)

b. Dutch onset condition:
C_1 = [-sonorant] and the sonority-distance of C_1 and C_2 is minimally 1.25 on the scale in (29)

The fact that final *-ln* and *-rl* clusters are permissible in German (*Köln, Kerl*), but not in Dutch, are not accounted for by different representations of coronals in German and Dutch, but rather by different sonority restrictions. In particular, in German, the sonority sequencing principle involves that the sonority-level of the consonant in nucleus position is higher than the sonority-level of the coda consonant on scale (59). The two segments may be adjacent on that scale. In Dutch, the consonant in nucleus and the consonant in coda position may not have the same sonority-level and, in addition, they may not be adjacent on the sonority scale in (29).

With respect to consonantal places of articulation, I propose that phonotactic restrictions refer to the C-Place features Labial and Coronal and that velars lack a C-Place feature. In particular, I have argued that the feature Labial prefers the left edge of onsets and the right edge of rhymes. The appendix is reserved for obstruents specified for the feature Coronal. Furthermore, lexical rules in German require Coronal to be present and Schwa-insertion in Dutch is best explained if we assume that "coronal fusion" takes place at certain morpheme boundaries. Coronal specification thus plays a crucial role in the phonology and morphology of German and Dutch.

Acknowledgements

I would like to thank Geert Booij, Tracy Alan Hall, Helga Humbert, Jan Kooij, Martin Krämer, Martin Neef, Roland Noske, Albert Ortmann, Ruben van de Vijver, and the editors of this volume for valuable comments.

References

Altjohann, Anja (1997): *Die Vokal/Konsonanten-Alternation im Belauischen*. Ms. Düsseldorf.

Avery, Peter & Keren Rice (1989): Segment Structure and Coronal Underspecification. *Phonology* 6, 179-200.

Booij, Geert (1995): *The Phonology of Dutch*. Oxford: Clarendon Press.

Clements, G.N. (1989): *A Unified Set of Features for Consonants and Vowels*. Ms. Cornell University.

Hall, Tracy Alan (1992): *Syllable Structure and Syllable-Related Processes in German*. Tübingen: Niemeyer.

— (1995): Remarks on Coronal Underspecification. *Proceedings of the First HIL-Phonology Conference*. Leiden, 187-203.

Hulst, Harry van der (1984): *Syllable structure and stress in Dutch*. Dordrecht: Foris.

— (1985): Ambisyllabicity in Dutch. *Linguistics in the Netherlands* 1, Dordrecht: Foris, 57-66.

Hume, Elizabeth (1992): *Front vowels, coronal consonants and their interaction in non-linear phonology*. Ph.D. dissertation, Cornell University, Ithaca, N.Y.

Jespersen, Otto (1904): *Lehrbuch der Phonetik*. Leipzig: Teubner.

Kohler, Klaus J. (1990): Comments on German. *Journal of the International Phonetic Association* 20, 48-50.

McCarthy, John J. (1988): Feature Geometry and Dependency: A Review. *Phonetica* 43; 45, 84-104.

— (1996): *Faithfulness in Prosodic Morphology & Phonology: Rotuman Revisited*. Ms. University of Massachusetts, Amherst.

McCarthy, John & Alan Prince (1995): *Faithfulness and Reduplicative Identity*. In: Jill N. Beckman et al., (eds.): *Papers in Optimality Theory*. University of Massachusetts Occasional Working Papers 18. UMass, Amherst: GLSA, 249-384.

McCarthy, John & Alison Taub (1992): Review of Paradis and Prunet 1991. *Phonology* 9, 363-370.

Ní Chiosáin, Máire (1991): *Topics in the Phonology of Irish*. Ph.D. dissertation, University of Massachusetts, Amherst.

Ní Chiosáin, Máire & Jaye Padgett (1993): *On the Nature of Consonant-Vowel Interaction*. Report no. LCR-93-09. Linguistic Research Center, UC Santa Cruz.

Paradis, Carole & Jean-François Prunet (1989): On Coronal Transparency. *Phonology* 6, 317-348.

— (eds) (1991): *The Special Status of Coronals: Internal and External Evidence*. San Diego: Academic Press.

Ramers, Karl-Heinz & Heinz Vater (1995): *Einführung in die Phonologie*. Hürth: Gabel Verlag.

Rice, Keren (1996): Default Variability: The Coronal-Velar Relationship. *Natural Language and Linguistic Theory* 14, 493-543.

Selkirk, Elisabeth O. (1984): On the major class features and syllable theory. In: M. Aronoff and R.T. Oehrle (eds), *Language Sound Structure*. Cambridge, Mass.: MIT Press, 107-136.

Trubetzkoy, Nikolai (1939/1969): *Grundzüge der Phonologie / Principles of Phonology*. (C. Baltaxe, translator), University of California Press.

Vater, Heinz (1992): Zum Silben-Nukleus im Deutschen. In: Peter Eisenberg, et al. (eds): *Silbenphonologie des Deutschen*. Tübingen, 100-133.

Vennemann, Theo (1982): Zur Silbenstruktur der deutschen Standardsprache. In: Theo Vennemann (ed.): *Silben, Segmente, Akzente*. Tübingen: Niemeyer, 261-305.

— (1988): *Preference Laws for Syllable Structure and the Explanation of Sound Change*. Berlin: Mouton.

Wiese, Richard (1991): Was ist extrasilbisch im Deutschen und warum? In: Karl-Heinz Ramers & Richard Wiese (eds): *Zeitschrift für Sprachwissenschaft* 10, 112-133.

— (1996): *The Phonology of German*. Oxford: Clarendon Press.

Zonneveld, Wim (1978): *Formal Theory of Exceptions in Generative Phonology*. Dordrecht: Foris.

Albert Ortmann

Consonant epenthesis: its distribution and phonological specification

1. Introduction[1]

This article is concerned with the phonological and distributional aspects of productive consonant epenthesis in hiatus position. I characterise the segmental and prosodic environment of inserted consonants as well as their segmental shape. In addition to analyses of *r* in British English and *n* in High Alemannic, a universal characterisation of possible epenthetic consonants is proposed that makes use of minimalist feature specifications.

The article is composed as follows: I will start with a classification of the various types of consonant epenthesis, followed by a brief discussion of the well-known example Axininca Campa. In section 3, I recapitulate the facts of British English intrusive *r* and then propose an analysis based on the notion of feature spreading. Section 4, the major part of the paper, is a detailed study of High Alemannic 'Binde-*n*'. I will argue that the *n* -∅ alternation in its entire complexity is not merely the result of a general, unrestricted epenthesis rule. Rather, it comes about by either a more specific rule of epenthesis or by lexical prespecification of the segment *n*, which is only parsed under resyllabification. Section 5 introduces a universal restriction on consonant phonemes which can occur in systematic epenthesis. The main results are summed up in section 6.

2. Consonant epenthesis - an overview

The phenomenon of consonant epenthesis is widely spread among the world's languages. The best-known example seems to be *t*-insertion in Axininca Campa. However, productive epenthesis is also found in the Germanic languages, namely in English and High Alemannic (to be discussed in 3. and 4., respectively). I will first provide an informal classification of the phenomenon in its broader sense.

[1] This work was carried out in the Special Research Programme „Theorie des Lexikons" (SFB 282), supported by the German Science Foundation (DFG). I am particularly indebted to Janet Grijzenhout for valuable discussion. I would also like to thank Peter Gallmann, Birgit Gerlach, Wolfgang Kehrein, James Kirchner, Martin Krämer, Damaris Nübling, Tobias Scheer, Carsten Steins, Richard Wiese, Dieter Wunderlich, and Susi Wurmbrand. Last but not least, thanks go to the audience of an oral presentation of this paper, especially to Geert Booij and Paul Kiparsky.

2.1 Classification

Rather than being a uniform strategy, consonant epenthesis is a heterogeneous phenomenon. It occurs in various segmental shapes, as well as in different phonotactic and prosodic contexts. To start with the latter, we find consonant epenthesis in the following environments:

- in hiatus position, as the *r* in *law [r] and order*
- in sonority clashes, e.g. *t* in the history of German, as in *hoffentlich* 'hopefully'
- intrusive stop formation after a nasal within a consonant cluster, for example in *warm[p]th*, or French *chambre* 'room' < Romance *cam(e)ra* (see Hock 1991 and Picard 1989)
- to fill a C-slot in a morphological template where no lexically underlying consonant is available (see Broselow 1995:182 and references therein)
- as a means to avoid otherwise empty onsets, which are universally dispreferred

Epenthesis also differs with respect to shape, that is the segmental properties of the inserted consonant. The following strategies of associating segmental material to the epenthetic C-position are attested:

- the placeless consonant segment, i.e. the glottal stop, will be inserted on a phonetic level if no phonemic consonant is available in the language, as in German *Auto* [ʔaʊto] 'car'
- a stop that receives its place specification from an adjacent segment, like in *warm[p]th* above
- glide insertion, which can be described as spreading of vocalic features
- a specific and invariant consonant phoneme of the language

I will be concerned with the latter type only, that is, a specific consonant phoneme, the 'default' consonant in a sense to be made precise in section 5, of the language in question. For more information on some of the other types, the reader is referred to Picard (1989) and Hock (1991).

2.2 An introductory example

Probably the best-known example of productive consonant epenthesis in the literature is from Axininca Campa. It was first described in Payne (1981). Let us consider the treatment of underlying forms with two adjacent vowels. From underlying */noN-pisi-i/*, for example, we get *[nompisiti]*, a form with *t* between the vowels on the surface.

(1) Axininca Campa (Arawakan language, Amazon):

/noN-pisi-i/	→	*[nompisiti]*	'I will sweep'	(Itô 1989:237)
/noN-piyo-i/	→	*[nompiyoti]*	'I will heap'	
/i-n-koma-i/	→	*[iŋkomati]*	'he will paddle'	

There are two assumptions associated with epenthesis in Axininca that are widely held in the literature. The first is an implicit one and says that consonant epenthesis is a general rule in Axininca, and also in other languages, and the only question is what kind of consonants are epenthesised. The second assumption has often been made explicit (see for example the contributions in Paradis & Prunet 1991): [coronal] is underspecified in phonological representation; therefore, coronals must be the typical epenthesis consonants in the world's languages.

Consequently, *t* has been described as the unmarked consonant for Axininca (Payne 1981, Itô 1989; accordingly, *a*, which is used for vowel epenthesis, is treated as the unmarked vowel). However, with respect to these assumptions it must be stated that the first is wrong and the second is only half true. As for Axininca Campa, this point has been made already by Spring (1994). She shows that in this language consonant epenthesis is by no means a general phonological rule. Rather, it is restricted to the morphological context of verbal suffixation. In other affixation contexts, hiatus is avoided by vowel deletion:

(2)	verb prefixation:	*pi-ook-i-ro*	*[pookiro]*	(Spring 1994)
		2-leave-FUT-3f	you will leave it	
	noun prefixation:	*no-inki-ni*	*[niŋkini]*	
		1-peanut-POSS	my peanut	
	noun suffixation:	*manii-iriki*	*[maniiriki]*	
		ants-DIM	little ants	

In the first and in the third example *i* is deleted, and in the second one, *o* is deleted. The theoretical point to be noted is that like in the case of Axininca, it is very typical of consonant epenthesis that it underlies morphological or syntactic restrictions, as will become clearer in section 4.

As to the second assumption in the literature, it must be stated that it is doubtful whether coronals really should be treated as unspecified. In fact, this idea has often been rejected in the more recent literature; see Grijzenhout (1998) and references therein. And even for Axininca, Spring gives evidence in terms of velar deletion and nasal assimilation that coronals, unlike velars, have to be specified. Thus instead of the assumption of coronal underspecification, I will propose that an epenthetic consonant is *minimally* specified within its phonemic system, that is in terms of one node or feature specification only. Accordingly, Axininca *t* can be represented with the only underlying specification [coronal], and the fact that labials or velars are not found in systematic epenthesis must follow from principles other than the representation of consonant segments. These reflections will be given more substance in section 5, after detailed analyses of two other cases of consonant epenthesis.

3. British English intrusive *r*

British English intrusive *r* represents the hiatus type of consonant epenthesis in its most typical origin, namely reanalysis of a consonant that has historically been lost in coda position. My analysis will particularly draw on the complementary distribution with glide formation.

3.1 The facts

In many varieties of English, like Standard British English with its pronunciation called 'RP' (Received Pronunciation), *r* does not occur in coda position. Historically, this absence is a loss due to a vocalisation process: depending on the height of the preceding vowel, the process has resulted in either a monophthong, as in *far* [fɑː], or in a diphthong, as in *stair* [stɛə]. However, these so-called non-rhotic varieties of English still realise former coda *r* (which was formerly realised exactly where the orthography indicates it, and where the rhotic dialects such as American English have maintained it) if the following syllable begins with a vowel. Here, the *r* functions as the onset of this syllable. For illustration consider the words in (3), both in isolation (a) and with a following vowel (b):

(3)	a.	*far [fɑː]*	*spider [spaɪdə]*	*fear [fɪə]*	*door [dɔː]*
	b.	*fa[r] away*	*the spide[r] is*	*in fea[r] of*	*the doo[r] is*

The (a) examples are all pronounced with a final vowel. In the (b) examples, *r* 'links' the syllable to a following vowel initial syllable, as it constitutes the onset of the latter. Let me emphasise again the fact that in RP syllables can never have *r* in the coda[2]

From this use of /r/, traditionally called 'linking *r*', the alternation *r* - ∅ is generalised to stems where *r* has never been present underlyingly, giving rise to the 'intrusive *r*' in hiatus contexts, as in the examples in (4).

(4)	*the idea [r] of*	*the cinema [r] is*	*a raw [r] egg*
	law [r] and order	*China [r] or Japan*	*draw[r]ing*

Thus for most speakers of Standard British English, *r* is the general means of avoiding hiatus. In other words, a reanalysis in the phonotactic behaviour of the phoneme /r/ has taken place in terms of the scenario in (5a), which can be described by an informal rule inversion as in (5b).[3]

(5) a. *r* occurs also in codas > *r* gets lost in codas, but is retained under resyllabification, i.e. when realised in onset position (linking *r*) > all syllables ending in a non-high vowel show *r* when followed by a vowel (intrusive *r*)

b. /r/ → ∅ is reanalysed into ∅ → /r/

---

[2] In particular, speakers of American English sometimes find it hard to accept that in British English, words like *far* and *bar* have the same rhyme as *bra*, and *spider* the same as in *China*, *here* or *beer* the same as in *idea*, and *door, floor* as in *law*.

[3] The same kind of reanalysis happened in the case of German schwa: full vowels are reduced to schwa > reduced vowels get dropped except where they are needed for syllabification > epenthesis of schwa.

Turning now to the synchronic restrictions of intrusive *r*, the crucial phonological factor is that *r* is not inserted after high vowels. Rather, in this environment the high vowel spreads to the initial consonant position and is realised as a glide.

(6) [i]: **see /r/ it* *see /j/ it* [u]: **too /r/ old* *too /w/ old*

It is thus clear that the distribution of intrusive *r* is phonologically governed by the surrounding vowels; a fact that the phonological representation in the following subsection will have to account for. On the morphosyntactic side, however, there are no restrictions: *r* is not blocked after any morphological or syntactic category; nor is it limited to the word boundary, as can be seen from word-internal *r* as in *draw[r]ing, saw[r]ing.*[4] In this regard, intrusive *r* behaves differently from virtually all other examples of epenthesis of a consonant phoneme.[5]

---

4 As McCarthy (1993) points out, in a variety very close to British English, viz. Massachussetts English, a morphosyntactic restriction appears to exist, namely a ban against intrusive *r* after function words. However, McCarthy shows that this restriction is in fact a phonological one, following from the prosodic status of function words as proclitics rather than prosodic words of their own. Moreover, in Colloquial British English, *r* is possible even after reduced function words such as *to, you, do*, as is clear from examples like *I'm gonna ask [gənə-r-ɑːsk]* or *something to eat [tə-r-i̥ːt]*; hence our conclusion that morphology plays no role for intrusive *r*.
I should also mention that in his article, McCarthy provides an Optimality Theoretic analysis of intrusive *r*. His analysis, however, aims at capturing the exact prosodic environment of the variety in question, whereas the present account is primarily concerned with the segmental properties of the epenthetic consonant.

5 The more common situation for consonant epenthesis is the opposite situation of English, namely non-productive, construction-specific epenthesis, without a general phonological rule. In other words, consonant epenthesis is often restricted to morpheme-specific environments, or it is lexicalised in other cases. Let me mention three examples in order to make clear what this article is *not* concerned with: first, there is French formal style inversion as in *Pourquoi a-t-il ....* No phonological rule can be assumed here, rather, perhaps, a lexical variant of the auxiliary, like in the case of the *a* vs. *an* alternation of the English indefinite article.
A second example is the Dutch *d* - zero alternation, which is restricted to *[r-ˈr], a sequence that never surfaces in Dutch. It seems to be banned because otherwise sonority (or OCP) conflicts would arise:

(i)	*ver - verder*	*klaar - klaarder*	*leren - leerder*	*Almére - Almeerder*
	'far - further'	'clear - clearer'	'learn - student'	A.(place) - A.(inhabitant)

However, *[rər] is not avoided by the existence of a phonological rule of d-insertion, but rather, as Booij (1998) points out, by allomorphy selection; cf. *Amsterdam-er* (*-er* as default), *Diemen-aar, luister-aar* (*-aar* in prosodically strong position). In other words, there is no rule of *d*-epenthesis in Dutch. For example, ***d*** is not available in other types of word formations.
Third, consider derivations formed by the suffix *-lich* in Standard German, where an otherwise unpreferred syllable contact is avoided (cf. Löhken 1995):

(ii)	*eigen**t**lich,*	*wesen**t**lich,*	*orden**t**lich,*	*hoffen**t**lich,*	*wissen**t**lich*	*morgen**d**lich*
	'actually'	'essentially'	'properly'	'hopefully'	'knowing'	'morning...'

There is no general ban against sonorant clusters in German, and again, consonant epenthesis is not a general rule, cf. *morgen**d**lich* 'morning... (ADJ.)' (< *Morgen+lich*) vs. *Morgen**l**icht* 'morning light' (< *Morgen+Licht*), in the same prosodic environment. Many other more or less idiosyncratic instances of consonant epenthesis can easily be found; cf. Hock (1991). These cases often have properties different from productive epenthesis, e.g. as far as the epenthetic consonant is con-

Summing up our description of the facts of intrusive *r*, we can state the following: (i) British English consonant epenthesis is not restricted by the morphology, but rather by a general phonological rule of the language, and (ii) a consonant that is historically lost in the coda but is retained in the onset is a good candidate to be reanalysed as an epenthetic consonant, since it alternates with zero. Subsequent reanalysis can lead to epenthesis as 'emergence of the unmarked'. Let me now present a phonological account of the phenomenon.

3.2 Representation: intrusive *r* as the result of spreading

The analysis that will be presented in this subsection starts out from the following premises: (i) *r* insertion can be described without reference to morphology or syntax, hence as a purely phonological phenomenon. Therefore, a general hiatus rule can be assumed; (ii) as the synchronic phonotactic distribution of *r* shows, the choice of this phoneme as the epenthetic consonant is immanent to the phonological system: *r* is never underlying in codas, and there is no rule that deletes *r*; (iii) intrusive *r* and glide insertion are in complementary distribution.

To account with one single rule for (iii), the complementary distribution of *r* and glide insertion, I will make use of an idea in Broadbent (1991). Broadbent treats intrusive *r* as the result of spreading, more precisely as glide formation, parallel to the occurrence of *j* and *w* in (6). In a Government Phonology based analysis she proposes that the vocalic element 'A' (basically for 'low'), which is present in all non-high vowels, spreads into the empty onset of the following syllable, the assumption being that unlike the 'genuine' glides *r* is [-high][6] Given that *r* and the glides *j* and *w* are the most sonorous consonants, and that they are traditionally looked upon as a natural class, namely 'approximants', a treatment in terms of one rule is very convincing. Obviously, however, it is not an appealing solution to treat *r* literally as a glide[7] I thus follow Broadbent only in assuming that intrusive *r* comes about by spreading of vowel height, not, however, in treating *r* as a glide.

What I propose, then, in terms of feature geometry, is that both the glides and *r* in British English have a 'vocalic' node[8] This enables an analysis under which the empty consonant position, introduced by the general hiatus rule in (7a), is provided with its features by the

---

cerned (like *d* in (i), which will be predicted to be an impossible candidate for productive epenthesis in section 5.), and no claim is made here as to their specific conditions.

6 Assuming a third (viz. non-high) glide is not uncommon. For example, Golston & Kehrein (1997), in their treatment of onsets in Mazatec, assume a labial, a palatal and a dorsal glide. In this language, glides are generally associated with onset consonants. They are contrastive, thus not the result of spreading. Crucially, however, the dorsal glide is not an *r* sound. The reason why an underspecified dorsal approximant surfaces as a glide in Mazatec but as *r* in English is, I assume, that the former has no phoneme *r*. The interpretation of consonants with 'vocalic' nodes is thus immanent to the particular system of the language in question.

7 This problem remains even if one disregards a theory-internal problem in Broadbent's account, making wrong predictions about mid vowels.

8 My use of the vocalic node is due to Clements & Hume (1995:283f). It is simply for convenience that I do not stick to their representation of vowel height in terms of a separate aperture node (next to a V-place node for the place features) but rather to the more familiar feature [high].

spreading of the vocalic node from the preceding vowel as in (7b). Note that the vowel features relevant for height and frontness are the only ones to be underlyingly specified under the [vocalic] node; in particular, features such as [labial] (or [round], more traditionally), are not involved since they are not distinctive in the vowel system of English.

(7) a. *hiatus rule:* $\varnothing \rightarrow \begin{bmatrix} +\text{cons} \\ +\text{son} \end{bmatrix}$ / $\text{V}]_\sigma \ {}_\sigma[\ \_\_\ \text{V}$

b. *specification of epenthetic segment:*

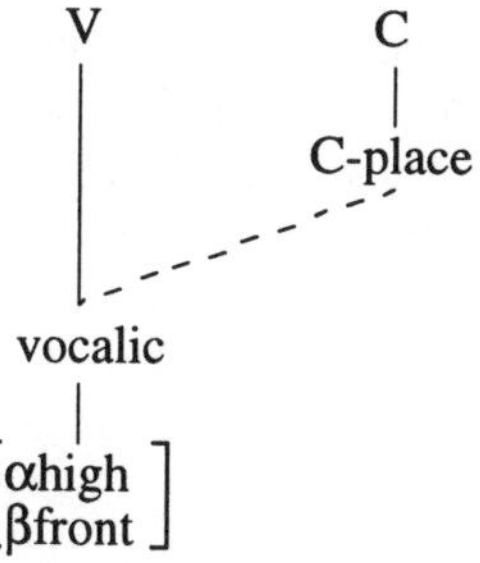

This analysis gives us the correct results if we assume the feature representation of the three consonants involved to be like in (8).

(8)

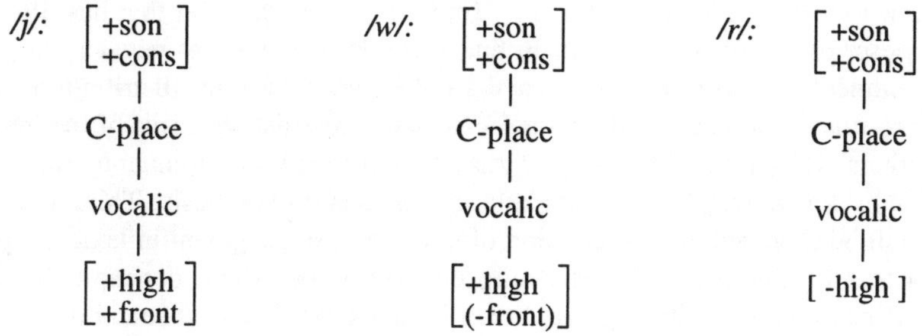

The glides are specified as [+high], and *r* is specified as [-high]. The dominating nodes are filled in by universal well-formedness restrictions, for example [high] implies the presence of vocalic, or vocalic for consonants implies C-place. The only information that must be present underlyingly, besides the root node features [cons] and [son], are the specifications for [high] and [front].

Note that there is an interaction of a universal and a specific part: the universal part is the hiatus rule[9], which is otherwise operative in the phonetic component, where C can be filled by a non-phonemic segment, like the glottal stop. The specific part is the representation of *r* and the occurrence of the feature [high]. Spreading to glides in, for example, Dutch (or in German) is not restricted to a preceding high vowel and makes only reference to the feature

[9] Next to epenthesis, of course, there are various conflicting universal rules by which hiatus is avoided on the surface, such as glide formation, vowel deletion or coalescence. See Rosenthal (1997) for illustration and an Optimality account of the variation found across languages; Casali (1997) offers an account of the strategy of vowel deletion.

[front] instead, which can be seen from the Dutch forms *theater* [teː'(j)aːtər] 'theatre' and *zoals* [zoː'(v)als] 'like; as if'.

To conclude this section, let me sum up the advantages of my analysis of intrusive *r*. The complementary distribution of glides and intrusive *r* is immediately explained by spreading, and by the default nature of *r* in RP: *r* is the default approximant. The epenthesis consonant is thus minimally specified: the feature [-high] suffices to characterise *r*. It is sufficiently distinguished from the glides, which are [+high], and from all other consonants, which do not have a vocalic node.[10] RP glide formation is thus structure-preserving, in the sense that its results are all immanent to the phonological system. The spreading analysis also motivates why *r* is not generally inserted in empty onsets: when there are no features to spread, viz. initially of prosodic domains higher than the prosodic word, the onset is filled by the placeless glottal stop.

In the next section, I will provide another case study of the hiatus type, namely epenthesis of *n* in High Alemannic.

4. 'Binde-*n*' in High Alemannic

In this section, I will provide an account of 'Binde-*n*', a phenomenon that has often been observed in descriptions of Swiss German, but to my knowledge has never been given a theoretical treatment.[11] It will be seen to have a rather heterogeneous distribution, such as cliticisations to functional heads, inflectional ə-suffixes, alternative forms of the indefinite article, and others. The discussion will show that these different environments cannot all be accounted for by a general phonological rule of consonant epenthesis. Three theoretical alternatives will be sketched; the assumption of *n* as a floating segment in lexical representations (next to a productive epenthesis rule) enables a consistent, conceptually simple treatment of Binde-*n* and is to be preferred over both a solution based solely upon cliticisation and a deletion rule.

4.1 Basic facts

High Alemannic is mainly spoken in Switzerland, known as Swiss German, and also in the very south west of Germany as well as in western parts of Austria. My data are from descriptions of Swiss dialects, for which references are provided in each case, and otherwise from a variety in Germany, spoken in the south of the Black Forest and the Upper

---

10 Note that the specification [-high] is necessary, and simply 'vocalic' would not suffice, in order to avoid the application of (7b) for lexically underlying *r* in, e.g., *he rides*, which would lead to the incorrect result **he [j]ides*.

11 I should mention that in some syntactic studies *n*-epenthesis has been taken as a diagnostic for clitics (for example Bader & Penner 1988, Cooper 1995). Being regarded as a diagnostic, however, its status is taken for granted rather than being an object of investigation by itself, as in the present study.

Rhine valley (all examples from this variety are represented in orthography).[12] The epenthetic *n* is glossed as 'EP' throughout. The examples in (9) provide a first illustration of the phenomenon.

(9)	*grösser wie-n-i* taller than-EP-I 'taller than I'	*gang zu-n-ere* go to-EP-her go to her'
	bi-n-ene at-EP-them 'with them'	*so, wie-n-er gsait hätt* so as-EP-he said has 'right as he said'
	säll ha-n-i scho this have I already 'I have this already'	*däs Stuck, wo-n-ere id gfalle hätt* the play REL-EP-her not pleased has 'the play she didn't like'

These data show that hiatus as in **wie i* or **zu ere* is avoided throughout by inserting *n* in that position. Traditionally, the phenomenon is called 'Binde-*n*'. It is often mentioned in the descriptive literature, for example in Heusler (1888). However, hardly any effort is made in the literature to give a comprehensive characterisation of the environment where epenthesis occurs and where it does not occur.

As far as the historic origin is concerned, Binde-*n* is similar to English intrusive *r*. The development is also initiated by the loss of a consonant in coda position. This is illustrated by the words in (10). All of these words had *n* in the coda in former diachronic stages (and still have in Standard German: *Mann, Zahn, kann, braun, von,...*), but synchronically there is no reflex of it; note that the vowel is not even nasalised.

(10)	*Maa,*	*Zah,*	*schö,*	*bru,*	*vo,*	*scho,*	*cha,*	*ha,*	*bi*
	man	tooth	beautiful	brown	from	already	can	have	am

The same holds for inflectional suffixes, like in *die alte̲ Lüt* 'the old people'. Historically, the inflectional suffixes *-en* and *-an* had various functions for nouns, adjectives and verbs. While in varieties like Standard German the form -ən is retained (cf. *die alt<u>en</u> Leute*), in Alemannic - like in many other dialects of German - it is reduced to schwa; thus the development *-an/-en* → -ən → -ə.

As the next diachronic step, and again parallel to the case of English *r*, the alternation *n* - ∅ is generalised to positions where *n* was never part of the words involved. Note that in none of the examples in (9) (with the exception of *ha*) was *n* underlying in any previous diachronic stage of Alemannic. In other words, a rule deleting a sonorant in the coda is reversed into a rule introducing it, that is, deletion turns into epenthesis. Our analysis will take this historic scenario into account.

---

[12] Special thanks go to Peter Gallmann for confirming the data in all relevant aspects for his dialect (Schaffhausen).

4.2 Phonological restrictions

As far as its phonological environment is concerned, *n*-epenthesis takes place irrespective of the quality of the surrounding vowels. In particular, it does not alternate with glides after high vowels. Thus unlike English intrusive *r*, which is precluded in this segmental environment, Alemannic Binde-*n* also occurs after high vowels, as in the forms *zu-n-ere, bi-n-ere* in (9).

The only occasional exception to this generalisation involves *i* as the preceding vowel in varieties like Baseldeutsch ('Basel German'). According to Heusler (1888:110), *n* never appears after (tensed) *i*. However, this restriction is not found in all varieties, as (11c,d) shows. Moreover, note that it does not even hold for the dialect of Basel, as is clear from (11a,b), taken from Suter (1992:39):

(11)	a. *I bii-n-eBaasler*	b. *I gsii-n-ich*	c. *größer wie-n-i*	d. *so, wie-n-er gsait hätt*
	I am-EP-a B.	I see-EP-you(PL)	taller than-EP-I	so as-EP-he said has
	'I am from Basel'	'I see you'	'taller than I'	'right as he said'

There is thus only a marginal reservation to our observation that the epenthesis of *n* is not blocked by high vowels. More generally speaking, it is unrestricted after monophthongs. However, epenthesis is not found after non-syllabic high vowels, in other words after diphthongs with a high offglide. The following examples are taken from Heusler (l.c.:111).[13]

(12)	[kæɪ inə]	(*[kæɪ-n-inə])	[hæu-i]	(*[hæu-n-i])	[kæɪ-i]	(*[kæɪ-n-i])
	fall in		beat I		fall I	
	'fall into (it)'		'I beat'		'I fall'	

In this regard the segmental-phonological environment of Binde-*n* is similar to the one of English intrusive *r*. Note that in both languages the epenthetic consonant is also found after diphthongs with non-high offglide, more specifically with schwa, as in *(the) idea [r] is*, and *[duə-n-m nit]* (see (15) below) respectively; note further that in varieties where *wie* as in (11c,d) is pronounced [vɪə] epenthesis is just as obligatory. These details, however, are of little relevance for the analysis developed below. I will now turn to the morphosyntactic aspects of *n*-epenthesis.

4.3 Morphosyntactic restrictions: the role of functional heads

There are no varieties of Alemannic where *n* is epenthesised irrespective of the morphosyntactic context (which is the case with intrusive *r*, as will be remembered from section 3.1). For example, *n* is ungrammatical in all varieties in the following contexts:

[13] The phonetic transcription of Heusler slightly differs from the IPA conventions, to which I have adapted it where necessary.

(13)

bruchsch no (-n-) öppis?*	*wil's roh (*-n-) isch*	*irgendwo (*-n-) i dä Stadt*
need-2sg still something	because-it raw is	somewhere in the town
'Do you need something else?'	'because it is raw'	'somewhere in the town'
dä chunt morge früh (-n-) a*	*China (*-n-) un Japan*	*so (*-n-) isch's gsi*
DEF(m) comes tomorrow early on	China and Japan	so is it been
'he arrives tomorrow morning'	'China and Japan'	'that's how it was'

These data indicate that there are intricate morphosyntactic and lexical restrictions; note that *n*-insertion in these examples is not excluded for purely phonological reasons, as a look at some of the forms in (9) with the same segmental environment reveals.

The first crucial morphosyntactic generalisation is that epenthesis is excluded after non-finite verb forms. (14) shows that there is no Binde-*n* after monosyllabic infinitival forms, i.e. both infinitives and participles:

(14)

wo's ko (-n-) isch*	[væmər go əfaŋ]	[kse: uŋ keχt] (Heusler 1888:110)
when it come (-EP-) is	want we go start	seen and heard
'when it came'	'shall we go now?'	'seen and heard'

With finite verb forms, on the other hand, epenthesis is obligatory. This was already observed by Heusler (1888), who states that epenthesis typically occurs after finite modals and auxiliaries as well as in inversions. Heusler's examples are rendered here as (15a) for illustration; the forms in (15b) are inversions of (first person singular) subject and auxiliary.

(15) a.

[i lo:-n-iχ ko:]	[duə-n-m nit]	(Heusler 1888:111)
I let-EP-you(pl) go	do-EP-him nothing	
'I let you go'	'don't hurt him'	

b.

bi-n-i	*ha-n-i*	*mu-n-i*	*ka-n-i*	*du(e)-n-i*	*lo-n-i*
am-EP-I	have-EP-I	must-EP-I	can-EP-I	do-EP-I	let-EP-I
'I am,	I have	...'			

In order to account for this asymmetry based on finiteness, i.e. the contrast of (14) and (15), as well as for the data in (9) and (11), the role of the concept of host and clitic for *n*-epenthesis must be pointed out. The crucial point is that finite verbs, like certain other categories (see below) but unlike infinite verbs, are possible hosts for clitics. The clitics that are found in this context are basically the reduced forms of the personal pronouns, whereas full pronouns do not cliticise; e.g. *gib-mer däs* vs. *gib MIR däs* 'give me/ME that'. Now exactly this contrast governs the presence of epenthesic *n*, as is illustrated in (16).

(16) a.

wo-n-er ko isch	*vs.*	** wo-n irgendeine ko isch*
when-EP-he arrived is		when-EP someone come is
'when he arrived'		

b. *däs Stuck, wo-n-ere id gfalle hätt* vs. * *däs Stuck, wo-n allne gfalle hätt*
the play REL-EP-her not pleased has the play REL-EP-all.DAT.PL pleased has
'the play that she didn't like'

c. *grösser wie-n-i* vs. * *grösser wie-n alli andere*
taller than-EP-I taller than-EP all others
'taller than I'

d. *gang zu-n-ere* vs. * *gang zu-n IRE*
go to-EP-her go to-EP-her (free pronoun)
'go to her'

e. *däs mu-n-i kaufe* vs. * *däs mu-n öpper / irgendeine kaufe*
this must-EP-I buy this must-EP somebody / anybody buy
'I must buy this'

In (16a), for example, a reduced subject pronoun contrasts with an indefinite pronoun. Similarly, in (16d), a reduced indirect object form is in opposition to a stressed full form pronoun.[14] Given these contrasts on the one hand and abstracting over the categories that are possible hosts, viz. complementisers, conjunctions, prepositions, and finite verbs, on the other hand, we are able to state the informal generalisation in (17).

(17) **Generalisation:** *n* is epenthesised in hiatus position in cliticisations to the functional heads COMP (C^0) and P^0.

Given this generalisation, it is understood why epenthesis is ungrammatical in (13) and (17): neither C^0 nor P^0 are involved. Let us see, then, how (17) applies to (16a-e):

- *wo* is both a temporal conjunction meaning 'when', as in (16a), and a relative complementiser, as in (16b). Both uses are lexical instantiations of the syntactic category C^0.
- Treating markers of comparative (*than, like*) as in (16c) as lexical instances of C^0 is justified by their semantics: for the correct interpretation of a comparative phrase usually an entire propositions has to be reconstructed; e.g. the meaning of *(on a conference is a better place to sleep) than in the Cup Final* is something like '... than it is appropriate to sleep in the Cup Final'.
- The functional head analysis extends to prepositions such as *bi* as in (9) or *zu* as in (16d): P can be regarded as a functional category over the noun phrase (N and D projections; see below)·[15]

[14] Heusler (l.c.:111) observes the same contrast. Cf. also Cooper (1995:76-78) and Bader & Penner (1988).

[15] The use of *n* with prepositions is sometimes analogically generalised to non-hiatic positions, i.e. to prepositions ending in a consonant, as in *häsch mit-nem / mit-nere gschwätzt?* 'did you talk to him / to her ?'. It seems appropriate to assume lexical entries *nem, nere* here in addition to the otherwise expected forms *em* and *ere*. As is expected with such idiosyncrasies, there is considerable diachronic and dialectal variation here; cf. Nübling (1992:227f).

- Like Standard German, Alemannic is a 'verb second' language. Consequently, the finite verb is fronted to the C^0 position. This accounts for epenthesis in the inversion cases (15b), (16e) and with clitic object pronouns as in (15a).

There is some variation in the status of first person singular main verbs as hosts. For some varieties of Alemannic, including the German ones, first person singular has no suffix. As is expected, Binde-*n* is found if the verb is vowel-final: *zieh-n-i* 'pull I', *see-n-eu* 'see you(PL)' For most Swiss varieties, on the other hand, first person singular is marked with a syllabic suffix, viz. -ə. Consequently, epenthesis is obligatory here as well:[16]

(18) a. *säg-e-n-i* *styg-e-n-i* *lüg-e-n-i* Bern (Marti 1985:65)
say-1sg-EP-I step-1sg-EP-I lie-1sg-EP-I

b. [i ʃnefl-ə-n-epis] Basel (Heusler 1888:110)
I cut-1sg-EP-something
'I cut something (into pieces)'

Note that first person singular is the only finite verb form ending in a vowel. Like for the former varieties, epenthesis follows because the suffixed verb forms in (18) can host clitics, just like other finite verbs, by virtue of being fronted to C^0.

A remark on the treatment of prepositions as functional categories is in order. It is well known that prepositions can display properties of both functional and lexical categories, as far as criteria such as semantic content, participation in derivational morphology, or open vs. closed lexical class are concerned. Since Grimshaw (1991) it is common to treat P as a functional category over the noun phrase, which by itself is a projection of N and D. Grimshaw draws on the parallel role of C for clauses and P for noun phrases and introduces the concept of extended projections for CP and PP.

To account for the obligatoriness of *n*-epenthesis in cliticisations to the heads of extended projections in terms of a more explcit representation we can state the rule in (19). (Part b, the identification of *n* as the epenthetic segment, will be dealt with in section 5.)

(19) a. *hiatus rule:* $\varnothing \rightarrow \begin{bmatrix} +\text{cons} \\ +\text{son} \end{bmatrix}$ / $[\,[\,\ldots\ V\,]_{PrWd}\ \_\ V \ldots\,]_{PrWd}$

morphosyntactic context: hiatus rule applies to C^0, P^0

b. *specification of epenthetic segment:* [+coronal]

As is generally assumed, enclitics are treated as integrated into (here: adjoined to) the prosodic word; see 4.5 for more discussion. The prosodic domain that the application is restricted to is the prosodic word. The specification of the morphological context ensures

[16] Historically, the first person singular verb forms of the Old High German 'weak' classes II and III as well as some irregular verbs ended in *-n*. From these forms *n* was analogically extended to other verbs in these varieties (Marti 1985:65) and later subject to deletion and reanalysis as sketched in 4.1.

that there is no epenthesis in clitic contexts involving a host other than the head of an extended projection, as in (14), or (arguably) in (26) below.

In the following subsection we will see that not all occurrences of Binde-*n* can be reduced to epenthesis in cliticisation.

4.4 Non-epenthetic occurrences of Binde-*n*

In addition to the instances of Binde-*n* just characterised as the result of a productive rule of *n*-epenthesis, I will now present further occurrences of Binde-*n*. The question discussed in 4.4.2 is if the account based on cliticisation developed so far can be extended to these occurrences, for example along the lines of Booij (1996). It turns out that the data are not analysable in the same manner. Therefore, the possibility of a rule of *n*-deletion, next to *n*-epenthesis, will also be considered. Eventually, in 4.4.3 I will argue that the data can be naturally accounted for with the concept of floating segments.

4.4.1 Binde-*n* with inflectional morphemes

The alternation *n* - ∅ is also found with inflectional schwa suffixes. Consider the suffix-final participles and infinitives in (20):

(20)	*blieb-e-n-isch*	*gang-e-n isch*	*lach-e-n un singe*
	stay-PART-n is	go-PART-n is	laugh-INF-n and sing
	'has stayed'	'has gone'	'to laugh and sing'

In environments other than hiatus these infinitival forms are realised as *bliebe*, *gange*, *lache*. The same alternation occurs in the noun forms in (21), which in non-hiatus environments have the plural forms *Löie* and *Hirte*:

(21)	*D Löi-e-n im Gheg*	*D Hirt-e-n uf em Fääl*	Bern (Marti 1985:66)
	the lion-PL-*n* in.the(DAT) cage	the shepherd-PL-*n* on the(DAT) field	
	'the lions in the cage'	'the shepherds in the field'	

In addition, there are different shapes of the indefinite article. Its form in isolation is *e*, as in *e Baasler, e Fèlse* (MASC), *e Gschicht* (FEM). (Whether there is a separate form *en* for masculine gender or not is a matter of variation.) When preceded by a vowel, however, the article shows initial *n*:

(22)	*I bii-n-e Baasler*	*soo-n-e Gschicht*	*wie-n-e Fèlse*	Basel (Suter 1992:39)
	I am *n*-a Basel-er	so*n*-a story	like *n*-a rock	
	'I am from Basel'	'such a story'	'like a rock'	

Obviously, *ne* in hiatus environment contrasts with *e* after a consonant or in isolation. Like with *a* and *an* in English, there appears at first sight to be lexical allomorphy for the indefinite article: *e,* and *ne* (and *en*, for varities that have *e* rather than *es* as the neuter indefinite article, as in *en Auto* 'a car'). However, the goal of this section is to provide an account that relates (22) to (20) and (21).

To sum up, (20) - (22) thus also exhibit the alternation *n* - *Ø*, which is governed by the presence or absence of hiatus, just like with the previous examples. Unlike the latter, however, the examples presented here cannot be reduced to cliticisation to function words. Now from a theoretical perspective it is not desirable to call for heterogeneous devices in order to capture one alternation, viz. *n* - *Ø*. Therefore, let us discuss next wether it is possible to extend the cliticisation analysis presented in 4.3.

4.4.2 The generalised epenthesis approach

Booij (1996:227) mentions an epenthesis phenomenon in Dutch which is similar to Alemannic. In Dutch, hiatus resulting from cliticisation is for many speakers also resolved by epenthesis of *n*.

(23)	ik zette-n-et	hij wilde-n-et	wilde-n-ie	het gekke-n-is	dat je-n-et
	'I put it'	'he wanted it'	wanted he'	'the strange thing is'	'that you it...'

Booij treats these examples as 'word + enclitic combinations', where the clitic forms a prosodic word with the host. (Contrary to our treatment of enclitics as adjoined to the prosodic word, Booij (l.c.:229) argues that Dutch enclitics „are incorporated into the preceding prosodic word", that is dominated by the same foot. This discrepancy, however, is of no relevance.) Thus, similar to our treatment of Alemannic, the prosodic word is assumed to be the domain of application for the rule of *n*-insertion (on which Booij does not comment any further, except that it is optional, hence postlexical).

Compared to our account, Booij makes a more general use of the environment of host and clitic, as there are no restrictions concerning the category of the host. Note that (23) involves verbs next to (nominalised) adjectives and pronouns. As these environments are very similar to the ones just illustrated for High Alemannic one would wish to simply transfer Booij's analysis. What we would have to do is to revise the rule proposed in (19) as to apply regardless of a morphosyntactic context, hence as a general phonological rule.

However, while Booij's account may work for Dutch, there is sufficient evidence that it cannot be transferred to High Alemannic: First, it is unclear why there is no epenthesis in the afore-mentioned examples like *ko(*-n-) isch* 'come-is'. Obviously, the context is the same as in (20) and (23), which involve epenthesis. Second, there are also systematic occurrences of *n* between adjectives with schwa suffixes and nouns. In fact, Weinhold (1863:171) regards this as the typical environment of Binde-*n*. Consider the following inflected adjectives followed by a vowel-initial noun:[17]

[17] Binde-*n* with adjectives does not occur in in all varieties. It is not found, for example, in the dialect of St. Gallen and Vorarlberg; cf. Berger (1913:146), who explicitly states the lack of *n* in this environment:

(i) [də grøə œpfɪl]
the green apple
'the green apple'

(24) a. *mit mim dreckig-en Auto* b. *Amene süess-en Öpfel* (Marti 1985:65)
'with my (DAT) dirty car' 'on a (DAT) sweet apple'

c. *(du hesch) e lieb-en Unggle* d. *di schön-en Ouge* (Marti 1985:65)
'(you have) a nice uncle' 'the beautiful eyes'

e. [en unntsitigə-n epfl] (Heusler 1888:110)
'an unripe apple'

Note that the distributuion of *-e* vs. *-en* in attributive adjectives is not ruled by number or case for the varieties in question: preceding a consonant, all the adjectives in (24) would end in *-e*, e.g. *mit mim dreckig-e Traktor* 'with my dirty tractor', *amene süess-e Kueche* 'on a sweet cake', etc.

As Binde-*n* is found between two major category words here, it is obvious that a cliticisation approach fails: the prosodic domain of adjective and noun is a higher one than the prosodic word, viz. the prosodic phrase. Moreover, with two phonologically non-reduced major category words it is unclear what would be the clitic and what would be the host.

Since the general cliticisation approach must be rejected, one might look for a solution that captures all the cases with an unrestricted epenthesis rule, that is not bound to any prosodic domain. However, a general epenthesis rule is also bound to fail, as the occurrence of *n* is lexically restricted. In addition to the cases in (13) and the behaviour of the monosyllabic participles in (14), consider nouns and adjectives followed by a vowel: on the one hand, in contrast to the vowel-final forms in isolation of the type *bru, schö* illustrated in (10) above, we find Binde-*n* with the same words when followed by a vowel:

(25) *(wil's) schö-n isch* *(wil's) bru-n isch* *(wil's) grüe-n isch*
'(...) is beautiful' '(...) is brown' '(...) is green'

We thus have a further example of the alternation *n* in hiatus vs. Ø elsewhere. However, *n* in (20) cannot be the result of a general rule of *n* epenthesis. This is evident from other nouns and adjectives with vowel-final base forms where *n* is excluded, as in (26).

(26) *(wil's) en Floh(*-n) isch* *(wil's) im Zoo(*-n) isch*
'(because it) is a flee' '(because it) is in the zoo'

(wil's) roh(-n) isch* *(wil-er) froh(*-n) isch*
'(because it) is raw' '(because he) is happy'

Although the phonological and morphosyntactic context is the same as in (25), namely hiatus in a noun or adjective followed by an auxiliary form, epenthesis is precluded in (26). Note that those words where Binde-*n* is found in this context also exhibit *n* in inflected forms:

(27)	*schö - schöner,*	*bru - brune*	*grüe - grüene*
	beautiful - more beautiful	brown - brown(inflected)	green - green(inflected)
vs.	*Floh - Flöh,*	*roh - rohe,*	*froh - frohe*
	flee - flees	raw - raw(inflected)	happy - happy(inflected)

The occurrence of *n* in nouns and adjectives followed by a vowel is thus lexically restricted. Recall that the examples in (25) belong to the type illustrated in (10) above, where historically, *n* is underlying in the coda. The words in (26) on the contrary never had *n*. The synchronic reflex is that *n* is still found in the inflected forms of the former, whereas the latter are inflected without *n*, hence *Flöh, rohe* and *frohe*. It is thus clear that a generalised epenthesis approach fails to account for the complexity of Binde-*n*, no matter if epenthesis is assumed to be prosodically unrestricted or to be bound to cliticisation.

The question, then, is how to implement the historical facts just described into a synchronic analysis. It is clear that the presence of *n* in (25) is not the result of epenthesis, as the ban against *n* in the same phonological context in (26) would remain unexplained. Rather, (unlike English 'intrusive *r*') it is a lexical property of some words and not of others to have an underlying *n* in the coda.

Suppose we treat *n* in contexts like (25) as a fixed part of the lexical entries of the nouns and adjectives in question, for example */bruːn/*. Under this account, next to the rule in (19) that epenthesises *n*, a deletion rule would have to be assumed to capture the fact that *n* does not surface in coda position. This rule is sketched in (28).

(28) $n \rightarrow \varnothing \; / \; \_\_\,]_{\sigma}$

Even though it is clear that something like (28) must have been operative in the history of Alemannic it is problematic to assume a synchronic status of a deletion rule, for the following reasons: (i) it is not desirable on conceptual grounds to have both an epenthesis rule and a deletion rule to account for just one alternation, namely *n* - *∅*; (ii) it makes wrong empirical predictions: though it would adequately capture (20) - (25), it would also have to apply to words such as *wenn* 'if', *Bahn* 'train', *Zaun* 'fence', *Sohn* 'son', *Ton* 'sound', *Japan* (id.), which in fact are always realised with final *n*. Hence the possibility of *n*-deletion must also be rejected.

4.4.3 The floating segment approach

I will now present a solution that is based on the observations made so far and that avoids the shortcomings of the alternatives discussed so far by making use of the concept of prespecified (or floating) segments. As in the previous account, *n* in (20) - (25) is treated as a segment that is present in the underlying representation. Crucially, however, it is not associated to a syllable position, hence it cannot be parsed unless a suitable timing slot is available. I will assume that an empty onset position is available under resyllabification within the phonological phrase, provided that it is not associated to a lexically underlying segment.

With these prerequisites, how are the facts to be captured? Recall that we are dealing with lexical items behaving in three different ways: on the one hand there is *n* - *Ø* alternation as in *schö* - *schö-n-isch*, *bru* - *brune*, on the other hand there are forms without *n* even in hiatus (*froh* [fro:] - *frohe*), and finally there are words invariably realsed with *n*, even in the coda. This is represented by the three-way opposition of absence, preassociation and fixed association of *n*; consider (29c):

(29) a. 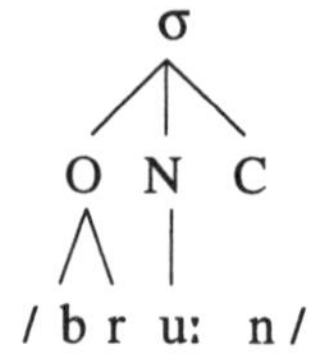 b.  c. 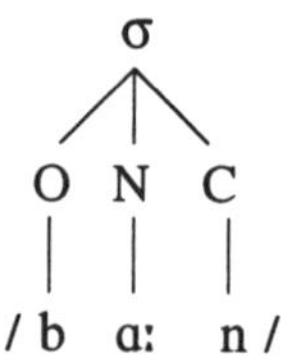

The entry in (29a) consists of three segments, only two of which are associated to constituents of the syllable (onset, nucleus, and coda, respectively). Hence the final segment *n* cannot be realised unless an appropriate position is introduced by a following word under resyllabification. This accounts for the *n* - *Ø* alternation, while non-alternating items are represented as in (29b-c): entries of the type in (b) have no segment *n* in their lexical representation. Consequently, no consonant can be parsed in the onset after resyllabification, hence the contrast in (27) above. The same holds for *no, früh, China, so...* as in (13). (29c) illustrates how to treat words like *Bahn* [bɑ:n] 'train', where *n* invariably occurs, that is also in syllable-final position: the *n* is underlyingly linked to a syllable constituent, as any other segment is. This is the situation found in a few native items as well as in some more recent loan words.

This solution extends naturally to Binde-*n* with inflectional morphemes as illustrated in 4.4.1. A lexical treatment of the alternation immediately accounts for the different behaviour of the suffixed participle forms (*n* in *blieb-e-n-isch, gang-e-n isch...*) and the monosyllabic participle forms in (14) above, which do not allow *n* (*ko(*-n-) isch*). This contrast follows from assuming monomorphemic entries without a floating *n* for the latter vs. *-e(n)* as the suffix of the former. A suffix of the same phonological form signals verbal infinitives, noun plurals, and various gender/number/case distinctions in the paradigm of attributive adjectives (such as dative of all genders in the weak declension, or structural case with masculine in the strong declension; cf. the examples in (24) above). If this is accepted, all that is necessary to account for the facts is the following representations:

(30) a. inflectional suffix *-e(n)*: 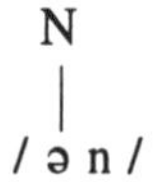 b. indefinite article *(n)e*: 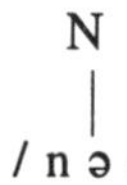

The inflectional schwa suffix (in all its functions, as plural marker, adjective suffix, and irregular participle ending) can be treated as in (30a). The same treatment accounts for the *e* - *ne* alternation of the indefinite article. Here the floating segment is initial rather than final. Note that *n* in *so-n-e Gschicht* cannot be a segment of *so*, as this would incorrectly predict *n* in *so (*-n-) oder so* 'anyway', *so (*-n-) alte Gschichte* 'such old stories', hence the entry (30b) (the neuter form *nes* as in *wie-n-es* can be treated accordingly).

As many other languages, Alemannic has resyllabification across word boundaries, the domain being the phonological phrase. In order for the analysis to work, it must be assumed that an empty onset is available under resyllabification. To this position the floating consonant in entries like the ones in (29a) and (30) can be associated, hence be realised on the surface. This is illustrated here with *dreckigen Auto* 'dirty car':

(31)

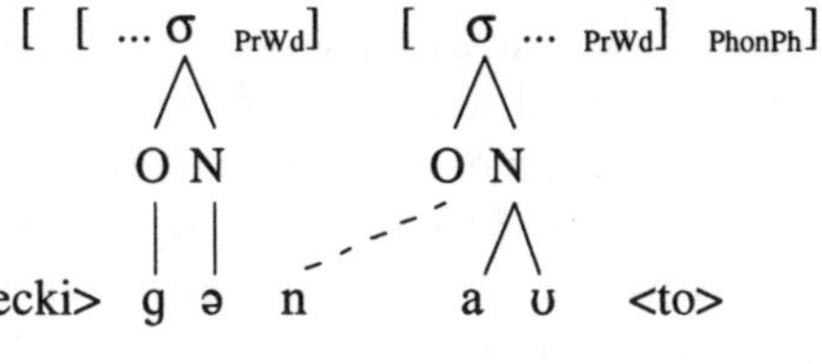

Similarly, in (30b) the initial *n* will be associated to the empty onset if the preceding syllable provides no other consonant to fill this position under resyllabification: *so ne Gschicht* 'such a story' vs. *für e* [fy.rə] *Gschicht* 'for a story'.

Requiring an empty C-position for the floating segment to be parsed accounts for the fact that in none of the lexical items with floating *n* this consonant is realised in a context other than hiatus. We have thus arrived at a homogeneous solution; a unified account could be presented for phenomena that superficially look as diverse as involving the devices of epenthesis, deletion and lexical allomorphy. Note that on a more intuitive level, the status of the consonant *n* as both being diachronically lost and being inserted is also immediately captured by the 'floating' analysis.

4.5 Summary

In this section I have presented an account of High Alemannic Binde-*n* in its various environments. It results from epenthesis in cliticisations to functional heads; it is found in inflectional ə-endings as well as in the indefinite article; and, finally, it occurs in a lot of lexical items where it belongs historically and is retained only in hiatus position without generalising *n* to other items in the same phonological context.

It was shown that while there is productive epenthesis in cliticisation, the other occurrences of Binde-*n* cannot be accounted for by a general, unrestricted epenthesis rule. The theoretical alternatives that were discussed comprise (i) the approach in Booij (1996), which is based on a more general concept of cliticisation, (ii) a synchronically active deletion rule, and (iii) the concept of prespecified (or floating) segments. I have come to the conclusion that the latter solution, in addition to an epenthesis rule with a specific context, captures the complexity of the facts most successfully and elegantly: Binde-*n* in contexts other than clitic environments is treated lexically as a floating segment which is only parsed under resyllabification within the phonological phrase.

5. The phonological specification of epenthetic consonants

A look at the role of epenthesis in the literature reveals a striking asymmetry: on the one hand, vowel epenthesis has extensively been dealt with.[18] We have some understanding of what are possible candidates for a non-underlying vowel position, viz. ə or ɪ, or occasionally *a*. On the other hand, consonant epenthesis has so far drawn much less attention.[19] While the previous sections have been concerned with the question of where and how consonant epenthesis applies (and the often much more intricate question why it does not apply), this section looks at the possible 'shape' of the inserted segment. For this purpose I will take a more cross-linguistic perspective and speculate on a general restriction on segments that can productively surface as epenthetic consonants.

As we have seen from both English intrusive *r* and Alemannic Binde-*n*, consonant epenthesis can arise by reanalysis of an originally underlying sonorant in the coda which has been lost in this position. The reanalysis starts from those contexts where the consonant is immediately followed by a vowel, which prevents the consonant from being delinked by resyllabification, that is by associating it to an onset position. An important synchronic corollary of the loss of those consonants in coda position is the observation that inserted consonants are 'simple' within the phonological system of the language in question.[20] More formally, this means that the epenthetic consonant is to be specifiable *minimally*, in a sense to be made precise now. In the remainder of this section, I will thus argue for the following claim:

(32) In a language where a specific consonant phoneme is designated for epenthesis, this consonant bears no more than one underlying specification [F]. Likewise, [F] is the only specification of the segment specification part of the hiatus rule.

Note that the notion 'specific consonant phoneme' excludes postlexical (as opposed to phonological) glide formation, which is not dealt with here. What (32) says is that the underlying form of the epenthetic consonant phoneme is to be represented by only one feature or only one node. As a consequence, the universal hiatus rule (Ø-> C / V_V ...) requires for each language a minimal specification to identify the specific epenthetic consonant of the language (see part b of the rules (8) and (19) above).[21] This generalisation, I

---

[18] To mention one detailed case study, Wiese (1986) provides a comprehensive analysis of German schwa epenthesis.

[19] One of the few exceptions is Picard (1987).

[20] The idea of 'simplicity' fits to the observation that consonants get lost only via the by-and-by loss of their properties. For example, the typical way for obstruents to get lost in the course of change is via a previous change to the laryngeals *h* or / , that is by loss of oral place features (Lass 1984:332ff). Similarly, I assume that sonorants in coda position get lost only via vocalisation, that is by loss of their root features, yielding nasalisation, velarisation or vowel lengthening of the nucleus vowel.

[21] Richard Wiese (p.c.) points out the possibility that in one and the same language, more than one consonant is specified minimally. For example, in (Standard) German the consonants *t, l, n, h* arguably all have only one underlying specification (Wiese 1996:165ff). The question arises which consonant out of several 'minimal' ones is the one to be used in productive epenthesis. However,

claim, holds for all systematic (as opposed to morpheme-specific) cases of consonant epenthesis, regardless of the exact distribution in a particular language.

Note that my analysis is based on the commonly accepted assumption that the root node hosts the features [±consonantal] and [±sonorant], cf. McCarthy (1988); for discussion see also Clements & Hume (1995:268f). In accordance with the latter authors, I assume that these features are present in underlying representation anyway; therefore they are irrelevant for (32).

The simplicity that (32) calls for in the representation of the epenthesised segment captures the two major characteristics observed with consonant epenthesis: (i) Sonorants often both get lost and are, due to reanalysis, subsequently inserted. This is represented most naturally in terms of minimal complexity of these segments. (ii) Epenthetic consonants can be regarded as universally unmarked as opposed to other consonants (immediately evident for obstruents, on sonorants see below).

Let us see if (32) holds for the consonants found cross-linguistically in productive epenthesis, that is *r, n, l, t,* ʔ, and *w/j* . (33) lists the consonants, together with the minimal specifications they are characterised by in the languages in question.

(33) Consonants found in productive epenthesis and their specifications:

[ʔ]	/t/	/n/	/l/	/r/	/w, j/
([-sonorant])	[+coronal]	[+coronal]	([+sonorant])	[-high]	[+high]
	([-sonorant])	([+sonorant])		([+sonorant])	([+sonorant])

In the following, each of the consonants is discussed in turn:

ʔ: The simplicity of this consonant is uncontroversial and immediately accounts for its use as epenthetic consonant in languages where it is phonemic, as in Ilokano:

(34)	*/lailo/*	*[la.ʔi.lo]*	'affectionate'	Rosenthal (1997:144)
	/daulo/	*[da.ʔu.lo]*	'leader'	

Given the specification [-sonorant] at the root node, no further positive information is needed to identify the default obstruent. The articulatory simpleness of the placeless segment also accounts for phonetic insertion into empty onsets as in, for example, Sierra Miwok, Baka, or in German: *Theater* [teʔa:tər]'theatre', *Auto* [ʔaʊto:] 'car'.

t: *t* is probably the only non-laryngeal obstruent found in productive epenthesis. Its use is frequent, examples are Axininca Campa, as illustrated in 2.2, or Amharic. For these languages *t* is analysed as having [coronal] as the only underlying specification. (The status of 'coronal' with respect to the other place features will be discussed at the end of this section.)

n: The only underlying specification for languages with *n*-epenthesis, such as High Alemannic or Dutch, is [+coronal]. This specification excludes other sonorants than a nasal because *l* and *r* require the additional specification [+liquid] (and *r* is not a coronal at least

(32) does not predict all minimal segments to be epenthetic (note that Standard German does not have systematic consonant epenthesis at all). This indicates that the specification part (b) of the epenthesis rule is not necessarily a redundancy statement but rather an indispensable part of the grammar of the language in question.

in Alemannic). As these languages exhibit no phonological processes such as the spreading of [nasal], I assume (following a proposal of Janet Grijzenhout, p.c.) that this feature is not present here. Finally, as the feature [sonorant] is specified at the root node, namely as [+sonorant] here, *n* is predicted rather than *t* - hence the minimal specification of the segmental part b in the epenthesis rule in (19) gives the correct result.

l: *l* is epenthesised in Baka, a Niger-Kongo language of Cameroon (data and analysis due to Kleinhenz 1992). *l* is both inserted between identical vowels (optional), as in (35a), and in derived environments, (35b):

(35) a.	*mɛɛ*	→	*mɛlɛ*	'make'	(Kleinhenz 1992:10, 12)
	soò	→	*solò*	'dry (verb)'	
	moò	→	*molò*	'kill'	
b.	*sià* + ɛ	→	*siàlɛ*	*mɛɛ*+ ɛ → *mɛɛlɛ*	
	watch - PERF			make- PERF	

As Kleinhenz points out, *l* is the unmarked consonant in Baka. This is clear from the substitution of consonants with more specifications, as in *gogogo* -> *gogolo*, or from reduplication, for example *ngé* 'big' - *ngèngélé* 'size' (l.c.:30f). Baka *l* can thus be represented with no other specification than the root node feature [+sonorant]: there is no *r* in the language (hence no feature [lateral] is needed), and it contrasts with *n* which has the underlying specification [+coronal] in addition.

r: In 3.2 I have already argued for a minimal specification of *r* in British English in terms of the feature [-high]. That *r* can be represented minimally gains further support by an analysis by Akinlabi (1993), who draws on the similar status of this phoneme in Yoruba. Akinlabi points out that *r* is the only consonant to be transparent for a rule of regressive spreading of vowel quality, hence „therefore it must lack a place specification since the rule spreads the place node" (l.c.:156). In particular, Akinlabi provides evidence that *r* in Yoruba, unlike obstruent coronals, contains no [coronal] specification. Thus while details like the role of the feature [-high], as I have proposed for English, may differ between the two languages, the point is that *r*, apparently a rather complex phoneme, can have a default character both in its behaviour and in its representation.

Some further examples of epenthesis with exactly these consonants are discussed in Lombardi (1997) (albeit with a different conclusion). What Lombardi does not consider is that glides also feature as epenthetic segments:

the glides *w* and *j*: The specification of glides is of interest only for languages where glide epenthesis is phonological, i.e. it is not the result of phonetic spreading. One such language is West Greenlandic (Rischel 1974:100-121). In this language, glide epenthesis is one means to avoid sequences of long vowels followed by another vowel. That glide epenthesis is not phonetic here is clear from the fact that the glide „is complementary in quality to the vowels: /ii + i, uu + u/ become /iivi, uuju/" (l.c.:101):

(36)	*/qii+iaʳppaa/*	→	*/qiiviaʳppaa/*	'he removes his white hair'
	/puu+uciga/	→	*/puujuciga/*	'my bag'

If this distribution can be captured by an output constraint forbidding VVC sequences to share one place node, then all that must be specified for epenthesis is, in addition to [+son] at the root node, [+high] as the common feature of the two glides (also cf. the structure in (8) in subsection 3.2).

All other specifications that are part of the full feature geometries of the consonants discussed here are filled in per default or per well-formedness constraints. For example, in the case of *t*, the features [-continuant], [-voiced], which distinguish *t* from *s* or *d*, are assigned their negative values per default. Similarly, for British English *r* with the underlying specification [-high], the dominating 'vocalic' node and in turn the C-place node are filled in per interpolation in order to satisfy the restrictions on dominance of features (Clements & Hume 1995).

A final matter remains to be discussed. Recall that in 2.2. the question was addressed whether the place feature [coronal] is underspecified in phonological representation, and I have been assuming here that the coronal node has to be specified underlyingly just like labial or dorsal. Given this, the following objection might be raised against our requirement of minimal specifications: 'If coronals are underlyingly specified in terms of a place node, why is it that one does not find labial or velar consonants in productive epenthesis instead of only coronals and laryngeals? Under the assumption that the coronal node has to be specified underlyingly just like labial or dorsal, for example *p* with the specification [labial] is no more complex than *t* with [coronal] and hence would be expected to occur in epenthesis. And after all, we still feel that coronals are unmarked as opposed to the others.'

The answer to this objection is as follows: Coronals are indeed unmarked as opposed to other places of articulation. For example, appendices to the syllable are typically coronal (like *s* and *t* in German); coronals are more prone to processes of weakening; for more examples cf. Paradis & Prunet (1991). However, asymmetries like these based on place of articulation should not be accounted for in terms of the representation of segments. This issue is specifically dealt with in Grijzenhout (1998). Grijzenhout gives evidence for the underlying specification of [coronal] on the basis of processes such as schwa-insertion or lenition that coronals do not undergo, which can only be captured by reference to an underlying specification of that place feature.

The asymmetry of place features thus should be implemented into the grammar by principles or constraints which refer to labials and velars only, but not to coronals. What this means with respect to consonant epenthesis is, in terms of Optimality Theory, that constraints like 'FILL labial' (or 'DEP(ENDENCY) labial', according to more recent conceptions) or 'FILL dorsal' are higher ranked than 'FILL coronal'. This also accounts for other asymmetries than with respect to epenthetic consonants; for example the fact that an underspecified nasal *N* surfaces as *n* rather than *m* in surroundings where there are no place features to spread, as in *inability*.

A more explicit proposal in this direction has in fact been made recently by Lombardi (1995:240f, 1997), which she calls the 'constraint ranking approach to markedness'. According to her, it is only laryngeals and not coronals that may be characterised as placeless. On the other hand, as both the laryngeal *ʔ* and coronals are typical epenthetic segments, she assumes the ordering in (37). Coronals are treated as also having a place specification but the constraints referring to them are dominated by the ones referring to labials and dorsals in a universal constraint ranking:

(37) *Dor, *Lab >> *Cor >> *Phar (Lombardi 1997:157)

Consequently, an output candidate with a coronal, like *t*, will always win over a labial or dorsal in the same position, like *p* or *k*. Under such a perspective, the apparent contradiction resolves easily: while it is true that coronals are the typical epenthesis consonants (we find *t, r, n,* and not *k* or *p*), this asymmetry does not imply a represention in terms of underspecification of the [coronal] node. Rather, the fact that, so to speak, coronals out of nothing are cheaper than labials or dorsals, is implemented in constraint ranking. While the latter concept accounts for the preference of, for example, ʔ, *n, t* over *p, m, k,* ŋ as epenthetic segments, the preference of ʔ, *t* over *h, s, d* is accounted for by the complexity of underlying representation.

To sum up the idea of this section, I have argued that where consonant epenthesis is a productive rule of a language, the epenthesised consonant is minimally specified, in the sense that it has one underlying feature specification only. In interaction with independently motivated constraints referring to the place features we can characterise a possible epenthesis consonant relative to the phonemic system of the language.

6. Conclusion

The purpose of this article was to show how consonant epenthesis is restricted by phonological (both segmental and prosodic) and morphological factors. One phonological factor is the quality of the two vowels in hiatus position. As far as the height of these vowels is concerned, it is only the first vowel in hiatus position that is able to influence the nature of the inserted consonant, i.e. a high vowel tends to spread to the epenthetic C-position, yielding a glide where otherwise a designated epenthetic consonant is found. Thus in British English, glides in hiatus position after *i* and *u* contrast with intrusive *r* elsewhere. I have proposed a spreading analysis that accounts for both the complementary distribution of the three segments and for the choice of *r* as the epenthetic consonant in terms of the minimal specification [-high].

Although only two languages were investigated more closely here (apart from English, we saw that High Alemannic Binde-*n* is sometimes excluded following *i*), there seems to be no counterexample to our generalisation that the height of the following vowel shows no effects on the inserted consonant.[22]

Another phonological factor concerns the prosodic restrictions on epenthesis. The concept of cliticisation, conceived as adjunction to the prosodic word, turned out to be crucial for the application of *n*-epenthesis in High Alemannic, next to the phonological phrase as the domain of resyllabification. The discussion of Alemannic has shown that the assumption of *n* as a floating segment of certain nouns and inflectional ə-suffixes next to a

[22] In glide formation, on the other hand, the choice of the glide may well be determined by the frontness value of the following vowel, as in Wolof: *woo-y-e* 'to call from' vs. *yee-w-u* 'to wake oneself up' (Ka 1994:100f). However, the height of this vowel is irrelevant again.

productive epenthesis rule provides a comprehensive, conceptually simple treatment of Binde-*n* and is to be preferred over solutions solely based on cliticisation or involving a deletion rule.

As regards its morphosyntactic conditions, consonant epenthesis is a largely restricted phenomenon. British English intrusive *r* seems to be the only case where both the morphosyntactic and the prosodic context plays no role in the application of epenthesis. It is only here that intrusive *r* can be accounted for by a general epenthesis rule in hiatus without further context. Apart from the majority of totally unproductive cases, in which what looks like epenthesis is either lexicalised or found with a particular morpheme only, and which were not further discussed, even productive consonant epenthesis usually gets bound to specific syntactic categories before it becomes a general, unrestricted rule. Examples are verbal suffixes in Axininca Campa, as well as functional categories in High Alemannic as hosts for cliticisation.

As to the segmental properties of the epenthesised consonant, I have argued that where consonant epenthesis is a productive rule in the phonology of a language, the consonant is minimally specified, that is, it contains only one underlying segmental specification. This accounts for both the loss and the (historically subsequent) productive epenthesis of one and the same consonant, as underlying representations and surface forms differ but minimally for both deletion and epenthesis.

References

Akinlabi, Akinbiyi (1993): Underspecification and the Phonology of Yoruba /r/. *Linguistic Inquiry* 24, 139-160.

Bader, Thomas & Zvi Penner (1988): A GB-Account of the Complementizer System in Bernese Swiss German. *University of Berne, Linguistic working papers 25*.

Berger, Jakob (1913): *Die Laute der Mundarten des St. Galler Rheintals (und der angrenzenden vorarlbergischen Gebiete).* Frauenfeld (CH): Huber & Co.

Booij, Geert (1996): Cliticisation as Prosodic Integration: The Case of Dutch. *The Linguistic Review* 13, 219-242.

— (1998): Phonological Output Constraints in Morphology. In: Wolfgang Kehrein & Richard Wiese (eds.): *Phonology and Morphology of the Germanic Languages.* Tübingen: Niemeyer, 143-163.

Broadbent, Judith (1991): Linking and Intrusive r in English. *UCL Working Papers in Linguistics* 3, 281-302. University College London.

Broselow, Ellen (1995): Skeletal Positions and Moras. In: Goldsmith, John A. (ed.): *The Handbook of Phonological Theory.* Oxford: Blackwell, 175-205.

Casali, Roderic F. (1997): Vowel Elision in Hiatus Contexts: which Vowel Goes? *Language* 73, 493-533.

Clements, G. N. & Elizabeth V. Hume (1995): The Internal Organization of Speech Sounds. In: John A. Goldsmith (ed.): *The Handbook of Phonological Theory.* Oxford: Blackwell, 245-306.

Cooper, Kathrin E. (1995): Topics in Zurich German Syntax. *Groninger Arbeiten zur germanistischen Linguistik (GAGL) 38*, Rijksuniversiteit Groningen.

Golston, Chris & Wolfgang Kehrein (1997): Mazatec Onsets and Nuclei. Ms., California State University Fresno and Philipps-Universität Marburg.

Grijzenhout, Janet (1998): The Role of Coronal Specification in German and Dutch Phonology and Morphology. In: Wolfgang Kehrein & Richard Wiese (eds.): *Phonology and Morphology of the Germanic Languages*. Tübingen: Niemeyer, 27-50.

Grimshaw, Jane (1991): Extended Projections. Ms., Waltham: Brandeis University.

Heusler, Andreas (1888): Der Alemannische Consonantismus in der Mundart von Baselstadt. In: Stefan Sonderegger (ed., 1970): *Andreas Heusler, Schriften zum Alemannischen.* Berlin: de Gruyter.
Hock, Hans-Henrich (1991): *Principles of Historical Linguistics.* Berlin: de Gruyter.
Itô, Junko (1989): A Prosodic Theory of Epenthesis. *Natural Language & Linguistic Theory* 7, 217-259.
Ka, Omar (1994): *Wolof Phonology and Morphology.* Lanham: University Press of America.
Kleinhenz, Ursula (1992): Zum Lexikon isolierender Sprachen: Baka (Kamerun). *Arbeiten des Sonderforschungsbereichs 282 „Theorie des Lexikons"* Nr. 28. Universität Düsseldorf.
Lass, Roger (1984): *Phonology. An Introduction to Basic Concepts.* Cambridge: Cambridge University Press.
Löhken, Sylvia (1995): Consonantal Epenthesis in German: Phonological and Morphological Aspects in Sound Change. Paper presented at the International Conference on Historical Linguistics, Manchester.
Lötscher, Andreas (1983): *Schweizerdeutsch.* Stuttgart.
Lombardi, Linda (1995): Laryngeal Neutralization and Alignment. In: Beckman, Jill, Urbanczyk, Suzanne & Walsh, Laura (eds.): *Papers in Optimality Theory.* Amherst: GSLA (= *University of Massachusetts Occasional Papers in Linguistics 18*), 225-247.
— (1997): Coronal Epenthesis and Markedness. *University of Maryland Working Papers in Linguistics 5*, 156-175.
Marti, Werner (1985): *Berndeutsch-Grammatik.* Bern.
McCarthy, John (1988): Feature Geometry and Dependency: A Review. *Phonetica* 43, 84-104.
— (1993): A Case of Surface Constraint Violation. In: C. Paradis & D. LaCharité (eds): Constraint-based Theories in Multilinear Phonology (= *Canadian Journal of Linguistics* 38), 169-195.
Nübling,, Damaris (1992): *Klitika im Deutschen. Schriftsprache, Umgangssprache, alemannische Dialekte.* Tübingen: Narr (= Script Oralia 42).
Paradis, Carole & Jean-François Prunet (eds.; 1991): *The Special Status of Coronals: Internal and External Evidence.* San Diego: Academic Press.
Payne, D.L. (1981): *The Phonology and Morphology of Axininca Campa.* Summer Institute of Linguistics Publications in Linguistics 66, University of Texas.
Picard, Marc (1987): On the General Properties of Consonant Epenthesis. *Canadian Journal of Linguistics* 32, 133-142.
— (1989): Consonant Epenthesis as a Regular Sound Change. *Diachronica* VI, 223-236.
Rischel, Jørgen (1974): *Topics in West Greenlandic Phonology. Regularities Underlying the Phonetic Appearance of Wordforms in a Polysynthetic Language.* Copenhagen: Akademisk Forlag.
Rosenthal, Sam (1997): The Distribution of Prevocalic Vowels. *Natural Language & Linguistic Theory* 15, 139-180.
Spring, Cari (1994): Combinatorial Specification of a Consonantal System. *West Coast Conference on Formal Linguistics (WCCFL)* 12.
Suter, Rudolf (1992): *Baseldeutsch-Grammatik.* Basel.
Weinhold, Karl (1863): *Alemannische Grammatik.* Berlin.
Wiese, Richard (1986): Schwa and the Structure of Words in German. *Linguistics* 24, 695-724.
— (1996): *The Phonology of German.* Oxford: Clarendon.

Tomas Riad

Towards a Scandinavian accent typology*

1. Introduction

Traditionally, the pitch accent systems of Scandinavia have been investigated from the bottom up, by collecting phonetic data of a particular kind from a particular dialect. This method has resulted in several fine, if somewhat disparate, descriptions of the prosodic systems of individual dialects (e.g., Klintberg 1885; Kallstenius 1902; Rutberg 1924; Meyer 1937, 1954). Sometimes, conclusions regarding the prosodic phonology have been drawn, in a few cases leading to the formulation of new questions and directed experiments (e.g., Bruce 1974, 1987; Kristoffersen 1990). The task of working out the prosodic phonologies of many individual dialects remains staggering, and presumably this has limited the pursuit of typological work on the accent systems beyond the most salient parameters of variation (quality of central tones, lexical distribution of accents in compounds).

Here, I attempt to make some headway into the phonological aspects of the accent typology. First, I propose a new typology of tonal makeup for the four major dialect groups. Second, I lay out a set of constraints that are required to describe the best known aspects of Scandinavian pitch accent systems. Third, I show how the ranking of these constraints in an optimality grammar (Prince & Smolensky 1993) can generate the pitch accent dialects studied. The advantage of using this model in the present context is that it allows us to state separately the several different properties that affect the tonal structure in any one dialect. These can then be individually manipulated to generate and predict different pitch accent systems. We thus get a transparent descriptive framework which makes clear predictions at a rather fine level of detail. Both of these properties are key to an argument that seeks to unify the analysis of the several pitch accent dialects in Scandinavia.

Many of the claims made here are based on previous work on the typology of Scandinavian accents (Meyer 1937, 1954; Öhman 1967; Gårding 1977; Bruce & Gårding 1978; Gårding, Bruce & Willstedt 1978; Lorentz 1995; Riad 1996) and on the synchronic analysis of the best studied Swedish dialect—Stockholm (Central Swedish)—e.g., in work by Bruce (1977, 1987) and Engstrand (1995, 1997). Where needed, the empirical base has been broadened by information available in a number of dialect descriptions, of varying degrees of sophistication and depth.

The available information practically restricts this investigation to the core properties of accent realization that show in the narrow context of citation forms. However, this still admits the comparison of simplicia and compounds, which is an important dimension of the typology. Thus, we shall pay considerable attention to long compounds, since they allow us

* I would like to thank Gösta Bruce, Chris Golston, Carlos Gussenhoven and Wolfgang Kehrein for highly valuable input at various stages of the development of the ideas presented here.

to see the behaviour of individual tones much clearer than do simplicia and short compounds.

There is considerable homogeneity across dialects with regard to tonal grammar. If we allow ourselves to extrapolate, mildly, from what appear to be stable features in the better known dialects, we can formulate some hypotheses concerning specific properties of the Scandinavian typology. This will be the general method used. The goal, then, is not so much to provide a comprehensive analysis of the typology—that would be premature—but to arrive at reasonably clearly formulated hypotheses which could subsequently be discussed and/or tried out in further, preferably instrumentally supported, analysis of individual dialects.

We will compare the following seven dialects of Swedish and Norwegian, representing different types: Stockholm, Göta, Oslo, Narvik, Bergen, Färnebo, Malmö. (Several other dialects belonging to these types are mentioned in (26) below.) Constraints expressing the different properties exhibited within the typology will be introduced as we lay out the basic grammar of the dialect of Stockholm (Central Swedish accentual variety). It is appropriate to use Stockholm as example because of the relative complexity exhibited by this dialect, and because of the attention it has received in previous research.[1]

A general finding is that Scandinavian dialects lend themselves to uniform description and analysis. For instance, geographic distance between dialects is not correlated with a difference in grammar. The lexical pitch accent opposition can be uniformly described as privative (i.e., accent 1 has no lexical specification while accent 2 does), although, to do this, we need to assume a new segmentation of the tonal contour in some dialects. The central tones obey the OCP in a strikingly uniform manner, and invariably occur in the same order: Lexical, Prominence, Boundary. There is some typological variation concerning how the Prominence tone holds itself vis-à-vis the Lexical tone on the left, vis-à-vis the right boundary, and whether or not it spreads. Other areas of variation concern the definition of tone-bearing unit and the extent of tonal association, as opposed to tonal concatenation and flotation.

The paper is structured as follows. Section 2 contains a description of basic properties of Scandinavian pitch accent. Section 3 is a detailed analysis of the Stockholm system. Here we shall introduce all constraints needed for the typology except one. In section 4 we turn to the typological aspects, regarding tonal specification (4.1, 4.2) and grammatical variation (4.3) with a focus on the behaviour of the Prominence tone. Towards the end of that section we discuss predictions of typology presented (4.5) and give a general overview in terms of constraint ranking(4.6). Other proposals regarding the segmentation of the tonal string are briefly reviewed in section 5, before concluding (section 6).

---

[1] The analysis of Scandinavian tonal grammar proposed here is a developed and expanded version of Riad (1996), both as regards the basic segmentation of tones and organization of constraints.

2. Basic description

By 'pitch accent' I mean a lexically distinctive tonal accent, which occurs at most once in a word. Tradition has given us the terms 'accent 1' and 'accent 2' (and, 'acute' and 'grave') to use for the description of the contrast. I will continue to use these as cover terms, but there are two things about them that may create confusion. First, the term 'accent' is often used for the realization of the whole contour, which consists of tonal material contributed by several different prosodic levels. In the phonological analysis, obviously, the different tones must and will be kept apart, by explicit reference to their origin. Second, as one school of analysis has long maintained for certain dialects, accent 1 is the *absence* of lexical tonal material (Sweet 1877:155; Haugen & Joos 1952; Haugen 1967). Thus, accent 1 is the case where the tonal contour is made up of tones from the prosodic phrase and up only.

2.1. Geography

Pitch accent dialects occur all over Scandinavia, except the northernmost parts of Norway and Sweden, most Swedish dialects in Finland, and most Danish dialects. In addition, there are a few smaller areas which lack distinctive accent, such as eastern Uppland and the area surrounding Bergen. There is no accent distinction in Iceland or the Faroe Islands. It is usually assumed that the Danish stød/zero alternation is a counterpart of the tonal accent distinction, but this is not uncontroversial. For instance, while stød corresponds to accent 1 in many cases, there is also a robust correspondence with accent 2 in compounds (Riad forthc.). Also, the segmental conditioning that stød requires, limits the correspondences. The status of stød need not concern us here, however, since the typology I shall describe concerns the (more obviously) tonal dialects only.

2.2. The lexical opposition

The accent distinction is largely superfluous, it would seem. As mentioned, several dialects lack it completely, and in the dialects that have it, the number of minimal pairs is limited in several syntactic, semantic and phonological ways. Elert (1972) counts about 350 minimal pairs in Standard Swedish. For Norwegian, the corresponding list is much longer—about 3000 pairs according to the recent count in Leira (1998). Norwegian vowel reduction is an important source for the difference between Swedish and Norwegian (Claes-Christian Elert p.c.). The distinction is limited structurally to polysyllabic words containing at least one syllable following primary stress. This means that a large chunk of the lexicon is not even eligible for accentual distinction.

While functionally dubious, the pitch accent opposition is phonologically very real. Accent 2 contains a real Lexical tone, which accent 1 lacks (Haugen 1963, 1967; Kristoffersen 1990: 254ff.; Ladd 1996:159; Lorentz 1995; Engstrand 1997). The privative nature of the opposition is simple and desirable from the theoretical point of view, and we adopt it here for all pitch accent dialects of Scandinavia. It is, however, not uncontested (Bruce 1977).

(1) The lexical tonal opposition is privative (Stockholm):
accent 1: Ø
accent 2: H*

2.3. Lexical distribution

The lexical distribution of accents in simplicia and most derivations is strikingly stable across Scandinavian pitch accent dialects. To mention but a few instances, disyllabic infinitives and derivations on, e.g., *-ig* (*mysig* 'cosy'), *-ing* (*teckning* 'drawing'), *-ad* (*månad* 'month') get accent 2, while derivations on *-is* (*dagis* 'kindergarten'), *-isk* (*komisk* 'comic') and forms prefixed by *be-* (*beröva* 'bereave') or *för-* (*förbjuda* 'forbid') get accent 1, regularly and across dialects.

The situation with accent in compounds is different, and subject to extensive variation (Bruce 1973, 1974; Withgott & Halvorsen 1984, 1988; Kristoffersen 1992). Broadly speaking, dialects appear to choose between a lexical treatment of compounds, in which the accent of the compound is determined by, e.g., the lexical accent of the first member, and a prosodic treatment, where the presence of more than one stress (clashing or otherwise) automatically leads to pitch accent 2. Stockholm (and Central Swedish generally), for instance, has accent 2 in nearly all compounds, while several other dialects exhibit mixed systems (Bruce 1973; Withgott & Halvorsen 1984). In this paper we shall only look at the phonology of accent 2 compounds. Dialects which have accent 1 compounds, treat them phonologically the same way as regular simplicia.[2]

2.4. Tones and constituents

The discussion of the tonal features of the pitch accent dialects centers around what is sometimes called the three central tones: Lexical tone, Prominence tone and Boundary tone. All dialects lend themselves to analysis in terms of these three central tones. Homogeneity is even stronger; while the central tones may have different values in different dialects, the *order* of the three central tones appears to be stable across dialects. This is illustrated in (2).

---

[2] The source of the crucial difference between the stability of simplicia, etc., and the variability of compounds would seem to be the number of stresses. Nearly all compounding (and some derivation) cause the output to contain two stresses, while most derivation and inflection of simplicia does not add to the single stress of the root.

(2) Tone sequences

Lex	*Prom*	*Bound*	*Dialect*
H*	LH	L]	Stockholm
L*	HL	H]	Malmö
H*	L	H]	Göta, Oslo
L*	H	L]	Färnebo, Bergen, Narvik

Lorentz (1995:40) expresses the stable linearization as in (3), where the brackets refer to constituents of the prosodic hierarchy.

(3) ((Lexical tones) Prominence tones) Boundary tones

Tones, then, are properties of constituents (Pierrehumbert & Beckman 1988:21ff., 119; Fretheim & Nilsen 1989). Realization of the tones depends on several factors, including the function of the tone and the availability of tone-bearing units. Generally, the Lexical tone and the Prominence tone tend to occur near stressed syllables, the primary stressed syllable in particular, while the Boundary tone occurs near the right edge of constituents. Since there is only one tone tier, tones are necessarily sequenced. The picture below illustrates the structure contributing the central tones, and how the tones line up on the tone tier in these single-word utterances.

(4) Prosodic structure and the tone tier (accent 2, Stockholm)

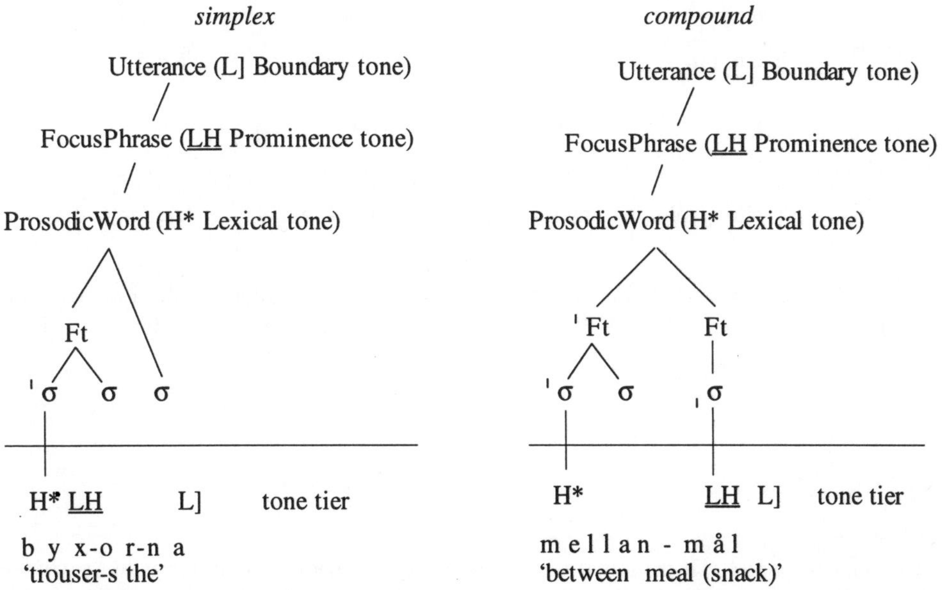

The primary stress is always the first stress of a word, and the sequence of central tones always begins there.[3] Let us now turn to a detailed analysis of the pitch accent system of Stockholm.

3. The tonal grammar of Stockholm (Central Swedish)

Lexical tone invariably occurs first of the three central tones, with the intonational tones (Prominence and Boundary) following. In accent 1, where there is no Lexical tone, the intonational tones will begin directly at the syllable carrying primary stress. (5) illustrates the parts and the order of the tonal features. Simplicia occur in either accent. Compounds are invariably accent 2 in Stockholm, but reveal properties of the grammar that accent 2 simplicia conceal.

(5) Accents 1 and 2 in Stockholm

	Lexical tone	Prominence tone	Boundary tone	Stylized tracings
Accent 1 simplex 'tobacco'	ˈt o b a k	LH ˈt o b a k	LH L] ˈt o b a k	ˈt o b a k
Accent 2 simplex 'mustard'	H* ˈs e n a p	H* LH ˈs e n a p	H* LHL] ˈs e n a p	ˈs e n a p
Accent 2 compound 'the snack'	H* ˈmellan,målet	H* LH ˈmellan,målet	H* LHL] ˈmellan,målet	ˈmellan,målet

The second peak of accent 2 and the only peak of accent 1 are functionally identical, and phonetically similar, as Bruce (1977) shows. This observation is now a corner-stone of any description of the tonal string in Scandinavian dialects.

[3] It is sometimes said that the initial syllable receives secondary stress in forms like *elimiera* 'eliminate' and *multiplikation*. If so, this stress is rhythmic and of no consequence to the prosodic phonology. Unlike German (cf. Alber 1998) and English, foot structure preceding the primary stress is very hard to ascertain in Swedish and Norwegian.

3.1. Association

As seen in (5), only one tone is associated to a syllable in the two simplex words. In accent 1 it is the Prominence tone. In accent 2 it is the Lexical tone, while the Prominence tone remains unassociated. This directly reflects the findings of Bruce (1977, 1987). In each case, the association point is the syllable carrying primary stress. When there is only one stressed syllable, Lexical tone association has precedence over Prominence tone association as seen in *senap* (simplex, accent 2) above. I will follow Bruce (1987) and Gussenhoven & Bruce (forthc.) here in assuming that the Prominence tone floats, when it cannot associate. Other factors than association will thus determine where and how such a floating Prominence tone is realized. In the compound, there are two stresses, and the Prominence tone can associate, not to the primary stress, but to the secondary stress.

As for the Boundary tone, it is arguably never associated in the usual way (Bruce 1977). While this tone tends to coincide with the prosodic boundary, there is no stable timing with, say, the last syllable, which would warrant an associative relationship between the Boundary tone and some TBU. It would seem more adequate to think about the Boundary tone as *aligning* with the edge of the prosodic domain. There is a L target on the tone tier, but whether that L is fully reached within the stretch of segmental material is subject to variation. Sometimes, it will be, other times, only the cues of an anticipated L target are actually realized.

The association of tones and the alignment of tones, I take to be two different ways that tones can get licensed (or 'parsed'). The distinction appears to be very important for the characterization of Scandinavian accent systems. An *associated* tone is in a stable timing relationship with a TBU, i.e., it has an association line in the autosegmental representation. *Alignment* means for a tone to be oriented towards some edge. By allowing both of these relations as licensing mechanisms for tone, I depart from the traditional autosegmental view, where association is taken as the way for a tone to get a phonetic interpretation. The objective here is to take the phonetic findings of Bruce and others seriously, and try to reflect the differences of tonal behaviour rather directly in the grammar.

The Lexical tone is associated by virtue of meeting the following constraint (Riad 1996:140).

(6) ASSOC(Lex) ASSOCIATE (LexicalTone, TBU)
'The Lexical tone is associated to a TBU'

Lexical tone is always associated (to primary stress), and hence this constraint is undominated.

The Prominence tone (whether single of contour) is always associated in accent 1. In some dialects, and Stockholm is among them, Prominence tone also associates in accent 2 compounds. An association constraint is therefore warranted for the Prominence tone, too.

(7) ASSOC(Prom) ASSOCIATE (ProminenceTone, TBU)
'The Prominence tone is associated to a TBU'

Importantly, it is the L tone of Prominence LH which is associated. As Gussenhoven & Bruce (forthc.) discuss, the H tone of Prominence LH is clearly not associated, either in accent 1, or in accent 2 compounds.

As mentioned, the Lexical tone has precedence over the Prominence tone in associating to the syllable carrying the primary stress. The means that the dominance relation between the association constraints is as in (8).

(8) ASSOC(Lex) >> ASSOC(Prom) (all dialects)

This dominance relation is the same in all dialects.

(9) Simplex, 'abbess'

2	Stockholm	ASSOC (Lex)	ASSOC (Prom)
a. ☞	H* LH | abbe'dissa]$_{PrWd}$		*
b.	H* LH | abbe'dissa]$_{PrWd}$	*!	

In (9a) Lexical H* associates to the exclusion of Prominence LH. In (9b) things are the other way around. When we look at this limited candidate set, these two constraints, thus ranked, can select the correct winner. However, a putative candidate in which both tones are associated fares better than either of (9a) or (b), on these particular constraints. More must therefore be said to stop tones from associating to just any syllable. In particular, we should restrict the associations points, the TBUs, to stressed syllables. I propose to formalize the familiar correspondences of Goldsmith's (1976) in the following way.

3.2. Tone-bearing unit (TBU)

I take the notion of *tone bearing unit* to mean 'unit which bears one tone' in the unmarked case (Leben 1973; Goldsmith 1976).[4] As mentioned, the phonetic correlate of an association relation between a tone and a TBU is primarily stable phonetic timing.[5] Unequivocal association would seem to hold only in stressed syllables, and in many

4 The one tone–one TBU information could be formulated as a separate constraint if need be (Riad 1996:139). That would be a closer map to the original conceptualization by Goldsmith (1976).

5 In other systems segmental conditioning or positional lexical contrast (Gussenhoven forthc.) may also help in determining association.

dialects only in the syllable bearing primary stress.[6] Notably, there is no evidence for association of tones in unstressed syllables. This indicates that while the stressed syllable is the association point for the Lexical tone, the syllable is not itself the tone bearing unit in the phonological sense. Rather, it is the foot or the prosodic word which is TBU, while their heads are stressed syllables. As pitch accent languages, Swedish and Norwegian have, at most, one accent per word. This would make it seem natural to have the prosodic word as the preferable TBU, i.e., the phonological target of a tone.[7] The realization of the word accent involves percolation to the prosodic head, thus typically (the first mora in) a stressed syllable.

One way of thinking about the notion of TBU, then, is to make available the whole set of categories in the prosodic hierarchy.

(10) TBU = μ, σ, Ft, Wd, Ph ...
'The tone bearing unit is a mora, a syllable, a foot, a word, a phrase ...'

These will all represent constraints with a fixed internal order. Thus, if a tone has the prosodic word as TBU, and associates, then it automatically satisfies all the higher ranked constraints of being associated to the lower categories of the prosodic hierarchy (Ft, σ, and μ). There is thus transitivity. The relevant TBU constraints required for the dialect typology presented here are given in (11).

(11) TBU=Ft >> TBU=Wd (universal ranking)[8]

The interest of having this scaling of TBU-constraints for present purposes is twofold. First, we expect Lexical tones to associate sooner to the primary stress than to a secondary stress, simply because violation is minimal (Smolensky & Prince 1993). Second, it provides the means of expressing the behaviour of the Prominence tone in compounds, by allowing the constraints in (11) to be interleaved with ASSOC(Prom).

(12) TBU=Ft >> ASSOC(Prom) >> TBU=Wd

In Stockholm, ASSOC(Prom) is ranked between the two TBU constraints, whereby TBU=Ft is respected and TBU=Wd may be violated. The reverse is not possible. To illustrate this, we look at two types of context: compounds with three stresses and simplicia with one stress.

---

6 Our interpretation of the notion of TBU is very near that of Gussenhoven & Bruce (forthc.) but differs from Kristoffersen (1993), Lorentz (1995) and Bye (1996). A brief discussion is given in Riad (1996:138-141).

7 I will not go into the issue of whether or not compounds are single prosodic words. It is clear that they can only contain one accent, but that would not seem to be sufficient to settle the issue (cf. Booij 1985 for other evidence bearing on the status of the prosodic word).

8 The ranking TBU=Wd >> TBU=Ft makes no sense, since that would lead to the contradiction that an unstressed syllable could be the prosodic head of a prosodic word.

(13) Compound, 'the snack bun'

2	Stockholm	TBU=FT	ASSOC (Prom)	TBU=WD
a. ☞	H* (ˈmel-) LH (-ˌbul-): ˈmellan-ˌmåls-ˌbullen]$_{PrWd}$			*
b.	H* (-ˌmåls-) LH (-ˌbul-): ˈmellan-ˌmåls-ˌbullen]$_{PrWd}$			**!
c.	H* (ˈmel-) LH (unassociated): ˈmellan-ˌmåls-ˌbullen]$_{PrWd}$		*!	
d.	H* (-lan-) LH (-ˌbul-): ˈmellan-ˌmåls-ˌbullen]$_{PrWd}$	*!		*

Beginning from the bottom, (13d) is out because one tone is associated to an unstressed syllable (*-lan-*). This incurs a violation on TBU=Ft, and TBU=Wd by transitivity. (13c) fails to associate the Prominence tone. (13b) associates both tones to stressed syllables, but neither of those stresses is the primary stress, hence TBU=Wd is violated twice. In the winning candidate, (13a), ASSOC(Prom) forces a violation of TBU=Wd by having the Prominence tone associated to a secondary stress. The Lexical tone, however, finds the primary stress and violation of TBU=Wd is thus minimal.

(14) Simplex, 'the people'

2	Stockholm	TBU=FT	ASSOC (Prom)	TBU=WD
a. ☞	H*LH (LH associated to ˈmän-, H* unassociated): ˈmänniskorna]$_{PrWd}$		*	
b.	H* LH (both associated to ˈmän-/-ni-): ˈmänniskorna]$_{PrWd}$	*!		*
c.	H* (ˈmän-) LH (-kor-): ˈmänniskorna]$_{PrWd}$	*!		*

We should here compare (14a) with (13a), and (14b, c) with (13d). In accent 2 simplicia, ASSOC(Prom) cannot be accomodated lest the Prominence tone be associated to an unstressed syllable (14b). But this would mean violating TBU=Ft, which is higher ranked than ASSOC(Prom).

It might seem here that the phonetic difference between (14a) and (b) would not be very large. To better see the behaviour of the Prominence tone we must look at it in other contexts, notably long compounds, and then put our grammar together.

3.3. Prominence tone and alignment

Regarding the Prominence tone (LH), there are two interesting properties to keep in mind in the analysis: 1) The L of Prominence LH follows directly and crisply after the Lexical H*, in simplicia as well as in compounds. 2) When there are TBUs (secondary stresses) available, the L of Prominence LH will choose to associate to the *right*most stress, i.e., far away from the Lexical H*. The reconciliation of these leftward and rightward orientations is achieved by spreading in the relevant forms. In (15), stylized tracings are given on the left and corresponding autosegmental representations on the right. The arrows are used to symbolize spreading of the Prominence tone from its point of association towards the Lexical tone.

(15) Stockholm compounds

Stylized tracings	*Autosegmental representation*
 kaˈmel-ˌdrivare 'camel-driver'	H* LH L] (H* and LH associated) kaˈmel-ˌdrivare
 ˈmid-ˌsommar-ˌdanserna 'the midsummer dances'	H* ◄—— LH L] (H* and LH associated) ˈmid-ˌsommar-ˌdanserna
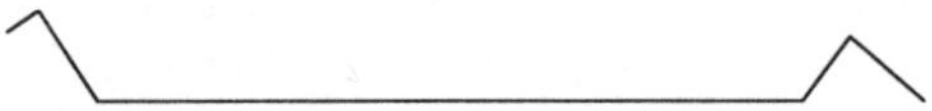 ˈutˌrikes-departeˌments-ˌråds-ˌsommar-ˌbyxorna 'the foreign office counsellor summer trousers'	H* ◄———————— LH L] (H* and LH associated) ˈutrikesdepartementsrådssommarbyxorna

Lexical H* associates with the syllable carrying primary stress. The pitch then falls to a low point and then rises again when the last stress of the word has been reached. This is the Prominence LH tone. In the compound *kaˈmelˌdrivare*, the Prominence rise will occur directly after the primary stress, much as in disyllabic simplicia (cf. *ˈsenap* 'mustard' in (5)), but this is only for reasons of space. In longer compounds we see that the Prominence tone actually looks for, and associates with, the last stressed syllable. Specifically, it is the

L of LH which associates to the last stressed syllable, the rise immediately following (Gussenhoven & Bruce forthc.).

To express the rightward orientation of the Prominence tone, within the Focus phrase, we need an alignment constraint.

(16) R-ALIGN(Prom) ALIGN (ProminenceTone, RIGHT; FocPh, RIGHT)
'The Prom. tone occurs at the right edge of the Focus phrase'

In Stockholm, R-ALIGN(Prom) thus sees to it that the rightmost available TBU will be preferred by the Prominence tone in long compounds. This is illustrated below. We leave out the arrow symbolizing spreading below, for clarity.

(17) Compound, 'the midsummer dances'

2	Stockholm	TBU=FT	ASSOC (Prom)	R-ALIGN (Prom)
a. ☞	H* LH L] ˈmid-ˌsommar-ˌdanserna] $_{PrWd}$			
b.	H* LH L] ˈmid-ˌsommar-ˌdanserna] $_{PrWd}$			Ft!
c.	H* LHL] ˈmid-ˌsommar-ˌdanserna] $_{PrWd}$		*!	
d.	H* LHL] ˈmid-ˌsommar-ˌdanserna] $_{PrWd}$	*!		

In (17a), the Prominence tone is associated to the rightmost, legitimate TBU. While not entirely aligned with the right edge, the Prominence tone only violates R-ALIGN(Prom) minimally.[9] In (17b), R-ALIGN(Prom) is gratuitously violated in that the leftmost TBU of the two TBUs available is selected. In the last two candidates, Prominence tone aligns perfectly with the right edge, but either fails to associate (17c), or associates to an illegitimate TBU (17d).

The effect of R-ALIGN(Prom) is logically distinct from association. Thus, it is entirely possible for a Prominence tone to exhibit rightward orientation without associating to a TBU (cf. Göta in (28) below).

[9] No interesting interactions at a finer level of detail are apparent in the dialects studied. Therefore, we do not register violations to R-ALIGN(Prom) below the size of a foot.

In accent 1, the constraints controlling the Prominence tone can all be met, more or less. The rightmost stress is the only stress, and there is no Lexical tone occupying it.

(18) Simplex, 'the syphilis'

1	Stockholm	ASSOC (Prom)	R-ALIGN (Prom)
a. ☞	<u>LH</u> L] | ˈsyfilisen]$_{PrWd}$		
b.	<u>LH</u>L] ˈsyfilisen]$_{PrWd}$	*!	

3.4. Tone concatenation

The transition between the Lexical tone and the Prominence tone is the next point of interest. This transition is quite crisp, and is not coordinated with the points of association. Instead, the Prominence tone seems to spread leftward until it reaches the Lexical tone. In simplicia it simply glues on to the Lexical tone without associating, as we have seen. In keeping with Riad (1996), I will assume that this is a case where a syntagmatic relation between tones on the tone tier is grammatically controlled. Thus, the hypothesis is that spreading need not be mediated by a syllable-by-syllable association on the tier of the TBUs. Rather, spreading can be effectuated directly on the tone tier. I shall tentatively assume that the responsible constraint, CONCATENATE, is of the alignment type.

(19) CONCAT ALIGN (ProminenceTone, LEFT; LexicalTone, RIGHT)
'The Prominence tone follows directly after the Lexical tone'

CONCAT sees to it that the Prominence tone always follows directly after the Lexical tone. In accent 2 simplicia, where the Prominence tone is unassociated, CONCAT accounts for why all of the Prominence tone is near the primary stress, where the Lexical tone is associated. In compounds (accent 2), CONCAT accounts for why Prominence tone spreads leftwards, from however far away to the right, cf. (15) above.

(20) Compound, 'the midsummer dances'

2	Stockholm	ASSOC (Prom)	CONCAT	R-ALIGN (Prom)
a. ☞	H* ◄——— <u>LH</u> L] | | 'mid-ˌsommar-ˌdanserna] PrWd			
b.	H* - - - - - <u>LH</u> L] | | 'mid-ˌsommar-ˌdanserna] PrWd		*!	
c.	H* <u>LH</u> L] | 'mid-ˌsommar-ˌdanserna] PrWd	*!		Ft

The winner here meets all three constraints. In candidate (20b), the interrupted line indicates tonal interpolation, i.e., a tonally unspecified distance between two targets (cf. section 4.3.3). In order for CONCAT to be met, however, the <u>L</u> of <u>LH</u> must spread, and thus come to directly follow the Lexical tone. Candidate (20b) fails to do this. In (20c) CONCAT is met, but the Prominence tone does not associate at all (in violation of ASSOC(Prom)) even though there are legitimate TBUs available.

CONCAT is an attempt at directly expressing the observed phonetic behaviour of Prominence tone in simplicia and in long compounds. Let us briefly review the phonetic testimony regarding the floating status of Prominence tone in Stockholm.

Gussenhoven & Bruce (forthc.) make it quite clear that while the Lexical tone is firmly associated, the Prominence tone holds itself freer with respect to syllable structure. One source of evidence for this is the adjustments that take place on the tone tier as the size of the focussed domain is varied. Bruce (1987) shows that the Prominence tone (his 'Focal accent') is indeed sensitive to the size of the Focus phrase. A strict timing relationship (=association) between tones and syllables does not seem to have phonetic reality, except at the initial boundary of the stress group. In other words, the Lexical tone is unambiguously associated to the stressed syllable, but the Prominence tone may shift location somewhat depending on the size of the focussed domain (see (21) below).

Bruce's analysis of the tone sequence is different from mine (cf. section 5 below). I assume that all of Prominence <u>LH</u> floats although the floating behaviour is clearer for the latter part of the contour. The phonetic figure does not contradict this analysis, as the associated Lexical tone can be expected to have crisp edges (unless it spreads). The first floating tone following the Lexical tone would thus tend begin at a fairly stable point.

(21) Timing of F0 in Focus phrases of varying lengths (Figure 4, Bruce 1987; reprinted with permission)

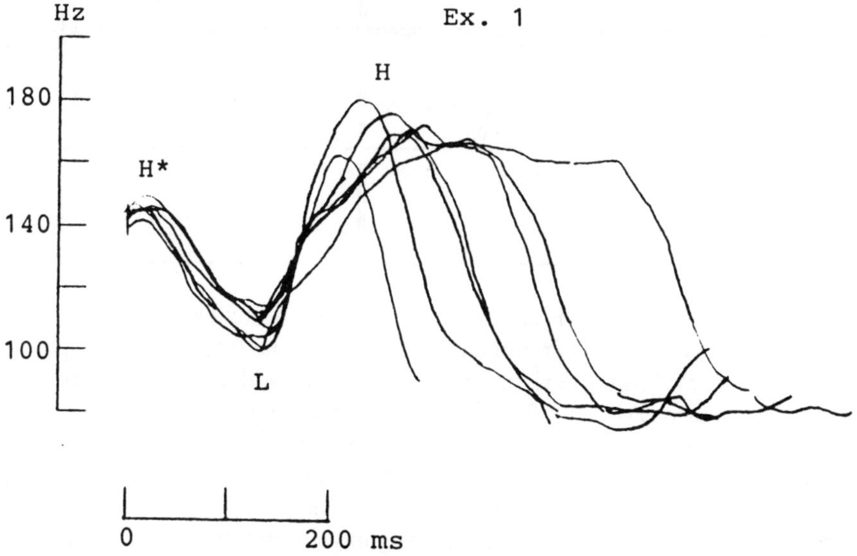

Trisyllabic simplicia provide another indication of the floating status of Prominence tone in Stockholm. In these simplicia, the Prominence tone can either occur in the usual place directly after the Lexical tone, or align with the right edge. The variation may be controlled by contextual factors, but these have not been described, as far as I know.

(22) Variable realization of Prominence tone. Trisyllabic simplicia (Stockholm).

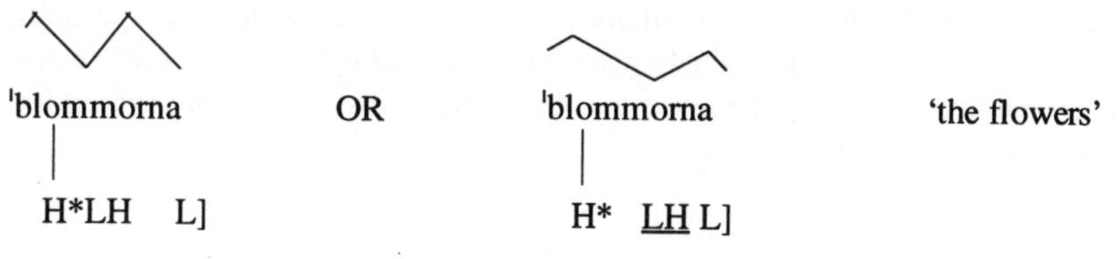

Non-compounds exhibiting accent 2 have at least one post-tonic syllable, and the second peak usually occurs in that syllable (in citation form). In trisyllabic simplicia, the second peak may occur in either the second or third syllable. The very variability, whatever causes it, suggests that the Prominence tone is not associated to a syllable, in accent 2 simplicia. The tonal grammar, as formalized so far, accomodates the trisyllabic variation rather straightforwardly.

(23) Simplex, ‘the flowers’

2	Stockholm	CONCAT	R-ALIGN (Prom)
a.	H*<u>LH</u> L] | 'blommorna] PrWd		?
b.	H* <u>LH</u>L] | 'blommorna] PrWd	?	

The constraints CONCAT and R-ALIGN(Prom) are in no obvious conflict in Stockholm, since spreading allows for the Prominence tone to be at the left and right edges simultaneously. In a simplex form, the right and left edges are within one foot. Therefore, it is questionable whether candidate (23a) qualifies as incurring a R-ALIGN(Prom) violation, and whether (23b) qualifies as a CONCAT violation. In view of the observed variation in trisyllabic simplicia in (22), an attractive interpretation is that there is no conflict here, but a slightly underspecified grammar, allowing for the variation.

CONCAT is separate from a putative left-aligning constraint (L-ALIGN(Prom)), mostly in its predictions. CONCAT says that some tone navigates according to a specific other tone, which is adjacent on the tonal tier. It is thereby ensured that the Prominence tone will follow the Lexical tone (if there is one in the domain). Putative L-ALIGN(Prom) would not itself stop the Prominence tone from occurring to the left of the primary stress, if there were syllables available.

Another way of analyzing the tight sequencing of the Lexical and Prominence tones is crowding. One could assume that when both tones opt to associate with the primary stressed syllable, the result would be that either both get in (under duress), or one gets in and the other stays right outside. This approach is taken in Lorentz (1995) and Bye (1996) and appears successful in simplicia, where there is only one stress. In longer compounds, however, the crowding analysis fails to account for spreading; if the general desideratum is to associate, and Prominence tone associates to the rightmost stress, why should it try to get into the primary stress as well?

3.5. The Boundary tone

The Boundary tone is controlled by the following constraint.

(24) R-ALIGN(Bound) ALIGN (BoundaryTone, RIGHT; Utterance, RIGHT)
‘The Boundary tone occurs at the right edge of the Utterance’

As mentioned above, the phonetic situation suggests that the Boundary tone is not associated to some specific target (Bruce 1977). This is in fact now predicted by our analysis. If the TBU constraints are the way they are, it would be surprising if the Boundary tone *could* associate to an unstressed syllable at the end of the word. The behaviour of the Lexical and Prominence tones shows sensitivity down to secondary stress level (no violations of TBU=Ft). Why should the Boundary tone not obey the same grammatical constraints?

We have now covered the constraints that play a role in the synchronic grammar of Stockholm (Central Swedish). In the discussion of the typology below, we shall introduce one more constraint, UNITY, which inhibits spreading in some dialects (cf. (31) below). Beyond that, the other dialects will be generated by changes in the specification of tone values, and the reranking of the proposed constraints. Before moving on, let us cast an eye on the general ranking relations of Stockholm.

(25) Stockholm, constraint ranking

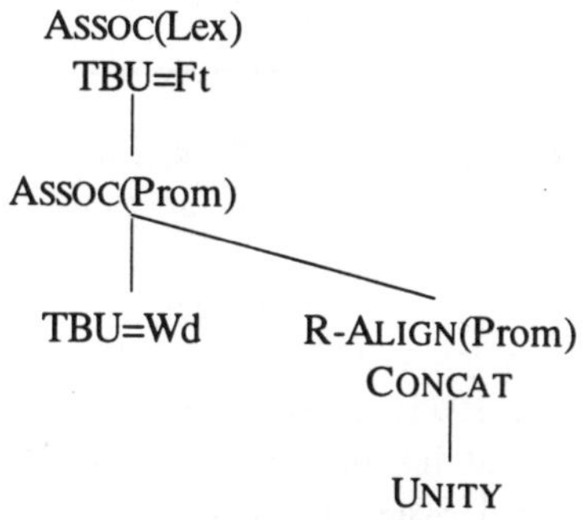

4. Typology

Dialects vary tonally in at least three major respects: 1) the specification of the central tones, 2) the behaviour of the Prominence tone, and 3) the lexical treatment of compounds. In this section, I shall discuss the first two, which are of direct phonological interest.[10]

4.1 Specification of central tones

The specifications of the central tones for the dialects studied are given in (26). When we look at the tone values only, we get four tonal types, which correspond to those reported in the typology of Gårding (1977) and Bruce & Gårding (1978). The seven dialects I use as representatives for different types are set in boldface, and a few other dialects, known to fit into the chart, have been added.

[10] The distribution of accent in compounds in dialects which have a contrast in that domain is an interesting topic but orthogonal to the discussion of representation of tonal structure.

(26) Central tones and dialect types

"accent 1"	*Lexical tone "accent 2"*	*Prominence (Focus tone)*	*Boundary tone*	*Dialect*
Ø	H*	LH	L]	**Stockholm**, Älvdalen, NSw, Stavanger, Snappertuna
Ø	L*	HL	H]	**Malmö**
Ø	H*	L	H]	**Göta, Oslo**
Ø	L*	H	L]	Värmlands bergslag/**Färnebo**, Dala, Gotland/Lau, **Bergen**, Nås, NNw/**Narvik**
Ø	Ø	H	L]	Helsinki

There is no relationship between tone value and function. Thus, even if two dialects "sound" different as a result of using different tones for different functions, they may have the same tonal grammar. The constant part in these pitch accent dialects is the required phonological tones (Lexical, Prominence, Boundary), not their values (H, L, HL, LH).

The position of the *Obligatory Contour Principle* (OCP, Leben 1973) in Scandinavian pitch accent dialects is quite prominent (Lorentz 1995). This is apparent in (26). Combination of functional tones strictly obey the OCP, and this alternation between H and L tones, regardless of function, holds in all dialects. Indeed, Scandinavian tonal dialects may be, and have been, described as different cut-outs of the same string of alternating high and low tones (Meyer 1937, 1954:appx.; Fintoft et al. 1978; Mjaavatn 1978; Lorentz 1995).

(27) OCP Avoid adjacent identical tones (undominated)

The OCP gives a good measure of predictability to the tonal string, whatever piece of known information one starts with, cf. (26).

Looking at average phonetic contours of the accents one can see that geographically adjacent dialects differ phonetically but systematically by the gradual displacement of pitch peaks and pitch troughs. The appendix in Meyer (1954:82ff.) is a good place to study this, where tonal contours of many dialects are listed next to one another. This means that the phonological interpretation of one dialect type will contain several slightly but systematically different realizations of the tone sequence vis-à-vis the phonological string. At some point the phonology identifies a categorically different dialect. Meyer's sample is impressive, but not enough for ascertaining whether transitions between different phonologies (in our interpretation) can be completely smooth phonetically.[11]

The proposed typology of tone specifications in (26) only displays complex tones in the Prominence tone function. If we value the privative nature of the lexical distinction highly, this provides a better null hypothesis than assuming that Lexical tones could be complex.

[11] Öhman (1967) makes an attempt at interpreting Meyer's data in precisely this regard, resulting in what he calls the Scandinavian accent orbit (Fig. II-B-14; reproduced in Gårding 1977:96). However, while very suggestive, the orbit does not make much geographic sense.

With complex Lexical tones, a privative opposition would appear less well motivated. Thus, e.g., H ~ Ø is a more natural privative distinction than HL ~ Ø, since complexity usually follows the exhaustion of the simple contrasts. The Prominence tone, on the other hand, does not enter into a lexical opposition (Gussenhoven & Bruce forthc.).

4.2. Stylized tracings of the dialects

Let us first get an overview of the dialects. In the table below, stylized tracings and autosegmental representations are given for the compound *'mid,sommar,dansen* 'the midsummer dance' (accent 2) for each dialect. The representations for simplex forms (accent 1 and accent 2) are predictable from the compound representations, once we recognize the homogeneity across dialects with respect to association (primary stress is always preferred; Lexical tone always has precedence) and concatenation (in the absence of available TBUs).

(28) Overview

Dialects	*Stylized tracings*	*Autosegmental representations*
Stockholm H* LHL]	 ˈmid-ˌsommar-ˌdansen	H* ◄—— LH L] ˈmid-ˌsommar-ˌdansen]$_{PrWd}$
Malmö L* HLH]	 ˈmid-ˌsommar-ˌdansen	L* HL ——► H] ˈmid-ˌsommar-ˌdansen]$_{PrWd}$
Göta H* L H]	 ˈmid-ˌsommar-ˌdansen	H* ◄— L —► H] ˈmid-ˌsommar-ˌdansen]$_{PrWd}$
Oslo H* L H]	 ˈmid-ˌsommar-ˌdansen	H* L - - - - - - - H] ˈmid-ˌsommar-ˌdansen]$_{PrWd}$
Färnebo L* H L]	 ˈmid-ˌsommar-ˌdansen	L* - - - - - H L] ˈmid-ˌsommar-ˌdansen]$_{PrWd}$
Narvik L* H L]	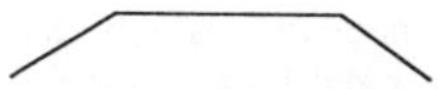 ˈmid-ˌsommar-ˌdansen	L* ◄—— H L] ˈmid-ˌsommar-ˌdansen]$_{PrWd}$
Bergen L* H L]	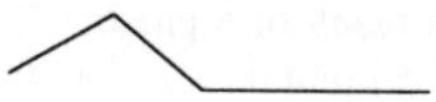 ˈmid-ˌsommar-ˌdansen	L* H - - - - - - - L] ˈmid-ˌsommar-ˌdansen]$_{PrWd}$

It should be clear that the dialects have fairly different melodic characteristics. Some of this variation is due to the choice of functional tones, other variation reflects grammatical properties, to which we turn now.

4.3. Grammatical variation

Given that the Lexical tone and the Boundary tone are quite fixed in their locations, it is not very surprising that the Prominence tone is the major player in the typological variation. The grammatical variation is primarily of three kinds, all relating to the Prominence tone: 1) association (yes/no), 2) directional orientation (right/left), and 3) spreading vs. interpolation.[12] With the several stresses made available in long compounds, we can determine whether a Prominence tone associates or not, when the syllable bearing primary stress is occupied. Long words also allow us to study the phonetic implementation of the space between fixed points for tones. The distinction between spreading and interpolation concerns *how* the transition between tones takes place.

4.3.1. Association of Prominence tone

The issue of whether the Prominence tone associates or not arises only in compounds, since compounds have the property of providing potentially legitimate TBUs (stressed syllables), while at the same time having the preferred TBU, the primary stress syllable, occupied by the Lexical tone.[13] As seen above, association to a secondary stress was legitimate in Stockholm. The dialects pattern as follows.

		yes	*no*
(29)	Association to secondary stress?	Stockholm	Malmö
		Färnebo	Göta
		Narvik	Oslo
			Bergen

Whether the Prominence tone ever gets to associate to some other foot than the head of the prosodic word, or whether it floats, is a major typological parameter, which is determined

[12] These aspects of Prominence tone behaviour have not been extensively discussed in a typological context before. This may be due to the fact that one must look at long compounds in order to notice the behaviour clearly. The traditional disyllabic simplicia (*flicka* 'girl', *springa* 'to run', etc.), often used to exemplify accent 2, conceal all three properties.

[13] Calling this the Lexical tone is a little idiosyncratic in view of the fact that accent 2 is not a lexical specification of compounds, but rather the productive result of a prosodic generalization or some other lexical specification (e.g., the first member of the compound). For simplicity, we stick with the terminology.

by the ranking of the TBU constraints with respect to ASSOC(Prom), in the individual dialects.[14] Compare the following constraint rankings.

(30)	a.	TBU=Ft	>> ASSOC(Prom)	>> TBU=Wd	Stockholm, Färnebo, Narvik
	b.	TBU=Ft	>> TBU=Wd	>> ASSOC(Prom)	Malmö, Göta, Oslo, Bergen
	c.	ASSOC(Prom)	>> TBU=Ft	>> TBU=Wd	unattested

In dialects of the Stockholm type (30a), ASSOC(Prom) can force the association of Prominence tone, even if this means that not only the primary foot is employed as TBU. In a dialect of the Malmö type (30b), association of the Prominence tone will take place only in accent 1, i.e., when the primary foot is available. The several dialects of this type have a floating Prominence tone in all accent 2 words (simplicia and compounds). Indeed, dialects of this type make no tonal prosodic distinction between simplicia and compounds. (30c) represents the case where a dialect would permit association of the Prominence tone to an unstressed syllable. None of the dialects studied here have this property, which would be more typical of tone languages than of pitch accent languages. We have to go to Danish or Roermond Dutch (Gussenhoven forthc.) to find cases where some association constraint must dominate TBU=σ, i.e., cases where the association of tones to individual moras is phonologically relevant.

4.3.2. Directional orientation of Prominence tone

As seen above, association of Prominence tone is by no means self-evident in compounds, in Scandinavian dialects. In the dialects which permit association to a secondary stress (Stockholm, Färnebo, Narvik), it is always the *right*most secondary stress which is selected. We attributed this to the constraint R-ALIGN(Prom) in the analysis of Stockholm in (17) above. None of our seven dialect types associates the Prominence tone to the *left*most secondary stress. The rightward orientation of phrasal accent (instantiated by Prominence tone) would thus appear to be constant. How far to the right it goes can be determined by the ranking of the TBU constraints and R-ALIGN(Prom) in unison, that is, what passes as a legitimate TBU (cf. above) will decide whether the Prominence tone can associate near the

[14] This view of association and TBU predicts that association of more than one tone within the prosodic head should be marked, just as in classical autosegmental theory (Leben 1973; Goldsmith 1976). A contour tone on a long vowel, for instance, should only take place under duress. Supporting examples of this are close at hand. In Kiparsky's (1995) and Ito & Mester's (1997) analyses of stød in Livonian and Danish, respectively, the tonal configuration giving rise to stød is precisely a HL contour tone realized on two tautosyllabic sonorant moras. In so-called no-stød words, the same tonal sequence is realized on separate syllables. In stød words, faithfulness requires both tones to be realized in the same syllable, which is what forces the phonetically marked, even exotic, realization.

	hu:'s 'house'		hu:se 'houses'
stød	H̲ L]	no stød	H̲ L]

right edge or not. However, a rightward orientation can also be instantiated by R-ALIGN(Prom) alone. Thus, the Prominence tone can spread in both directions without being associated.

This leads us to formalize another factor which is evident in the typology, namely spreading and no spreading. Phonology can manipulate the inclination of tones to spread (Goldsmith 1976), and this can be formalized with either spreading or no spreading as the default. We will use an anti-spreading constraint, UNITY.

(31) UNITY 'Tones do not spread'

This constraint expresses that there is a cost to spreading tones, while interpolation is default. I will only consider the spreading behaviour of the Prominence tone.

UNITY interacts primarily with CONCAT and with R-ALIGN(Prom), which represent the left- and rightward orientation, respectively. Consider Färnebo, a dialect where Prominence tone may associate to the rightmost secondary stress in compounds.

(32) Compound, 'the midsummer dance'

2	Färnebo	UNITY	CONCAT
a. ☞	L* - - - - - <u>H</u> L] | | ˈmid-ˌsommar-ˌdansen] PrWd		*
b.	L* ◄——— <u>H</u> L] | | ˈmid-ˌsommar-ˌdansen] PrWd	*!	

In candidate (32b), the <u>H</u> Prominence tone spreads leftward and would yield a high plateau (similar to Narvik, cf. (28), but not identical). However, Färnebo in fact exhibits a *rise* between the Lexical tone and the Prominence tone, which we interpret as an interpolation. In this analysis, then, it is the ranking of UNITY which controls spreading.

In other dialects, where Prominence tone cannot associate to a secondary stress, it may well stay near the left edge. Bergen is a case in point.

(33) Bergen
L* <u>H</u> L]

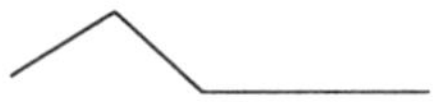

ˈmid-ˌsommar-ˌdansen

L* <u>H</u> - - - - - - - L]
|
ˈmid-ˌsommar-ˌdansen] PrWd

The contrast with a spreading alternative may be considered in the following tableau.

(34) Compound, 'the midsummer dance'

2	Bergen	UNITY	CONCAT	R-ALIGN (Prom)
a. ☞	L* <u>H</u> - - - - - - - L] | 'mid-ˌsommar-ˌdansen] $_{PrWd}$			Ft
b.	L* <u>H</u> ——————► L] | 'mid-ˌsommar-ˌdansen] $_{PrWd}$	*!		

The candidate in (34a) wins because even if it violates R-ALIGN(Prom), it does not spread the Prominence tone (34b). The orientation issue remains highly relevant in the discussion of spreading and interpolation, which we turn to next. We summarize the typology in this domain jointly in (37) below.

4.3.3. Spreading and interpolation

Spreading and interpolation concern the nature of the transitions between the central tones. Immediate transitions between tonal targets are occasioned by juxtaposed association points (*ka'melˌdrivare*), by crowding for lack of space (*flicka*), or by spreading (*'utrikes-departementsrådssommarˌbyxorna*). In contrast with spreading, interpolation is the less direct transition between tonal targets, through syllables which are unspecified for tone (Pierrehumbert & Beckman 1988; Kristoffersen 1993:113f.).

Let us look at a contrast in rightward spreading/interpolation of Prominence tone, in the dialects of Göta and Oslo. These dialects are usually considered to belong to the same pitch accent dialect area. They have the same constituent tones and are geographically adjacent. However, they contrast with respect to the ranking of UNITY. Rightward spreading may occur in dialects in which the Prominence tone fails to associate to a secondary stress in compounds. In such a case, CONCAT will require the Prominence tone to be near Lexical tone, while R-ALIGN(Prom) will pull the other way. Both constraints can only be met if they dominate UNITY (in Göta, as opposed to Oslo). As usual, arrows mark spreading and the broken line marks interpolation.

(35) Spreading vs. interpolation

Göta
H*<u>L</u>H]

'mid-ˌsommar-ˌdansen

H* ◄— <u>L</u> —► H]
|
'mid-ˌsommar-ˌdansen] $_{PrWd}$

Oslo
H*<u>L</u> H]

'mid-ˌsommar-ˌdansen

H* <u>L</u> - - - - - - - H]
|
'mid-ˌsommar-ˌdansen] $_{PrWd}$

The first transition from H* to L is immediate in both dialects, while the second transition from L to H] is markedly different. In Göta there is a Low plateau until the last syllable (the stress status of which is irrelevant) where the pitch jumps up to Boundary H]. I interpret this as spreading. Since the spreading tone is not associated, the question of direction is moot, hence the two arrows in (35). In Oslo, by contrast, there is a steady rise from L until the end, viz. interpolation. Thus, there is no sense in which the L Prominence tone is present at the right edge. Below is the grammar of Göta.

(36) Compound, 'the midsummer dance'

2	Göta	CONCAT	R-ALIGN (Prom)	UNITY
a. ☞	H* ◄— L —► H] | 'mid-ˌsommar-ˌdansen] $_{PrWd}$			*
b.	H* L - - - - - - - H] | 'mid-ˌsommar-ˌdansen] $_{PrWd}$		*!	

Candidate (36b) is a loser in Göta, but a winner in Oslo. To get the Oslo pattern, we should simply rerank R-ALIGN(Prom) and UNITY.

The typological pattern with regard to directional orientation, spreading and interpolation is summarized in (37).

(37) a. CONCAT, R-ALIGN(Prom) >> UNITY — Sto., Nar., Mal., Göta

b. UNITY >> R-ALIGN(Prom) >> CONCAT — Färnebo

c. UNITY, CONCAT >> R-ALIGN(Prom) — Oslo, Bergen

The distinction between spreading and interpolation is very clear in transitions from L to H, as in (35) above. In transitions from H to L, however, the distinction is not apparent. H never seems to fall to L over several syllables. This leaves us with no evidence for a distinction between the two autosegmental representations of the Bergen contour in (38) below.

(38) Bergen
L*H L]

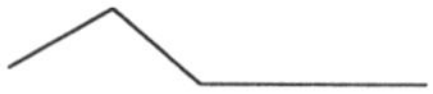

'mid-ˌsommar-ˌdansen

a. L* H - - - - - - - L]
|
'mid-ˌsommar-ˌdansen] $_{PrWd}$

b. L* H◄——— L]
|
'mid-ˌsommar-ˌdansen] $_{PrWd}$

Both (38a) and (38b) would yield the typical Bergen accentual contour. This matter obviously invites careful phonetic study. Phonologically, it may be possible to understand this asymmetry in terms of a L default, and the general tendency to downdrift—as opposed to updrift—in tonal realization. For now, I will simply assume that spreading and interpolatory transitions between H and L cannot be distinguished in Scandinavian accent systems. This limits the scope of predicted tonal grammars considerably. I take representation (38a) to be the least costly, and therefore the one we want for Bergen.

In the seven dialects studied, there is very little interpolation between the Lexical tone and the Prominence tone. Only Färnebo seems to have it, and here we rely on a single and fairly old source (Kallstenius 1936).

(39) Färnebo
L*H̲ L]

ˈmid-ˌsommar-ˌdansen

L* - - - - - H̲ L]
| |
ˈmid-ˌsommar-ˌdansen]PrWd

The status of this feature in Scandinavian tonal grammar will therefore have to remain tentative, in the absence of closer phonetic study. Our grammar captures this interpolation by the following ranking.

(40) b. UNITY >> R-ALIGN(Prom) >> CONCAT Färnebo

Thus, it is more important for the Prominence tone to stay unified, than to spread and satisfy CONCAT, in Färnebo. Also, association obeys R-ALIGN(Prom) sooner than CONCAT. This is illustrated below.

(41) Compound, 'the midsummer dance'

2	Färnebo	UNITY	R-ALIGN (Prom)	CONCAT
a. ☞	L* - - - - - H̲ L] | | ˈmid-ˌsommar-ˌdansen] PrWd			*
b.	L* H̲ - - - - - - L] | | ˈmid-ˌsommar-ˌdansen] PrWd		Ft!	
c.	L* ◄——H̲ L] | | ˈmid-ˌsommar-ˌdansen] PrWd	*!		

Candidates (41a) and (b) illustrate the struggle between R-ALIGN(Prom) and CONCAT. In (41b) CONCAT is met (or nearly so if the first member of the compound were longer), but R-ALIGN(Prom) is violated. Candidate (41c) violates UNITY by spreading the Prominence tone. Färnebo is the only dialect in the sample which appears to have all three of these constraints ranked with respect to each other. Clearly, we should look for a dialect in which the ranking of R-ALIGN(Prom) and CONCAT is the reverse, to see if such a grammar is possible.[15] Let us now turn to consider some other predictions of the analysis.

4.4. Predicted dialects

When we consider what other tonal dialects may occur, a parallel set of dialects to that studied here is predicted. For every grammar we formulate (our seven dialects to the left, below) there should be a corresponding one with the tones inverted, every thing else being equal. The unattested ones are written in italics, the attested in bold. Autosegmental representations have been arranged under the examples to facilitate comparison.

(42) Tonal behaviour

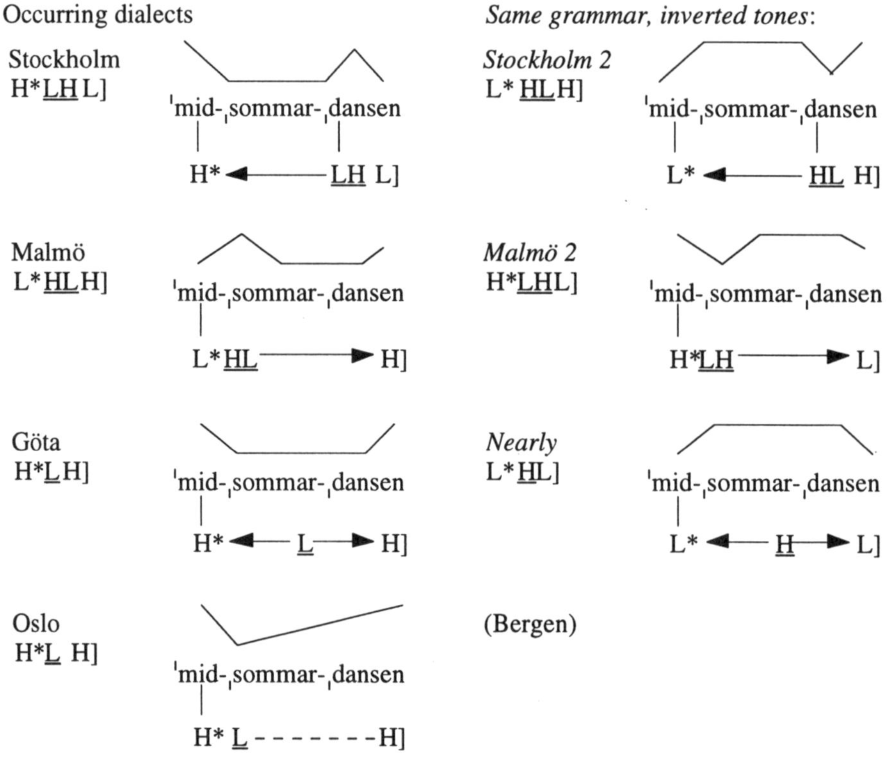

[15] Such dialects might be found Nordfjordeid (Odd Monsson p.c.) and Älvdalska (Gunnar Nyström p.c.), where the first post-tonic stress seems at least a possible position to be selected for Prominence tone association.

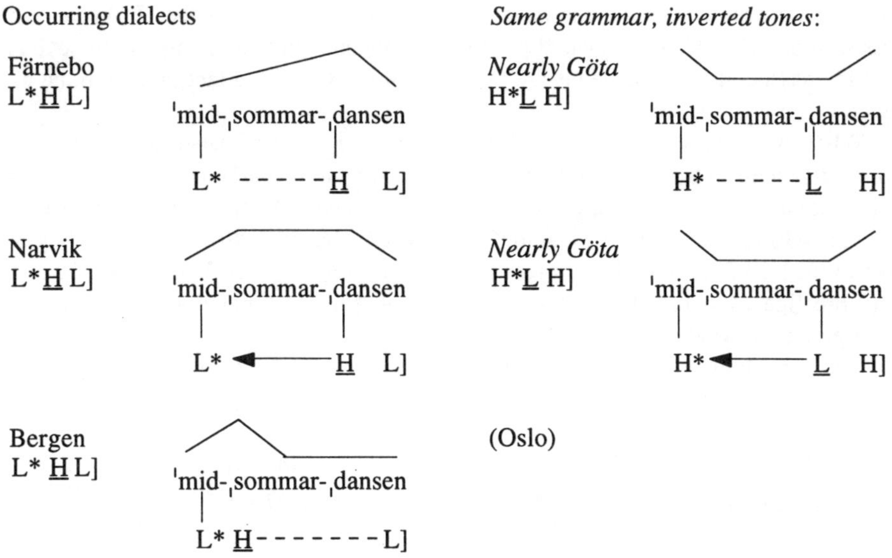

The Prominence tone is a contour tone in Stockholm and Malmö, which makes these dialects into four-tone dialects. The status of the final Boundary H] in Malmö does not seem to be quite as clear as the Stockholm Boundary L].[16]

Concerning the putative dialects on the right, we should note first that they presuppose no phonological asymmetries between H and L. We have already noted a phonetic asymmetry, though, regarding transitions (falling vs. rising interpolation). This asymmetry is further reflected in a pattern among the Boundary tones. When the Boundary tone is H], it never "reaches into" the word (cf. Malmö, Göta, Oslo), while when it is L], it may (cf. Bergen). The simplest analysis here is that the Boundary tone is preceded by interpolation in both instances. As a consequence, we assign the same tonal grammar to Oslo and Bergen. The same goes for Färnebo and hypothetic Nearly Göta (whose tracing is not a mirror image of Färnebo). The only difference between these pairs is that they happen to have opposite tones in each function. The difference in transitions (certainly in need of explanation) follows from this fact.

The inverse of Narvik and Färnebo, respectively, should be one and the same dialect (Nearly Göta), if the asymmetry concerning interpolation stands. The only difference between Nearly Göta and Göta is the association of the Prominence tone to the last secondary stressed syllable, which we do not find in Göta, but which is there in Narvik and Färnebo. Nothing we have said so far would lead us to expect that Nearly Göta is non-existent.

The inverse of Göta, similarly, would be a dialect not unlike Narvik, hence Nearly Narvik. This dialect would have a H Prominence tone which would not associate to the last stressed syllable, unlike Narvik proper (but like Göta, *mutatis mutandi*). This would also appear to be a completely reasonable dialect, under the analysis proposed. However, what

[16] Informal checking of some other dialects from the same dialect area as Malmö (Skåne) give the auditory impression that the final rise is not typically present in citation forms. If the final Boundary H] is removed we are left with a Bergen type of system.

might be a problem with Nearly Narvik, and with Malmö 2, is the H plateau without an association point. Unassociated H plateaus are not encountered in any of our seven dialects, while unassociated low plateaus are (Malmö, Göta, Bergen), a fact that might be of importance.

When we look at the inverse of Stockholm and Malmö, these may be less expected, since it would appear that four-tone dialects are more marked than three-tone dialects. Stockholm 2 amounts to something quite similar to Narvik, but with a contour Prominence tone, resulting in an extra twist at the end. Malmö 2 has the extra twist in the beginning. As mentioned, Malmö would seem less stable a four-tone dialect than Stockholm, which has the prestige of being the historically original type of tonal dialect, according to one interpretation (Riad 1998).

The behaviour of the Prominence tone with respect to association gives rise to one further predicted dialect.[17]

(43) Stockholm
H* LHL]

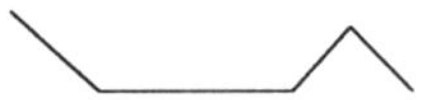

ˈmid-ˌsommar-ˌdansen
H* ◄—— LH L]

Stockholm 3
H* LHL]

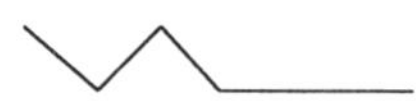

ˈmid-ˌsommar-ˌdansen
H* LH- - - - - - L]

Stockholm 3 would have the same tonal grammar as Oslo and Bergen. Basically it would treat compounds and simplicia in the same way, i.e., as simplicia. This is not uncommon among Scandinavian dialects.[18]

The absence of all these variant dialects is, one would hope, not entirely accidental. Progress could presumably be made either by improving the model and thus slimming down the predictions, or by looking for asymmetries in the interaction of H and L tones, or indeed, by looking for dialects that match the predictions (e.g., Nearly Narvik and Nearly Göta). Closer study of tonal change and dialect transition should also help to clarify what to expect and what to exclude.

4.5. Overview of the typology

The general picture of the typology is given below. The tree depicts the tonal grammars in terms of the constraints discussed. Lines indicate dominance relations. The dialects are listed at the bottom and arranged in two rows according to quality of Lexical tone, here shorthand for the information in (26) above.

---

[17] The ASSOC(Prom)-obeying variant of Malmö is identical to Stockholm 2.

[18] Stockholm 3 in fact ties in with the variation of accent in compounds that occurs in some dialects. As mentioned, compounds get their accent either via a prosodic generalization (2 stresses > accent 2, as in Stockholm), or lexically (accent of the first element > accent of the whole compound). Lexical accent in compounds is described for Southern Swedish dialects (Malmö, Kristianstad, Halmstad) and from East Norwegian. Presumably, a shift from prosodic to lexical accent in compounds is preceded by the loss of the Prominence tone association in compounds.

(44) Typology

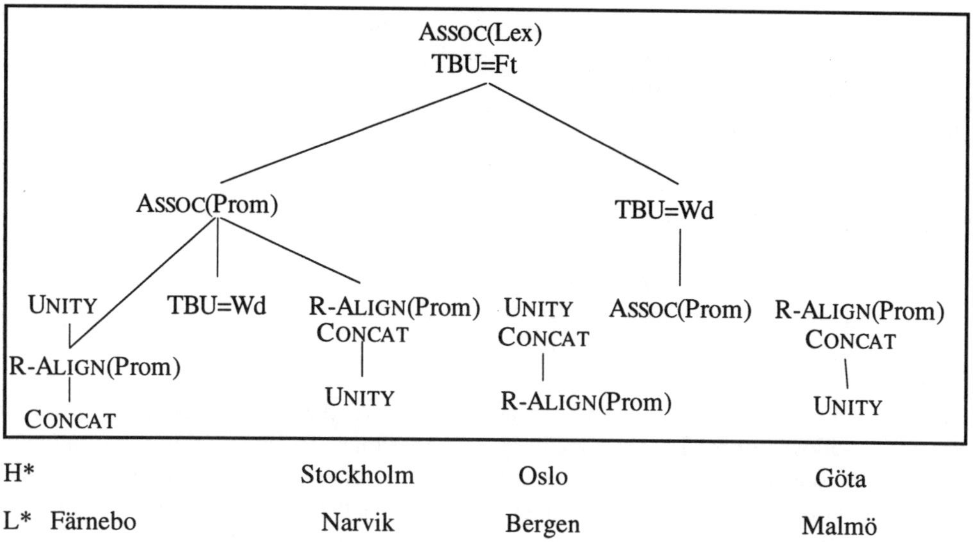

All dialects always associate a Lexical tone, and no dialect permits association of tones to unstressed syllables. From there we get a first split into dialects which associate the Prominence tone to a secondary stress and those which do not. The former group, on the left, will thus make a prosodic difference between accent 2 simplicia and accent 2 compounds (which have two or more stresses). This word-encompassing prosody is sometimes referred to as 'connective accent', since it can be taken to signal the semantic coherence of compounds. By contrast, the group of four dialects on the right, treat compounds the same way as simplicia, by stacking Lexical and Prominence tone where the primary stress occurs, typically at the left edge of the word.

5. Comparing tonal segmentation

There is some disagreement in the phonetic and phonological analysis concerning the segmentation of the string of tones into the three functions: Lexical, Prominence, Boundary (compare Bruce 1977 and Engstrand 1995, 1997). Let us briefly review the issue.

If we accept the functions and their linearization as given, the issue of segmentation arises only in the dialects that have four central tones, that is, more tones than functions (Stockholm and Malmö). Three different segmentations of the Stockholm (Central Swedish) dialect are given below. Our segmentation, largely inspired by the findings of Engstrand (1995, 1997), and used above, is given in (45c). Epenthetic tones are given in outline.

(45) Stockholm: 3 analyses

a.

		Lex	Prom		Bound	
acc2		H*L	H		L]	(Bruce 1977; Riad 1996)
acc1		HL*	H		L]	

b.

	Epen	Lex	Prom	Epen	Bound	
acc2		H*	L	H	L]	(Lorentz 1995)
acc1	H	Ø	L	H	L]	

c.

		Lex	Prom		Bound	
acc2		H*	LH		L]	
acc1		Ø	LH		L]	

The segmentation in (45a)—often seen as the standard theory for Stockholm (Central Swedish)—allows for the Lexical tone to be a contour tone. The most prominent feature of this theory, sometimes called the 'time shift model', is the fact that it assumes distinctive timing, rather than a privative tone/zero opposition. Thus, the tonal accents 1 and 2 are both represented as identical lexical sequences, but with different designated points of association, marked by the star (H*L vs. HL*). This means that the lexical distinction is not taken to be privative in the traditional sense (Trubetzkoy 1967). In other dialects—those with a single Lexical tone in the typology of Bruce and Gårding (1978), which is based on the same framework—the distinction is always privative, however. This yields a perhaps unnecessarily heterogeneous typology.

The other two segmentations both represent the tonal distinction as privative in all dialects treated. Neither of them allows contours as Lexical tones. However, it is not possible to extend a one tone–one function program without additional measures, since in a dialect like Stockholm there are more tones (four) than functions (three). The proposal in (45b) here introduces epenthetic tones, the insertion of which is driven by the OCP. The proposal in (45c) gets away from generating epenthetic tones by allowing a contour Prominence tone. More importantly, however, the latter proposal denies the phonological relevance of the pretonic H tone in accent 1. Bruce (1977:46ff.) argues that there is reason to assume that there is a H tone preceding the associated L in accent 1. Recently, however, Engstrand has shown that pretonic H in accent 1 is not stable, and that it is better derived from contextual factors (e.g. stress status of the pretonic syllable), than from word level phonological specifications. This hypothesis was arrived at by analyzing spontaneous speech (Engstrand 1997). By systematically manipulating the intonational context preceding the focussed word, Engstrand (1995) was able to show that the presence or absence of a pretonic fall could be predicted from intonation. In accent 2, however, the fall is affected by contextual factors, but never removed. It should be noted that the stable accent 2 H is *in* the tonic syllable, and therefore not dependent on the presence of a pretonic syllable.[19]

[19] Whatever other effects should be derived from the stress status of the syllable in which a putative word tone is contained is not discussed in Engstrand's papers.

A few other considerations give further motivation for why we should prefer (45c) over (45a,b).

On the theory-internal side we get a simpler typology if the time shift model of Bruce (1977) can be dropped in favour of a straightforward privative opposition, which is needed anyway for dialects such as Göta, Narvik and Oslo (East Norwegian; cf. Lorentz 1995).

Another theory-internal argument, relates to the spreading behaviour of tones. With the proposed system (45c), we can confine spreading to the Prominence tone, across dialects, leading to a tighter and more stream-lined typology (hence a better null hypothesis).

Finally, it would seem a good thing if we could do without the two epenthetic ℍ tones of (45b) (Lorentz 1995), since they are motivated only within the context of one dialect and the OCP. Why are there no dialects with fewer central tones but which employ epenthesis (e.g. L*LH] showing up as L*ℍLH])? Phoneticians agree that the second H peak has the function of marking focus. Our proposal (45c) retains this function by making H part of the Prominence tone LH, while (45b) mechanically makes it epenthetic, hence basically a tone without a linguistic function.

6. Conclusion

In this paper, I have presented a typology of Scandinavian pitch accent, both as regards inventory and grammar. A new segmentation of the tonal sequence is made in order to secure privative oppositions in all dialects. On the grammatical side, the typology presented here shows quite clearly that the Prominence tone is involved in most of the typological variation. Many other aspects (order of tones, fixity of Lexical tone, OCP) are remarkably stable across dialects. One of the major methodological points made in the paper is that there is much to learn from long compounds, since they allow us to study the behaviour of the Prominence tone.

In the pitch accent systems of Sweden and Norway, tones have a tendency to occur near stresses. At the same time, there are noticeable differences regarding whether a tone is really anchored in stressed syllables, or just occurs near it (Bruce 1987; Gussenhoven & Bruce forthc.). The analysis of Scandinavian pitch accent dialects presented here attempts to capture these behaviours by a few measures. One is the formalization of TBU as a sequence of constraints modeled on the prosodic hierarchy, with a fixed internal order (... TBU=σ >> TBU=Ft >> TBU=Wd ...). Scandinavian dialects exhibit interesting interactions only in two of the lower ranked constraints, which effectively limit tone association to heads of feet, i.e., stressed syllables. The familiar one tone-one TBU maxim (Goldsmith 1976) is incorporated into the notion of TBU and it is thereby expected that the Prominence tone will often float.

It has also been proposed that association should not be considered the only way for a tone to get phonetic interpretation. Rather, we opened for the possibility of syntagmatic licensing of tones. In particular, the Prominence tone could get licensed by concatenation with Lexical tone, and the Boundary tone by aligning with the boundary of the prosodic Utterance. The observed floating status of Prominence tone in Stockholm supports such an approach, as does, e.g., the spreading behaviour of the completely unassociated Prominence tone in Göta.

On the empirical side, we have identified seven different pitch accent dialects, to be compared with the four that tonal specification alone make available. A few more putative dialects were predicted in a general way, and with that, the goal of the article can be said to have been reached. Thus, we have developed a reasonably detailed and specific hypothesis about the Scandinavian pitch accent systems to the point where it makes quite clear predictions about what other members of the same general system should look like.

References

Alber, Birgit (1998): Stress preservation in German loan-words. In: Wolfgang Kehrein & Richard Wiese (eds.): *Phonology and Morphology of the Germanic Languages*, 113-141. Tübingen: Niemeyer,

Booij, Geert (1985): Coordination reduction in complex words: a case for prosodic phonology. In: Harry van der Hulst & Norval Smith (eds.): *Advances in nonlinear phonology,* 143-160. Dordrecht: Foris.

Bruce, Gösta (1973): Tonal accent rules for compound stressed words in the Malmö dialect. *Working papers* 7, Phonetics laboratory, Lund University.

— (1974): Tonaccentregler för sammansatta ord i några sydsvenska stadsmål. In: Christer Platzack (ed.): *Svenskans beskrivning* 8, 62-75. Dept. of Scandinavian languages, Lund University.

— (1977): *Swedish word accents in sentence perspective.* Lund: CWK Gleerup.

— (1987): How floating is focal accent? In: Kirsten Gregersen & Hans Basbøll (eds.): *Nordic Prosody* 4, 41-49. Odense: Odense University Press.

Bruce, Gösta & Eva Gårding (1978): A prosodic typology for Swedish dialects. In: Gårding et al., 219-228.

Bye, Patrik (1996): *Correspondence in the prosodic hierarchy and the grid.* Cand. philol. thesis. Institutt for språk of litteratur. University of Tromsø.

Elert, Claes-Christian (1972): Tonality in Swedish: Rules and a list of minimal pairs. In: Evelyn S. Firchow, Kaaren Grimstad, Nils Hasselmo & Wayne O'Neil (eds.): *Studies for Einar Haugen*, 151-173. The Hague: Mouton.

Engstrand, Olle (1995): Phonetic interpretation of the word accent contrast in Swedish. *Phonetica* 52, 171-179.

— (1997): Phonetic interpretation of the word accent contrast in Swedish: Evidence from spontaneous speech. *Phonetica* 54, 61-75.

Fintoft, Knut, Per Egil Mjaavatn, Einar Møllergård & Brit Ulseth (1978): Toneme patterns in Norwegian dialects. In: Gårding et al., 197-206.

Fretheim, Thorstein & Randi A. Nilsen (1989): Terminal rise and rise-fall tunes in East Norwegian intonation. *Nordic journal of linguistics* 12, 155-181.

Goldsmith, John (1976): *Autosegmental phonology.* diss. New York: Garland.

Gussenhoven, Carlos (forthc.): The lexical tone contrast of Roermond Dutch in Optimality Theory. In: Merle Horne (ed.): *Prosody: Theory and Experiment.* Amsterdam: Kluwer.

Gussenhoven, Carlos & Gösta Bruce (forthc.): Word prosody and intonation. *Word Prosodic Systems.* European Science Foundation project in typology. Mouton.

Gårding, Eva (1977): *The Scandinavian word accents.* Lund: CWK Gleerup (=Travaux de l'institut de linguistique de Lund 11).

Gårding, Eva, Gösta Bruce & Ursula Willstedt (1978): Transitional forms and their position in a prosodic typology for Swedish dialects. In: Gårding et al., 197-206.

Gårding, Eva, Gösta Bruce & Robert Bannert (eds.) (1978): *Nordic prosody. Papers from a symposium.* Lund University (=Travaux de l'Institut de Linguistique de Lund 13.).

Haugen, Einar (1963): Pitch accent and tonemic juncture in Scandinavian. *Monatshefte für deutschen Unterricht* 55, 157-161.
— (1967): On the rules of Norwegian tonality. *Language* 43, 185-202.
Haugen, Einar & Martin Joos (1952): Tone and Intonation in East Norwegian. *Acta Philologica Scandinavica* 22, 41-64. (Reprinted in: Ernst Håkon Jahr & Ove Lorentz (eds.) (1983): *Prosodi/Prosody*, 178-202. Oslo: Novus.)
Itô, Junko & Armin Mester (1997): Støˀdet i dansk. Handout, Hvalfjarðarströnd, Iceland.
Kallstenius, Gottfrid (1902): *Värmländska Bärgslagsmålets ljudlära*. Stockholm: Norstedt & Söner.
Kiparsky, Paul (1995): Livonian stød. Handout, Workshop on diachronic prosody, Nijmegen.
Klintberg, Mathias (1885): *Laumålets kvantitet ock aksent*. Stockholm: Norstedt & Söner (=Svenska landsmål ock svenskt folklif VI.1).
Kristoffersen, Gjert (1990): *East Norwegian prosody and the level stress problem*. ms. University of Tromsø.
— (1992): Tonelag i sammensatte ord i østnorsk. *Norsk lingvistisk tidsskrift* 10, 39-65.
— (1993): An autosegmental analysis of East Norwegian pitch accent. In: Björn Granström & Lennart Nord (eds.): *Nordic prosody* 6, 109-122. Stockholm: Almqvist & Wiksell International.
Ladd, D. Robert (1996): *Intonational Phonology*. Cambridge: Cambridge University Press.
Leben, William (1973): *Suprasegmental phonology*. diss. MIT.
Leira, Vigleik (1998): Tonempar i bokmål. *Norskrift* 95, 49-86.
Lorentz, Ove (1995): Tonal prominence and alignment. *Phonology at Santa Cruz* 4, 39-56.
Meyer, Ernst A. (1937): *Die Intonation im Schwedischen I. Die Sveamundarten*. Helsingfors: Fritzes bokförlags AB. Mercators tryckeri.
— (1954): *Die Intonation im Schwedischen II. Die norrländischen Mundarten*. Uppsala: Almqvist & Wiksell. (=Stockholm studies in Scandinavian Philology 11).
Mjaavatn, Per Egil (1978): Isoglosses of toneme categories compared with isoglosses of traditional dialect geography. In: Gårding et al., 207-216.
Pierrehumbert, Janet & Mary Beckman (1988): *Japanese tone structure*. Cambridge, MA: MIT Press.
Prince, Alan & Paul Smolensky (1993): *Optimality theory: Constraint interaction in generative grammar*. Ms, Rutgers University and University of Colorado, Boulder.
Riad, Tomas (1996): Remarks on the Scandinavian Tone Accent Typology. *Nordlyd* 24, 129-156.
— (1998): The origin of Scandinavian tone accents. *Diachronica* XV:1, 63-98.
— (forthc.): The Origins of Standard Danish Stød, Eskilstuna-curl and Generalized accent 2 in Mälardalen. In: Aditi Lahiri (ed.): *Markedness in Language Change (Proceedings from the Maurach workshop)*, Cambridge: Cambridge University Press.
Rutberg, Hulda (1924): *Folkmålet i Nederkalix och Töre socknar*. Stockholm: Norstedt & Söner.
Sweet, Henry (1877): Sounds and Forms of Spoken Swedish. *Transactions of the Philological Society* 1877. 478-543.
Trubetzkoy, Nikolai S. (1967): *Grundzüge der Phonologie*. 4 Auflage. Göttingen: Vandenhoeck & Ruprecht.
Withgott, Meg & Per-Kristian Halvorsen (1984): Morphological constraints on Scandinavian tone accent. *Report no. CSLI-84-11*, Stanford University.
— (1988): Phonetic and phonological considerations bearing on the representation of East Norwegian accent. In: Harry van der Hulst & Norval Smith (eds.): *Autosegmental studies on pitch accent*, 279-294. Dordrecht: Foris.
Öhman, Sven (1967): Word and Sentence Intonation: A quantitative model. *Speech Transmission Laboratory Quarterly Progress and Status Report* (STL-QPSR) 2-3.20-54. Dept. of Speech Transmission, Royal Institute of Technology, Stockholm.

Section II: Prosodic morphology

Birgit Alber

Stress preservation in German loan-words

1. Introduction

It has been a well known fact from the very beginning of generative phonology that morphologically complex forms often inherit characteristics of related, morphologically less complex forms (Chomsky & Halle 1968). Take for example the contrast in stress pattern of the English words *Tatamagouchi* and *originality*, both consisting of the same number of (light) syllables preceding main stress.[1] Secondary stress falls on the first syllable of the underived

(1) Tà.ta.ma.góu.chi

but on the second syllable of

(2) o.rì.gi.ná.li.ty

due to the fact that a main stress is assigned to the second syllable of the morphologically simpler

(3) o.rí.gi.nal

In other words, the main stress of *o.rí.gi.nal* is preserved as a secondary stress in *o.rì.gi.ná.li.ty*.

Traditionally the phenomenon of stress preservation has been analyzed in terms of cyclic rule application or, in the model of lexical phonology, as the result of interleaving morphological and phonological processes. More recently, the similarities between morphologically related forms have been reanalyzed within the framework of optimality theory (Prince & Smolensky 1993) as being the result of faithfulness constraints targeting related output forms (cf. Benua 1995, McCarthy 1995, Kenstowicz 1996). Specifically, in Kenstowicz (1995), Pater (1995), Benua (1997) and Kager (forthcoming a), (forthcoming b) the preservation of stress is interpreted as the effect of constraints requiring identity between the distribution of stress in morphologically related forms.[2]

In this paper I offer a contribution to the discussion on stress preservation from the domain of German loan-word stress. This case study provides a straightforward illustration of the advantages of an approach in terms of optimality theory to this phenomenon. As

[1] cf. Liberman & Prince (1977).
[2] Faithfulness constraints referring to stress can also be found in Alderete (1995).

Pater and Benua (for English stress) and Kager (for stress in Dutch, Palestinian Arabic and Tripoli Arabic) show, if we view stress preservation as the result of a faithfulness constraint, this constraint can interact in various ways with the set of constraints regulating the overall stress pattern of a language. In other words, the stress pattern of the base of affixation may not be preserved as a whole, in all its details, in the affixed form, or - on the contrary - be disregarded completely. Rather, we expect there to be languages where single, high-ranked, stress pattern constraints may be observed, while other, lower-ranked ones, may be violated, if dominated by the constraint requiring faithfulness between morphologically related forms. As a result, the stress pattern of the stem might be preserved only in part. For example, let X and Y be stress pattern constraints of a certain language, where X dominates Y, a ranking which can be established by the behavior of underived words. We may then have a constraint F, requiring morphologically related words to be identical, which is ranked below X, but above Y:

(4) X >> F >> Y

As a result, stress will be preserved at the cost of violating the constraint Y, but stress preservation will not occur when the satisfaction of X is at stake. Note that an approach in these terms makes more restrictive predictions about the possibilities of stress preservation than an approach in terms of cyclic rule application. Given the ranking X >> Y of metrical constraints in a language, stress preservation may occur across the board, if F is top-ranked in the language under discussion, or it may never occur, if F is bottom-ranked. Finally, we can have a language with stress preservation only in certain contexts, if the ranking is as in (4). But we should not find a language with X >> Y where F is satisfied at the cost of X while stress preservation does not occur when Y is at stake.[3] Another advantage of viewing stress preservation as the result of a faithfulness constraint is that it can give us additional evidence for the hierarchy of stress pattern constraints, in that we can check the position of F in the constraint hierarchy against the position of the metrical constraints established on independent grounds for underived words. For example, if the hierarchy of metrical constraints of a language can be established as being

(5) V >> ... X >> Y >> ... >> Z

and we can establish that X dominates F, which in turn dominates Y, as in (4), then we predict also that stress preservation can occur only at the cost of the constraints lower-ranked than Y (e.g. Z), but never when this would cause the violation of the constraints higher ranked than X (e.g. V). Thus the position of F in the constraint hierarchy provides a testing ground also for the correctness of the hierarchy of constraints determining the stress pattern of underived words. This point was stated first by Pater (1995) who observed that it is striking that the cases of stress preservation in the metrical system of English require the

3 At least, if we assume that we do not have any reranking of constraints when we are dealing with morphologically complex forms. This is the most restrictive claim and thus it should be pursued, if possible. It means that there is only one grammar, valid for morphologically simple and morphologically complex forms.

same constraints to be high ranked, and the same constraints to be low ranked, as the analysis of words where stress preservation is not at stake.

In what follows, I will first present a case where stress preservation occurs in certain contexts, but not in others, in the domain of German loan-words. These facts will be analyzed as being the result of a constraint requiring correspondence between morphologically related forms which is ranked above certain stress pattern constraints, but below others. The analysis will then be compared to a derivational analysis, to show that an analysis in terms of violable constraints is more restrictive. Moreover, placing a faithfulness constraint responsible for stress preservation in the middle of the constraint hierarchy of stress pattern constraints leads to a set of implications about the interaction between F and the stress pattern constraints. Basing myself on previous work on secondary stress in underived words (Alber 1997b) I will discuss some of these implications and show that they are indeed borne out.

2. Preservation of stress in German loan-words

In this paper I will concentrate on the stress pattern of German loan-words. This subpart of the lexicon has been chosen because loan-words are longer than native words, thus a rich pattern of secondary stress can be observed. Morphologically simple native words generally consist of a single heavy syllable (cf. Golston & Wiese 1998) and hence cannot display any alternating rhythm.

In what follows I will be mainly concerned with the distribution of secondary stress, the distribution of main stress will not be discussed in any detail. Unlike secondary stress, main stress is not completely predictable in German loan-words. Main stress is assigned close to the right edge of the prosodic word to one of the last three syllables of the word (cf. Wurzel 1970, 1980a, 1980b; Benware 1980; Giegerich 1985; Hayes 1986; Eisenberg 1991; Vennemann 1990; Féry 1995; Wiese 1996; Alber 1997a for a discussion of main stress assignment in loan-words). A possible analysis of main stress assignment is to say that in one class of words stress is placed on the head of the rightmost trochee, for another class of words it must be assumed that constraints of the NONFINALITY type (cf. Prince & Smolensky 1993) prevent main stress from being final (cf. Alber 1997a). A typical example of the idiosyncratic nature of main stress assignment in loan-words are words with similar segmental make-up but different main stress placement such as *Pén.sum*, with penultimate stress vs. *Kon.súm,* with final stress. The distribution of secondary stress in the examples given throughout the text are based on the judgment of 12 native speakers of German, including myself. I am following Giegerich (1985) and Ramers (1992) in assuming that syllables containing a long vowel or a diphthong and syllables closed with a consonant are heavy, while open syllables containing a short vowel are light. Long vowels are shortened in the domain of secondary stress (cf. Wurzel 1980b: 930), hence the only heavy syllables that can influence the pattern of secondary stress either contain a diphthong or are of the CVC type. To facilitate concentration on secondary stress in the examples only the quantity of the syllables preceding main stress has been noted.

To illustrate the preservation of stem stress in German loan-words, words have been chosen which have been affixed with the stress attracting suffix *-ität*. The reason for this choice is that *-ität,* along with *-ion* and *-ie,* is one of the most frequent noun-forming loan-suffixes (cf. Fleischer & Barz 1995). Differently from *-ion* and *-ie*, however, the stress bearing final syllable in *-ität* is always preceded by an unstressed syllable, which creates a buffer against a possible stress clash with the stress inherited from the stem. Stress preservation is not possible when it would create a stress clash among adjacent syllables and therefore choosing a suffix like *-ität* increases the possibilities of stress preservation considerably. The suffix *-ität* attaches to adjectives and, less frequently, to nouns. The stems may themselves be derived via suffixation (e.g. *Kontinent* 'continent' → *kontinent-al* 'continental' → *Kontinent-al-ität* 'continentality') or not be analyzable morphologically (e.g. *naiv* 'naive' → *Naiv-ität* 'naiveté'). The suffix *-ität* consistently attracts main stress, but there are cases where the main stress of the stem is preserved as a secondary stress in the derived word, and other cases where this does not happen.

For instance, stress preservation takes place in words where the main stress of the stem falls on the fourth syllable. Note that it is of no importance whether the third syllable is heavy or not. A secondary stress will inevitably fall on the fourth syllable in the suffixed form: [4]

(6)	ù.ni.ver.**sál**	→ [[Ù.	ni.	ver.	**s à.**	l]i.	t´ät]	'universal',	'universality'
		'L	L	H	'L	L			
	kòn.ti.nen.**tál**	→[[Kòn.	ti.	nen.	**tà.**	l]i.	t´ät]	'continental',	'continentality'
		'H	L	H	'L	L			
	Ò.ri.gi.**nál**	→ [[Ò.	ri.	gi.	**nà.**	l]i.	t´ät]	'original',	'originality'
		'L	L	L	'L	L			
	ì.rra.tio.**nál**	→ [[Ì.	rra.	tio.	**nà.**	l]i.	t´ät]	'irrational',	'irrationality'
		'L	L	L	'L				
	è.mo.tio.**nál**	→ [[È.	mo.	tio.	**nà.**	l]i.	t´ät]	'emotional',	'emotionality'
		'L	L	L	'L				
	ì.lle.gi.**tím**	→ [[Ì.	lle.	gi.	**tì.**	m]i.	t´ät]	'illegitimate',	'illegitimacy'
		L	L	L	L	L			
	hè.te.ro.**gén**	→[[Hè.	te.	ro.	**gè.**	n]i.	t´ät]	'heterogeneous',	'heterogeneity'
		L	L	L	L	L			

4 From now on the syllable which is the potential target of stress preservation will be noted in bold face, also in the cases where eventually no stress preservation occurs. Light syllables are indicated by "L", heavy syllables by "H".

It is clear that stress preservation is indeed at play here, when we compare the pattern of the examples above with the distribution of stress in otherwise comparable words where preservation of stress from a morphologically simpler form cannot be at stake (cf. Alber 1997b for an analysis of secondary stress in German loan-words). For example, take words with a sequence of five light syllables preceding main stress.

(7) Là. ti. tù. di. na. rís. mus 'latitudinarianism'
'L L 'L L L

Notwithstanding the same syllabic make-up of the pretonic string as in *Ò.ri.gi.nà.li.t´ät*, in *Là.ti.tù.di.na.rís.mus* secondary stress falls on every odd-numbered syllable, counting from the left. In this case, stress cannot be inherited from a morphologically simpler stem, *latitudinar* is not attested as a word. In fact, most speakers will not even know the word *Latitudinarismus*,[5] nevertheless the stress pattern is clear. The same is true for

(8) Lè. pi. dòp. te. ro. ló. ge 'butterfly expert'
'L L 'H L L

with an LLHLL sequence before main stress, just as in *Ù.ni.ver.sà.li.t´ät*, but with stress on the third, instead of the fourth syllable. Again, the connection to the scientific name *lepidóptera,* used in zoological classification for the order of insects comprising the butterflies is arguably not transparent for most speakers and even when it is, there might remain some doubt as to whether the main stress should fall on the antepenultimate or the penultimate syllable of the word.[6] Nevertheless, the pattern of secondary stress in *Lè.pi.dòp.te.ro.ló.ge* is clearly alternating, from the left to the right.

Below, more examples are given which show that secondary stress falls on every odd-numbered syllable counting from the left when stress preservation is not at stake:[7]

(9) ò. no. mà. to. po. é. tisch[8] 'onomatopoetic'
'L L 'L L L

---

[5] According to the *Duden* (1994), *Latitudinarismus* is "a tendency originated in the 17th century in the Anglican church, characterized by confessional tolerance and openness towards the findings of modern science" [my translation].

[6] The Brockhaus encyclopedia destroys any hope of treating stress on *-dòp-* as inherited by giving the germanized form *Lepidoptéren*, with stress noted on the syllable following *-dop-*

[7] But see below for cases where the alternating pattern of secondary stress can be disrupted by an even-numbered heavy syllable in examples such as *Àu.to.de.tèr.mi.nís.mus.*

[8] This word could of course be analyzed as being morphologically complex, i.e., [[onomato]poetisch], but there is no loan-word *onomato*, from which the secondary accents on the first and third syllable could be inherited.

È.	pi.	dè.	mio.	lo.	gíe[9]		'epidemiology'
'L	L'	L	L	L			
È.	o.	sì.	no.	phi.	líe		'eosinophilia'
'L	L	'L	L	L			
Kò.	le.	òp.	te.	ro.	ló.	ge	'beetle expert'
'L	L	'H	L	L			
Sì.	pho.	nàp.	te.	ro.	ló.	ge	'flea expert'
'L	L	'H	L	L			

In conclusion, the stress pattern of these words shows us that the examples in (6) must be cases of stress preservation, while those in (7), (8) and (9) reflect the regular stress pattern. If the examples in (6) were not cases of stress preservation, secondary stress in German loan-words would have to be described in the following way: 'place stress on the first syllable of the word and on the second syllable to the left of the main stressed syllable' but this would leave the examples in (7) through (9) unaccounted for.

In parallel to the cases just discussed, we have words with a very similar morphological structure, where the main stress of the stem is not preserved as a secondary stress in the derived form. These words are shorter and the main stress of the underived word falls on the second syllable. As before, different sequences of heavy and light syllables before main stress give the same results.

(10)	lo.**yál**	→[[Lò.	**ya**.	l]i.	t´ät]		'loyal',	'loyalty'
		'L	L	L				
	Ri.**vá**.le	→[[Rì.	**va**.	l]i.	t´ät]		'rival',	'rivalry'
		'L	L	L				
	la.**bíl**	→[[Là.	**bi**.	l]i.	t´ät]		'weak',	'weakness'
		'L	L	L				
	sta.**bíl**	→[[Stà.	**bi**.	l]i.	t´ät]		'stable',	'stability'
		'L	L	L				

[9] I disregard here an alternative pronunciation, preferred by some speakers, where the high vowel in the fourth syllable is not pronounced as a glide and hence the word is syllabified as *E.pi.de.mi.o.lo.gie.*
The stress pattern *È.pi.dè.mio.lo.gíe* 'epidemiology' could in principle be connected to *È.pi.de.**míe*** 'epidemic', but if the stress pattern of this word was preserved in *È.pi.dè.mio.lo.gíe* we should have stress on the fourth, not on the third syllable in the derived word.

ku.**riós**	→[[Kù. **rio** .s]i. t´ät][10] 'L L L	'odd',	'something odd'
per.**vérs**	→[[Pèr. **ver**. s]i. t´ät 'H H L	'perverse',	'perversity'
ab.**súrd**	→[[Àb. **sur**. d]i. t´ät] 'H H L	'absurd',	'absurdity'
ner.**v´ös**	→[[Nèr. **vo**. s]i. t´ät] 'H L L	'nervous',	'nervousness'
mo.**dérn**	→[[Mò.**der**. n]i. t´ät] 'L H L	'modern',	'modernness'

No stress preservation occurs in these cases. Instead the derived forms behave exactly as loan-words where stress cannot be treated as inherited by a morphologically simpler form: a secondary stress falls on the first syllable of the word, if more than one syllable precedes main stress, as we can see in the following examples.[11]

(11)	Drè.pa. no. clá. dus 'L L L	'a genus of moss'
	Ò. ri. gi. nál 'L L L	'original'
	Àn.tho. lo. gíe 'H L L	'anthology'
	Kà. lei. do. skóp 'L H L	'kaleidoscope'
	Dè.ter. mi. nís. mus 'L H L	'determinism'

[10] As for *Epidemiologie*, also for *Kuriosität* some speakers prefer a pronunciation without a glide where the word is syllabified as *Ku.ri.o.si.tät*.

[11] There is some variation among speakers in cases where the first syllable of the word is light and the second is heavy, as in *A.dap.ta.tion*. Some speakers, generally of northern extraction, tend to stress the second, heavy syllable. This tendency seems to be stronger in cases like *A.dap.ta.tion,* where the heavy syllable contains an [a] and less strong when it contains a non-low vowel, as in *De.ter.mi.nis.mus*. It could therefore be interpreted as a case of stress driven by sonority (cf. Kenstowicz 1994). For the purpose of this paper only judgments of speakers who consistently stress the first syllable of a word have been considered.

À. dap. ta. tíon 'adaptation'
'L H L

à. mor. ti. síe. ren 'to amortize'
'L H L

Descriptively, stem stress is preserved word-medially (and hence in words that are long enough to show rhythmic alternation in this context) but not at the left edge of the word (and hence not in short words, where the stem's main stress falls close to the left edge of the word).

We have now seen words with main stress falling on the fourth syllable, and others where main stress falls on the second syllable of the stem. When a suffix like *-ität* is added, stress is preserved in the former case, but not in the latter. The cases still missing from the paradigm are those where the stem stress falls on the first or the third syllable. They are less interesting for our purpose since preservation of the stem stress leads exactly to the pattern expected also for underived words. Hence no cases can be observed of stress preservation violating the pattern of underived words, or cases of failed stress preservation following the pattern of underived words. Thus, when stems with initial main stress are suffixed, the derived word will have an initial secondary stress, just as the underived examples in (9) and (11) above:

(12) **Plú**.ral → **Plù**.ra. li. t´ät 'plural', 'plurality'
'L L L

rár → **Rà**.ri. t´ät 'rare', 'rarity'
'L L

The same is true when the stem stress falls on the third syllable. A secondary stress falls on the third syllable of the derived word, just as in underived words with a pretonic string of light syllables (e.g. in (9)):

(13) lè.gi.**tím** → Lè. gi. **tì**. mi. t´ät 'legitimate', 'legitimacy'
'L L 'L L

rì.go.**rós** → Rì. go. **rò**. si. t´ät 'rigorous', 'rigorousness'
'L L 'L L

The challenge then is how to account for the fact that stress is preserved in cases like *Ù.ni.ver.**sà**.li.t´ät*, while it is not preserved in cases like *Lò.**ya**.li.t´ät.* As a matter of fact, we have a triple puzzle. First, the suffix *-ität* is stress attracting: the main stress of the stem is not preserved as a main stress, but at most as a secondary stress, i.e., the stress pattern of the stem is never preserved in all its characteristics. Second, we do have stress preservation to some extent, if the main stress of the stem falls further to the right than the second syllable. Third, we do not have stress preservation, if the main stress of the stem falls on the second syllable. This nonuniformity of stress preservation is one of the central arguments that make Pater (1995) argue for an analysis in terms of violable constraints and against the cyclic application of rules.

3. Analysis

In my analysis I propose that the nonuniform behavior of stress preservation in German loan-words can be explained as the result of ranking the faithfulness constraint requiring identity to the stem's stress pattern below certain stress pattern constraints and above others. I will first show that the faithfulness constraint is ranked below a constraint ALIGN (PRWD, L, FT, L), requiring every prosodic word to begin with a foot, but above the *weight-to-stress principle* (WSP, henceforth) which militates against unstressed heavy syllables. Basing myself on the constraint hierarchy worked out for German loan-words in previous work (Alber 1997b), I will then verify whether the interaction between the faithfulness constraint and other stress pattern constraints is as we would predict it to be. All constraints dominating ALIGN (PRWD, L, FT, L) should be observed even if this means that main stress is not preserved. All constraints ranked below the WSP should be violated when stress preservation is at stake. But first of all it is necessary to define what is meant by "faithfulness to the stress pattern of the stem".

3.1. Faithfulness to stem stress

In principle there are several different ways of thinking about a constraint requiring faithfulness to the stress pattern of the stem of affixation. We can treat stress preservation as being the result either of a faithfulness constraint requiring identity between two output forms (O/O-faithfulness) or of a faithfulness constraint targeting an input and an output form (I/O-faithfulness). The case of stress preservation presented here cannot add anything new to the discussion about this topic, but I want to make clear the reasons that make me follow an analysis like Kager's (forthcoming a), where faithfulness to stem stress is defined as an O/O-faithfulness constraint.[12]

If we do not want to distinguish between I/O-faithfulness and O/O-faithfulness in the domain of affixation[13] we could try to maintain the model of lexical phonology, assuming that affixation proceeds cyclically and that each cycle of affixation forms the input for the

---

[12] Pater (1995) does not distinguish between an I/O-faithfulness constraint responsible for lexical stress and an O/O-faithfulness constraint responsible for stem stress preservation. However, he mentions in the appendix that such a distinction might indeed be necessary for English secondary stress. Cf. also Benua (1997) for an analysis of stress preservation in terms of O/O-faithfulness.

[13] But see McCarthy & Prince (1995), McCarthy (1995), Benua (1995), Kenstowicz (1996), Kager (forthcoming b) for cases outside of the domain of affixation where constraints requiring identity between output forms seem to be required in any case.

next cycle of affixation. Candidates will then be evaluated at each level by the constraint hierarchy and since the output of one cycle forms the input for the next the faithfulness constraint which links the two cycles could be conceived of as being an input-output faithfulness constraint. An approach along similar lines, with a cyclic evaluation of candidates, is argued for in Booij (1996). Booij also points out that there is no straightforward contradiction between a cyclic candidate evaluation and an approach in terms of violable constraints, since the former reflects a specific position taken with respect to the theory about the organization of the grammar (in this case the interaction between morphology and phonology) while the latter makes a claim about the form phonological generalizations take.

Nevertheless, I will follow here the proposal of Kager (forthcoming a) who analyzes stress preservation as the result of a requirement of identity between surface forms. As Kager points out, this approach has the immediate advantage that it predicts that only characteristics of surface forms (but not, e.g., of bound roots) can be transferred, a fact that an analysis in terms of cyclic suffixation has to stipulate. Kager discusses a striking case - the distribution of the adjectival suffixes *-ig* and *-lijk* in Dutch - where stress preservation cannot be seen as satisfying a requirement of identity to the output of the preceding cycle. These suffixes require stress to fall on the preceding syllable, a requirement which induces stress shift, when they are attached to compounds. So we have

(14) nóod-lot 'fate' → [[nood-lót]-ig] 'fatal'

But the same strategy of stress shift is not available for affixed forms: here, instead of shifting stress to the affix, no suffixation of *-ig* and *-lijk* is possible at all:

(15) schóon-heid 'beauty' → *[[schoon-heid]-ig]

Leaving aside the details of constraint ranking, in Kager's analysis the fact that compounds allow for stress-shift, and therefore for suffixation with *-ig/-lijk,* is due to the fact that stress shift in this case does not violate a constraint requiring that the stress peak of the derived word have a correspondent stress peak in some base.[14] The stress peak in *[[nood-lót]-ig]* matches the stress peak of an indirect base of *[[nood-lót]-ig]*, the output form *[lót]*. A word like **[[schoon-héid]-ig]* would violate this constraint, since the affix *-heid* is not a possible output form, therefore *-ig* cannot be attached to words of this kind. What is interesting about this case is that the stress peak of an output form becomes relevant which, in derivational terms, is not present at the moment of suffixation. In other words, if *[nóod-lot]* was the input for *[[nood-lót]-ig]*, we could not make reference to I/O-faithfulness to explain the different behavior of the suffixes *-ig* and *-lijk* with respect to compounds versus affixed words. Kager's analysis therefore shows that an O/O-faithfulness constraint targeting stress peaks is needed in any case.

---

[14] For Kager, the base of a derived word is " ... a fully prosodized, independently occurring *word,* which is also *compositionally related* to the output". The 'base-of-the-base' is referred to as 'indirect base' (Kager forthcoming a).

There is one additional consideration which makes an approach in terms of O/O-constraints more desirable. If we assume that there is just one faithfulness constraint that links input to output as well as the output of one cycle to the output of the next, we make predictions about the behavior of lexical stress systems that are by no means borne out. We would have to say that languages that do not preserve stress specified already at the level of underlying representation also do not have instances of cyclic stress preservation. In fact, if a language does not have any lexical stress, this means that the faithfulness constraint under discussion is bottom-ranked: even if there should be some stress peak specified underlyingly, it could never surface, because other constraints that regulate the distribution of stress would prohibit it.[15] The constraint therefore should be bottom-ranked also at subsequent levels, if we do not want to postulate that the grammar of a language can change at every level of affixation.[16] Hence, no stress preservation could ever occur. Likewise, in a language where lexical stress surfaces to some extent cyclic stress preservation should occur to exactly the same extent: when the constraints dominating faithfulness to stress peaks are not violated.[17] Clearly, to settle the issue more work on lexical stress systems is needed and, in general, on the question of what and at what levels can be preserved.

For the purpose of this paper I will adopt the definition of faithfulness to stress peaks given in Kager (forthcoming a)[18], formulated in terms of correspondence theory (McCarthy & Prince 1995):[19]

(16) PK-MAX (B/O)
Let α be a segment in B and β be its correspondent in O
If α is the stress peak of B, then β is the stress peak of O
(from Kager (forthcoming a))

where O stands for output and B for a base[20] of the output.

3.2. Nonuniform stress preservation in German loan-words

The examples in (11) showed us that German loan-words have a secondary stress on the initial syllable,[21] a fact that I interpret as the effect of a constraint requiring that prosodic words begin with a foot:

15 This consideration holds, if we assume with Prince & Smolensky (1993) that there are no constraints on the input (cf. their concept of *richness of the base*).

16 But see Benua (1997) for the indexation of affix classes to different O/O-faithfulness constraints.

17 This observation may not be so important for secondary stress, since arguably secondary stress is never specified underlyingly (Paul Kiparsky, p.c.), although the question remains why this should be so. However, it has consequences for the assignment and preservation of main stress.

18 But see also the constraint HEAD-MAX in McCarthy (1995) and Alderete (1996) requiring faithfulness to the prosodic head of a word.

19 Kager proposes also a faithfulness constraint PK-DEP (B/O) which requires that a stress peak in an output form have a correspondent in some base. This constraint is not relevant for the case discussed below.

20 cf. fn. 14.

(17) Align (PrWd, L, Ft, L):
∀ prosodic word ∃ foot such that the left edge of the prosodic word and the left edge of the foot coincide. (McCarthy & Prince 1993)

This constraint holds even when the second syllable is heavy, as, e.g., in

(18) Dè.ter. mi. nís. mus 'determinism'
'L H L

Thus, ALIGN (PRWD, L, FT, L) dominates a constraint requiring heavy syllables to be stressed:

(19) WSP = weight-to-stress principle: heavy syllables are prominent (cf. Prince 1990; Prince & Smolensky 1993)

The competition of the two constraints is shown in the following tableau:

Candidates	ALIGN (PRWD, L, FT, L)	WSP
☞ (a) (Dè.ter).mi.nís.mus		*
(b) De.(tèr).mi.nís.mus[22]	σ!	

Tableau 1

Candidate (a) has a trochaic ('LH) foot aligned with the left edge of the prosodic word. Therefore it wins against candidate (b), which would satisfy the WSP by stressing the second, heavy syllable. There are other candidates, which would satisfy both ALIGN (PRWD, L, FT, L) and the WSP, but which would violate constraints that turn out to be higher ranked than ALIGN (PRWD, L, FT, L).[23] This is the case for the following parsing:

(20) (De.tèr). mi. nís. mus → violates TROCH
(L 'H) L

[21] This requirement is violated just in case main stress falls on the second syllable of the word and the initial syllable would form a degenerate foot consisting of a single light syllable, as, e.g., in *E.lán* 'spirit' (cf. discussion below).

[22] I am assuming that ('HL) trochees are banned in German, due to the influence of a constraint ITL (for *I*ambic-*T*rochaic-*L*aw, cf. Hayes 1985, 1995) banning uneven trochees (cf. Alber 1997b for a discussion of this constraint). Thus candidate (b) is parsed here as *De.(tèr).mi.nís.mus* and not as *De.(tér.mi).nís.mus*. But nothing in the analysis of stress preservation hinges crucially on this assumption. Uneven ('LH) trochees are allowed at the beginning of a word, as in the winning candidate (a), because ALIGN (PRWD, L, FT, L) dominates the ITL.

[23] As a matter of fact, the three constraints mentioned below seem to be undominated in German loan-words: there are no cases where an iambic foot would have to be posited, there are no observable cases of stress clash in loan-words and there are no cases where a foot consisting of a single light syllable must be assumed (cf. Alber 1997b).

An (L'H) iamb violates TROCH, a constraint requiring left-headed feet:

(21) TROCH = ALIGN (FT, L, HEAD(FT), L)
∀ foot ∃ head of the foot such that the left edge of the foot and the left edge of the head of the foot coincide.
(cf. RHTYPE=T in Prince & Smolensky 1993; McCarthy & Prince 1993)

On the other hand, the following candidate, with stress on both the first and the second syllable creates a stress clash and parses the initial syllable into a degenerate monomoraic foot:

(22) (Dè).(tèr).mi. nís. mus → violates *CLASH and FT-BIN
('L) ('H) L

Thus it violates *CLASH, a constraint militating against adjacent, stress bearing syllables:

(23) *CLASH: adjacent syllables must not bear stress
(used as a violable constraint in Kager 1994; Pater 1995)

and, with its initial degenerate foot, FT-BIN, requiring feet to be either bimoraic or disyllabic.

(24) FT-BIN: feet must be binary at some level of analysis (μ, σ)
(Prince 1980; McCarthy & Prince 1986; Prince & Smolensky 1993)

Although ALIGN (PRWD, L, FT, L) dominates the WSP, we can see effects of the latter constraint in words which contain a word medial heavy syllable. Although secondary stress generally falls on every odd-numbered syllable, counting from the left (see examples (7) through (9)), an even-numbered *heavy* syllable is stressed word-medially when this does not lead to a clash with the main stress: [24]

(25) Àu. to. de. tèr. mi. nís. mus 'self-determinism'
('H) L L ('H) L

---

[24] As to the first example, for some speakers *Àu.to.dè.ter.mi.nís.mus*, with stress on the third syllable, is also a possible pronunciation. To me this pronunciation sounds somehow artificial, with a pause at the morphological boundary and I would suggest that this second pro-nunciation can be interpreted as two prosodic words, i.e., *[$_{PrWd}$ Àu.to.][$_{PrWd}$ dè.ter.mi.nís.mus]*, each with a stress falling on the initial syllable. On the other hand, the pronunciation in (25) would reflect a parsing in one prosodic word. Words with this sequence of syllables are hard to find, and in fact the second example is a nonexistent though possible word. Note that stress on the fourth syllable cannot be an effect of stress preservation in any of the two cases: ***Dè****.ter.mi.nís.mus* bears secondary stress on the first, not on the second syllable and the main stress of *Àn.te.****zé****.dens* 'antecedent' falls on the third, not the fourth syllable. Such examples are discussed at length in Alber (1997b).

Àn. te. ze. dèn. ta. lís. mus 'antecedentalism'
('H) L L ('H) L

Let us now see how the two constraints ALIGN (PRWD, L, FT, L) and WSP interact with PK-MAX (B/O), the constraint requiring identity between stress peaks of morphologically related forms. Compare a case of stress preservation as, e.g.,

(26) ù.ni.ver.**sál** →[[Ù. ni. ver. **sà**. l]i. t´ät] 'universal','universality'
('L L) H ('L L)

with a case of failed stress preservation:

(27) lo.**yál** →[[Lò. **ya**. l]i. t´ät] vs.*[[Lo. **yà**. l]i. t´ät] 'loyal', 'loyalty'
('L L) L L ('L L)

The first example shows us that stress is preserved at the cost of leaving a heavy syllable unstressed, i.e., PK-MAX (B/O) dominates the WSP. In the second example stress is not preserved because satisfaction of PK-MAX (B/O) would violate the requirement to align the left edge of the prosodic word with the left edge of a foot, hence ALIGN (PRWD, L, FT, L) dominates PK-MAX (B/O). The constraint hierarchy that we obtain is the following:

(28) Align (PrWd, L, Ft, L) >> Pk-Max (B/O) >> WSP

The tableau below shows the interaction of PK-MAX (B/O) and the WSP:

Base: ù.ni.ver.**sál**	ALIGN (PRWD, L, FT, L)	PK-MAX (B/O)	WSP
☞ (a) (Ù.ni).ver.(**sà**.li).(t´ät)			*
(b) (Ù.ni).(vèr).**sa**.li.(t´ät)		*!	

Tableau 2

In cases of more than one secondary stress, the constraint PK-MAX (B/O) can show its force, once ALIGN (PRWD, L, FT, L) is satisfied by the first secondary stress. Therefore candidate (a) wins, where the stress peak of the stem on the fourth syllable is preserved, although candidate (b), with stress on the third, heavy syllable, would satisfy the WSP.

On the other hand, we do not have stress preservation when ALIGN (PRWD, L, FT, L) is challenged:

Base: lo.**yál**	ALIGN (PRWD, L, FT, L)	PK-MAX (B/O)	WSP
(a) Lo.(**yà**.li).(t´ät)	*!		
☞ (b) (Lò.**ya**).li.(t´ät)		*	

Tableau 3[25]

Here the unfaithful candidate (b) wins, because candidate (a), although satisfying PK-MAX (B/O), does not satisfy the higher ranked ALIGN (PRWD, L, FT, L).

3.3. Stress preservation under a derivational approach

Let us stop here for a moment before considering the interaction of PK-MAX (B/O) with other stress pattern constraints. We have just pinpointed the exact hierarchical position of the faithfulness constraint requiring correspondence between morphologically related forms: it is ranked below the constraint ALIGN (PRWD, L, FT, L), but above the WSP. Of course we could explain the data above also with an analysis in terms of cyclic rule application. For example, we could analyze the two examples that were discussed above by considering the assignment of main stress to be a cyclic rule, with stress assigned on a previous cycle being carried over to subsequent cycles. We would then have two postcyclic rules, one saying something like "assign stress to the initial syllable" and another that says "assign stress to heavy syllables".[26] At the end of the derivation we would need two destressing rules, one that - under clash - destresses the second, but not the initial syllable of the word (Destress I), and another one that eliminates the clash between two syllables by destressing the first of them (Destress II).[27] The two rules are crucially ordered with respect to each other. This would lead to the following Derivation of *Universalität:*

(29)	1st cycle:	"assign main stress"	→	univers**ál**
	2nd cycle:	"assign main stress"	→	Univers**à**lit´ät

[25] See below for a discussion of the candidate *(Lo.yà).li.(t´ät)*, which would satisfy all three constraints.

[26] Note that both rules are necessary to derive words where stress preservation is not at stake as, e.g., *Kà.lei.do.skóp* ("assign initial stress") and *Àu.to.de.tèr.mi.nís.mus* ("assign stress to heavy syllables", in this case the fourth, heavy syllable).

[27] Actually, we would need yet a third destressing rule destressing syllables preceding a syllable bearing main stress, in order to derive the correct output for *lo.yál*. This destressing rule should be ordered before Destress I, otherwise the generated output would be *ló.yal.*

Postcyclic rules:

	"assign initial stress"	→	Ùniver**sà**lit´ät
	"assign stress to heavy syllables"	→	Ùnivèr**sà**lit´ät
	Destress I	→	n.a.
	Destress II	→	Ùniver**sà**lit´ät
			---------------------
	output	→	Ùniver**sà**lit´ät

The derivation for *Loyalität*, on the other hand, would run as follows:

(30)	1st cycle:	"assign main stress"	→	lo**yál**
	2nd cycle:	"assign main stress"	→	Lo**yà**lit´ät

Postcyclic rules:

	"assign initial stress"	→	Lò**yà**lit´ät
	"assign stress to heavy syllables"	→	n.a.
	Destress I	→	Lò**ya**lit´ät
	Destress II	→	n.a.
			---------------------
	output	→	Lò**ya**lit´ät

Destress I and Destress II must be ordered with respect to each other, so that in the case of *Loyalität* the first rule bleeds the application of the second rule, otherwise we would get the wrong output *Lo.**yà**.li.t´ät.*

The derivation proposed here is perhaps oversimplified, and a number of other possible derivational analyses are imaginable, but hopefully the main idea has become clear: the result of stress preservation in one case (*ù.ni.ver.**sál** → Ù.ni.ver.**sà**.li.t´ät*) vs. lack of stress preservation in the other (*lo.**yál** → Lò.**ya**.li.t´ät*) is attributed to the definition of two destressing rules and their ordering with respect to each other. The crucial point now is that we could equally well imagine a language minimally different from German, where the definition of the destressing rules diverges slightly from what we have just seen. Let us call this language German_D and assume that the stress pattern for underived words is just the same as for German_A, that is, actual German. German_D could have the destressing rules Destress I_D, saying "destress the initial syllable of the word under clash" and Destress II_D, saying "destress the second of two clashing syllables". The output of a derivation including these rules would then be the mirror-image of the derivation presented before: no stress preservation word-medially (*ù.ni.ver.**sál** → Ù.ni.vèr.**sa**.li.t´ät*), but on the second syllable instead (*lo.**yál** → Lo.**yà**.li.t´ät*):[28]

[28] Changing the destressing rules makes it also necessary to change the order of the rule "assign stress to heavy syllables" with respect to them: this rule must now be ordered after Destress I_D, otherwise we could not generate correctly the underived *Kà.lei.do.skóp*, where the second, heavy syllable does not bear any stress. But this move has no consequences for the examples under discussion.

(31)	1st cycle:	"assign main stress"	→	univer**sál**
	2nd cycle:	"assign main stress"	→	Univer**sà**lit´ät
Postcyclic rules:				
		"assign initial stress"	→	Ùniver**sà**lit´ät
		Destress I_D	→	n.a.
		"assign stress to heavy syllables"	→	Ùnivèr**sà**lit´ät
		Destress II_D	→	Ùnivèr**sa**lit´ät
		output "$German_D$"	→	Ùnivèr**sa**lit´ät

(32)	1st cycle:	"assign main stress"	→	lo**yál**
	2nd cycle:	"assign main stress"	→	Lo**yà**lit´ät
Postcyclic rules:				
		"assign initial stress"	→	Lò**yà**lit´ät
		Destress I_D	→	Lo**yà**lit´ät
		"assign stress to heavy syllables"	→	n.a.
		Destress II_D	→	n.a.
		output "$German_D$"	→	Lo**yà**lit´ät

These derivations show us, that a language like "$German_D$" is perfectly possible under a rule based approach. It is not a possible language, though, if we attribute stress preservation to the effects of a constraint like PK-MAX (B/O), a constraint that has a specific position in the constraint hierarchy. If we limit our attention for the moment to the three constraints discussed above, ALIGN (PRWD, L, FT, L), PK-MAX (B/O) and the WSP, there are exactly three positions, where PK-MAX (B/O) could be located in a language like German. It could be ranked in between the other two constraints, and in this case we would have a language like actual German, "$German_A$", where we have stress preservation in certain contexts, but not in others:

(33) $German_A$: ALIGN (PRWD, L, FT, L) >> PK-MAX (B/O) >> WSP

ù.ni.ver.**sál**	→	Ù.ni.ver.**sà**.li.t´ät
lo.**yál**	→	Lò.**ya**.li.t´ät

We could then have a language, "$German_B$" where stress preservation occurs in all cases. This would be a language where PK-MAX (B/O) is ranked above the other two constraints:

(34) $German_B$: PK-MAX (B/O) >> ALIGN (PRWD, L, FT, L) >> WSP

ù.ni.ver.**sál**	→	Ù.ni.ver.**sà**.li.t´ät
lo.**yál**	→	Lo.**yà**.li.t´ät

Finally, there could be a language, "German $_C$", where PK-MAX (B/O) is ranked lowest, with no stress preservation to be observed at all:

(35) German$_C$ ALIGN (PRWD, L, FT, L) >> WSP >> PK-MAX (B/O)

ù.ni.ver.**sál** → Ù.ni.vèr.**sa**.li.t´ät
lo.**yál** → Lò.**ya**.li.t´ät

But what we do predict not to exist, is a language like "German$_D$", where stress preservation occurs at the cost of ALIGN (PRWD, L, FT, L), but not when the WSP would be violated:

ù.ni.ver.**sál** → Ù.ni.vèr.**sa**.li.t´ät
lo.**yál** → Lo.**yà**.li.t´ät

In order to generate this language, we would have to invert the hierarchical order of the stress pattern constraints, leading to a hierarchy that is at odds with the hierarchy established for underived words:

(36) *German$_D$: WSP >> PK-MAX (B/O) >> ALIGN (PRWD, L, FT, L)

If we want to maintain that a language has one grammar, hence one constraint hierarchy without the possibility of reranking constraints, we predict that a language like "German$_D$" does not exist. On the other hand, a rule based approach as outlined above has no major problems in accommodating "German$_D$" in the general picture of stress preservation. The reason resides in the fact that destressing rules do not have to be linked in any way to the principles governing the general stress pattern of the language. If we want to give the derivational analysis the same restrictiveness that the constraint based analysis has, we would have to specify that destressing rules can resolve a clash only in such a way that the final output does not disturb "important" requirements on the stress pattern of the language (e.g. for German: initial syllables must be stressed). But this would just mean to introduce wellformedness constraints on the output into the rule system so that what we obtain at the end is a mixed system of rules and constraints. In conclusion we can say that an analysis of stress preservation in terms of violable constraints has the advantage of being more restrictive: its predictions can be falsified more easily, something every theory should aim at.

3.4. The interaction of PK-MAX (B/O) with other stress pattern constraints

In what follows, I want to illustrate yet another advantage of treating stress preservation as the result of a violable constraint, an advantage that becomes quite clear also in Pater's (1995) and Benua's (1997) work. In a language like German, where PK-MAX (B/O) is ranked above certain stress pattern constraints, but below others, we can predict the interaction of this constraint with the other stress pattern constraints of the language. For example, if we can establish for German underived words that certain stress pattern constraints dominate ALIGN (PRWD, L, FT, L), then those constraints will also dominate

PK-MAX (B/O): stress preservation will never occur if they would be violated. Conversely, all stress pattern constraints ranked below the WSP can be violated if it serves the selection of an output where stress is preserved. The insertion of a constraint responsible for stress preservation into the hierarchy of stress pattern constraints thus provides an excellent testing ground for the correctness both of the analysis of stress in underived words as well as for the position of PK-MAX (B/O). I will take as a starting point the hierarchy worked out in Alber (1997b) for stress in underived German loan-words. The constraint PK-MAX (B/O) is inserted in the position established above:

(37)

```
              FT-BIN, TROCH
                    |
                RIGHTMOST
                    |
   ALIGN (PRWD, L, FT ,L), *CLASH
                    |          /
 ┌──────────────────────────────────┐
 │           PK-MAX (B/O)           │
 └──────────────────────────────────┘
                    |
                 WSP, ITL
                    |
                 PARSE σ
                    |
                 ALL-FT-L
```

For reasons of space I will not discuss here all the aspects of this constraint hierarchy (see Alber 1997b for a detailed account of the ranking arguments), but just give a summary of the resulting stress pattern and then concentrate on single aspects of the ranking and its effects on stress preservation. The feet parsed in German loan-words are trochaic and at least bimoraic, a fact expressed by the high ranking of the constraints TROCH (requiring left-headed feet) and FT-BIN (requiring feet to be either bimoraic or disyllabic). There are no cases where the presence of iambs or degenerate feet consisting of a single light syllable must be assumed. The constraint RIGHTMOST summarizes the requirements of main stress assignment:[29] main stress is generally assigned close to the right edge of the prosodic word, precisely to one of the last three syllables. The high position of this constraint reflects the fact that the placement of main stress cannot be altered in order to satisfy one of the other stress pattern constraints which are ranked lower in the hierarchy. Secondary stress, all things being equal, is assigned from left to right to every odd-numbered syllable, as we have already seen in the examples in (9). Exhaustive left-to-right parsing is analyzed as the ranking of the constraint PARSEσ over ALL-FT-L. The two constraints are defined as follows:

(38) PARSEσ: syllables must be parsed into feet
(Prince & Smolensky 1993)

[29] But see below for a definition of this constraint for a specific class of words.

(39) ALL-FT-L = ALIGN (FT, L, PRWD, L):
∀ foot ∃ prosodic word such that the left edge of the prosodic word and the left edge of the foot coincide.
(McCarthy & Prince 1993)

This alternating pattern is interrupted in words where a word-medial heavy syllable attracts stress (as, e.g., in example (25)). The stress attracting force of heavy syllables is accounted for by the ranking of the WSP over PARSEσ and ALL-FT-L. The WSP itself can be violated when higher constraints are at stake. Thus we have seen in example (11) that it can be violated to satisfy ALIGN (PRWD, L, FT, L), requiring a trochee at the left edge of the prosodic word. The WSP can also be violated when assigning stress to a heavy syllable would create a stress clash as, e.g., in sequences of heavy syllables, where alternating stress is preferred to stress on every heavy syllable, as, e.g., in the word

(40) Pèr.ver. si. t´ät 'perversity'
'H H L

The constraint *CLASH, militating against adjacent stress bearing syllables, is undominated in the hierarchy, reflecting the fact that no cases of stress clash can be observed in this part of the lexicon. Finally, there is the constraint ITL that bans uneven trochees from the foot repertory (cf. fn. 22), but which will not play any role in what follows.

If the constraint hierarchy as proposed here is correct, then certain implications with respect to stress preservation must hold. Let us first consider the constraint ALL-FT-L. If it is true that the WSP dominates ALL-FT-L, then also PK-MAX (B/O) must dominate this constraint. Hence stress preservation will be possible even at the cost of violating this bottom-ranked constraint. Schematically we can express the predicted implication as below:

(41) If PK-MAX (B/O) >> WSP and WSP >> ALL-FT-L
then PK-MAX (B/O) >> ALL-FT-L

We have already shown in Tableau 2 that PK-MAX (B/O) dominates the WSP. The following tableau illustrates that the WSP dominates ALL-FT-L. The crucial examples have already been discussed in (25):[30]

(42) Àu. to. de. tèr. mi. nís. mus 'self-determinism'
('H) L L ('H) L

Àn. te. ze. dèn. ta. lís. mus 'antecedentalism'
('H) L L ('H) L

[30] Candidates which parse ('HL) feet, as, e.g., *(Àu.to).de.(tèr.mi)(.nís.mus)* have not been considered here, since they violate the ITL, the constraint against uneven trochees, which is assumed to be ranked above PARSEσ. Note, however, that even if we allowed for ('HL) feet, this would not change the general argument that in this context heavy syllables do attract stress in spite of violating left alignment of all feet.

The tableau shows us, how the WSP can force a disruption of the alternating pattern.

Candidates	WSP	PARSE σ	ALL-FT-L
☞ (a) (Àu).to.de.(tèr).mi.(nís.mus)		***	σσσ
(b) (Àu).to.(dè.ter).mi.(nís.mus)	*!	**	σσ
(c) (Àu).to.de.ter.mi.(nís.mus)	*!	****	

Tableau 4

Since McCarthy & Prince (1993) exhaustive parsing of feet has been analyzed as the ranking of PARSEσ above such constraints as ALL-FT-L, requiring all feet to be left-aligned. If the ranking were the inverse, candidate (d) should win, with a single foot,[31] which is perfectly aligned to the left edge of the prosodic word. But even with the ranking of PARSEσ over ALL-FT-L, all things being equal, candidate (b) should win, since this candidate counts fewer violations than (a) on both constraints. It is the WSP that makes this candidate fail and (a) win, where the fourth, heavy syllable is stressed.

If the WSP is ranked above PARSEσ and hence above ALL-FT-L, and PK-MAX (B/O) is ranked above the WSP, by transitivity PK-MAX (B/O) should also be ranked above ALL-FT-L. In examples consisting of a pretonic string of light syllables we see that this is indeed the case:

(43)	Ò.	ri.	gi.	**nál**	→	Ò.	ri.	gi.	**nà**.	li.	t´ät	'original', 'originality'
	('L	L)	L			('L	L)	L	('L	L)		

The main stress of *Ò.ri.gi.**nál*** is preserved as a secondary stress in *Ò.ri.gi.**nà**.li.t´ät*, although this means that the second foot is aligned worse to the left edge of the prosodic word than it would be in a word of similar structure where stress preservation is not at stake (cf. (9)). The tableau shows the interaction between PK-MAX (B/O) and ALL-FT-L:

Base: Ò.ri.gi.**nál**	PK-MAX (B/O)	PARSE σ	ALL-FT-L
☞ (a) (Ò.ri).gi.(**nà**.li).(t´ät)		*	σσσ
(b) (Ò.ri).(gì.**na**).li.(t´ät)	*!	*	σσ

Tableau 5

Both candidates rate equally well on PARSEσ, but only (a) satisfies the constraint requiring that a stress peak of the base be also a stress peak in the derived word. (b), who fails on this requirement, must lose, although its second foot misses left alignment only by two syllables.

[31] ALL-FT-L violations of the main stress foot are not counted here.

We see that the predicted implication is borne out: when constraints lower ranked than the WSP are at stake stress preservation can be enforced at the cost of violating them.

Now let us consider an implication involving constraints higher ranked than PK-MAX (B/O):

(44) If ALIGN (PRWD, L, FT, L) >> PK-MAX (B/O)
and RIGHTMOST >> ALIGN (PRWD, L, FT, L)
then RIGHTMOST >> PK-MAX (B/O)

If this implication holds, then stress preservation should not occur at the cost of violating the regularities of main stress assignment. Tableau 3 has made clear that ALIGN (PRWD, L, FT, L) dominates PK-MAX (B/O). Examples with an initial light syllable followed by main stress show that ALIGN (PRWD, L, FT, L) itself can be violated when the requirements of main stress assignment make it necessary:

(45) E. lán 'spirit'
L ('H)

As mentioned before, main stress placement is not entirely predictable in German loan-words, it can fall on one of the last three syllables of the word. I take *Elan* to belong to the class of loan-words where main stress falls on the head of a final trochee, that is a class of words where the requirement of main stress to be final is not dominated by any constraint requiring final syllables to be unstressed.[32] Thus, in this case the constraint RIGHTMOST can be defined without further provisions as an alignment constraint requiring the right edge of a prosodic word to be aligned with the right edge of its head.

(46) RIGHTMOST = ALIGN (PRWD, R, HEAD (PRWD), R)
∀ prosodic word ∃ head of the prosodic word such that the right edge of the prosodic word and the right edge of the head coincide (cf. EDGEMOST, Prince & Smolensky 1993)

In example (45), a secondary stress on the first syllable (candidate (d) in the following tableau) would violate all the high ranked stress pattern constraints. Building a degenerate foot out of the initial syllable would violate FT-BIN and creating a clash with the main stress would violate the constraint *CLASH. There would, however, be a possibility to build a trochee at the left edge of the prosodic word without violating these constraints: main stress could be assigned directly to the first syllable of the word. Since this option is not chosen we must conclude that main stress assignment overrides the requirement of aligning a trochee to the left edge of the prosodic word. In tableau 6 below, candidate (a) wins because it is the only one that satisfies the high-ranked stress pattern constraints, including RIGHTMOST. (b) would satisfy the requirement of a trochee at the left edge of the prosodic

[32] The word *Bál.kan*, with stress on the first syllable would be an example for the class of words where it is more important to satisfy a constraint of the NONFINALITY type, requiring final syllables to be unstressed, than to assign stress to the rightmost syllable.

word but fails because of misalignment of the main stress with the right edge of the prosodic word. There would be another possibility of satisfying all the constraints discussed so far, illustrated by candidate (c) that parses an iamb, a parsing that would be compatible with the observed output form. If this was the correct foot structure of the word, the constraint TROCH would have to be ranked below RIGHTMOST and ALIGN (PRWD, L, FT, L). But such a ranking would leave open the possibility to create iambs whenever RIGHTMOST wants to be satisfied, for example also by placing main stress on final light syllables, a case unattested in German (cf. Alber 1997b).

Candidates	*CLASH	FT-BIN	TROCH	RIGHT-MOST	ALIGN (PRWD, L, FT, L)
☞ (a) E.(lán)					σ
(b) (É.lan)				σ!	
(c) (E.lán)			*!		
(d) (È).(lán)	*!	*!			

Tableau 6

In order to see if the implication in (44) holds, we must show that stress preservation does not occur at the cost of a RIGHTMOST violation. Up to now we have not distinguished between preservation of a main stress of the base as secondary stress and preservation of the main stress as main stress. Pater (1995) discusses this problem of weak versus strong stress preservation and proposes for English to treat the constraint responsible for stress preservation as a gradient constraint. In his analysis the stress preservation constraint is violated twice if stem stress is preserved neither as main stress nor as secondary stress, but only once if the main stress of the base is preserved as a secondary stress. We can then see that perfect stress preservation is not possible in stems suffixed by *-ität* because this would mean to shift main stress away from the final syllable. We can take as an example a case of weak stress preservation such as

(47) ù.ni.ver.**sál** → Ù. ni. ver. **sà**. li. t´ät 'universal', 'universality'
'L L H 'L L

Base: ù.ni.ver.**sál**	RIGHT-MOST	ALIGN (PRWD, L, FT, L)	PK-MAX (B/O)	WSP
☞ (a) (Ù.ni).ver.(**sà**.li).(t´ät)			*	*
(b) (Ù.ni).(vèr).**sa**.li.(t´ät)			**!	
(c) (Ù.ni).ver.(**sá**.li).(t`ät)	σσ!			*

Tableau 7

If we treat PK-MAX (B/O) as a gradient constraint, the winning candidate (a) incurs one violation, because it preserves stem stress only as secondary stress. However, this is better than not preserving stress at all, as in (b). Candidate (c), finally, would be a case of perfect stress preservation, where main stress is preserved as main stress in the derived word. This is no option, though, because it would mean that the syllable bearing main stress is misaligned by two syllables with respect to the right edge of the prosodic word. Thus the implication in (44) holds: no stress preservation is possible at the cost of a constraint like RIGHTMOST that is higher ranked than ALIGN (PRWD, L, FT, L).[33]

We find more evidence for the correctness of this implication, if we turn to another type of suffixes which, like *-ität*, attract main stress, but consist only of one syllable as, e.g., the verb forming suffix *-ier*. The interesting case is the one where *-ier* attaches to a stem bearing final main stress, as, e.g., in

(48)	Kà. ta. **púlt**	→	kà. ta. **pul**. tíert	'catapult', 'launched with a catapult'
	('L L)		('L L) H	

An elegant means to preserve stress without creating a clash with the final main stress would be to simply assign main stress to the third, instead of the final syllable as in

(49) *kà.ta. **púl**. tiert

This would even preserve the prosodic head of the base as such. But again stress preservation is no option here, because of the ranking of RIGHTMOST over PK-MAX (B/O).

As a last example I will consider the interaction between the constraint TROCH and stress preservation. In the hierarchy proposed for German TROCH is ranked above RIGHTMOST. Thus the following implication must hold:

(50)	If	TROCH >> RIGHTMOST	and	RIGHTMOST >> PK-MAX (B/O)
	then	TROCH >> PK-MAX (B/O)		

We have just shown that RIGHTMOST dominates the constraint responsible for stress preservation. The domination relation between TROCH and RIGHTMOST can be seen in words with a final light syllable and stress on the penult:

(51)	Ès. pe. rán. to	'esperanto'
	('H) L ('H) L	

[33] Note, though, that the argument outlined here holds only, if we attribute strong and weak stress preservation to the effects of the same constraint. Ultimately, it could be necessary to postulate two separate constraints, one requiring the identity between stress peaks in general and one for the preservation of the role that a stress peak plays in the prosodic structure of a word, i.e., the status of head of the prosodic word in the case of main stress. But for the English cases Pater discusses and for the examples here there is no evidence for this distinction and therefore this alternative has not been pursued.

In principle, the best way to satisfy RIGHTMOST would be to assign stress to the final syllable in these cases. But main stress never falls on a final light syllable in German. This means that main stress must be assigned close to the right edge of the prosodic word, but not at the cost of parsing a final iamb (candidate (c)) or a degenerate foot (candidate (b)). Hence both FT-BIN and TROCH must be ranked above the constraint determining the assignment of main stress, as we can see in the following tableau:

Candidates	FT-BIN	TROCH	RIGHTMOST
☞ (a) Es.pe.(rán).to			σ
(b) Es.pe.ran.(tó)	*!		
(c) Es.pe.(ran.tó)		*!	

Tableau 8

Now let us consider what the high ranking of TROCH means for stress preservation. Above I discussed the lack of stress preservation in the case of

(52) lo.yál → Lò.ya. li. t´ät 'loyal', 'loyalty'

In tableau 3 we showed that ALIGN (PRWD, L, FT, L) dominates PK-MAX (B/O). But we did not consider a dangerous candidate which could satisfy both ALIGN (PRWD, L, FT, L) and PK-MAX (B/O), the candidate where an initial iamb is parsed, as in (c) below:

Base: lo.**yál**	TROCH	ALIGN (PRWD, L, FT, L)	PK-MAX (B/O)
(a) Lo.(**yà**.li).(t´ät)		*!	
☞ (b) (Lò.**ya**).li.(t´ät)			*
(c) (Lo.**yá**).li.(t´ät)	*!		

Tableau 9

The fact that this candidate fails as well shows us, that stress preservation cannot be obtained at the cost of a TROCH violation.

In sum, the implications above show how the constraint responsible for stress preservation interacts with some of the stress pattern constraints of the language. We have shown that it is dominated by such constraints as ALIGN (PRWD, L, FT, L), RIGHTMOST and TROCH and hence can be violated when it conflicts with them. On the other hand stress preservation takes place even when this leads to violation of lower ranked constraints such as the WSP and ALL-FT-L.

This analysis thus predicts a precise pattern of stress preservation with stress attracting suffixes like *-ität.* Stress preservation will be of the weak type, i.e., main stress, if preserved, will be preserved as secondary stress. Feet will be trochaic and consist of either two moras or two syllables also in morphologically complex words. Provided that no stress clash with the attaching suffix arises, the predicted cases of stress preservation are as follows:

- stress preservation will not take place when the stem's main stress falls on the second syllable. (Align (PrWd, L, Ft, L) is satisfied at the cost of Pk-Max (B/O))

(a) [σ´σ̲ ...] → [[`σ.σ̲...] σ ´σ] cf. (10)

- stress preservation takes place in all other cases. (ALIGN (PRWD, L, FT, L) is satisfied, WSP, ALL-FT-L and PARSEσ may be violated)

(b) [´σ̲ ...] → [[`σ̲ ....] σ ´σ] cf. (12)

(c) [`σσ ... ´σ̲ ...] → [[`σσ ... `σ̲ ....] σ ´σ]

e.g. [`σσ ´σ̲] → [[`σσ `σ̲] σ ´σ] cf. (13)
[`σσ σ ´σ̲ ] → [[`σσ σ `σ̲] σ ´σ] cf. (6)

As a final note I want to give an outlook on the possibilities that an analysis based on violable constraints offers for crosslinguistic comparison. It is striking that while English, just as German, seems to have a constraint requiring initial syllables to bear secondary stress, it does preserve stem stress at the cost of violating this constraint. Compare the two examples given at the beginning of this paper. Stress falls on the initial syllable of the underived

(53) Tà.ta.ma.góu.chi

but, because of stress preservation, on the second syllable of *originality*:

(54) o.**rí**.gi.nal → o.**rì**.gi.ná.li.ty

The reason for this differing behavior resides in the fact that the constraint ALIGN (PRWD, L, FT, L), differently from German, is bottom-ranked in English. In fact, as Pater (1995) shows, it is dominated by a number of constraints as, e.g., the WSP:

(55) WSP >> ALIGN (PRWD, L, FT, L)
(cf. Pater 1995)

Thus, while ALIGN (PRWD, L, FT, L) can show its force in words with a pretonic string of light syllables, as in *Tatamagouchi*, it will be violated when the second syllable is heavy:

(56) Mo.nòn.ga.hé.la

One of the constraints dominating ALIGN (PRWD, L, FT, L) is the faithfulness constraint requiring identity between morphologically related forms (STRESSIDENT, in Pater's terminology):

(57) STRESSIDENT >> ALIGN (PRWD, L, FT, L)
(Pater 1995)

Hence the requirement of initial secondary stress is given up in *o.rì.gi.ná.li.ty* in order to preserve stem stress. This does not mean, however, that stress is preserved across the board in English. Just as in German, the stem's main stress is preserved only as a secondary stress,[34] showing that the requirements of main stress assignment are more important than perfect preservation of stem stress. In Pater's work ALIGN (PRWD, R, HEAD(PRWD), R) is the constraint responsible for main stress assignment:

(58) ALIGN (PRWD, R, HEAD(PRWD), R) >> STRESSIDENT
(Pater 1995)

Summarizing, stress preservation is nonuniform, both in German and in English. The differences between the two languages can be explained by the differing overall stress pattern: in German the requirement of initial stress is high-ranked and dominates faithfulness to the stem stress, in English the same requirement is low ranked and dominated by faithfulness.

4. Conclusions

The case of stress preservation in German loan words suffixed by *-ität* makes clear some of the advantages of treating preservation of stem stress as the result of a violable faithfulness constraint and thus gives support to recent analyses of the phenomenon in these terms. Stress preservation in this subpart of the lexicon is context-specific: it occurs only where high ranked stress pattern constraints are observed, but not where they would be violated. A comparison of the predictions made by this model with respect to the predictions of a rule-based analysis makes clear that the former approach is more restrictive in that the interactions between the faithfulness constraint and the stress pattern constraints can be only of a certain type: stress preservation is predicted to respect the hierarchy established for underived words. Moreover, once we have placed the faithfulness constraint PK-MAX (B/O) in some intermediate position of the constraint hierarchy (below ALIGN (PRWD, L, FT, L), but above the WSP), we can show that it interacts in the predicted way with other stress pattern constraints such as ALL-FT-L, RIGHTMOST and TROCH. Stress preservation thus is closely linked to the principles that determine stress assignment, a result that cannot be easily obtained in a system based on the application of rules.

---

[34] This is true for level I suffixes like *-ity*.

Acknowledgments

For discussion, comments and/or examples of German loan-words with many syllables I want to thank Heinz Giegerich, Bettina Isensee, Wolfgang Kehrein, Paul Kiparsky, Ingo Plag, Tomas Riad and Richard Wiese. Special thanks go to Alan Prince for discussion on and beyond the topics of this paper.

References

Alber, Birgit (1997a): Il sistema metrico dei prestiti del tedesco. Aspetti e problemi della teoria prosodica. Ph.D. thesis, University of Padova.

— (1997b): Quantity Sensitivity as the Result of Constraint Interaction. In: Geert Booij & Jeroen van de Weijer (eds.): *Phonology in Progress - Progress in Phonology. HIL Phonology Papers III*, 1-45. The Hague: Holland Academic Graphics.

Alderete, John (1995): Faithfulness to prosodic heads, ms. University of Massachusetts, Amherst, ROA-94-0000, Rutgers Optimality Archive, http://ruccs.rutgers.edu/roa.html

— (1996): Prosodic Faithfulness in Cupeño, ms. University of Massachusetts, Amherst, ROA-131-0496, Rutgers Optimality Archive, http://ruccs.rutgers.edu/roa.html

Benua, Laura (1995): Identity Effects in Morphological Truncation. In: Jill Beckman, Laura Walsh Dickey & Suzanne Urbanczyk (eds.): *University of Massachusetts Occasional Papers in Linguistics* 18: *Papers in Optimality Theory*, 77-136. Amherst, MA: Graduate Linguistic Student Association.

— (1997): Affix Classes are defined by Faithfulness. In: *University of Maryland Working Papers in Linguistics*. Vol. 5, 1-26

Benware, Wilbur (1980): Zum Fremdwortakzent im Deutschen. *Zeitschrift für Dialektologie und Linguistik*, XLVII. Jahrgang, Heft 3, 289-312.

Booij, Geert (1996): Lexical Phonology and the derivational residue. In: Jacques Durand & Bernard Laks (eds.): *Current Trends in Phonology. Models and Methods.* Vol. 1, 69-97. Manchester: European Studies Research Institute.

Chomsky, Noam & Morris Halle (1968): *The Sound Pattern of English*. New York: Harper and Row. (Reprint 1990. Cambridge, Massachusetts: MIT Press).

Eisenberg, Peter (1991): Syllabische Struktur und Wortakzent: Prinzipien der Prosodik deutscher Wörter. In: Karl Heinz Ramers & Richard Wiese (eds.): *Zeitschrift für Sprachwissenschaft* 10,1. Themenheft: Prosodische Phonologie. 37-64.

Féry, Caroline (1995): *Alignment, syllable and metrical Structure in German.* University of Tübingen: SfS-Report-02-95.

Fleischer, Wolfgang & Irmhild Barz (1995): *Wortbildung der deutschen Gegenwartssprache.* Tübingen: Niemeyer.

Giegerich, Heinz (1985): *Metrical Phonology and Phonological Structure. German and English.* Cambridge Studies in Linguistics 43. Cambridge: Cambridge University Press.

Golston, Chris & Wiese, Richard (1998): The Structure of the German Root. In: Wolfgang Kehrein & Richard Wiese (eds.) *Phonology and Morphology of the Germanic Languages.* Tübingen: Niemeyer, 165-185.

Hayes, Bruce (1985): Iambic and Trochaic Rhythm in Stress Rules. In: M. Niepokuj, M. VanClay, V. Nikiforidou, D. Feder (eds.): *Proceedings of the XIth Annual Meeting of the Berkeley Linguistics Society*, 429-446.

— (1986): Review of: Giegerich (1985). *Journal of Linguistics* 22, 229-35.

— (1995): *Metrical Stress Theory. Principles and Case Studies.* Chicago: The University of Chicago Press.

Kager, René (1994): Ternary rhythm in alignment theory. Ms., Utrecht University. ROA-35-1094, Rutgers Optimality Archive, http://ruccs.rutgers.edu/roa.html

— (forthcoming a): Stem stress and peak correspondence in Dutch. To appear in: J. Dekkers, F. van der Leeuw & J. van de Weijer (eds.): *The Pointing Finger: Conceptual Studies in Optimality Theory*. Amsterdam: HIL.

— (forthcoming b): Surface opacity of metrical structure in Optimality Theory. To appear in: Ben Hermans, Marc van Oostendorp (eds.): *The Derivational Residue in Phonology*. ROA-207-0797, Rutgers Optimality Archive, http://ruccs.rutgers.edu/roa.html

Kenstowicz, Michael (1994): Sonority-Driven Stress, ms. MIT, ROA-33-1094, Rutgers Optimality Archive, http://ruccs.rutgers.edu/roa.html

— (1995): Cyclic vs. non-cyclic constraint evaluation. *Phonology* **12**, 397-436.

— (1996): Base-Identity and Uniform Exponence: Alternatives to Cyclicity. In: Jacques Durand, Bernard Laks (eds.): *Current Trends in Phonology: Models and Methods*, Vol.1. 363-393. Manchester: European Studies Research Institute.

Liberman, Mark & Alan Prince (1977): On Stress and Linguistic Rhythm. *Lingustic Inquiry* 8.2., 249-336.

McCarthy, John (1995): Extensions of Faithfulness: Rotuman Revisited, Ms. University of Massachusetts, Amherst. ROA-110-000, Rutgers Optimality Archive, http://ruccs.rutgers.edu/roa.html

McCarthy, John & Alan Prince (1986): Prosodic morphology. Ms. University of Massachusetts, Amherst, and Brandeis University.

— (1993): Generalized alignment. In: Geert Booij, & Jaap van Marle (eds.): *Yearbook of Morphology 1993*, 79-153. Dordrecht: Kluwer.

— (1995): Faithfulness and Reduplicative Identity". In: Jill Beckman, Laura Walsh Dickey & Suzanne Urbanczyk (eds.): *University of Massachusetts Occasional Papers in Linguistics* 18: *Papers in Optimality Theory*, 249-384. Amherst, MA: Graduate Linguistic Student Association.

Pater, Joe (1995): On the nonuniformity of weight-to-stress and stress preservation effects in English. Ms. McGill University. ROA-107-0000, Rutgers Optimality Archive, http://ruccs.rutgers.edu/roa.html

Prince, Alan (1980): A Metrical Theory for Estonian Quantity. *Linguistic Inquiry* 11, 511-62.

— (1990): Quantitative Consequences of Rhythmic Organization

Prince, Alan & Paul Smolensky (1993): *Optimality Theory: Constraint Interaction in Generative Grammar.* Ms. Rutgers University, New Brunswick, and University of Colorado, Boulder. [Forthcoming MIT Press].

Ramers, Karl Heinz (1992): Ambisilbische Konsonanten im Deutschen. In: Peter Eisenberg, Karl Heinz Ramers, Heinz Vater (eds.): *Silbenphonologie des Deutschen*, 246-83. Tübingen: Narr.

Vennemann, Theo (1990): Syllable structure and simplex accent in Modern Standard German. In: K. Deaton, M. Noske, M. Ziolkowski (eds.): *CLS 26-II: Papers from the Parasession on the Syllable in Phonetics and Phonology*, 399-412. Chicago: Chicago Linguistic Society.

Wiese, Richard (1996): *The Phonology of German.* Oxford: Oxford University Press.

Wurzel, Wolfgang Ulrich (1970): Der Fremdwortakzent im Deutschen. *Linguistics*, 56, 87-108.

— (1980a): Der deutsche Wortakzent: Fakten - Regeln - Prinzipien. *Zeitschrift für Germanistik* 3/80, 299-318.

— (1980b): Phonologie. In: K.E. Heidolph (ed.): *Grundzüge einer deutschen Grammatik*, 898-988. Berlin: Akademie-Verlag.

Geert Booij

Phonological output constraints in morphology

1. Introduction

Recent developments in phonological theory have made it clear that the notion 'output constraint' cannot be dispensed with in phonological analysis. Such output constraints form a central ingredient of phonological theories such as Optimality Theory (OT) (McCarthy & Prince 1993, 1994; Prince & Smolensky 1993).

The theoretical concept of output constraint also has a large potential for morphological analysis. This can be illustrated with a simple example from Dutch. In Dutch the nominalizing suffix *-erd* /ərd/ cannot be added to adjectival stems ending in /ər/; this is a phonological restriction on this kind of word formation (Schultink 1962: 203, Booij 1977: 124):[1]

(1)	*Adjectival stem*	*Noun*
	vies /vi:z/ 'dirty'	viez-erd /vi:z-ərd/ 'dirty person'
	goochem /ɣo:xəm/ 'smart'	goochem-erd /ɣo:xəm-ərd/ 'smart person'
	dapper /dɑpər/ 'brave'	*dapper-erd /dɑpər-ərd/'brave person'
	duister /dœystər/ 'obscure'	*duister-erd /dœystər-ərd/ 'obscurant'

This restriction can be expressed as an input constraint on the kind of stems that the suffix *-erd* takes, and it is indeed formulated as such in Booij (1977: 124). However, this fails to express the generalization that this gap in word formation arises from the necessity of avoiding the sequence /rər/ in Dutch, a sequence which is also avoided by other word formation processes. Moreover, the undesirability of this sequence also plays a role in allomorphy. For instance, by using the allomorph *-der* of the suffix *-er* in comparatives, /rər/ is also avoided:

(2)	vies /vi:z/ 'dirty'	viez-er /vi:z-ər/ 'dirtier'
	helder /hɛldər/ 'clear'	helder-der /hɛldər-dər/ 'clearer'

The postulation of an output constraint */rər/, or a generalized version thereof, is therefore called for if we want to formally express this generalization.

The avoidance of /rər/ is an instantiation of more general tendencies in languages to avoid sequences with identical sounds. These tendencies have been discussed by Dressler (1977), Stemberger (1981), and Menn & MacWhinney (1984) in papers on haplology. Interestingly, they already pointed out that the standard approach of generative phonology

[1] The high vowels are transcribed as phonologically long, because they behave as such, although phonetically they are short except before [r].

does not suffice to make the relevant generalizations, and that we need output constraints. Dressler, for instance, remarked that

(3) [t]he constraint applies at the level of word formation and either prevents actual derivation or calls for haplological simplification. But the structural description of the constraint is in terms of *surface* [my italics, GB] phonetics. (Dressler 1977: 45-46).

Dressler also pointed out that in a rule-based phonology this would lead to assume 'peeking rules', rules that can look ahead to see what kind of output they will lead to. Similarly, Menn & MacWhinney (1984: 529) concluded with respect to iterations of identical morphs that „there is a general output constraint which tends to prohibit sequences of phonological identical morphs".

These ideas are also found in recent work: Raffelsiefen (1996) and Plag (1997, 1998) have argued that certain gaps in word formation should be accounted for in terms of restrictions on the phonetic forms of the derived words, and a number of phonologists have shown that the selection of particular allomorphs should follow from output conditions (cf. Kager 1996, Mascaró 1996, Booij 1997a).

In this paper, which deals mainly with Dutch, I will also argue that certain gaps in word formation and certain patterns of affix and allomorph selection can best be accounted for in terms of phonological output constraints. This raises the question whether competition between affixes and allomorphs can always be accounted for in terms of output constraints. I will argue that this is not the case, and that we still need subcategorization frames for affixes, which must be complied with by Gen, the component of the grammar that generates the set of possible phonological candidates for a complex word.

2. Optimal parsing

In Dutch, some morphological processes apply in such a way that their outputs obey the constraint that a foot consists of two syllables. Dutch feet are preferably disyllabic trochees. However, monosyllabic feet are also allowed if necessary, provided that the vowel of that monosyllabic foot is a full vowel: a schwa can never function as the head of a monosyllabic foot. Since a foot is maximally disyllabic, syllables headed by schwa may be left over, i.e. they cannot be parsed into a foot. In that case, they will be dominated directly by the prosodic word node of the relevant word. I will assume the following constraints:[2]

(4)	ParseSyll:	syllables must be parsed into feet
	FootMin:	feet are minimally disyllabic
	FootMax:	feet are maximally disyllabic

[2] Löhken (1997: 107), who follows Daniel Everett in splitting the constraint of Foot Binarity into two constraints, FootMax and FootMin, assumes the same constraints for German.

In the following subsections, a number of morphological processes will be discussed where these constraints play a role in the selection of competing affixes or affixal allomorphs.

2.1. Pluralization of nouns

Dutch has two plural suffixes for nouns, /s/ and /ən/. The basic selection pattern can be formulated as follows:[3]

(5) -s after an unstressed syllable, -ən after a stressed syllable.

This pattern of selection is illustrated by the following examples:

(6)	kánon 'canon'	- kánon-s [ˈka:nɔns]
	kanón 'gun'	- kanónn-en [ka:ˈnɔnən]
	nátie 'nation'	- nátie-s [ˈna:tsi:s]
	geníe 'genius'	- geníe-ën [žəˈni:jən]

This selection principle also correctly predicts that monosyllabic nouns have *-en* as their plural suffix:

(7)	non 'nun'	- nonnen
	knie 'knee'	- knieën
	bal 'ball'	- ballen

Note that it is obvious that we cannot derive the plural suffixes from a common underlying form by means of general phonological rules (they have different historical origins). Nevertheless, as is the case in a number of languages (cf. Carstairs 1988), the distribution of competing affixes may be governed by purely phonological principles (I will use the term 'allomorph' if the competing affixes show a clear phonological similarity).

The formulation of the selection principle given above is formulated in terms of properties of the input forms for the pluralization process, the nominal stems, which are formally identical to the singular forms. However, such a formulation does not explain why this particular selection principle holds. In terms of complexity of the grammar, it would make no difference if Dutch were just the other way round, i.e. if *-s* occurred after stressed syllables, and *-en* after unstressed ones. My hypothesis is that the motivation behind this particular affix selection is that plural nouns will end in a disyllabic trochee since the disylla-

---

3 A systematic class of exceptions to this generalisation is formed by nouns ending in an unstressed syllable with a final /s/; these nouns, such as *cúrsus* 'course' and *dréumes* 'toddler' always take *-en* as their plural suffix. The reason for this is obvious: Dutch has no consonantal geminates, and therefore, the plural /s/ will not surface after a stem in /s/. That is, the constraint Morpheme Identity that requires that each morpheme receives a phonetic realisation so that it can be identifed, is ranked higher than the Foot constraints.

bic trochee is the preferred pattern of organization of syllables into higher prosodic units in Germanic languages.[4]

The following OT-tableaux show how the selection of the correct plural suffix takes place. Note that we extend the notion 'candidate' as normally used in OT-phonology because the set of candidates is not defined exclusively phonologically, but also morphologically: each combination of stem + competing affix/allomorph is the basis for a set of candidates (geminate consonants indicate ambisyllabicity after short vowels).

(8)

kánon+PL 'canons'	FootMax	ParseSyll	FootMin
☞ (ka:nɔn-s)$_F$			
(ka:nɔn)$_F$(n-ən)$_σ$		*!	
(ka:nɔnnən)$_F$	*!		

kanón+PL 'guns'	FootMax	ParseSyll	FootMin
(ka:)$_σ$(nɔn-s)$_F$		*!	*
(ka:)$_F$(nɔn-s)$_F$			**!
(ka:)$_σ$(nɔnn-ən)$_F$		*!	
☞ (ka:)$_F$(nɔnn-ən)$_F$			*

In these tableaux, FootMax is ranked higher than ParseSyll, so that we do not get trisyllabic feet. Furthermore, I do not consider the candidate in which a schwa-headed syllable forms a foot of its own, since it is an unviolable constraint that syllables with schwa cannot head a foot. ParseSyll is ranked above FootMin because monosyllabic feet are preferred to having an unparsed syllable, cf. (15) below.

The computation of the correct plural suffix presupposes that the stress pattern of the stem is already given, and cannot shift rightward in the plural form. This stress-neutrality can be obtained in two ways: by allowing for levels within OT, or by making use of output-output correspondence constraints (McCarthy & Prince 1995, Benua 1995; cf. Booij 1997a for discussion).

The constraint FootMin implies the choice of the plural suffix *-en* for monosyllabic nouns; FootMin is obviously violated by monosyllabic nouns in their singular forms, and also in plural forms of loanwords which keep the original suffix:

(9)

(9)	*English*	tram	- trams 'trams'
	French	paraplú	- paraplu's 'umbrellas'

Dutch children tend to regularize these patterns during the process of language acquisition, and create plural nouns such as *trammen* 'trams', and speakers of Southern Dutch use

[4] Van de Vijver (1998) argues that the trochee is universally the preferred pattern of organisation of syllables into feet.

experten instead of Standard Dutch *experts* as the plural form of *expert* 'id.', and *testen* instead of *tests*.

The output-based approach is not only superior in that it formally expresses the 'why' behind the selection principle, it also makes the prediction that simplex nouns ending in schwa have both /s/ and /ən/ because of the effect of prevocalic schwa-deletion (a schwa deletes before an adjacent vowel within the same prosodic word, cf. Booij 1995), which ensures that the addition of *-en* after a noun ending in schwa does not create a new syllable. This prediction is correct:[5]

(10)	kadə 'quay'	kadəs, kadən
	bodə 'messenger'	bodəs, bodən
	ladə 'drawer'	ladəs, ladən
	methodə 'method'	methodəs, methodən

In some cases, one of them may be preferred, but this is a matter of lexical convention, not a matter of wellformedness.

Complex words ending in a schwa-final suffix also have the two options, as is to be expected on the basis of the phonological properties, unless the suffix requires a particular plural suffix:

(11) *words with both suffixes*:

-adə	marinades 'marinades', balustraden 'balustrades'
-sə	extases / extasen 'ecstasies', hypotheses / hypothesen 'hypotheses'
-də	liefdes / liefden 'loves', kundes / kunden 'arts'
-tə	gedeeltes / gedeelten 'parts', koeltes / koelten 'cools'
-ismə	modernismes / modernismen 'modernisms', mechanismes / mechanismen 'mechanisms'
-inə	sonatines / sonatinen 'sonatines'
-idə	fluorides / fluoriden 'fluorides'

words with only -s:

with non-native suffixes borrowed from French

-airə	documentaire-s 'documentaries'
-agə	massage-s 'massages'
-asmə	orgasme-s 'orgasms'
-essə	secretaresse-s 'female secretaries'
-ierə	cabaretiere-s 'female cabaretiers'
-eusə	masseuse-s 'female massagist'
-icə	directrice-s 'female directors'

[5] Below, the schwa is represented by its IPA symbol for reasons of clarity; in Dutch orthography, the schwa is mostly represented by *e*, and sometimes by *i, u* or *ij*. Word-final schwa is always represented by *e*.

-iennə	lesbienne-s 'female homosexuals'
-ettə	wasserette-s 'launderettes'
-urə	doublure-s 'duplications'

with native suffixes

-ə	acrobate-s 'female acrobats'
(t)jə	toetje-s 'desserts', boekje-s 'booklets'

words with only -(ə)n

-ə	blonde 'blonde' - blonden (nominalizing deadjectival suffix)

The importance of these data is that they show that the selection of one of the plural suffixes cannot always be accounted for in terms of phonological output conditions. For instance, diminutive nouns allow for *-s* only, although a diminutive like *toetjen* would not violate the constraints discussed. So we have to conclude that the selection may be governed by a particular suffix in cases where phonology cannot make a choice.

The output-based analysis of affix and affix-allomorph selection makes it also possible to give a proper account of the interaction between stem allomorphy and selection of plural suffix in words ending in *-or*, *-on* and *-ol.* These words have two stem allomorphs, with the last syllable containing either a short vowel or its long counterpart. It is only the short allomorph that occurs as independent word. In the case of the allomorphs with the long final syllable such as *motoor*, main stress must be located on that syllable because it is superheavy (long vowel plus consonant in the rhyme).

(12)	mótor 'engine'	mótors [ˈmo:tɔrs] /motóren [mo:ˈto:rən] *motóors [mo:ˈto:rs] / *mótorrən [ˈmo:tɔrən]
	proféssor 'id.'	proféssors/professóren
	néutron 'id.'	néutrons/neutrónen

The long stem allomorphs must be selected obligatorily before non-native suffixes, and can also, and this is exceptional, occur in plural nouns. What is explained under the present analysis is why the short allomorphs choose the plural suffix *-s*, and the long allomorphs the suffix *-en*.

The conspiracy of stem allomorphy, stress location (weight-sensitive assignment of primary stress) and choice of plural suffix follows directly from an output constraint approach.[6]

---

6 A similar generalisation concerning the form of plural nouns in terms of the required output can be made with respect to German (leaving aside the special category of plural nouns ending in *-s*), as pointed out by Wiese (1996: 106): "plural nouns in Modern Standard German must end in a bisyllabic foot, with the second syllable being a schwa syllable". Cf. also Golston & Wiese (1996).

2.2. Derived nouns

The working of the prosodic output constraints given in (4) can also be related to the allomorphy of the denominal and deverbal nominalizing suffix *-er* /ər/ that has the allomorph -*aar* /a:r/ after stems ending in schwa plus a coronal sonorant:

(13) *denominal nouns*

Bloemendaal /blu:mənda:l/	Bloemendal-er 'inhabitant of B.'
Diemen /di:mən/	Diemen-aar 'inhabitant of D.'
Uddel /œdəl/	Uddel-aar 'inhabitant of U.'

deverbal nouns

spin /spɪn/ 'to spin'	spinn-er 'spinner'
luister /lœystər/ 'to listen'	luister-aar 'listener'
bedel /be:dəl/ 'to beg'	bedel-aar 'beggar'
reken /re:kən/ 'to compute'	reken-aar 'computer'

The distribution of these two allomorphs is describable in phonological terms, but there is no regular phonological process that can derive *-aar* from *-er*, or vice versa. Both derive historically from the Latin suffix *-arius*. The allomorph *-aar* is the more restricted allomorph; it only occurs after stems ending in schwa followed by /l,r,n/. The non-phonological nature of the allomorphy involved here is also clear from the following observations:
- the allomorph *-aar* is not available for comparatives, which are also formed by suffixation with /ər/. Instead, the allomorph *-der* is used after stems in *-er*. Thus, we get a comparative like *duisterder* 'darker' instead of the prosodically more optimal **duisteraar*.
- we find *-aar* also exceptionally in words like *dien-aar* 'servant', *ler-aar* 'teacher', *winnaar* 'winner', and *zond-aar* 'sinner', i.e. after a syllable with a full vowel. The condition that the preceding consonant must be a coronal sonorant is never violated.

The distribution of these two allomorphs can now be related to the parsing constraints, because it is the choice of *-aar* after a stem ending in a schwa-syllable that avoids the creation of a sequence of two schwa-headed syllables of which the second cannot be parsed into a foot. On the other hand, for a word like *Amsterdam* the optimal inhabitant name is that with *-er*, and similarly, the optimal form for the verb *eten* 'to eat' is *eter*, and not **etaar*. In order to make the correct selection in the case of *eter*, we also have to invoke the constraint Superheavy:

(14) Superheavy: superheavy syllables must head a foot

A superheavy syllable has a threepositional rhyme: a long vowel followed by a consonant, or a short vowel followed by two consonants. This constraint is ranked higher than Foot-Min because Dutch words that end in a superheavy syllable, bear the word stress on that syllable, which must therefore form a monosyllabic foot, as in the example *kantóor* 'office' given above.

The following tableaux show how the selection proceeds for the base words *Diemen* and *spin* 'to spin':

(15)

	SuperH	FootMax	ParseSyll	FootMin
(di:mən-ər)$_F$		*!		
(di:mə)$_F$(n-ər)$_σ$			*!	
☞ (di:mə)$_F$(n-a:r)$_F$				*
(di:mə)$_F$(n-a:r)$_σ$	*!		*	

	SuperH	FootMax	ParseSyll	FootMin
☞ (spɪn-ər)$_F$				
(spɪn-a:r)$_F$	*!			
(spɪ)$_F$(n-a:r)$_F$				*!*

The word *Diemenaar* ends in a monosyllabic foot that bears secondary stress. This is apparently preferable to leaving the syllable unparsed, and hence, the form with *-aar* is selected. In the case of the verb *spin*, it is the form with *-er* that is selected.

It should be noted that the allomorph *-aar* is not always available when it would help to avoid violation of the ParseSyll constraint: after stems ending in /m/ such as *bezem* 'to sweep', we get *bezemer* /be:zəmər/ 'sweeper' rather than *bezemaar*, i.e. a form with a final unfooted syllable. This also holds for the restricted number of verb stems that end in an obstruent such as *vonnis* /vɔnəs/ 'to sentence': the corresponding deverbal agent noun is *vonnisser*. That is, the more restricted allomorph *-aar* must be subcategorized as appearing only after coronal sonorant consonants. In other words, phonological output constraints must be supplemented by other conditions, just as in the case of the nominal plural suffixes discussed in the preceding section, where morphological properties of the nominal stems appeared to play a role.

The ParseSyll constraint also plays a role in the formation of feminine nouns. In Dutch, the feminine suffix *-ster* /stər/ creates feminine nouns, and takes as its base either verbs or nouns:

(16)

verbal base	*feminine noun*
bak /bɑk/ 'to bake''	bak-ster
verdedig /vɛrde:dəɣ/ 'to defend'	verdedig-ster
nominal base	
kruidenier /krœydəni:r/ 'grocer'	kruidenier-ster
vliegenier /vli:ɣəni:r/ 'pilot'	vliegenier-ster

In the case of deverbal agent nouns, the choice between a nominal or a verbal base now appears to be determined by the principle of avoiding a sequence of two unstressed syllables, as pointed out by Shannon (1991): if the verbal stem ends in a schwa-syllable, *-ster* selects the deverbal noun in *-aar* as its base, and if the verbal stem ends in a syllable headed by a full vowel, the verbal stem is selected as the base (there is no meaning difference between these two kinds of feminine nouns):

(17)	*verb*	*deverbal noun*	*feminine noun*
	bak /bɑk/ 'to bake'	bákk-er /bɑkər/	bák-ster, *bákker-ster
	loop /lo:p/ 'to walk'	lóp-er /lo:pər/	lóop-ster, *lóper-ster
	dobbel /dɔbəl/ 'to gamble'	dóbbel-àar /dɔbəla:r/	*dobbel-ster, dóbbelàar-ster
	reken /re:kən/ 'to compute'	réken-àar /re:kəna:r/	*reken-ster, rékenàar-ster

It will be clear that in the analysis proposed here these data can be accounted for by the ParseSyll constraint: the grammar generates two morphologically well-formed feminine nouns, one from the verbal stem, and one from the deverbal noun, and ParseSyll will select words like *bak-ster* /bɑkstər/ over *bakkerster* /bɑkərstər/, and *dobbelaarster* /dɔbəla:rstər/ over *dobbelster* /dɔbəlstər/.

2.3. Inflected adjectives

In present-day Standard Dutch, adjectives in attributive position are inflected: the stem is followed by schwa, except when the adjective forms part of an indefinite NP headed by a neuter noun. In the latter case, there is no overt inflection. Traditionally, these forms are called uninflected adjectives. This is strange from a conceptual point of view: if a particular syntactic configuration requires inflection of a word class (i.e. contextual inflection, cf. Booij 1994), then members of this word class are by definition inflected. It is only in the case of inherent inflection such as pluralization of nouns that speakers have the option not to inflect a noun. Therefore, we should say that the inflectional morpheme involved is the zero-morpheme. In the examples below, *boek* 'book' is a neuter noun, and *tafel* 'table' is a non-neuter noun.

(18)	een goed-ø boek	'a good book'
	het goedə boek '	the good book'
	(de) goedə boeken	'(the) good books'
	een goedə tafel	'a good table'
	de goedə tafel	'the good table'
	(de) goedə tafels	'(the) good tables'

When the stem of the adjective ends in /ən/, however, the schwa does not appear:

(19)	het opən-ø boek	'the open book'
	de hout-ən-ø tafel	'the wooden table'
	de ge-slag-ən-ø room	'the whipped cream'
	de ver-get-ən-ø jas	'the forgotten coat'

The absence of the schwa in this position does not follow from a purely phonological rule of schwa apocope, because there is only absence of schwa if the schwa is the inflectional morpheme of the adjective. In other cases, the schwa remains, e.g. in the nominalized forms of adjectives:

(20)	het ge-slag-ən-ə	'the beaten' (neuter)
	de ge-slag-ən-ə	'the beaten (person)' (non-neuter)

Moreover, it is only after /ən/ that the inflectional schwa does not surface; it does surface after other consonants, and after the combination full vowel + /n/:

(21)	de mager-ə /ma:ɣərə/ vrouw	'the lean woman'
	de lelijk-ə /le:ləkə/ man	'the ugly man'
	de edel-ə /e:dələ/ mens	'the noble man'
	de groen-ə /ɣru:nə/ stoel	'the green chair'

That it is the output configuration /ənə/ only that is to be avoided, can be concluded from the fact that past participles used as attributive adjectives do have a final inflectional schwa if they have an exceptional form ending in full vowel + /n/, which is the form for the verbs *doen* /du:n/ 'do', *gaan* /ɣa:n/ 'go', *staan* /sta:n/ 'stand', *zien* /zi:n/ 'see' and their derivatives:

(22)	ge-dan-ə /ɣə-da:n-ə/ zaken	'lit. done business, finished matters'
	door-stan-ə /do:r-sta:n-ə/ moeite	'lit. suffered effort, efforts'
	be-gan-ə /bə-ɣa:n-ə/ wegen	'trodden paths'
	een ge-zien-ə /ɣə-zi:n-ə/ collega	'lit. a seen colleague, a respected colleague'

Furthermore, the same pattern can be observed for infinitives with *te* used in attributive position. After infinitives in -/ən/, the inflectional schwa does not occur, whereas the four exceptional infinitives for the verbs *doen, gaan, slaan* and *zien*, mentioned above, and the verb *slaan* 'strike' do have the final schwa:

(23)	nog te nemən-ø /ne:mən/ maatregelen	'lit. still to take measures'
	versus	
	nog te doen-ə /du:nə/ zaken	'matters still to be done'
	nog te gan-ə /ɣa:nə/ wegen	'ways that must be gone'
	nog te door-stan-ə /do:rsta:nə/ beproevingen	'trials still to be suffered'
	niet af te slan-ə /sla:nə/ voorstellen	'proposals not to be rejected'
	niet te zien-ə /zi:nə/ organismen	'organisms that cannot be seen'

In sum, the inflectional schwa of words used as attributive adjectives has a zero-allomorph if the stem ends in /ən/. In addition, the zero allomorph also occurs after adjectives that end in an unstressed vowel (cf. Van Oostendorp 1995). Compare:

(24) een blíj-ə dag 'a cheerful day'
een wée-ə pijn 'a sickly pain'
versus
een príma-ø lezing 'an excellent lecture'
een séxy-ø vrouw 'a sexy woman'

In a rule-based analysis of this kind of schwa apocope, we would have to assume the following rule:

(25) $ə \rightarrow \quad ø \,/\, \left\{ \begin{matrix} ə\ n \\ V_i \end{matrix} \right\} \_\_]_A$ Condition: V_i is =unstressed

Such a description does not express, however, why it is only in this context, that is after a preceding schwa, that the final schwa deletes. A rule with the context '[+voc] n __' , i.e. a rule that deletes schwa after /n/ whatever the preceding vowel, would be formally simpler. Yet, it is obvious that it would not be simpler from the point of view of the overall systematics of the grammar. It is obvious that the occurrence of the zero-allomorph is related to the prosodic constraints discussed above, which imply the avoidance of sequences of unstressed syllables and the creation of disyllabic feet.

The parsing constraints can be violated however, since we do find words with a sequence of two schwa-syllables, even if the word ends in a schwa, as in the following cases:

(26) (a) in inflected adjectives with another consonant than /n/, e.g. edələ mens 'noble man'
(b) in the inflected present participle: lopənd-ə mensen 'walking people'
(c) if the schwa is a nominalizing suffix: het opən-ə 'the open, neuter', de gebor-ən-ə 'the born person'.

Violable constraints are an essential ingredient of OT. In this case, the prosodic constraints can be assumed to be dominated by Morpheme Identity (cf. fn. 3):

(27) het opən-ə

	MorphI	SuperH	FootMax	ParseSyll	FootMin
☞ $(o{:}pə)_F(n\text{-}ə)_σ$				*	
$(o{:}pən\text{-}ə)_F$			*!		
$(o{:}pən)_F$-<ə>	*!				

The question thus arises how we account for the difference between the behaviour of the inflectional schwa of adjectives, which alternates with zero, and the other word-final schwas which always appear on the surface. Such differences in behaviour could be accounted for in terms of different constraint rankings. However, I do not want to assume affix-specific rankings of constraints, because this implies that the language learner would have to acquire a number of affix-specific grammars for his native language, not a very attractive position from the learnibility point of view. Therefore, I prefer an analysis in which the inflectional schwa has a zero-allomorph listed in the morphological module of the grammar.

This zero-allomorph of inflected adjectives only appears after a stem ending in /n/ and after adjectives ending in an unstressed vowel. Thus, the zero-allomorph has to be subcategorized for appearing after vowels or /n/. Again, as in the case of the suffix *-aar*, subcategorization is required as an additional mechanism:

(28)

	MorphI	SuperH	FootMax	ParseSyll	FootMin
$(\text{o:pə})_F(\text{n-ə})_\sigma$				*!	
☞ $(\text{o:pən-ø})_F$					

The second form, with the allomorph ø, does not violate ParseSyll, and is therefore to be preferred. The inflectional schwa of adjectives must therefore be assumed to have a zero-allomorph which is subcategorized for appearing after /n/. Note that we do not have to subcategorize this zero-allomorph for appearing only after /n/ if it is preceded by schwa, because the necessary presence of a preceding schwa follows from the constraint FootMin already discussed in the preceding section. That is, it follows automatically that the zero-allomorph does not appear after /n/ preceded by a full vowel, as is the case for an adjective like *groen* 'green':

(29)

	MorphI	SuperH	FootMax	ParseSyll	FootMin
☞ $((\text{ɣru:})_\sigma(\text{n-ə})_\sigma)_F$					
$((\text{ɣru:n-ø})_\sigma)_F$					*!

In other words, if Dutch has the option to create a word that ends in a disyllabic foot, it will do so, and not choose the zero-allomorph that results in a less optimal phonetic form. As in the cases discussed in the previous sections, the distribution of the two allomorphs is not completely accounted for by the output condition. In this case, we have to subcategorize the zero-allomorph for appearing after /n/ and vowels only. There are also a few adjectives, ending in /ər/, that have the zero-form of the inflectional ending: denominal geographical adjectives such as *Limburger* and *Groninger*, and the adjectives *linker* 'left' and *rechter* 'right'. In other words, the zero-allomorph of the adjectival inflection must also be specified as being permitted to appear after such geographical adjectives in *-er*. This zero-allomorph will then be selected by the constraint system proposed above, because forms like **linkere* [lɪŋkərə] will be less optimal. However, this zero-allomorph is not allowed for all adjectives in ər: comparatives, which end in *-er*, do have the schwa. This implies that the specification of the context of the zero-allomorph has to refer to specific classes of adjectives.

The effect of the ParseSyll constraint on the form of inflected adjectives with a stem in /ən/ can also be seen in Frisian (Dyk 1996), but in this language the zero-allomorph is optional. In this respect it mirrors the historical development of Dutch: in Middle Dutch, the inflectional schwa was obligatorily present, but gradually its absence became an option, leading to the situation in Modern Dutch where the absence of this schwa is obligatory (cf. Raidt 1968).

Phonological output conditions may also be invoked to explain particular word formation patterns. As pointed out by Neef (1996), German has a circumfix *Ge ... e* /gə ... ə/ used to derive nouns from verbs:

(30) Gehopse 'dancing', Gesinge 'singing', Gerede 'speaking'

However, if the verbal stem ends in a schwa-syllable, another form may be chosen for the deverbal noun, without a final schwa. For instance, the noun for the verbal stem *hampel*, with the meaning 'stumbling', has the following possible forms in addition to the form *Gehampele*:

(31) gə-hampəl, gə-hamplə

(in the first form, we may also have a syllabic [l] instead of [əl]). In this way, a sequence of two unstressed syllables is avoided.

One may ask the question under which conditions zero-allomorphy is allowed for. As far as zero-allomorphy in inflection is concerned, an important point to be noted here (also mentioned by Dyk 1996) is that the kind of inflection involved is what has been called weak (Kiparsky 1982) or contextual (Booij 1994) inflection: is is inflection that is completely dependent on and governed by the syntactic context, and has no independent information content. Therefore, it is omissible from the informational point of view.

As observed by Kiparsky (1971) [1982: 67], it is contextual inflection that gets lost first:

(32) Morphological material which is predictable on the surface tends to be more susceptible to loss than morphological material which is not predictable on the surface.

A number of illustrations of this principle can be found in Booij (1994). For instance, Romance languages such as Spanish, Italian and French have lost their case endings (mainly contextual inflection), whereas the formal distinction between singular and plural nouns (inherent inflection) has been kept. In conformity with this generalization, schwas that have a non-predictable function, e.g. the function of nominalizer (changing an adjective into a neuter or a non-neuter noun) always surface, and do not have a zero-allomorph.[7] Menn & MacWhinney (1984: 815) also observed that "[v]acuous application [=ø-allomorphy, G.B] is common only in inflectional morphology, however, where it has the support of sentential redundancies. Derivational morphology is supported by far fewer redundancies". In the German examples of *Ge*-nominalizations in (30), a case of derivational morphology, the prefix *Ge-* can be seen as the expression of the nominal nature of these words, hence the schwa-suffix can be omitted.

---

[7] In his LSA summer school lectures, Cornell, 1997, Kiparsky has pointed out that in Finnish it is structural cases only that exhibit zero allomorphy, thus supporting this generalisation.

These considerations with respect to the occurrence of zero-allomorphs are of a functional nature, and are not claimed to be part of the set of formal constraints.

In Frisian, where this kind of schwa-apocope is optional, the zero-allomorph after /n/ is optional, and not an obligatory allomorph. The optionality of the allomorph suggests that phonology has not yet completely won the victory over morphology. In the classical rule-based framework we would say that Frisian has an optional rule of inflectional schwa-deletion, and this is in conformity with the following generalization (Kiparsky 1982: 68):

(33) Grammatically conditioned variability in the application of optional rules favours optimal outputs.

It is interesting to see how in the formulation of this generalization the notion 'output' already plays a direct role. A similar kind of variation is found for Dutch inflected adjectives of which the stem already ends in two schwa-headed syllables:

(34)	het onvermijdələk(ə) gevolg	'the unavoidable consequence'
	ons hartələk(ə) weerzien	'our cordial meeting again'
	gebruikələkər(ə) gevallen	'more usual cases'
	een voorzichtəgər(ə) formulering	'a more prudent formulation'

A parallel development can be seen in the form of inflected infinitives. In Middle Dutch, infinitives could be inflected: the preposition *te* assigned dative case, expressed by the ending -ə:

(35)	te copene /ko:pənə/	'to buy'
	te kerene /ke:rənə/	'to turn'
	te vellene /vɛlənə/	'to fell'

In Modern Dutch, this inflectional ending is no longer found. Again, this inflection is a case of contextual, syntactically determined inflection, which can be lost without loss of information.

3. OCP-effects

As pointed out in the introduction, the sequence /rər/ is to be avoided in Dutch, by means of blocking of morphological processes such as *-erd*-suffixation, and also by using particular allomorphs, as we will see below (a point also made by Shannon 1991) .

The non-occurrence of /rər/ can be seen as an instantiation of a much more general constraint: a schwa cannot be preceded and followed by the same consonant. Since the schwa is the neutral vowel of Dutch, it has no features except on the root node (Van Oostendorp 1995). Therefore, in a sequence /C_iəC_i/, we get adjacency of identical features, thus violating the Obligatory Contour Principle (OCP).[8] The only sequences of this type that are permitted in native words of Dutch are those with the coronal consonant /n/:

(36)	linnən	'linen'
	binnən	'inside'
	bonnən	'tickets'

This analysis correctly predicts that it is only identical consonants separated by a full vowel with its own place features that are possible:

(37)	pap	'porridge'
	kak	'shit'
	lol	'fun'
	raar	'strange'
	mam	'mom'
	non	'nun'
	sis	'sizzle'

Thus, there are no words in Dutch that contain the sequence /C_iəC_i/ except /nən/.

The occurrence of a sequence like /n ən/ is not excluded by OCP if /n/ is not specified for place at the underlying level because it has the default place of articulation of consonants, the coronal place. However, the invisibility of unmarked place features for such constraints should probably be expressed in a different way, i.e. not by underspecification, because, as pointed out in the literature, there are also rules that crucially refer to, for instance, the set of coronal consonants (cf. Booij 1995: 74). For instance, one could assume that OCP will not take the Place features of the default consonant of a language into account, /n/ being defined as the default consonant of Dutch.

OCP plays two roles: it blocks certain word formation processes, and it governs the selection of allomorphs. In an output constraint based grammar, blocking is interpreted as 'null parse'. For instance, the ill formed word *dappererd* given in the introduction should be blocked as there is no allomorph of this suffix available that would avoid violation of OCP:

(38)

	OCP
dapər-ərd	*!
☞ dapər-<ərd>	

In this respect, we see a difference between derivation and inflection: a particular derivation can be avoided because derivation is optional: we can always use either an alternative word formation process, or a syntactic construction to express a particular meaning, whereas (contextual) inflection is obligatory. This may explain why inflection makes use

---

8 The C_iəC_i-constraint also holds for Frisian (Visser 1997).

only of competing allomorphs and affixes, and not of blocking, i.e. null parse.[9] This difference between derivation and inflection is thus of a primarily functional nature. It could be incorporated into a set of formal constraints by assuming a condition that prohibit null-parse in the case of inflectional morphemes: *Null-parse-Inflection, which is ranked above the phonological constraints that might require null-parse in order not to be violated.

For the suffix *-erd* the alternative suffix *-ling* exists, and this suffix is then used after stems ending in /r/:

(39)	*deadjectival nouns:*		*denominal nouns:*	
	goorling	'dirty person'	kamerling	'valet'
	zuurling	'crab'	voedsterling	'nursed animal'
	zuiderling	'Southerner'	kleurling	'coloured person'
	ouderling	'presbyter'	zilverling	'silver coin

Similarly, the suffix *-ig* /əɣ/ cannot be attached to a stem ending in /ɣ/. Instead, another suffix has to be used, *-achtig* /ɑxtəɣ/:

(40)	berg	'mountain'	*berg-ig / berg-achtig	'mountainous'
	dwerg	'dwarf'	*dwerg-ig / dwerg-achtig	'dwarfish'

If OCP is not violated, both suffixes can be used, e.g. both *rod-ig* and *rood-achtig* with the same meaning 'reddish' are wellformed.

Dutch has a number of *-er*-suffixes, the comparative suffix, the deverbal nominalizing suffix, and the denominal nominalizing suffix. All of them have the allomorph /dər/ to be used after a stem ending in /r/.

(41)	*adjective*		*comparative:*
	duister /dœystər/	'dark'	duisterder
	helder /hɛldər/	'clear'	helderder
	noun		*denominal noun*
	Bijlmermeer /bɛilmərme:r/		Bijlmermeerder
	Almere /ɑlme:rə/		Almeerder
	verb		*deverbal noun*
	leer /le:r/	'to learn'	leerder
	beroer /bəru:r/	'to touch'	beroerder

As pointed out above, the nominalizing *-er* also has the allomorph *-aar*. I will now illustrate how the selection of the right allomorph is made for *Bijlmermeer*.

9 The lacking of inflectional gaps is not exceptionless. For instance, as mentioned in Halle (1973), Russian verbal paradigms exhibit certain gaps, but these gaps are not due to violation of phonological constraints.

(42)

	OCP	SuperH
$(\text{bɛilmər})_F(\text{me:r-ər})_F$	*!	
$(\text{bɛilmər})_F(\text{me:r-a:r})_F$		*!
☞ $(\text{bɛilmər})_F(\text{me:r-dər})_F$		

In the case of *Amsterdam*, we have to account for the choice between *Amsterdammer* and *Amsterdamder* (the form *Amsterdammaar* is excluded due to violation of SuperH, cf. above). The correct choice (*Amsterdammer*) can be effected in two ways: one solution is to assume that the NoCoda constraint prefers *Amsterdammer* to *Amsterdamder* because the third syllable of the latter is a closed syllable. Note, however, that in *Amsterdammer* the /m/ of the third syllable is ambisyllabic because the preceding vowel is short (Booij 1995). In other words, this solution only works if we assume that the NoCoda constraint is not violated if the relevant consonant is ambisyllabic. The alternative is to assume that the allomorph *-der* is subcategorized for appearing after /r/ only. As we have seen above, such phonological subcategorization requirements cannot be dispensed with in other cases.

There is evidence for the autonomous existence of the allomorph *-der* in that it also occurs in a number of other complex words after stems that do not end in /r/ but in another kind of sonorant consonant:

(43)

dien-der /di:n-dər/	'lit. servant, policeman'
vil-der /vɪldər/	'skinner'
maal-der /ma:ldər/	'miller'
Afrikaan-der /a:fri:ka:ndər/	'id.'

The allomorph /dər/ also occurs in certain suffix combinations which synchronically function as one suffix, *-er-ig* /ərəɣ/ and *-er-ij* /ərɛi/:

(44)

zeur-der-ig	'nagging'
klier-der-ig	'nagging
boer-der-ij	'farm'
grossier-der-ij	'wholesale trade'
poelier-der-ij	'poulterer's firm'
maal-der-ij	'mill'

Again, the allomorphy serves to avoid the sequence /rər/ which violates OCP.[10]

An interesting interaction of the constraints OCP and ParseSyll can be observed in the formation of denominal geographical adjectives. Geographic nouns in *-en* have a shortened

---

[10] Two exceptional words that violate OCP are *hoererij* [hu:rərɛɪ] 'whoredom' and *narrerij* 'foolish behaviour'. In addition, as Jaap van Marle pointed out to me, some speakers of Dutch claim that they find words like the comparative *barrer* [bɑrər] 'more awful' acceptable. In the latter two examples, the first /r/ is also part of the first syllable because the preceding vowel is short. This suggests that for those speakers the /rər/-constraint would only hold for completely tautosyllabic identical consonants.

allomorph without this sequence, and this shortened stem is used before *-er* in order to avoid violation of ParseSyll:

(45)	*noun*	*adjective*
	Assen /ɑsən/	Ass-ər (*Assen-er)
	Beilen /bɛilən/	Beil-ər (*Beilen-er)
	Groningen /ɣro:nɪŋən/	Groning-ər (*Groningen-er)

However, in the case of the geographical noun *Haren* /ha:rən/, a short stem without /ən/ would create a violation of OCP in the adjective **Harer* /ha:rər/. Therefore, the adjective for *Haren* is *Harener* /ha:rənər/ (as in *Harener Weekblad* 'Harener weekly') because OCP is ranked higher than ParseSyll:

(46)

	OCP	ParseSyll
$(\text{ha:r-ər})_F$	*!	
☞ $(\text{ha:rə})_F(\text{n-ər})_\sigma$		*

The number of morphological processes that could give rise to OCP-place violations is rather restricted for other consonants than /r/. There are two relevant suffixes with /l/: the no longer productive diminutive suffix *-el* /əl/, and the allomorph *-elijk* /ələk/ of the adjectival suffix *-lijk.* As predicted, the suffix *-el* (as in *eik-el* 'acorn' and *drupp-el* 'drop') never occurs after stems ending in /l/, and after /l/-final stems it is always the suffix allomorph *-lijk* /lək/ which is preferred to *-elijk* /ələk/, as in *adel-lijk* /a:dəl-lək/ 'noble' with the phonetic form [a:dələk].

The avoidance of the sequence /rər/ can also been seen in post-lexical phonology. Dutch has a number of clitics spelled as *'r*, with the form /ər/ or /dər/. This clitic always fuses with the preceding word into one prosodic word (Booij 1995, 1996), which is the domain of the OCP-constraint discussed here. A compound like *ere-rij* /e:rərɛi/ 'row of honour' is wellformed because the sequence /rər/ is distributed across two prosodic words. Since the clitic form /ər/ (the feminine pronoun *er* and the adverbal pronoun *er*) has the allomorph /dər/, it is this allomorph that is obligatorily used after a host word ending in /r/:

(47)	(Ik) koester 'r	'I cherish her'	*[ku:stərər], [ku:stərdər]
	(Ik) boor 'r	'I drill there'	*[bo:rər], [bo:rdər]

Again, the selection of the right allomorph of these clitic forms follows from the OCP-constraint proposed above. This suggests that this constraint also applies to prosodic words created postlexically. For clitics of the form /əC/, with C being /m/ or /t/, there is no allomorph available, and hence we do find sequences like [tət] and [məm], as in *ziet 't* [zitət] 'sees it' and *noem 'm* [numəm] 'name him' respectively: the clitic must surface somehow due to Morpheme Identity.

4. Conclusions

In this paper I have shown that making use of phonological output constraints is essential for a proper account of the choice between competing affixes, and between allomorphs of affixes and stems in the morphology of Dutch. Thus, it is possible to express the fact that there are general phonological constraints that are relevant for more than one morphological process, and to account for the observation that the selection process can be governed by output forms.

However, the set of phonological conditions on morphological operations cannot be completely reduced to output conditions, and thus to phonology. The set of coocurrence restrictions on morpheme concatenation that form part of the definition of the set of wellformed complex words of a language also comprises subcategorization requirements on the phonological forms of these morphemes. These phonological subcategorization features form part of a larger set of subcategorization features of affixes and stems that serve to define morphological welformedness. For instance, affixes also impose requirements as to the syntactic category of the stems they attach to, and to the layer of the lexicon to which the stem should belong, for instance the non-native stratum. We might therefore assume that the morphological module of the grammar contains a generator that generates the set of possible complex words within the boundaries set by such constraints. By locating these requirements within the morphological generator, they are correctly qualified as unviolable constraints. The phonological module will then serve to make a choice between those candidate complex words that obey the Gen-constraints but differ in the selection of affix or allomorph. In the case of derivation, this evaluation procedure will also include the possibility of null-parse, and thus the blocking of a particular complex word. This view also implies that morphology cannot be equated with the morpheme-concatenating function of the Generator. Morphology is an autonomous module of the grammar (cf. Booij 1997b) in that it imposes its own, non-reducable requirements on the forms of complex words.

Acknowledgements

Previous versions of this paper were read at the Conference on the Phonology and Morphology of Germanic Languages, Marburg, August 1997, at the opening session of the 1997-1998 academic year of HIL, Leiden, September 1997, and in the series of lectures of the Department of Language and Linguistics, University of Essex, Colchester, November 1997. The comments on a previous draft of this paper by Gjert Kristoffersen, Marc van Oostendorp, Ingo Plag, Willem Visser, and the editors of this volume are gratefully acknowledged.

References

Benua, Laura (1995): Identity effects in morphological truncation. *University of Massachusetts Occasional Papers in Linguistics 18.*
Booij, Geert (1977): *Dutch morphology. A study of word formation in generative grammar*. Dordrecht: Foris.
— (1994): Against split morphology. In: Geert Booij & Jaap van Marle (eds.) *Yearbook of Morphology 1993*. Dordrecht: Kluwer, 27-51.
— (1995): *The phonology of Dutch*. Oxford: Clarendon Press.
— (1996): Cliticization as prosodic integration: the case of Dutch. *The Linguistic Review 13*, 219-242.
— (1997a): Non-derivational phonology meets Lexical Phonology. In: Iggy Roca (ed.) *Derivations and constraints in phonology*. Oxford: Clarendon Press, 261-288.
— (1997b): Allomorphy and the autonomy of morphology. *Folia Linguistica* 31, 25-56.
Carstairs, Andrew (1988): Some implications of phonologically conditioned suppletion. In: Geert Booij & Jaap van Marle (eds.) *Yearbook of Morphology 1988*. Dordrecht: Foris, 67-94.
Dressler, Wolfgang U. (1977): Phono-morphological dissimilation. In: W.U. Dressler & O. E. Pfeiffer (eds.) *Phonologica 1976*. Innsbruck: Institut für Sprachwissenschaft, 41-48.
Dyk, Sybren (1996): From inflected material adjectives to the history of schwa apocope in West Frisian: diverging influences on a sound change. In: *A Frisian and Germanic Miscellany. Published in Honour of Nils Århammar on his Sixty-Fifth Birthday*. Odense: Odense University Press/Bredtsedt: Nord-Friisk Instituut, 55-67 (= *Nowele* 28/29).
Golston, Chris & Richard Wiese (1996): Zero morphology and constraint interaction: subtraction and epenthesis in German dialects. In: Geert Booij & Jaap van Marle (eds.) *Yearbook of Morphology 1995*. Dordrecht: Kluwer, 143-159.
Halle, Morris (1973): Prolegomena to a theory of word formation. *Linguistic Inquiry* 4, 3-16.
Kager, René (1996): On affix allomorphy and syllable counting. In: Ursula Kleinhenz (ed.), *Interfaces in phonology*. Berlin: Akademieverlag, 151-171.
Kiparsky, Paul (1971): Historical linguistics. Reprinted in Kiparsky 1982, 57-80.
— (1982): *Explanation in phonology*. Dordrecht: Foris.
Löhken, Sylvia (1997): The emergence of complex consonantal clusters in German. In: Marina Nespor & Norval Smith (eds.), *Dam phonology. HIL phonology papers II*. The Hague: Holland Academic Graphics, 103-122.
Mascaró, Joan (1996): External allomorphy as emergence of the unmarked. In: Jacques Durand & Bernard Laks (eds.), *Current trends in phonology: Models and methods*. Salford: ESRI, University of Salford, 473-484.
McCarthy, John J. & Alan Prince (1993): Prosodic Morphology I. Constraint interaction and satisfaction. Ms. Univ. of Mass., Amherst and Rutgers Univ.
— (1994): Generalized alignment. In: Geert Booij & Jaap van Marle (eds.) *Yearbook of Morphology 1993*. Dordrecht: Kluwer, 79-153.
— (1995): Faithfulness and reduplicative identity. *University of Massachusetts Occasional Papers in Linguistics* 18.
Menn, Lise & Brian MacWhinney (1984): The repeated morph constraint: toward an explanation. *Language* 60, 519-541.
Neef, Martin (1996): Wortdesign: Das Lexembildungsmuster *Gehopse* und die Kopflosigkeit von 'Ableitungen'. *Zeitschrift für Sprachwissenschaft* 15, 61-91.
Oostendorp, Marc van (1995): *Vowel features and syllable projection*. Ph. D. diss, Katholieke Universiteit Brabant.
Plag, Ingo (1997): *Morphological productivity. Structural constraints in English derivation*. Habilitationsschrift, Philipps-Universität Marburg.
— (1998): Morphological haplology in a constraint-based morpho-phonology. In: Wolfgang Kehrein and Richard Wiese (eds.): *Phonology and Morphology of the Germanic Languages*. Tübingen: Niemeyer, 199-215.

Prince, Alan & Paul Smolensky (1993): *Optimality Theory: constraint interaction in generative grammar*. Ms. Rutgers Univ./Univ. of Colorado.

Raffelsiefen, Renate (1996): Gaps in word formation. In: Ursula Kleinhenz (ed.) *Interfaces in phonology*. Berlin: Akademie Verlag, 194-209.

Raidt, Edith H. (1968): *Geskiedenis van die byvoeglike verbuiging in Nederlands en Afrikaans*. Kaapstad etc.: Nasou Beperk.

Schultink, Hendrik (1962): *De morfologische valentie van het ongelede adjectief in modern Nederlands*. Den Haag: Van Goor Zonen.

Shannon, Thomas F. (1991): On the relation between morphology and syllable structure: universal preference laws in Dutch. In: Thomas Shannon & Johan Snapper (eds.): *The Berkeley Conference on Dutch Linguistics 1989*. Lanham MD: University Press of America, 173-205.

Stemberger, Joseph (1981): Morphological haplology. *Language* 57, 791-817.

Vijver, Ruben van de (1998): *The iambic issue. Iambs as a result of constraint interaction*. The Hague: HAG (HIL dissertations, 37).

Visser, Willem (1997): *The syllable in Frisian*. The Hague: Holland Academic Graphics (HIL dissertations, 30).

Wiese, Richard (1996): *The phonology of German*. Oxford: Clarendon Press.

Chris Golston and Richard Wiese

The structure of the German root

'Nur das Geheimnis der Wurzeln oder des Benennungsgrundes der Urbegriffe lassen wir unangetastet.' (Bopp 1833)

0. Goals[1]

The goal of the present study is to make the notion of the root more accessible to morphology and phonology by looking at a large corpus of roots and describing the frequency of different types of root in a constraint-based grammar.

Our research is based on a computer-readable data base of German roots compiled by Ortmann (1993) from ten different sources. We identify a number of phonological properties of roots and demonstrate that unmarked root shapes are much more common than marked ones. To base the research in a theoretical framework we use Direct OT (Golston 1996b), according to which underlying forms are represented solely in terms of markedness, as sets of constraint violations. Our goals are to show that phonologically unmarked roots are more common than marked ones, and to contribute to the theory of morpheme structure constraints.

1. Morphemes and roots

Every serious theory of language is based on morphemes. This is true even of theories that explicitly deny them. We know that aside from a grammar a language learner must learn a large number of arbitrary pairings of signals-to-meanings. The overwhelming majority of such pairings are of the familiar type in (1):

(1) Typical morpheme

 <=> [kæt]

---

[1] The present paper has benefitted from discussions with many colleagues, in particular at the universities of Arizona, Düsseldorf, Jena, and Marburg. Wolfgang Kehrein's comments on the paper have been very useful. The invaluable help of Carmen Scherer, Marburg, in the work with the data base deserves a special mention.

The classic definition runs something like this: a morpheme is 'eine Gruppe von ein bis mehreren Lauten mit einem bestimmten Bedeutungskern' [a grouping of one to several sounds with a specific semantic core] (Liebich 1899, 5). We have a more refined notion of all this now, with morpheme tiers and floating features, but the essential insight is the same: some signal is related to a meaning. We can quibble over whether people store roots or stems or processes or constraints or whatever, but the central fact remains unchanged: the basic pairing of signal to meaning in any language is completely idiosyncratic and memorized. To allay all doubts, though, let's look at claims in the literature that roots and morphemes do not exist.

Anderson (1992) proposes a completely processual morphology that abjures the use of morphemes altogether. Roots are thrown out with the morphemic bathwater: 'a theory that questions the status of morphemes in linguistic analysis has little room for such a construct' (1992, 4). But the evidence that any morphology must be processual is scant: the clearest case is subtractive morphology of the type found in Tohono O'odham and even that can be reanalyzed non-processually (Benua 1995, Golston 1996b, Fitzgerald & Fountain 1995). And even Anderson does not propose that *roots* are processes, so he too has fairly traditional morphemes at the base of his grammar.

Other approaches which downplay the usefulness of the root or which reject the notion altogether include the work of Matthews (1974, 1993), Becker (1990), Lieber (1992), Raffelsiefen (1995) and Neef (1996, 1998). Bat-El argues 'that there is no consonantal root in the morphology' of Hebrew either (1994, 594). But none of these authors would deny that there is an arbitrary pairing of signal and meaning that must be memorized in learning a language or that there's a difference between affixes and the things they attach to.

Aronoff (1976, 1992, 1994) has proposed that morphology is stem-based, rather than morpheme-based; but his stems are essentially of the type in (1). For Aronoff roots are somewhat derivative, but nonetheless real: 'A root is what is left when all morphological structure has been wrung out of a form' (1992, 15). Unanalyzable stems (roots) are fairly easy to come by in a language like German.

A number of researchers have proposed that morphemes are really *constraints* that regulate the sound-meaning relation. This is the claim of Declarative Phonology (Bird 1995, Coleman 1991, Scobbie 1991), for instance, which treats *all* of grammar as constraints. Within OT it has been proposed that all morphemes be treated as constraints as well (Hammond 1995; Russell 1995). And this is also the central claim of *Wortdesign* (Neef 1996), but only for affixes, not for roots. None of these proposals circumvents the need for morphemes, only the formal means by which they are encoded.

One often reads in the standard OT literature that there are no constraints on underlying representations (which is true), but this has nothing to do with the existence of morphemes. A language learner must posit some underlying form for *cat* in OT as in any other theory of grammar. The standard assumption in OT is that morphemes are encoded as strings of segments, as brief perusal of any OT article will verify. Golston (1996b) has proposed that morphemes aren't encoded as strings of segments (standard OT) or as constraints (Declarative Phonology, etc.) but as constraint violations. This doesn't do away with morphemes either, it just recasts how they are encoded in a grammar.

We can take the synactic road as well and deny any independent existence to morphology. But even if morphology is just word-syntax (Selkirk 1982, Höhle 1982, di

Sciullo & Williams 1987, Lieber 1992), we still have morphemes. More than ever, in fact, because now all terminal nodes in a syntactic tree are morphemes.

So let's not worry about claims that language makes no use of morphemes: the concept exists in any explicit theory of grammar and the details of analysis need not blind us to the necessity of the concept. This is particularly clear for roots. Roots are called unanalyzable stems in stem-based morphology and we'll be happy to call them that too if it helps avoid confusion. They are called morpheme constraints in Declarative Phonology and some corners of OT, and we are comfortable with that terminology as well. Likewise with treating roots as sets of constraint violations, as proposed in Direct OT or *even* as strings of segments, the path well-trodden from Saussure to Smolensky.

We want to look at what generalizations arise when we look at the type of thing in (1) in German and we want to see if these generalizations can be related to what we know about phonology generally. The question we want to look at here is not 'What is a root?,' but 'What properties do roots have?' Using a large computer corpus of roots collected independently by others, we'll propose that roots in a given language tend to have a basic shape and that such a shape is inherently related to markedness universals in phonology. The claim will be that less marked shapes have greater numbers of roots than more marked shapes. For English this would mean that there are less roots like *strict* than like *tea.*

2. A data base for German roots

Any large scale study of roots faces the problem of finding an adequate empirical domain over which all generalisations and claims are supposed to range. We see two problems here. The first is the decision of what to treat as native or borrowed. Native speakers usually don't know the difference, so it's not clear that the distinction is psychologically real or in any way important for grammar. Given that the number of foreign words can be huge and that words are usually assimilated to the host language, the issue is not trivial. There is good evidence that the stock of morphemes used in a language is not uniform. Itô & Mester (1995), e.g., have convincingly argued that the over-all set of Japanese morphemes consists of various subsets, normally called strata, which differ on a number phonological properties: a set of native morphemes (*Yamato*), a set of Sino-Japanese roots, a set of foreign roots, and a set of mimetic morphemes.

Second, the division into morphemes (affixes and roots) can itself be difficult. Following Aronoff's dictum that roots are what remains when affixes are stripped off can still leave a large number of dubious cases. To take up just one case from German, many nouns display a final schwa, as in [ʔaugə] 'eye', [naːzə] 'nose', [vaŋə] 'cheek'. The data base of frequent nouns by Ruoff (1981) yields 1484 such nouns, 19% of the total of 7863. For various reasons, it is unclear whether this final schwa should be regarded as a suffix or not. If so, it's not clear what the suffix marks. If not, it could be seen either as part of the root or as epenthetic material, not belonging to any morpheme. Deciding one way or the other makes a big difference for many of the statistics below: removing schwa from the root morpheme removes one syllable and makes the preceding consonant root-final. Wiese

(1986, 1996a) and others have argued that schwa is generally a vowel of epenthesis and not an underlying segment and we will incorporate this into our analysis of German roots. The database introduced below does not treat final schwa as part of the root; it contains roots such as /aug/, /na:z/ and /vaŋ/.

We think it best that the selection of roots and their analysis be made independently of each other. Fortunately, there already exists for German a good deal of work in this area. Our starting-point is a computer-readable data base of *Kernmorpheme* (core morphemes) of German, compiled by Ortmann (1993), who based it on several extant root dictionaries.[2] The dictionaries used are of various sorts and span 80 years, from about 1890 to 1970. Together the resulting dictionary of Ortmann's can be regarded as a fairly complete set of German roots.

The work by Augst (1975) constitutes Ortmann's major source. This large-scale study consists of a three-volume dictionary of German morphemes; it is strictly synchronic, structuralist in orientation, and based mainly on two recent dictionaries of Standard German, Wahrig (1968) and Duden (1968). Augst notes variants of morphemes, related morphemes and borrowings, and marks them as such. In general, decisions made in Augst (1975) for morphemic segmentation were taken over by Ortmann. However, a fairly large number of simplex morphemes postulated by Augst were segmented further by Ortmann (1993: XLI). Among these are many words with final schwa, with a prefix *be-* or *ge-* (/bəgɪn/ 'beginning', /gəʃtalt/ 'gestalt'), and with various other types of formal changes. While these decisions could be regarded as problematic, we did not reverse them.

In setting up the data base, Ortmann made a number of further non-trivial decisions on the organization of his material. The four decisions which are quantitatively and qualitatively most important are the following:

1. A large number (several thousand) of words classified as foreign in Augst (1975) are simply omitted (*Abbé* 'abbot', *Schafott* 'scaffold', *Tohuwabohu* 'id.'...).
2. Words from a second list are singled out and listed in an appendix of Ortmann's data base (*Abenteuer* 'adventure', *add-* 'add', *Akt* 'act', *Scharlach* 'scarlet fever'). This list comprises 792 items. We interpret these as nativized loans in contrast to the foreign words mentioned in 1.
3. Of words such as *Gemälde* 'painting', which are listed in Augst under *mal* as being related to the latter, Ortmann isolates a 'core' *mäld*, and includes these in his list. Also, the endings *-e* and *-er* are truncated by Ortmann in a number of cases (*Schaffner* 'conductor' in Augst, *Schaffn* in Ortmann).
4. For more than 600 morphemes which are marked as capable of being umlauted in Augst, Ortmann generates a separate umlauted entry. That is, for *Buch* 'book', the data base contains both /bu:x/ and umlauted /by:ç/ as separate entries.

The last three decisions, the exclusion of assimilated loan words, the inclusion of roots such as *mäld* or *schaffn*, and the treatment of umlauted variants as separate roots, we regard as

[2] Wolf Dieter Ortmann, Munich, has kindly made available his computer-readable database of the German „Kernmorpheme". On the basis of this database, Carmen Scherer, Marburg, has provided an Excel datasheet of the complete database and helped with the present calculations. At a later stage, we plan to make the database available through the internet.

problematic. First, putative *mäld* appears in *Gemälde* only, *schaffn* is obligatorily followed by *-er* in the word *Schaffner*, and has no other status in the language. For umlauted forms, the inclusion of two forms leads to a duplication of forms which are otherwise completely identical. Second, Wiese (1996b) has argued that umlaut is a (lexical) phonological rule. In consequence, we have retraced the final three steps in the data base, but have remained faithful to Ortmann's first step. In this case, there was no choice here, anyway. Augst's several thousand *Fremdwörter* (3771, according to Ortmann 1993, p. XX) could have been added by hand only. The resulting list in our data base comprises 6512 entries.[3] Not a single entry has been altered, added or removed, even if there seemed to be good reasons for doing so, except for the correction of a few obvious spelling errors. The list of roots is thus (almost) completely based on the independent proposals made by Ortmann and by the dictionaries his work is based upon. Entries exist in orthographic and surface-phonemic form, as part of a (rather large) standard data base, at present an Excel sheet.

We take this data base to be the best current list of German roots. The process of arriving at this guess involves three steps. First, dictionary makers made their own decisions of classification and segmentation, which may or may not have been independent of each other.[4] Second, Ortmann (1993) made a number of carefully documented decisions in setting up his data base, as described above. Finally, we have changed it slightly as detailed above. Through this three-way filtering process, we arrive at a reasonable set of German roots. To see the amount of filtering which has occurred here, consider the fact that a good-sized German dictionary has 120,000 *words* (Duden 1989), while our list yields a mere 6512 *roots*. Etymologically, this set largely derives from the native Germanic vocabulary; else, an item is nativized to such an extent that it can be included in the same class of items. The class we have extensionally defined by our procedure may be compared to the *Yamato* items discussed by Itô & Mester (1995).

3. (Direct) Optimality Theory

Both traditional accounts and those informed by recent phonological theory tend to describe roots as strings of segments. We will depart from this view in a way to be described now. We start with the central claims of Optimality Theory (Prince & Smolensky 1993). While we do not want to provide here an introduction to Optimality Theory (OT), we summarize its major claims in (2) and provide an example for its application immediately below. For published introductions to OT, we refer the reader to McCarthy & Prince 1993, and to three edited volumes, Beckman et al 1995, Archangeli & Langendoen 1997 and Roca 1997.

---

3 A number of forms (about 600) have multiple entries in Ortmann's morpheme list; this is because they had been assigned to several „word families" in Liebich's (1899) dictionary. As these families are etymological in nature, and as the shapes of the morphemes with multiple entries are always identical, we have removed this multiplication. Otherwise, the number of entries would be 7,134.

4 It is of course well-known that new dictionaries are normally compiled on the basis of existing dictionaries.

(2) Principles of Optimality Theory:
- Constraints express universal grammatical preferences.
- Constraints evaluate surface forms as to the fulfillment of these constraints.
- Grammars differ in constraint ranking alone, not in the constraints they contain.

Grammaticality of a linguistic form is defined as best-fulfillment of a given constraint hierarchy: constraints and constraint violations are the stuff of which grammar is built. No rules, principles or parameters play any role in OT.

Here, we illustrate the concept by means of an example from German. Like all languages, German prefers syllables that begin with a consonant (CV) to those that begin with a vowel (V). Also like other languages, German avoids epenthesis whenever possible. Following work in OT, let us call the constraints responsible ONSET and FILL-C:

(3) ONSET 'Syllables begin with consonants.'

(4) FILL-C 'No epenthesis of consonants.'

The two constraints conflict with a vowel-initial word like aχt 'eight'. If we respect ONSET, [ʔaχt], we violate FILL-C (by inserting the glottal stop) but if we respect FILL-C we violate ONSET: [aχt]. The issue is resolved by weighting or 'ranking' ONSET above FILL-C:

(5) ONSET >> FILL-C

The correct output will be generated in an OT grammar by penalizing [aχt] more than [ʔaχt], as follows:

(6) Glottal stop epenthesis

aχt	ONSET	FILL-C
☞ ʔaχt		*
aχt	*!	

The first candidate isn't perfect but it's better-formed than the second. Both candidates violate a constraint but the violation of ONSET is fatal (!) to the second because it is worse than the violation of FILL-C incurred by the first.

It turns out that the constraints used in standard OT are so varied and so many that violations of them can be used to specify morphemes: linguistic forms can be characterized as specific sets of constraint violations. This makes standard representations redundant since constraint violations can be used both to evaluate forms and to represent them. This is the central claim of Direct OT:

(7) Direct OT (Golston 1996b)

Morphemes are represented by the constraints they violate.

This equivalence between standard representations and sets of constraint violations is illustrated for the German word [ɑχt] *'8'* below. Consider a standard autosegemental representation of the surface form of [ɑχt]:

(8) Autosegmental representation of ɑχt:

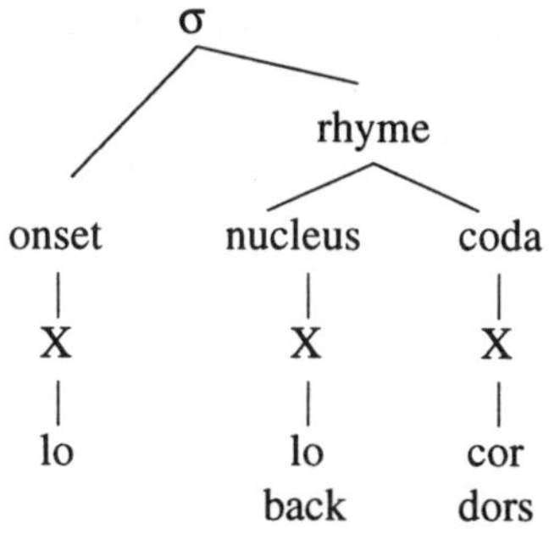

There are a bunch of things that are marked in (8) including the empty onset, the coda [χ] and the extrasyllabic stop [t] (Wiese 1996a: § 3.2.3). In addition, the tongue must be lower and further back in the mouth for the vowel than it is for quiet breathing and the dorsum must be low in the mouth to contact the uvula. The representation in (8) will be evaluated as violating ONSET, NOCODA, NODORSAL, etc. in the course of the grammar. If we freeze the grammar at this point and note just how marked our form is we will have something like (9) which says what is bad about [aχt] purely in terms of markedness. These distinctive violations or desiderata constitute a grammatical address for the meaning *8*:

(9) Desiderata for [aχt] '8'

ONSET	NO CODA	NO DORSAL	NO CONT	NO STOP	NO CORONA L	NO LO
8	8	8	8	8	8	8

The idea is that the listener will select the meaning *8* just in case the utterance she hears has no onset, does have a coda, has a dorsal articulation, etc. Note that (9) says nothing about linear order (the ranking of the constraints is irrelevant): the fact that the consonants all come after the vowel has to be inferred from the violation of ONSET and NOCODA.

Empirical evidence for encoding morphemes in terms of constraint violations (9) instead of autosegmental representations (8) comes from various types of morphology generally regarded as problematic for sign-based models. Such types of morphology include truncation, zero-affixation and reduplication. These receive a natural interpretation in Direct OT. Let's look at two examples to see how this is done. Tohono O'odham has a well-studied alternation involving perfective verb stems in which the perfective is marked by deletion of the stem-final syllable (Zepeda 1983).

(10)

Stem	Perfective		
cikapana	cikapa	'worked'	(surface [cik^{h}p^h])
bisiceka	bisice	'sneezed'	(surface [bisc^h])

Subtractive morphology of this sort can be characterized as distinctive violation of the faithfulness constraint PARSESYLLABLE, part of a family of faithfulness constraints in standard OT (Prince & Smolensky 1993; PARSE is recast as MAX in McCarthy & Prince 1995). The desideratum for the Tohono O'odham perfective (pf) is then simply:

(11) Tohono O'odham perfective

PARSE SYLL
pf

The hearer accesses the meaning PERFECTIVE just in case she *cannot* locate one syllable of the verbal stem in the utterance. The fact that it is the *final* syllable of the word that is underparsed is attributed to a constraint that aligns distinctive features with the beginning of a word: ALIGN-L (*f*, WD): underparsing any non-final syllable would alter the distinctive (mis-)alignment of features.

Alignment constraints (McCarthy & Prince 1993) are distinctively violable as well. Recall that German has roots that surface with a final schwa when they stand alone but without schwa when suffixed or compounded: [li:bə] 'love', but [li:blo:s] 'loveless' or [li:bçən] 'darling'; [ʔaugə] 'eye', but [ʔaugʔapfl̩] 'eye-ball'; [na:zə] 'nose' but [na:shorn] 'rhinoceros', and so on. The surface peculiarity of the unaffixed forms is that the root is misaligned from the end of the prosodic word by what appears to be an epenthetic vowel [ə]: roots like [li:b] and [na:z] *never* occur at the end of the word in German while roots like [zi:b] 'sieve' and [gʀa:z] 'grass' do (modulo the effect of Final Devoicing). Assuming a constraint ALIGN-R (ROOT, WD),we may specify that roots of the [li:bə] and [na:zə] type violate it distinctively: they never surface word-finally. In the event that they are suffixed or compounded, the constraint is satisfied trivially (the root is not word final in [li:blo:s] or [na:shorn]). In the event that they are not suffixed, an epenthetic schwa is inserted to meet the desideratum. In this way we can capture the insight that the vowel is epenthetic but lexically idiosyncratic (Wiese 1986, 1996a), an otherwise difficult thing to do:

(12) Desideratum for final schwa in [ha:zə] 'bunny':

ALIGN-R (RT, WD)

The hearer accesses the meaning BUNNY just in case (inter alia) she locates a misaligned root.[5]

Floating features that mark specific morphological categories are handled analogously. Ladefoged & Maddieson (1996, 69) report on a causative morpheme in Burmese whose sole phonetic reflex is aspiration of word-initial consonants:

(13) Burmese causative

state		*causative*	
páuʔ	'be pierced'	p^{h}áuʔ	'pierce'
céʔ	'be cooked'	c^{h}éʔ	'cook'
nôu	'be awake'	n̥ôu	'waken'
láʔ	'be bare'	l̥áʔ	'uncover'

The causative morpheme violates the constraint against a spread glottis, a marked state for the vocal tract. Direct OT represents the morpheme as follows:

(14) Desideratum for Burmese causative

NOSPREAD GLOTTIS
caus

Here the hearer accesses the meaning CAUSATIVE if she notices a spread glottis configuration. The location of the spread glottis feature is independently given by alignment constraints.

In general, DOT represents every morpheme in terms of a non-null set of constraint violations. This opens a new view on what properties must be categorically true for some item: it will be the expected situation that a particular linguistic item violates a constraint holding for many other items of the same type. For example, if syllables are expected to be open in some language, a closed syllable will simply be represented as one violating the constraint NOCODA.

4. Root markedness

In this section we'll try and substantiate one of the predictions of Direct OT, viz. that less marked roots are more common within a given language than more marked shapes. We'll

[5] Golston & Wiese (1996) argue that the German plural suffix -ə is epenthetic as well, the result of an alignment constraint affecting inflected forms.

cover both constraints that are never violated and those that are rarely violated, basing our frequency on the corpus described above.

4.1. Minimality

Like the lexical roots of Sanskrit (Steriade 1988), Greek, Latin, English (Golston 1991) and Proto-Indo-European (Golston 1996a), lexical roots in German are minimally bimoraic, CVC or CVː. Examples include the following:

(15)	...VC		...VV		*...V
	ʀɛt	'save'	ʀeː	'deer'	*ʀɛ
	kʊs	'kiss'	kuː	'cow'	*kʊ
	ʃtat	'city'	ʃtau	'traffic jam'	*ʃta

As has often been discussed in the literature on German phonology, stressed syllables cannot end in one of the short full vowels [ɪ, ʏ, ɛ, œ, ʊ, ɔ, a]. Given that lexical roots must be stressed, they cannot consist of **bɪ*, **bɛ*, etc or of **b*, **k*, etc. Assuming that the mora is the unit of which a light syllable contains one, and a heavy syllable two, the relevant constraint is one which requires every root to contain a bimoraic foot:

(16) CONTAIN (RT, FT) 'Every root contains a bimoraic foot.'

CONTAIN (RT, FT) is an absolute constraint in German desiderata (no subminimal roots exist in the lexicon) and in the grammar (roots never become subminimal as a result of deletion).

An absolute constraint is never violated in the grammar or by the desiderata for morphemes. The result is an exceptionless skewing away from subminimal roots:

(17) No subminimal roots in German

root-shape	#	%	CONTAIN (RT, FT)
huː, etc.	6512	100	
hʊ	0	0	R

This constraint is not distinctively violated ('R') by any root in German.

4.2. Maximality

German roots tend to be short, usually maxing out at one vowel or two syllables. Vowel and syllable count diverge in German because of large numbers of what we might call syllable-

and-a-half roots, roots with a full syllable followed by a schwa (as discussed above) or syllabic sonorant:

(18) Short roots

Monosyllable		*Schwa*		*Syllabic sonorants*	
hu:t	'hat'	li:b(ə)	'love'	be:zn̩	'bowl'
man	'man'	vi:z(ə)	'meadow'	laɪtʀ̩	'ladder'
ze:	'sea'	bak(ə)	'cheek'	e:zl̩	'donkey'

The precise distribution and characterization of the relevant syllables and vowels has been a matter of some debate ever since the phonemic status of these vowels was questioned by Moulton (1947); for a recent line of discussion see Giegerich (1985), Wiese (1986, 1996a) and Neef (1996). All we are saying at this point is that syllables of this type are best regarded as syllables without vocalic features like [hi] [lo] and [rd].

We capture all of this with the constraints in (19) and (20):

(19) ALIGN-L (V*f*, RT) 'Every vocalic feature is root-initial.'

(20) ALIGN-R (V*f*, RT) 'Every vocalic feature is root-final.'

A vocalic feature in the second syllable of a root is one syllable peak away from the left edge of the root in violation of ALIGN-L (V*f*, RT); a vocalic feature in the first syllable of a two syllable root is one peak away from the right edge in violation of ALIGN-R (V*f*, RT). Roots that respect both alignment constraints above are monosyllabic: [gu:t] 'good', [maχ] 'make', [ze:ʀ] 'very'. Those that violate the second are syllable-and-a-half roots: [ze:gl̩] 'sail', [ʔa:tm̩] 'breath', [ʔa:bn̩d] 'evening'—most of these ends in orthographic-*el* or *-er* such as *Hagel* [ha:gl̩] 'hail' or *Ruder* [ʀu:dʀ̩] 'oar'. Roots that violate the first are quite rare: [ʔaʀbaɪt] 'work,' [ʔalaɪn] 'alone.' Figures for the frequency of each type are given below, alongside a tableau that indicates the markedness of each type with respect to the alignment constraints discussed above:

(21) Short roots in German

root-shape	#	%	ALIGN-L (V*f*, RT)	ALIGN-R (V*f*, RT)
hu:t	5149	79		
ze:gl̩	1227	19		R
ʔaʀbaɪt	131	2	R	R
ʔale:gʀo	5	0	RR	RR
kalifɔʀnjən	0	0	RRR	

The five roots in our corpus that violate the alignment constraints twice are all loans and felt to be such by most speakers: [ʔale:gʀo] 'allegro,' [baldʀia:n] (name), [ʔɛntsia:n] (name), [fe:bʀuaʀ] 'February,' and [januaʀ] 'January.' Longer roots that do not occur in the data base are obvious loans and are interpreted as such [kalifɔʀnjən], [ʔalaba:ma], etc. These are possible German words (they can be pronounced) but their shapes are so marked in the language that they only occur as loans.

Similar restrictions on maximal length are found in many language families. Here we mention but two. Many Mon Khmer languages also have both syllable and syllable-and-a-half roots, but with exactly the opposite alignment effects of German: syllable-and-a-half roots begin with the half-syllable and end with the full one. Consider root shapes in Sre (Manley 1972) and German:

(22) Root shapes in Sre and German

	Sre	*German*
CVX	√	√
Cə	*	*
CəCVX	√	*
CVCə	*	√

Both languages have mostly bimoraic monosyllabic roots and neither has any monomoraic roots. Sre allows half-syllables initially but not word-finally; German allows them finally but not initially. The general picture in (21) is very clear: monosyllabic forms account for a large majority of roots; monovocalic polysyllabic forms are in a large minority, whereas the number of polyvocalic forms is very small. A similar case is found in the Mayan language Mam (England 1983, 93):

> Most Mam roots are of the shape CVC, and in fact only noun, adjective and particle roots can have more than one vowel, and that rarely. Verbs, positionals, and affect roots are quite restricted as to shape.

So the type of maximal size restriction we find in German is not uncommon in the languages of the world. This adds a measure of support to our analysis, which represents German roots by distinctive violation of universal constraints.

Alignment constraints like these restrict the size of the lexicon considerably. Given *n* possible syllables, there are *n* monosyllabic potential roots, but *n* to the power of *m* possible roots containing *m* vowels. Assuming 2000 syllables, there are 8 billion trisyllabic (and smaller) roots!

4.3. Root alignment

A different type of alignment constraint makes roots begin crisply with a syllable boundary:

(23) ALIGN-L (RT, σ) 'Every root begins with a syllable.'

This seems trivial, but it is necessary for ruling out roots that begin with an unsyllabifiable consonant, like *mhu: or *tku::[6]

(24) No misaligned roots in German

root-shape	#	%	ALIGN-L (RT, σ)
ku:, etc..	6512	100	
tku:	0	0	R

The constraint is also necessary for correctly deriving surface forms of morphologically complex words. Consider a vowel-initial root like [aʀbaɪt] 'work' which takes a prefix /g/ (schwas are non-phonemic!) and a suffix /t/ in the preterite. We might expect the verb to surface as *[gaʀbaɪtət] but it does not. Rather, the root stays aligned with a syllable boundary and the prefix is forced into a degenerate foot:

(25) [gəɑʀbɑɪtət] *'worked'*[7]

root-shape	ALIGN-L (RT, σ)	FILL-V	ONSET
g[aʀ.baɪ.t]ət	*!	*	
☞ gə.[aʀ.baɪ.t]ət	R	**	*

The winning candidate is prosodically awful, with two epenthetic vowels and an unfilled onset; but the only serious competitor misaligns the root with the edge of the first syllable and so forfeits the competition.

A similar type of constraint explains an otherwise puzzling fact about German: despite the presence of many polymorphemic words like [gəaʀbaɪtət] 'worked' and [bəʃʀɪtn̩] 'stepped on', there are no monomorphemic words (roots) that begin with a syllable headed by schwa or a syllabic consonant.

(26) Roots begin with a full syllable
*[ʔəlaɪn]
*l̩ze:g
*m̩ta:
*bn̩da:

[6] We assume here that initial [ʃ] or [s] in roots such as *Stadt* 'town', *Spiel* 'play', *Skelett* 'skeleton' are not extrasyllabic, but are part of a complex segment (Wiese 1991).

[7] Note that the brackets used for candidates in (25) denote root boundaries.

We may attribute the lack of such roots to a constraint which prohibits roots from beginning with degenerate syllables:

(27) ALIGN-L (RT, V*f*) 'Every root begins with a vowel feature.'

Violations of this constraint are assessed in terms of syllable peaks that intervene between the edge of the root and a given vowel feature. This makes [ʔɑχt] '8' and [mɑχt] 'power' equally well aligned in terms of vocalic features.

There is a sizable class of *stems* that begin with orthographic *ge-* (gənau 'precise', gəzund 'healthy', gəʃtalt 'gestalt') or *be-* (bəʀaɪχ 'scope', bəʀaɪt 'ready'); all of these have schwa in the first syllable but none of them turned up in our database. This is partly because *ge-* and *be-* are prefixes in German; the forms that contain them are thus not roots, properly speaking, but stems. The *ge-* and *be-* prefixes no longer contribute to the meaning of the stem, but native speakers may recognize them as prefixes.

4.4. Initial consonants

One of the clearest generalizations about prosodic structure is that syllables tend to begin with consonants. The constraint has been introduced above and needs little discussion. What is interesting to note is just how many German roots respect it. Fully 94% of our corpus consists of consonant-initial roots.

(28) Vowel-initial roots in German

root-shape	#	%	ONSET
mɑχ	6147	94	
ɑχt	365	6	R

The marked status of vowel-initial roots couldn't be more clear. Direct OT marks this directly in lexical representation as violation of Onset. Consider the desiderata for '8' again, repeated below:

(29) Desiderata for /aχt/ *'eight'*

ONSET	NO CODA	NO UVULAR	NO CONT	NO STOP	NO CORONA L	NO LO
8	8	8	8	8	8	8

(The violation of NOCODA is for the uvular fricative, which surfaces in all forms of the root, even when suffixed, as in [ʔaχ.tsiç] 'eighty'.)

4.5. Final consonants

At the other end of the root we find the same story repeated: fully 96% of German roots are consonant-final. This cannot be attributed to syllable structure, of course, since syllables prefer to be open cross-linguistically. McCarthy (1993) has proposed a different type of constraint, however, according to which prosodic words want to end in a consonant in certain dialects of English. Golston (1996a) extends this to roots for Indo-European and we adopt his constraint here:

(30) FINAL-C 'Every root ends with a consonant.'

FINAL-C accounts for the skewing shown in the following table, where significantly more roots respect the constraint than violate it:

(31) Vowel-final roots in German

root-shape	#	%	FINAL-C
maχ	6268	96	
draɪ	244	4	R

Roots that violate this constraint bear a desideratum to that effect, as the following example makes clear:

(32) Desiderata for /drai/ *'3'*

NOCOMPLEX ONSET	NOCOMPLEX NUCLEUS	FINALC	NO COR	NO STOP	NO CONT	NO UVU	NO LO	NO HI
3	3	3	3	3	3	3	3	3

We exclude from consideration vowel-final roots that end in schwa, like [na:zə] 'nose'. As discussed above, we analyze the vowel here as epenthetic, since it fails to appear inside suffixed or compounded forms.

4.6. Schwa syllables

Let's look a bit more closely at root-final schwa syllables. As we have just seen, the most common of these by far are those whose syllable peak is occupied by a schwa rather than a syllabic sonorant.[8] Next come those whose peak is a syllabic liquid, followed by a syllabic nasal and so on, as shown in the chart below.

(33) Root-final schwa syllables in German

peak	#	%	NOCODA	*P/NAS	*P/LIQ
ə	1484	53.0			
l̩	620	22.0			*
R̩	593	21.0			*
n̩	50	2.0		*	
n̩d	10	.5	*	*	
n̩t	7	.5	*	*	
ət	5	.4	*		
R̩t	4	.3	*		
əm	3	.3	*		

We can understand the drop in frequency in terms of three constraints: one that prohibits codas entirely, two that prohibit nasals and liquids from forming syllable peaks. The ranking of the last two is not open to cross-linguistic variation: liquids are more sonorous (and thus form better peaks) than nasals in all languages. All three constraints are familiar in OT (Prince & Smolensky 1993):

(34) NOCODA 'Syllables end in a nucleus.'

(35) *P/NAS 'Syllable peaks do not contain nasals.'

(36) *P/LIQ 'Syllable peaks do not contain liquids.'

If we rank NOCODA above the constraints on what may occupy a peak, we predict the exact pattern found in German roots: the most common schwa syllables have (featureless) vowels, followed by syllabic liquids, syllabic nasals and finally syllabic sonorants with codas.

8 The frequency of such roots cannot be determined from our root data base because, as discussed above, the schwa is always stripped off. But we may take the figure 1484 (Ruoff 1981) as a reasonable estimate.

4.7. Stress

As a further case of an asymmetrical distribution of root-shapes, we look at stress. Obviously, this can only be done for polyvocalic ones, as the schwa syllables discussed above are always stressless. There are 136 polyvocalic roots in the corpus, 27 of which have a final schwa (foˈʀɛl(ə) 'trout', ʀoˈziːn(ə) 'raisin') which we do not treat as part of the root here.[9] This leaves us with 109 relevant polyvocalic roots, out of which more than 80% are stressed non-finally:

(37) Stress-final roots in German

root-shape	#	%	NON-FINAL
aʀbaɪt	89	82	
aˈpʀɪl	20	18	R

We assume that a constraint directly disallowing final stress (see Prince & Smolensky 1993: 40) is in charge here:[10]

(38) NONFINALITY 'Final syllables are unstressed.'

To state the result more dramatically, we could say that not more than 0.3 % of the roots in the data-base clearly bears final stress, presupposing that monosyllabic roots (the vast majority) are not distinctively marked for stress. It is also the case that almost all of the 20 stress-final roots are represented in only one of the dictionaries. (Some may even be in the list by mistake, like *Benzol* and *Burgund*.)

We note, however, that a number of common words are not found in our data base: balˈkɔŋ 'balcony', byˈʀoː 'office', idˈjoːt 'idiot', muˈziːk 'music', paˈkeːt 'package', naˈtuːʀ 'nature', kaˈpʊt 'broken' etc. These are not items of Germanic origin, to be sure, but we would have included them in the database simply because of their commonness. It may well be that these words were not included in the database because of their peculiar final stress, but this is something we can only speculate on. We have chosen not to tamper with the corpus for the present.

---

[9] The reason is that there is a strong stress principle in German which says that the vowel preceding a schwa must be stressed. That is, ˈʀoːzin(ə) is not a possible stress pattern for *Rosine* 'raisin'.

[10] Given that roots are predominantly monosyllabic or at least monovocalic, this system will become more apparent on the levels of stems and words, rather than roots; see, e.g., Wiese (1996b; ch. 8), Alber (1998).

4.8. Other root features

In principle, Direct OT predicts that every active constraint in a language should skew the morphemes in a lexicon in their favor: for any constraint C there should be more roots that respect C than violate it. We are not in a position to show this yet, though we hope to have shown that it is true for the constraints we consider above.

Let us briefly spell out, however, what we would expect to find. First, we have seen that vocalic features align leftwards in the root in German, and we expect consonantal features to do the same. Given a configuration of the type C_1VC_2, we expect a feature like NASAL or LABIAL will show up more often on C_1 than on C_2. Second, given constraints like NONASAL and NOLABIAL, we expect more roots to have oral stops than nasals and more roots to have plain stops than aspirates. Finally, given constraints against complex onsets, nuclei and codas, we expect more roots like [fɪʃ] 'fish' than like [fʀɪʃ] 'fresh', [ki:ʃ] 'quiche' or [zɪçt] 'view'. Future research will have to determine whether our predictions in these areas are supported or not.

One other comment is in order: some constraints will appear to be violated quite freely, as a result of constraint ranking. Consider the case of NOCODA. We know from cross-linguistic study that syllables prefer to be open (respecting NOCODA), but German *roots* prefer to be closed (respecting FINAL-C) and they prefer to right-align with a prosodic word. In German, the roots win out over the preferred syllable structure as the figures in (31) demonstrate. The grammar does of course provide various means—in particular the addition of final schwa in inflected forms and in uninflected words like [na:zə] 'nose'—which conspire to give words a shape that is more in accordance with syllabic well-formedness.

5. Conclusions

The full set of constraints we have looked at in this paper is given below:

(39)	ONSET	'Syllables begin with consonants.'	(3)
	FILL-C	'No epenthesis of consonants.'	(4)
	FILL-V	'No epenthesis of vowels.'	(12)
	CONTAIN (Rt, Ft)	'Every root contains a bimoraic foot.'	(16)
	ALIGN-L (V*f*, Rt)	'Every vocalic feature is root-initial.'	(19)
	ALIGN-R (V*f*, Rt)	'Every vocalic feature is root-final.'	(20)
	ALIGN-L (Rt, s)	'Every root begins with a syllable.'	(23)
	ALIGN-L (Rt, V*f*)	'Every root begins with a vowel feature.'	(27)
	FINAL-C	'Every root ends with a consonant.'	(30)

NOCODA	'Syllables end in a nucleus.'	(35)
*P/NAS	'Syllable peaks do not contain nasals.'	(35)
*P/LIQ	'Syllable peaks do not contain liquids.'	(36)
NONFINALITY	'Final syllables are unstressed.'	(38)

For each of these constraints we have seen that the number of roots that obeys them is much greater than the number of roots that violates them.

A few of the constraints are exceptionless in our database: ALIGN-L (RT, σ), CONTAIN (RT, FOOT) and ALIGN-L (RT, V*f*). These are naturally accounted for in any grammar that countenances morpheme structure constraints. The rest of the constraints admit of exceptions. These are most naturally accounted for with violable constraints, specifically OT. Relating the frequency of shapes to the constraints that they violate is most naturally accounted for in Direct OT, where representation is done purely in terms of markedness. And so we take our results as supporting constraint-based grammars generally, OT more specifically and Direct OT in particular.

Morpheme structure constraints have been problematic throughout the history of generative phonology, because many such constraints are similar or even identical to phonological rules, where the latter seemed to be needed independently (Kiparsky 1982) and because well-formedness constraints are somewhat alien in a rule-based grammar. But as the appeal of rule-based grammars has given way to more surface-oriented models the idea of morpheme structure constraints has become more tractable. This is true despite the fact that OT at least is incapable of putting constraints on underlying forms. Constraints in OT regulate only surface forms, but this is perfectly compatible with the regulation of the forms of roots on the surface as we have seen. Morpheme structure constraints are part and parcel of the grammatical machinery regulating phonology and morphology. The fact that of all possible morpheme structure constraints we are readily identifying those which hold for roots is probably not accidental either: among others, McCarthy & Prince (1995: 364) observe that faithfulness to roots is ranked higher than faithfulness to affixes.

We feel that our results argue for the reality of the root as a linguistic category. Emphasizing that at least some of the properties are not those which typically hold for the syllable, stem or word, we feel justified in concluding that our study provides evidence for the reality of the root in the phonology and morphology of German. The root is not something abstract; it is the core of the signal-to-meaning relation and has a number of phonological properties, some exceptionless, some merely strong tendencies.

Finally, we note that our study of roots in German adds substance to an old hypothesis of the Jakobsonian school of linguistics: markedness can be related formally to frequency. This is to be expected if representation is carried out purely in terms of markedness (Direct OT) but is somewhat surprising if representation and markedness are formally unrelated.

6. References

Alber, Birgit (1998): Stress Preservation in German Loan Words. In: Wolfgang Kehrein & Richard Wiese (eds.): *Phonology and Morphology of the Germanic languages*. Tübingen, Niemeyer, 113-141.
Anderson, Stephen R. (1992): *A-morphous Morphology*. Cambridge: Cambridge University Press.
Archangeli, Diana & D. Terence Langendoen (1997): *Optimality Theory: An Overview*. Oxford: Blackwell.
Aronoff, Mark (1976): *Morphology in Generative Grammar*. Cambridge Mass.: MIT Press.
— (1992): Stem and Root. In: William Bright (ed.): *International Encyclopedia of Linguistics, vol 4*. New York, Oxford: Oxford University Press, 76-77.
— (1994): *Morphology by Itself. Stems and Inflectional Classes*. Cambridge, Mass.: MIT Press.
Augst, Gerhard (1975): *Lexikon zur Wortbildung. Band 1 - 3*. Tübingen: Narr Verlag.
Bat-El, Outi (1994): Stem Modification and Cluster Transfer in Modern Hebrew. *Natural Language and Linguistic Theory* 12, 571-598.
Becker, Thomas (1990): *Analogie und morphologische Theorie*. München: Fink.
Beckman, Jill N., et al., eds. (1995): *Papers in Optimality Theory*. University of Massachusetts Occasional Working Papers 18. UMass, Amherst: GLSA.
Benua, Laura (1995): Identity effects in morphological truncation. In: Jill N. Beckman et al., (eds.): *Papers in Optimality Theory*. University of Massachusetts Occasional Working Papers 18. UMass, Amherst: GLSA, 77-136.
Bird, Steven (1995): *Computational Phonology: A Constraint-based Approach*. Cambridge University Press.
Bopp, Franz (1833): *Vergleichende Grammatik des Sanskrit, Send, Armenischen*. Vol. 1. Berlin: Dümmler.
Coleman, John (1991): *Phonological Representations*. Doctoral dissertation, University of York.
Di Sciullo, Anna Maria and Edwin Williams (1987): *On the Definition of Word*. Cambridge: MIT Press.
Duden (1968): *Duden. Rechtschreibung der deutschen Sprache und der Fremdwörter*. Mannheim: Dudenverlag.
Duden (1989): *Duden. Deutsches Universalwörterbuch*. Mannheim, Wien, Zürich: Dudenverlag.
England, Nora C. (1983): *A grammar of Mam, a Mayan language*. Austin: University of Texas Press.
Fitzgerald, Colleen and Amy Fountain (1995): The optimal account of Ţohono O'odham truncation. Paper presented at 1995 LSA.
Giegerich, Heinz (1985): *Metrical Phonology and Phonological Structure. German and English*. Cambridge: Cambridge University Press.
Golston, Chris (1991): *Both Lexicons*. UCLA doctoral dissertation.
—(1996a): Prosodic constraints on roots and words. In: Ursula Kleinhenz (ed.), *Interfaces in Phonology*. Berlin: Akademie Verlag, 172-193.
—(1996b): Direct Optimality Theory: Representation as pure markedness. *Language* 72, 713-748.
Golston, Chris and Richard Wiese (1996): Zero morphology and constraint interaction: subtraction and epenthesis in German dialects. *Yearbook of Morphology 1995*, 143-159.
Hammond, Michael (1995): There is no lexicon! Ms., University of Arizona.
Höhle, Tilman (1982): Über Komposition und Derivation: zur Konstituentenstruktur von Wortbildungsprodukten im Deutschen. *Zeitschrift für Sprachwissenschaft* 1, 76-112.
Itô, Junko & R. Armin Mester (1995): Japanese Phonology. In: John Goldsmith (ed.): *Handbook of Phonological Theory*, 817-838.
Kiparsky, Paul (1982): Lexical Morphology and Phonology. In: The Linguistic Society of Korea (ed.): *Linguistics in the Morning Calm: Selected Papers from SICOL-1981*. Seoul: Hanshin, 3-91.
Ladefoged, Peter & Ian Maddieson (1996): *The Sounds of the World's Languages*. Oxford: Blackwell.
Lieber, Rochelle (1992): *Deconstructing Morphology. Word Formation in Syntactic Theory*. Chicago: University of Chicago Press.
Liebich, B. (1899): *Die Wortfamilien der lebenden hochdeutschen Sprache als Grundlage für ein System der Bedeutungslehre*. Breslau.

Manley, Timothy M. (1972): *Outline of Sre structure*. Oceanic Linguistics Special Publication No. 12. University of Hawaii Press.
Matthews, Peter H. (1974/1993): *Morphology: an introduction to the theory of word-structure.* Cambridge: Cambridge University Press.
McCarthy, John J. (1993): A case of surface constraint violation. *Canadian Journal of Linguistics* 38, 169-95.
McCarthy, John J. and Alan S. Prince (1993): Generalized Alignment. *Yearbook of Morphology* 1993, 79-153.
— (1995): Faithfulness and reduplicative identity. In: Jill N. Beckman et al., (eds.): *Papers in Optimality Theory.* University of Massachusetts Occasional Working Papers 18. UMass, Amherst: GLSA, 249-384.
Moulton, William G. (1947): Juncture in Modern Standard German. *Language* 23, 212-26.
Neef, Martin (1996): *Wortdesign. Eine deklarative Analyse der deutschen Verbflexion.* Tübingen: Stauffenburg.
Neef, Martin (1998): A case study in declarative morphology: German case inflection. In: Wolfgang Kehrein & Richard Wiese (eds.): *Phonology and Morphology of the Germanic Languages.* Tübingen: Niemeyer, 219-240.
Ortmann, Wolf Dieter (1993): *Kernmorpheme im Deutschen. 4561 allgemeinsprachliche deutsche Morphemgestalten im Vergleich zwischen zehn Quellen.* München: Goethe-Institut.
Prince, Alan and Paul Smolensky (1993): *Optimality Theory: Constraint Interaction in Generative Grammar.* Ms, Rutgers University and University of Colorado, Boulder.
Raffelsiefen, Renate (1995): *Conditions for stability: the case of schwa in German*. Düsseldorf, Theorie des Lexikons. Arbeiten des Sonderforschungsbereichs 282, Nr. 69.
Roca, Iggy, ed. (1997): *Derivations and Constraints in Phonology.* Oxford: Clarendon Press.
Ruoff, Arno (1981): *Häufigkeitswörterbuch gesprochener Sprache: gesondert nach Wortarten alphabetisch, rückläufig-alphabetisch und nach Häufigkeit geordnet.* Tübingen: Niemeyer.
Russell, Kevin (1995): *Morphemes and Candidates in Optimality Theory.* Ms. University of Manitoba.
Scobbie, James (1991): *Attribute Value Phonology.* Doctoral dissertation, University of Edinburgh.
Selkirk, Elisabeth O. (1982): *The Syntax of Words*. Cambridge, Mass.: MIT Press.
Steiner, Richard (1992): Ancient Hebrew. In: William Bright (ed.): *International Encyclopedia of Linguistics, vol 2*. New York, Oxford: Oxford University Press, 110-118.
Steriade, Donca (1988): Reduplication and syllable transfer in Sanskrit and elsewhere. *Phonology* 5, 73-155.
Wahrig, Gerhard (1968): *Deutsches Wörterbuch.* Gütersloh: Bertelsmann.
Wiese, Richard (1986): Schwa and the structure of words in German. *Linguistics* 24, 697-724.
— (1991): Was ist extrasilbisch im Deutschen und warum? *Zeitschrift für Sprachwissenschaft* 10, 112-133.
— (1996a): *The Phonology of German.* Oxford: Clarendon Press.
— (1996b): Morphological vs. phonological rules: on German umlaut and ablaut. *Journal of Linguistics* 32, 113-135.
Zepeda, Ofelia. (1983): *A Papago Grammar.* Tucson: University of Arizona Press.

Harry van der Hulst and Jan G. Kooij

Prosodic choices and the Dutch nominal plural[1]

1. The problem

Unlike both English and German,[2] Dutch has two productive and competing plural suffixes for nouns: -s and -en ([ən], often realized as [ə] in standard pronunciation). Examples:[3]

(1)		boek	boeken	'book'
(2)		vader	vaders	'father'
(3)		opa	opa's	'granddad'
(4)	a.	toekan	toekans	'tucan'
	b.	kanón	kanónnen	'gun'

In this paper, we will first discuss the conditions for adding the suffixes -s or -en. We will claim that these conditions are prosodic, both globally and in considerable detail. At the same time, choice of -s rather than -en is also a stratal feature of Dutch morphology. Next, we will compare the distribution of plural suffixes with the conditions on the choice of diminutive suffixes in Dutch nouns, and draw a conclusion about the morphological status of plural formation and diminutive formation.

Our claim will be that plural formation, to a large extent, is a matter of output conditions. However, we will not present a formal analysis of constraints and constraint ordering, but rather concentrate on the nature and the interaction of the conditions involved.

---

1 We thank Wolfgang Kehrein, Richard Wiese and an anonymous reviewer for comments that have led to considerable improvement of an earlier version of this paper. The usual disclaimers apply.

2 On first sight, -s plurals have a marginal position in German, occurring in a few paradigms such as Opa - Opas, 'granddads', and in loanwords, truncations etcetera: Café - Cafés, 'bars' and Sozi - Sozis, 'socialists' (data from Neef (1997)). For arguments that, nevertheless, -s may be the default plural suffix, see Clahsen a. o. 1995.

3 Unless otherwise indicated, stress in the examples is initial. In Dutch orthography, long vowels in open syllabes are written with a single letter (v**a**der); short vowels are written with a single letter in closed syllables (toek**a**n, kan**ó**nnen). Furthermore, *oe* stands for /u/, *ie* for /i/, and both *ij* end *ei* for the diphthong /ɛi/.

2. A first generalization

Comparison between the plural forms of the common native words in (1)-(3), above, leads to the following tentative generalization:

(i) Plurals have -s if the base ends in a trochaic foot; if not, plurals have -(e)n.

Condition (i) is in conformity with the generalization found in many descriptions of Dutch - but not quite. Usually, it is said that -s is added when a noun ends in a syllable that does not carry stress.[4] We will try to show that it is foot formation rather than stress that determines the choice between -s and -en. For this purpose, we will, first of all, discuss more details of the native vocabulary.

2.1. In the native vocabulary, exceptions to the generalization given in (i) are few as far as monosyllabic words are concerned. Only a handful monosyllabic words that end in consonants take -s rather -en in the plural, for instance, kok - koks, 'cook', and maat - maats, 'companion' (which has an alternative plural maten). Plurals such as pak - *paks, 'package', or kop - *kops, 'head', are definitely impossible. It is, therefore, remarkable that monosyllabic loanwords that end in consonants, either from the large Romance Vocabulary of Dutch or from other languages, easily and preferably take -s plurals: bal - bals, 'dance party' (vs. [+native] bal - ballen, 'balls'), club - clubs, 'id.', Mig - Migs, 'id.', stop - stops 'id.' (vs [+native] stop - stoppen, 'plug'). This leads to a second, and also still tentative generalization:

(ii) Monosyllabic [-native] words take -s plurals

We will have ample opportunity to come back to the way in which conditions (i) and (ii) interact and compete. For the moment, the conclusion is warranted that the choice between the suffixes -s and -en is also determined by stratal features of the lexicon, which, as we will see, considerably complicates the picture.

2.2. A separate class of words that form exceptions to (i), above, are monosyllabic words and words with final stress that end in a full vowel. The [+native] vocabulary does not have many of these, and some of those have irregular plurals. But, as a rule, such words take -s plurals when they end in [a], [o], or [u] and -en plurals only when they end in diphthongs or in front vowels. Examples:

[4] For instance, Booij and van Santen (1995). Booij (1997) uses a formulation that is closer to ours. Notice, incidentally, that Dutch never developed alternants of -s like in English hous -houses; after stems ending in [s] or [z] the plural suffix is always -en.

(5)	a.	pa	[a]	pa's		'dad'
		po	[o]	po's		'bedpan'
		knie	[i]	knieën	[knijən]	'knee'
		reu	[ö]	reuen	[röjən]	'male dog'

The [-native] words of this type follow the same pattern:

(5)	b.	tabóe	[u]	tabóe's		'taboo'
		cadéau	[o]	cadéau's		'present'
		genié	[i]	geniéën	[ʒəníjən]	'genius'

Since condition (i) predicts that monosyllabic words have -en plurals, it appears that the application of (i) is preempted by the following more specific condition:

(iii) 'Avoid hiatus'

Condition (iii) is, actually, a general condition on the surface form of Dutch words, the details of which have been described in Zonneveld (1978). For our purposes, it suffices to observe that monosyllabic words as well as polysyllabic words with stressed final syllables, have plurals in -en when they end in the glides /j/ or /w/ or in one of the diphthongs [ɛi], [au], [ʌü] ((5c)). A stated above, words ending in a single long vowel sometimes also have plurals in -en). Here, the choice is determined by the nature of the vowel: -en plurals are found in words ending in the front vowels [i], [e], [ü], [ö] ((5d)). But notice that not a few loanwords ending in a front vowel still have plurals in -s ((5e)). That seems to indicate that the generalization (iii) about the [-native] vocabulary also refers to polysyllabic words ending in stressed syllables.

(5)	c.	haai	[j]	haaien	[hajən]	'shark'
		vrouw	[w]	vrouwen		'woman'
	d.	zee	[e]	zeeën	[zejən]	'sea'
		idée	[e]	idéeën		'idea'
		geníe	[i]	geníeën		'genius'
	e.	logé	[e]	logé's		'guest'
		bougíe	[i]	bougíes		'sparkplug'
		menu	[ü]	menu's		'menu'

2.3. With a few exceptions, words ending in schwa take -s plurals in both vocabularies:

(5)	f.	boete	boetes	'fine'
		garáge	garáges	'id.'

The other option is a plural form in -n, and since both boetes and boeten would be perfect trochees, condition (i) cannot make a prediction here about the choice of the plural ending. The preference for -s plurals in this type of word should rather be interpreted as a morphological condition: 'Plurals should be marked'. The general tendency in the standard language to drop final -n would make *boeten* PLUR indistinguishable from *boete* SING.[5]

3. Polyllables and trochaic form

3.1. So far, the descriptive evidence confirms that Dutch plural formation is subject to the conditions (i) - (iii), where (ii) and (iii) constrain (i). In polysyllabic words ending in consonants, however, the situation is more complex.

An important class of counterexamples to (i) are polysyllabic native words with an unstressed final syllable which contains a full vowel followed by a consonant. Such words have plurals in -en, also when the base is trochaic. This is true, first, for all words ending in the rhyme -ing, irrespective of whether -ing is (part of) a morpheme or not. Secondly, it is true of a small group of other words ending in consonants that have a short vowel or sometimes even a long vowel in the final syllable. Examples (where + indicates a morpheme boundary):

(6)	a.	haring	haringen	'herring'
		won + ing	won + ingen	'house'
		leer + ling	leer + lingen	'pupil'
	b.	leeuwerik	leeuweriken	'lark'
		havik	haviken	'hawk'
		schaduw	schaduwen	'shadow'
		lichaam	lichamen	'body'

These words sharply contrast in their plural formation with the frequent type of word with schwa in the final syllable. Apart from a few exceptions or alternative plurals in a more literary style, such words never have -en plurals in the modern language:[6]

---

5 The exception are words like blind + e, 'blind person', derived from the corresponding adjectives with a suffix -e. These always take an -n plural: blinden, 'blind persons'. The same applies to nouns formed on the basis of past participles like gewond, 'wounded', gewond + e, 'wounded person', plural gewonde + n, 'wounded persons'.

6 German words of the type Wagen, 'car', often have plurals with 0-endings and sometimes Umlaut; in Dutch, such words always take an overt plural ending -s, irrespective of grammatical gender.

(7)

wagen	wagens	'car'
lepel	lepels	'spoon'
bakk + er	bakk + ers	'baker'
bodem	bodems	'bottom'

Prosodically, the words exemplified in (6a) and (6b) are peculiar because they form a trochee with a non-reduced vowel in the final syllable, followed by a consonant (or even a cluster, as in the case of avond, 'evening', plural avonden). In this respect, they constitute the Dutch counterpart of words undergoing the 'Arab rule' in the stress pattern of English.

We therefore assume that, in the [+native] vocabulary, a full vowel cannot occupy the weak branch of a foot. Hence, the weak syllables in (6) form a foot head instead, leading to the following structures:

(8)

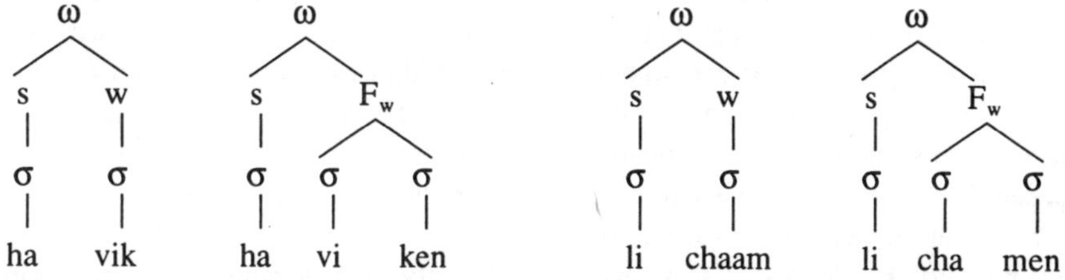

However, what happens in words like havik is not what happens with [-native] words of the same prosodic type. Polysyllabic words ending in obstruents like bivak, 'bivouac', kajak, 'id.', and almanak, 'almanac', and also words ending in sonorants like toekan, 'tucan', radar, 'id.', horizon, 'id.', and festival, 'id.', normally take -s plurals. So here, the two vocabularies diverge since in [-native] words a full vowel *can* occupy the weak branch of a foot.

There is a small class of exceptions that corroborate the prosodic analysis proposed above in an interesting way. A number of [-native] words with prefinal stress and a final syllable with a short vowel followed by a sonorant consonant can also have a plural in -en. Next to eléktron - eléktrons, 'id.', and rector, 'rectors', 'id.', we also have eléktron - elektrónen, and rector - rectóren, where stress shifts to the penultimate syllable, with concomitant lengthening of the vowel. That is, if the parsing is as in (9)a, below, the plural forms preserve the trochaic structure of the base form. If the parse is as in (10)b, with the final syllable not integrated, plurals are formed by adding -en and the formation of an additional foot.[7]

[7] Booij (1997) takes the position that alternative stems such as elektroon-, motoor- (which als occur in adjectival formations) should be listed as allomorphs. This question we will not discuss here.

(9)

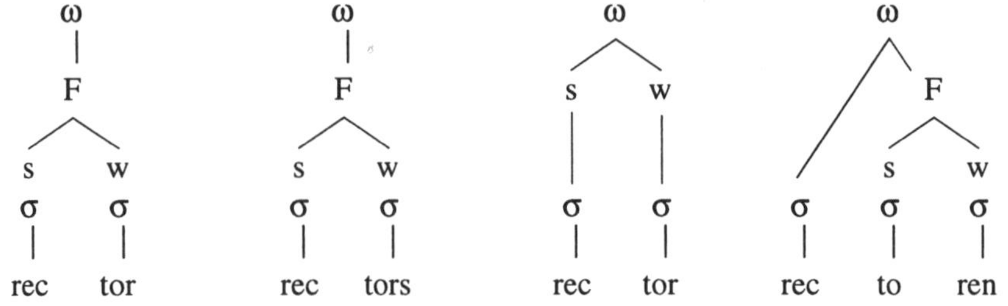

3.2. From these cases especially, it is clear that a generalization that is primarily based on the location of stress is not adequate. Wagen and woning, and bivak and havik have the same stress pattern, but different plurals. Therefore, we maintain that plural formation in nouns is, first of all, determined by foot structure. Formulated in terms of output conditions, Dutch seems to prefer plurals that preserve a trochee at the end of the word. At the same time, prosodic preferences are sometimes overridden by features of the lexicon and the morphology, in particular, the stratal feature [-native]. We saw earlier that [-native] monosyllabic words ending in a consonant prefer plurals in -s. A similar remarkable difference between the two vocabularies can be observed in the plural formation of a number of polysyllabic [-native] words with final stress. While condition (i) would predict an -en plural, many polysyllabic words of this type unexpectedly take -s rather than -en. Some typical examples of bisyllabic words of this type are given in (10a); examples of the same type of word with an -en plural are given in (10b).

(10)	a.	hotél	hotéls	'id.'
		balkón	balkóns	'balcony'
		pastóor	pastóors	'parish priest'
	b.	barón	barónnen	'baronet'
		kanón	kanónnen	'gun'
		kantóor	kantóren	'office'

The distribution of -s and -en in this category is largely unpredictable. Since, under any prosodic analysis, whether primarily based on stress or on foot structure, plurals such as balkón - balkóns are 'wrong', the reasonable conclusion is that the tendency for [-native] words to have plurals in -s is a true stratal feature of the lexicon and that plural formation is one of the features that mark the Dutch [-native] vocabulary as such.[8] Like we saw earlier in some examples of polysyllabic words ending in front vowels, words ending in sonorant

---

8 We use the feature [stratal] in the sense of Itô and Mester 1995. It would apear that their tripartite division of the Japanese vocabulary into Yamato, Foreign and Assimilated foreign, by and large corresponds to [+native], [foreign] and [-native] in Dutch. Interestingly, whereas words like agént - agénten have -en plurals, words that are more or less pronounced as if they were French, like expért, [ɛkspɛ́:ʁ], 'id.', take -s plurals: expérts [ɛkspɛ́:ʁs], not *expérten.

consonants also take -s rather than -en. However, -s plurals do not occur in polysyllabic loanwords ending in obstruents or clusters of sonorant and obstruent:

(10)	c.	florét	florétten	'fencing-sword'
		patát	patátten	'french fried'
		talént	talénten	'id.'
		ag + ént	agénten	'id.'
		debut + ánt	debutánten	'id.'

The same unexpected -s in loanwords with final stress turns up in some words with suffixes that are [-native], of which Dutch has quite a few. Generally, affixed words follow the general pattern of plural formation in monomorphemic words in both vocabularies (Booij and van Santen 1995:67), but there are some exceptions. For instance, a number of words with the [-native] suffixes -eur and -ier that form names of persons have plural froms with -s. These words, examples of which are given in (10d), are in clear contrast with the examples of suffixed words in (10e) and with the non-suffixed words in (10f):

(10)	d.	bank + iér	bankíers	'banker'
		regiss + éur	regisséurs	'movie director'
	e.	Arab + íer	Arabíeren	'Arab'
		Marokk + áan	Marokkánen	'Maroccan'
		Rom + éin	Roméinen	'Roman'
	f.	rivíer	rivíeren	'river'
		platáan	platánen	'plane-tree'
		koníjn	koníjnen	'rabbit'

But here too, -s plurals are the exception; the examples in (10e) and (10f) follow the general pattern that word stems ending in a superheavy syllable with long vowel followed by consonant take -en plurals.

3.3. We can now summarize the main conditions for plural formation in the following way ($]_{St}$ is right edge of the Stem, $]_{st}$ is right edge of the word).

(v) $*F\,]_{st}$ +en
(F branching: s w)

(vi) $*s/z\,]_{St}$ +s

(vii) $*V]_{St}$ +en

(viii) 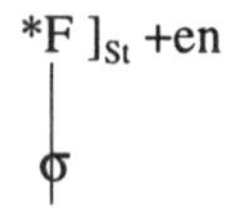 [-native]

(ix) 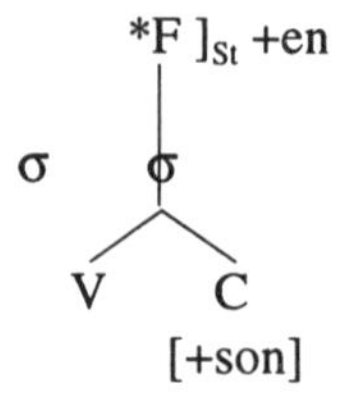 [-native]

The general condition is (v): if the word stem is a trochee at the right hand edge, the plural suffix to choose is -s. The specific conditions that restrict (v) are (vi) and (vii). These are valid for both vocabularies: stems ending in /s/ or /z/ do not have -s plurals; stems ending in full vowels do not take -en plurals in the unmarked case.

The formulation of condition (v) excludes the unbalanced trochees in [+native] words like havik, where the final syllables are parsed as separate feet. Condition (v), however, includes [-native] words like bivak and radar which take an -s prulal. The conditions (viii) and (ix) state that native words predominantly take an s-plural when monosyllabic, and when polysyllabic if the last syllable is stressed and ends in a sonorant consonant.

The two latter conditions replace the tentative generalization expressed in (ii), above: whereas there are categeories of [-native] words that unexpectedly take -s plurals, there are also types of loanwords (floret, Arabier) that regularly take a plural in -en.

This summary statement, to be sure, disregards a number of details and exceptions that were amply discussed above. We believe, however, that is gives a fair picture of the main tendencies and, especially, that is adequately summarizes both the convergence and the divergence of the two strata in the Dutch lexicon as far as plural formation is concerned.

4. Plurals and diminutives

4.1. Rather than going into more details of the formation of plurals, we would next like to discuss the relation between diminutive formation and plural formation, and draw some conclusions about the interaction of phonology and morphology.

Plural formation, as we have seen, is sensitive to both prosodic structure and to features of the lexicon and the morphology. More specifically, plural formation also generalizes over morphological and lexical categories. But that is not true, or to a much lesser extent, for the other process of word formation in Dutch that is highly sensitive to prosody, namely, diminutive formation. We will only discuss words ending in sonorant consonants here, since for words ending in obstruents and vowels, the situation is simple. Words ending in an obstruent have the diminutive ending -je, with only few exceptions, words ending in full vowels take -tje, usually regarded as the underlying or basic form. The alternations that are relevant to our purposes are exemplified in (11), below:

(11)	STEM	DIMINUTIVE	PLURAL	GLOSS
a.	bal	balletje		ball
	taal	taaltje	-en	language
	ring	ringetje		ring
b.	haring	haringkje		herring
	woning	woninkje	-en	house
	wandeling	wandelingetje		walk
	leerling	leerlingetje		pupil
c.	toekan	toekannetje		tucan
	motor	motortje	-s	engine
	festival	festivalletje		festival
d.	bacíl	bacílletje		bacillus
	tonéel	tonéeltje		stage
	bazín	bazínnetje	-en	boss FEM
	koníjn	koníjntje		rabbit

4.2. As the examples in (11a) show, diminutive formation is, first of all, sensitive to the moraic structure of the rhyme, plural formation is not. Bal and paal have the same plural but not the same alternant for the diminutive. The examples in (11b) show that diminutive formation is also sensitive to details of stress assignment. Words like haring take -tje, but words like wandeling, with secondary stress on the final rhyme, take -etje, just like bal in (1). Plural formation in the [+native] vocabulary disregards such differences; all words ending in -ing have -en plurals, irrespective of the details of their prosodic structure.

Interesting here is the example toekan in (11c). According to most analyses in the literature, a secondary stress on the final syllable, -kan, triggers diminutive formation with the suffix -etje rather than with -tje. More generally, words ending in -Vr, like motor, radar, will take -tje, whereas words ending in -Vn prefer the long alternant -etje. For the purpose of plural formation, however, these [-native] words are generally parsed as trochees: motors (but sometimes: motóren) and toekans rather than toekannen. Where plural formation and diminutive formation do coincide, however, is in the category of [-native] words with final stress, where, with the exception of words like balkón - balkóns, discussed earlier, the plural suffix is -en and the diminutive has the long form -etje and not -tje. The examples in (11d) again show that vowel quality overrides stress in diminutive formation: bacíl, with a short final vowel, selects -etje, but tonéel, with a long vowel, does not.

This confirms, first of all, the position taken in Trommelen 1983 that diminutive formation is a 'local' process. More specifically, it is sensitive to details of stress assignment that have not yet been spelled out when plural formation applies. This, we think, is an important conclusion because it shows that word forms do not necessarily have one, uniform prosodic shape at different levels of word formation. On the interface of phonological and morphological structure in Dutch, plural formation is an 'early' process that is sensitive to some aspects of the prosody but also to morphological category and stratal features, whereas a process such as diminutive formation is a late, postlexical process that is sensitive to details of prosodic and segmental structure, and not to morphological category; also, stratal features like [-native] do not play any role.

5. Conclusion

Our most important goal in this paper has been to show that the formation of Dutch nominal plurals is constrained by only a few prosodic conditions that interact in a complicated way. First of all, the basic condition, which we summarized as 'form a trochee at the right edge' has different consequences for the [+native] and for the [-native] vocabulary. Second, the [-native] vocabulary is, to an extent, subject to an independent and non-prosodic constraint: 'form plurals with the suffix -s'. In order to be able to focus on the cases where the vocabularies converge, we have assumed that -s plurals are a stratal feature of the language, rather than introducing the notion of 'co-phonologies'.[9] This also ties in with our claim that plural formation, unlike diminutive formation, is an early rule, at the lexical level, and therefore subject to morphological categorization.

References

Booij, Geert E. (1997): Non-derivational Phonology Meets Lexical Phonology. In: Iggy Roca (ed): *Derivations and Constraints in Phonology*, 261-288. Oxford: Clarendon Press.

Booij, Geert E. and A. van Santen (1995): *Morfologie: de woordstructuur van het Nederlands*. Amsterdam: Amsterdam University Press.

Clahsen, Harald, Gary Marcus, Susanne Bartke and Richard Wiese (1996): Compounding and Inflection in German Child Language. In: Geert E. Booij and Jaap van Marle (eds): *Yearbook of Morphology* 1995, 115-142. Dordrecht: Kluwer Academic Publishers.

Haeringen, C.B. van (1947): De meervoudsvorming in het Nederlands. *Mededelingen der KNAW, Afdeling Letterkunde,* Nieuwe Reeks, 10:5, 131-152.

Hayes, Bruce (1995): *Metrical Stress Theory*. Chicago, London: Chicago University Press.

Hulst, Harry van der and Jan G. Kooij (1997): Prosodische keuzes bij meervoudsvorming in het Nederlands. A. van Santen and M. van der Wal (eds): *Taal in tijd en ruimte*, 365-373 Leiden: SNL.

Inkelas, Sharon, Orhan Orgun and Cheryl Zoll (1997): The Implications of Lexical Exceptions for the Nature of Grammar. In: Iggy Roca (ed): *Derivations and Constraints in Phonology*. Oxford: Clarendon Press, 393-418.

---

9 For critical discussion of co-phonologies, see Inkelas, Orgun and Zoll (1997).

Itô, Junko and Armin Mester (1995): Japanese Phonology. In: John Goldsmith (ed): *The Handbook of Phonological Theory*. Cambridge, Mass.: Blackwell, 817-838.
Kager, René (1993): Alternatives to the Iambic-Trochaic Law. *Natural Language and Linguistic Theory* 11, 381-432.
— (1994): On Defining Complex Templates. *Proceedings of the Twelfth West Coast Conference on Formal Linguistics*, 19-34. Stanford.
Neef, Martin (1997): The Organization of German Nominal Inflection. Paper presented at the Marburg Conference on the Phonology and Morphology of the Germanic Languages.
Trommelen, Mieke (1983): *The Syllable in Dutch, with Special Reference to Diminutive Formation*. Dordrecht: Foris Publications.
Zonneveld, Wim (1978): *A Formal Theory of Exceptions in Generative Phonology*. Lisse: Peter de Ridder Press.

Ingo Plag

Morphological haplology in a constraint-based morpho-phonology

1. Introduction*

Morphological haplology is generally viewed as a dissimilatory process that interacts in some way with morphological structure. In spite of a long research tradition on this pervasive phenomenon, the exact nature of morphological haplology has remained obscure. The current state of affairs can still be characterized in the words of Maurice Grammont, published more than a century ago:

> The topic is not new. Everyone has talked about dissimilation, everyone has seen examples of it and has cited cases, but no one has ever established what it really is, dissimilation, under which conditions it occurs, and which rules govern it. (Grammont 1895: 9, my translation[1]).

More recent approaches to haplology have stressed that it is best described as the avoidance of identical phonetic or phonological material in morphologically complex words. Basically, two versions of this idea have been developed, the so-called Repeated Morph Constraint and so-called Stem-End Haplology. Consider the definitions in (1) and (2):

(1) Repeated Morph Constraint (e.g. Menn/McWhinney 1984)
the avoidance of adjacent identical morphs

(2) Stem-End Haplology (e.g. Stemberger 1981: 791)
the absence of "an affix or clitic [...] when the adjacent part of the stem is homophonous to it"

Several problems are still unresolved. The first problem concerns the universality of morphological haplology. Haplology, in one form or another, seems to occur in almost any language with enough morphology to create phonetically identical sequences. For example, in an impressive survey of cross-linguistic data, Dressler (1976) posits the strong universal constraint given in (3a), which is illustrated with two examples from German in (3b):

* I would like to thank Birgit Alber, Geert Booij, Wolfgang Kehrein, Roland Noske, Richard Wiese and the participants of the workshop for their critical comments and helpful suggestions. Remaining errors and shortcomings are, of course, my own.

[1] The original French text runs as follows:
"Le sujet n'est pas nouveau: tout le monde a parlé de la dissimilation; chacun en a rencontré des exemples et cité des cas, mais personne n'a jamais établi ce que c'est que la dissimilation, dans quelles conditions elle se produit et quelles en sont les lois".

(3) a. *...V_i C_j] V_i C_j...]
b. **honig-ig*, **Zauber-er-in*

Although apparently pertinent in a large number of different languages, (3a) appears to be too strong, since counterexamples can easily be found. In German adjectival inflection for instance, such sequences are readily admitted (cf. *eigen-en* 'own, pl.'). Thus morphological haplology seems to be universal in some sense but language-specific and even affix-specific in another sense. The latter has been argued for by Booij (1983: 257), who advocates the existence of affix-specific haplology rules also on the grounds that sometimes identity is avoided by the deletion of material (as in G. *Zauberin*, **Zauber-er-in* 'scorceress') and sometimes by the ungrammaticality of both the full complex form and the deleted form (cf. G. **honig-ig*, **hon-ig*).

Another problem concerns the interaction of haplology with other phonological properties, e.g. prosodic structure. In particular, I will show below that haplology sometimes depends on the suprasegmental properties of the complex word in question, such as syllabic structure and stress.

A third problem is which of the definitions in (1) and (2) is the more adequate one, i.e. more useful for the description and explanation of the data. The Repeated Morph Constraint restricts haplology to strictly morphological units whereas Stem-End haplology also includes cases where phonological identity of stem and an adjacent morpheme is sufficient to trigger haplology, irrespective of the morphological status of the material of the stem. This relates to the fourth problem, namely whether morphological haplology is essentially a morphological or a phonological phenomenon. Finally, it is unclear whether identity avoidance in complex words is best described in a rule-based or in a constraint-based model.

In the following I will try to find possible solutions to these problems by reexamining a number of pertinent phenomena from English, German and Dutch. The morphological categories involved are English *-ize* derivatives, German and English feminine person nouns, and the Dutch suffix *-er* in person nouns and comparatives. The analysis is couched in the framework of Optimality Theory (e.g. Prince and Smolensky 1993).

2. Proposal

I propose that morphological haplology results from a family of universal constraints on the repetition of identical phonological elements, OCP ('Obligatory Contour Principle', Leben 1973), which interact with other, phonological and morphological, constraints. By introducing universal violable constraints that are ranked in a language-specific and affix-specific way, the apparent paradox can be resolved that haplology seems to be universal and language- and affix-specific at the same time. The variability of haplology both across and within languages follows naturally from the interaction and the individual rankings of the constraints.

OCP constraints have been proposed before by Yip (to appear) in order to account for the Repeated Morph Constraint. She puts forward the following constraints:

(4) OCP (feature), OCP (segment), OCP (affix), OCP (stem)

I propose the following constraints instead:

(5) OCP (feature), OCP (segment), OCP (onset), OCP (nucleus), OCP (onset, coda)

My proposal differs from Yip's in important respects. I eliminate the two constraints making reference to morphological instead of phonological structure, i.e. Yip's OCP (affix) and OCP (stem), and elaborate the kinds of phonological structure OCP constraints can operate on.[2] This has two main consequences. First, in my approach, morphological haplology is exclusively triggered by phonological constraints, which, as we will see, is both empirically and theoretically preferable. The increase in the number of different OCP constraints is independently needed, as we will see below. Second, by eliminating OCP (affix) and OCP (stem) as constraints, I argue against the Repeated Morph Constraint. It will be shown that both the Repeated Morph Constraint and Stem-End-Haplology are the consequence of the same mechanisms. My claims are summarized in (6) and (7):

(6) Haplology results from the operation of the OCP constraints in (5), in interaction with other prosodic and morphological constraints relevant for the morphological category in question.

(7) The ranking of the pertinent constraints is language-specific.

In the following section I will present evidence for these claims on the basis of data from English, German and Dutch.

3. Illustration and evidence

3.1. English *-ize* derivatives

English verbs derived by the suffixation of *-ize* feature some peculiar and apparently variable phonological properties. Thus base-final segments are often deleted (as in *emphasis - emphasize*), base-final consonants may change (as in *Celtic - Celticize*), vowels may alternate (as in *gentile - gentilize*), consonants appear to be inserted between the base and the

---

[2] Although the account of haplology proposed below crucially rests on the notion of adjacency, nothing will be said about the representation of superficially non-adjacent subsyllabic constituents within one syllable (cf. OCP (onset, coda)) or across two adjacent syllables (cf. OCP (onset) and OCP (nucleus)). My model of haplology and the idea of OCP as such suggest that on some level or tier of the phonological representation the elements in question must be adjacent. It seems that current models of representation need to be revised to be able to account for the phenomena discussed in this paper. How exactly this may be done remains a matter of future research.

suffix (as in *stigma* - *stigmatize*) and even stress may be shifted (as in *cátholic* - *cathólicìze*[3]) or reduced (as in *géntìle* - *géntilìze*).[4] The phenomenon with which I will deal here is the truncation of base-final segments if the base word ends in a syllable in which onset and rhyme are identical. The data in (8) illustrate this regular phenomenon.

(8)	*femininize	feminize
	*minimumize	minimize
	*metathesisize	metathesize

In her account of these facts, Raffelsiefen (1996) proposes an output-oriented constraint which prohibits identical onsets in adjacent syllables in the derived word: $*O_iRO_i$. My term 'OCP (onset)' is only a different name for this constraint, which reflects that it is part of a larger family of related constraints. Raffelsiefen's account works for most of the data she presents, but the picture seems to be more complicated. Thus, in my sample of 284 20th century neologisms I have found 6 words that do not feature haplology, contra to Raffelsiefen's predictions. Consider the forms in (9):

(9)	strýchninìze	*strychnize
	clássicìze	*classize
	dilletántìze	*dilletize
	mírrorìze	*mirrize
	pótentìze	*potize
	térrorìze[5]	*terrize

On closer inspection, the contradictory data reveal a striking regularity, namely that all base words of the forms cited by Raffelsiefen in favour of the constraint are polysyllabic (*emphasize - emphasis, metathesize - metathesis, feminize - feminine, maximize - maximum*, etc.), whereas all the counterexamples (except one, *dilletante*, to be discussed shortly) are disyllabic. At first sight the constraint appears to be sensitive to the number of syllables. However, the violators and conformers also differ in the stress pattern. Thus, the base words of the haplological forms all have antepenultimate stress with two unstressed syllables following, i.e. they are dactyls, while all violators do not exhibit a stress lapse. That this stress-based description is superior to the simple counting of syllables is corroborated by the behavior of *dilletántìze*, whose base word has main stress on the final syllable (which all the other polysyllabic forms cited lack). In sum, the operation of OCP (onset) needs to be restricted to those cases in which a base with two unstressed syllables precedes *–ize*. By way of illustration, a form like **féemininìze* exhibits a stress lapse, which would only be tolerable if the last two onsets were not identical. Since they are identical,

---

3 Following established conventions, I use acute accent to indicate primary stress, grave accent to indicate secondary stress.

4 See Plag (1997: chapter 7.2) for a comprehensive account of the stem allomorphy of *-ize* derivatives.

5 Raffelsiefen considers *terrorize* a French borrowing. According to the *OED* this is incorrect. Semantically, this word is also completely regular (see Plag 1997, in press for a detailed account of the semantics of *-ize* derivatives).

**fémininìze* is an illicit formation. Derivatives like *térrorìze* do not exhibit a stress lapse, hence they behave according to the generalization.

In Plag (1997: 155-191) I have proposed a number of phonological constraints that govern the segmental and prosodic make-up of *-ize* derivatives. Of these constraints, the following are relevant for haplology:

(10) a. interacting constraints (see Plag 1997 for details):
OCP (onset): no identical onsets in adjacent syllables
IDENT HEAD: The prosodic head of the base is the prosodic head of the derivative (= no stress shift).
CLASH HEAD: Bases must not have a final prosodic head (= *-ize* may not attach to iambic bases).
b. constraint ranking:
IDENT HEAD >> CLASH HEAD >> OCP (onset)

IDENT HEAD is one of the constraints that ensures the recoverability of the base in a derived word by not allowing a stress shift. CLASH HEAD expresses the well-known fact that languages tend to avoid sequences of adjacent stressed syllables. Assuming that *-ize* carries secondary stress, iambic bases would lead to a clash of the two stresses. Such clashes are only tolerated with *-ize* derivatives in order to satisfy a higher ranked constraint. Consider the interaction of these constraints in the following tableau:

(11) OCP (onset) and *-ize* derivatives

Candidates	IDENT HEAD	CLASH HEAD	OCP (onset)
☞ féminìze			
féminìnìze			*!
☞ metáthesìze			
metathésisìze	*!		*
metáthesisìze			*!
☞ strýchn[ɪ]nìze			*
strýchn̄ze		*!	
☞ clássicìze			*
clássìze		*!	
☞ dilletántìze		*	*
dílletìze	*!		
dillétantìze	*!		*

On the one hand, derivatives on the basis of dactylic base words (*feminize, metathesize*) exhibit haplology because they would otherwise violate OCP (onset).[6] As shown in detail in Plag (1997), constraints against base truncation are ranked lower than the constraints in (10). On the other hand, derivatives on the basis of trochees are never truncated because this would lead to a violation of the higher-ranked CLASH HEAD. The candidate with an iambic base *dilletántìze* is optimal because the two lower-ranked constraints are violated in order to satisfy the highest constraint, IDENT HEAD. The haplological candidate **dílletize* is ruled out because of the stress shift.

The consistency of the patterns emerging from the operation of OCP (onset) is strong evidence not only for the reality of this constraint, but also for its interaction with other prosodic constraints. It is this interaction that triggers the apparent variability of haplology in *-ize* formations.

The proposed analysis has strong theoretical implications because it seriously challenges two widely-shared views on morpho-phonological processes. First, a number of people (e.g. Aronoff 1976, Booij 1977) have claimed that the truncation of stems always involves morphological constituents. Similarly, the Repeated Morph Constraint predicts that haplology can only occur if the adjacent elements are morphs. In my model, haplology effects are explained without making reference to the adjacency of identical morphs, i.e. the morphological status of the truncated strings does not play a role. In the following I will argue that restricting truncation to morphological entities is ill-advised.

Morphological truncation rules have been proposed, for example, in Aronoff (1976) or Booij (1977). The classic example of such a rule is the truncation of the verbal ending *-ate* when *-able* is attached (e.g. *demonstrate - demonstrable*). According to Aronoff (1976), this rule must make reference to the morphemic status of *-ate* since non-morphological *-ate* (as in *debate*) does not truncate (**debable*). As pointed out by Anderson (1992: 280), these facts can equally well be captured by a purely phonological generalization: only secondarily stressed *-ate* can be deleted, irrespective of the morphological status of the string [eɪt].

In general, it can be observed that truncation does often not involve morphological constituents. Corbin (1987: 345), for example, provides a whole range of French data which demonstrate that the deleted sequence at the end of the base cannot be a morpheme. The same is true for *-ize* derivatives. For example, the deletion of base-final [ɪ] in many of the neologisms under discussion can hardly be analyzed as the truncation of a putative morpheme *-y*, since [ɪ] does not seem to have morphemic status in words like *anthropólogy, (Madame) Bóvary, fántasy, mediócrity, Nórmandy* or *vaséctomy*, all of which form *-ize* derivatives under loss of *-y*. In particular, I am unaware of any claims that *-logy* or *-ity* are bi-morphemic suffixes, consisting of *-log-* and *-y*, or *-it-* and *-y*, respectively. What the six words really have in common is not the morphology of putative *-y*, but their prosody: they end in or are dactyls that end in a vowel. As demonstrated in Plag (1997), such a phonological structure leads to the truncation of the final vowel across the board, ignoring morphological structure: *anthropologize, bovarize, fantasize, mediocritize, Normandize, vasectomize*. This point is corroborated by the form *patinize*, where the final schwa of the base word *patina* does not represent a suffix either, but is nevertheles truncated because the

6 Consonant-final dactylic bases words that do not lead to an OCP violation are never truncated, cf. *federal - federalize*. See Plag (1997) for detailed discussion.

base conforms to the kind of prosodic structure that necessitates the deletion of the final vowel when *-ize* is attached. Similar arguments hold for the haplology cases, where *-ite* in *appetite*, or *-is* in *metathesis* can hardly be regarded as morphemes (if morphemes are units of sound and meaning).

Paul Kiparsky (personal communication, August 1997) pointed out to me that a form like *parallelize* is counter-evidence to my claims, because my model incorrectly predicts that the truncated form **parallize* be optimal. If, alternatively, only morphemic [əl] could be truncated, the existence of *parallelize* would be naturally accounted for.

This argumentation is not entirely convincing, however. First, *parallelize* is a very old form, first attested 1610, which means that it perhaps does not reflect the prosodic constraints of present-day productive morphology. This is corroborated by the fact that today's native speakers generally prefer the synonymous converted verb *parallel* to *parallelize* (see also the respective entries in the *OED*). Second, it seems that suffixal *-al* is equally almost never truncated (cf. *federalize* vs. **federize*), so that the argument in favor of morphological truncation collapses. Third, even if we allow *parallelize* to be a *possible* derivative (and not only an *actual* one), it is still conceivable that OCP (onset) needs to be further specified for phonological features. For example, [l] might be allowed to appear in identical onsets whereas other consonants might not. Unfortunately, there are no data that could show this, because all stems which can take adjectival *-al* and which end in [l] take *-ar* instead of *-al* as an adjectival suffix (cf. **polal* vs. *polar*).[7] In principle, the featural specification of OCP constraints is not unusual[8] and could also be used to solve the problem at hand. In view of the arguments just presented it is however preferable to assign idiosyncratic status to the word *parallelize*.

In summary, the idea of strictly morphological truncation has two main flaws. It necessitates the postulation of otherwise unmotivated morphological structure, and it cannot explain the robust phonological generalizations that hold across morphologically diverse derivatives.

We may now turn to other kinds of derivational processes which feature haplology.

3.2. German (and English) feminine person nouns

In German, derivatives ending in the person noun forming suffix *-er* may combine with the feminine suffix *-in* to denote female persons. The semantics of *-er* derivatives is rather flexible, they can for example denote agents or inhabitants (*Läufer* 'runner', *Marburger* 'person from Marburg'), hence the label 'person noun' used in this paper.[9] In the following we will consider some well-known phonological peculiarities of some of these forms when combined with the feminine suffix *-in*.

---

7 This is an interesting fact by itself, because it shows the operation of another OCP constraint (to be discussed below) which does not allow identical onset and coda in a single syllable.

8 For example, the occurrence of epenthetic schwa in English verbs and nouns involving the inflectional suffix *-s*, has been explained by a constraint which prohibits adjacent sibilants (see, for example, Yip (to appear), Russell 1997).

9 Note that *-er* derivatives may also denote instruments, as in *Öffner* 'opener'. See Booij (1986) for a semantic account of similar forms in Dutch.

Consider the data in (12):

(12)	a.	Zauber-er	Bewunder-er	Haiger-er
	b.	*Zauber-er-in	*Bewunder-er-in	*Haiger-er-in
	c.	%Zaubrerin	%Bewundrerin	?Haigrerin
	d.	Zauberin	Bewunderin	Haigerin
		'magician (m./f.)'	'admirer (m./f.)'	'male/female from Haiger'
	e.	Lehr-er-in, Fahr-er-in, Kassier-er-in		
		'teacher', 'driver', 'cashier' (all f.)		

While it is clear that the forms in (12b) are ungrammatical, the status of the derivatives in (12c) and (12d) is somewhat controversial. Some sources only allow (12d), others maintain that both patterns can be found. No matter how one wants to account for this variability, it seems that the data in (12c) and (12d) crucially have in common that they avoid the phonetic sequence *[ɐʁɐʁɪn] at the end of the derivatives. In essence, the sequence ✓[ɐʁɐ] is allowed (see 12a), the sequence ✓[ʁɐʁɪn] is allowed (see 12e), but not a combination of the two *[ɐʁɐʁɪn] These facts are usually analyzed as a haplology effect. A similar phenomenon can be observed in English with the corresponding suffixes *-er* and *-ess*:

(13) sorceress/*sorcereress, murderess/*murdereress

We will focus in our analysis on the fully productive pattern in German, since *-ess* is no longer productive in English. In principle, a parallel account could be devised for the English data, but an explanation in terms of lexicalized patterns seems preferable.

To return to the German data, one of the problems traditional rule-based accounts have to face is the nature of the deleted elements. Plank (1981) and Fleischer/Barz (1995) assume that the agentive morpheme *-er* is deleted, as in *Zauber#[er]#in*. However, a truncation of syllables works equally well: or *Zau.be.[re].rin*. I am not aware of any empirical arguments that could be adduced in favor of either solution. As we will shortly see, in an output-oriented model this problem disappears. I propose the following constraints on German feminine person nouns:

(14) Constraints on German feminine person nouns
OCP (nucleus): no identical nuclei in adjacent syllables
MAX: every segment of the input has an identical correspondent in the output (=no deletion)
DEP: every segment of the output has an identical correspondent in the input. (=no epenthesis)
COMPL ONS: no complex onsets in schwa syllables

The constraints in (14) should be uncontroversial, except perhaps COMPL ONS. In German schwa syllables, complex onsets are usually prohibited. The reason for this restriction is unclear, but it can be suspected that it is the combined effect of a number of general constraints on German syllable structure. Be that as it may, COMPL ONS can be seen either as an abbreviation of these constraints or as a constraint in its own right. For the purposes of this paper we can assume the latter, because the details of the prohibition of complex onsets in schwa syllables need not concern us here. The ranking of the constraints varies according to the permissibility of forms such as those in (12c) above. Let us first consider the grammar that rules out derivatives like *Zaubrerin*. I propose the following constraint ranking for this 'grammar 1':

(15) OCP (nucleus) >> COMPL ONS >> MAX (grammar 1)

(16) Haplology and German feminine person nouns, grammar 1

Candidates /tsaubr/-/r/-/in/	OCP (nucleus)	COMPL ONS	MAX	DEP
☞ Zau.be.rin			*	*
Zau.be.re.rin	*!			**
Zau.bre.rin		*		*

In accordance with most analyses in the literature (e.g Wiese 1996) I assume that schwa syllables do not contain a vowel underlyingly. Under this assumption, the derivative *Zauberin* involves a DEP violation (schwa has no correspondent in the input) and a MAX violation (one /r/ does not have a correspondent in the output). *Zauberin* is more optimal than *Zaubrerin* because the latter derivative violates the higher-ranked constraint prohibiting complex onsets in schwa syllables. In other words, in this grammar the loss of input /r/ is more easily tolerated than a complex onset in a schwa syllable.

Speakers who prefer *Zaubrerin* over *Zauberin* have a grammar ('grammar 2') where the ranking of COMPL ONS and MAX is reversed.[10] Consider (17):

(17) Haplology and German feminine person nouns, grammar 2

Candidates /tsaubr/-/r/-/in/	OCP (nucleus)	MAX	COMPL ONS	DEP
Zau.be.rin		*!		*
Zau.be.re.rin	*!			**
☞ Zau.bre.rin			*	*

The haplology data so far do not provide evidence for the exact ranking of DEP in either grammar, since all pertinent candidates violate this constraint, and the non-haplological candidate **Zaubererin* is ruled out anyway by OCP (nucleus).

[10] There are also speakers like one of the editors of this volume, Wolfgang Kehrein, who equally accept *Zaubrerin* and *Zauberin* (**Zaubererin* is impossible even with these speakers). In this kind of grammar ('grammar 3'), MAX and COMPL ONS are crucially non-ranked, yielding two optimal candidates.

It might be argued that the rejection of *Zaubererin* is not due to a violation of OCP (nucleus) but due to a violation of OCP (onset). This solution would work for the candidates in (16) and (17), but not for the forms in (12e), such as *Fahrerin* or *Lehrerin*. Thus, any account of haplology must be able to predict that in both grammars, *Fah.re.rin* is more optimal than *Fah.rin*. Consider the tableau in (18), which also features OCP (onset).

(18) Haplology and German feminine person nouns

Candidates /far/-/r/-/in/	OCP (nucleus)	MAX	OCP (onset)	DEP
☞ Fah.re.rin			*	*
Fah.rin		*		

The ungrammaticality of *Fah.rin* indicates that MAX must be ranked higher than OCP (onset), and that the decisive constraint in (16) and (17) must indeed be the one prohibiting identical nuclei.[11] For obvious reasons, COMPL ONS does not play a role in the evaluation of the two candidates *Fahrerin* and *Fahrin*.

Note that the truncation behavior of feminine person nouns cannot be accounted for by making reference to stress-related constraints instead of OCP. At first sight it looks as if a form like **Zaubererin* could be ruled out because of an undesired stress lapse, i.e. a violation of a constraint prohibiting adjacent stressless syllables (*LAPSE, see, for example, Plag 1997). Under this assumption *Fahrerin* would be optimal because there is no stress lapse, and truncation would result in an undesired stress clash. The problem is that with agent and instrument nouns the analysis is equivocal because two adjacent schwa syllables exhibit both identical nuclei and a stress lapse. There is, however, a set of data which show that a stress-related explanation of haplology effects is ill-advised, namely nouns denoting inhabitants. The haplological behavior of inhabitant nouns parallels the one of agent nouns (see, for example, the data in (12) above). Female inhabitant nouns whose base ends in two unstressed syllbales now illustrate that only identical nuclei trigger truncation, whereas non-identical nuclei do not. In other words, stress lapses are tolerated if the nuclei of the pertinent syllables are different. Thus, a female inhabitant of the town *Haiger* in Hessia is called *Haigerin*, not **Haigererin*, whereas a female from *Trebur* (stress only on the first syllable) is called *Treburerin*, not **Treburin*. This pattern is unexpected if *LAPSE (or CLASH) played a significant role. Under the OCP account developed above, however, the pattern is predicted.

To summarize, we can say that identity avoidance in some German feminine person nouns (and the lack thereof in others) can be accounted for by the same type of constraint that are at work with *-ize* derivatives, OCP. What makes the difference in behavior between the two morphological categories in the two languages is the overall ranking of the con-

[11] Of course, **Zaubererin* also violates OCP (onset), but this violation is not decisive, and was therefore not indicated in the tableaux (16) and (17).

straints involved. Furthermore, slight differences in the rankings can straightforwardly account for the variability found among German speakers.

We may now turn to our last case study, the Dutch suffix *-er*.

3.3. Dutch *-er*

In Dutch the suffix *-er* is used to derive denominal and deverbal agent and inhabitant nouns, similar to German and English. Unlike in English and German, however, the Dutch suffix exhibits a peculiar kind of phonologically conditioned allomorphy. There are three allomorphs whose distribution and orthographic and phonetic representation is given in (18):

(19)	a.	*-der*	[dər]	after stressed syllable ending in /r/
	b.	*-er*	[ər]	after stressed syllables not ending in /r/
	c.	*-aar*	[aar]	after unstressed syllable (i.e. elsewhere)

These generalizations are illustrated in (19):

(20)	a.	Bijlmerméer	Bijlmerméerder/*-aar/*-er	'person from B.'
		zéur-	zéurder/*-aar/*-er	'nagger'
	b.	Hoogevéen	Hoogevéener/*-aar/*der	'person from H.'
		Amsterdám	Amsterdámmer/*-aar/*der	'person from A.'
	c.	Díemen	Díemenaar/*-er/*-der	'person from D.'
		lúister-	lúisteraar/*-er/*-der	'listener'

How can this distribution be explained? It seems that any account of the allomorphy must make reference to the prosodic structure of the derivatives and to the fact that in general the sequence [rər] is avoided. The latter generalization can be interpreted as a haplology effect, since onset and coda of the last syllable may not be identical (if the nucleus is a schwa).

Booij (1998) assumes that there are three different suffixes available, of which the correct one is selected on the basis of five constraints: OCP-Place, Superheavy, FootMax, ParseSyll, FootMin, ranked in this order. OCP-Place prohibits an OCP violation on the place tier. Since schwa has no place features, sequences involving a schwa between two identical consonants are ruled out. The high ranking of this constraint ensures that /r/-final bases do not combine with /ər/, but only select one of the other allomorphs. In those cases, the lower-ranked constraints regulate the distribution of *-er* and *-aar* according to the prosodic structure of the derivative.

Booij's account of the haplology facts faces three problems. The first is that in Dutch, schwa is sometimes allowed between identical consonants. Thus, sequences involving /n/ as the consonant are readily allowed. As pointed out by Booij, underspecification of /n/ does not solve the problem, because /n/ must be specified at least for the feature [coronal], even if it is the default consonant in Dutch. He therefore proposes that OCP-place "will not take the place features of the default consonant of a language into account" (1998: 157). I fail to see any independent reason why that should be the case.

The second problem is that the avoidance of /rər/ is part of a larger generalization which includes schwa and all short vowels. For example, the sequences */rɔr/, */rɛr/, */rɑr/, */rur/ are impossible in Dutch (Booij 1995: 43). One can thus formulate a general constraint prohibiting the sequence */rVr/. Obviously, this haplological constraint cannot be explained by OCP-Place, because short vowels do have place features. Notice also that the patterning of schwa together with short vowels is unexpected, because in most, if not all, other environments, schwa behaves like a long vowel (Booij 1995: 19f).

The third problem concerns the nature of the allomorphy involved. Contrary to his earlier analysis (Booij 1995), Booij (1998) assumes that the three suffixes [dər], [ər], and [aːr] are phonologically unrelated and that the allomorphy is best analyzed in terms of allomorph selection. Under this approach, the close phonological similarity between the suffixes remains coincidental. One of Booij's arguments for the assumption of three different underlying representations is the claimed autonomy of the individual suffixes. Thus, there are a number of derivatives where the base does not end in /r/ and still /dər/ is chosen (e.g. *diender* 'policeman'), or where inspite of the stress clash, /-ar/ is chosen (e.g. *leeraar* 'teacher'). In my view, the existence of such lexicalized exceptions is not a compelling argument against a single underlying representation. For example, the fact that some English verbs choose the wrong one of the three phonologically conditioned allomorphs [d], [t], [əd] (e.g. *learn*[t] vs. *learn*[d], *spel*[t] vs. *spel*[d]) does not refute the existence of a phonologically conditioned allomorphy in the default case.

In view of these problems, I suggest an alternative solution, which makes use of an OCP constraint that prohibits syllables in which onset and coda are identical: OCP (onset, coda).

I assume that there is only one underlying representation of the suffix deriving inhabitant and agent nouns, not three. I take it that this underlying representation is /ar/. This assumption departs from earlier approaches which standardly assumed /ər/ as the underlying representation. The main reason for choosing /ar/ is that [ər] can be seen as the destressed realization of /ar/. In the form *Amsterdammer*, for example, the place features of the suffix vowel are lost in order to satisfy a constraint that prohibits adjacent stressed syllables, CLASH. This constraint is well-known in the OT literature and is functionally equivalent to Booij's Superheavy constraint, which prohibits superheavy syllbales in weak positions. (21) illustrates the computation of the optimal candidate:

(21)

Candidates	CLASH	MAX (feature)
☞ Amsterdámmer		*
Amsterdámàar	*!	

With trochaic base words the derivative in [-aar] is optimal because there is no stress clash. But let us turn to haplology. I suggest that the occurrence of [d] should be analyzed as a case of epenthesis, i.e. as a violation of DEP (see (14) above). DEP is violated in order to satisfy OCP (onset, coda). The latter constraint can be provisionally defined as in (22):

(22) OCP (onset, coda): Onset and coda of a single syllable may not be identical. (provisional)

Consider the form *zeurder* 'nagger' which is more optimal than **zeurer*, because lower-ranked DEP is violated in order to satisfy higher-ranked OCP (onset, coda).

(23)

Candidates	CLASH	OCP (onset, coda)	MAX (feature)	DEP
☞ zéurder			*	*
zéurer		*!	*	
zéuràar	*!	*		
zéurdàar	*!			*

Possible candidates in [-aar] are ruled out by CLASH. A potential problem for this kind of analysis arises with trochaic bases, however, which, contrary to the prediction, should end in [-daar] in order to avoid an OCP violation. Consider (24):

(24)

Candidates	OCP (onset, coda)	MAX (feature)	DEP
☜ [12]lúisteràar	*		
☞ lúisterdàar			*
lúisterer	*!	*	
lúisterder		*!	*

We are thus faced with contradictory constraint rankings. To make *luisteraar* the optimal candidate, DEP would have to be ranked higher than OCP (onset, coda). On the other hand, stress-final and monosyllabic bases require the opposite ranking (see (23) above). To solve this dilemma we must take into consideration the fact that in Dutch, long vowels are in general allowed following and preceding /r/, but short vowels are not (✓/rVVr/ vs. */rVr/, see e.g. Booij 1995: 43). This indicates that OCP (onset, coda) must be sensitive to the structure of the nucleus, which leads me to a reformulation of this constraint in terms of moraicity. Assuming that long vowels are bimoraic and that short vowels, schwa and /r/ (in the rhyme) are monomoraic, I propose the following constraint:[13]

---

[12] Hands pointing to the left are used to indicate attested outputs that run counter to the predictions of the model.

[13] Following Hayes (1989), I assume that trimoraic syllables are possible in some languages. For Dutch, others (e.g. van der Hulst 1984, Kager 1989) have already argued that there are superheavy

(25) OCP(onset, coda)/$\mu\mu$: Onset and coda of a bimoraic syllable may not be identical.

This constraint is ranked above MAX (feature) and DEP, which is illustrated in the following tableau:

(26)

Candidates	OCP (onset, coda) / $\mu\mu$	MAX (feature)	DEP
☞ lúisteràar			
lúisterdàar			*!
lúisterer	*!	*	
lúisterder		*!	*

The candidate *luisteraar* violates none of the constraints in (26), hence nothing can be gained by epenthesis or destressing.

CLASH is ranked higher than MAX. For stress-final or mono-syllabic bases ending in /-r/, the tableau looks as follows:

(27)

Candidates	CLASH	OCP (onset, coda) / $\mu\mu$	MAX (feature)	DEP
☞ zéurder			*	*
zéurer		*!	*	
zéuràar	*!			
zéurdàar	*!			*

In general, epenthesis is only allowed with /r/-final bases, because with non-/r/-final bases OCP does not play a role. Instead, epenthesis leads to an additional DEP violation, making each non-epenthesized candidate more optimal than its epenthesized counterpart. Thus the potential candidate **Amsterdamder* is ruled out because it violates DEP, which the optimal candidate *Amsterdammer* does not.

To summarize, the account presented above makes correct predictions concerning the allomorphy of the suffix and has the additional advantage of being able to explain the phonological similarity of the suffix variants. Notice that the proposed constraints yield correct results both under the allomorph selection assumption (à la Booij 1998) and under the phonologically triggered allomorphy approach advocated here. Thus, my model does not only rule out competing attested allomorphs, but also conceivable others (as in **roerdaar, *luisterdaar*, or **Amsterdamder*).

---

syllables, in other words, that the sequence /VVr/ is trimoraic in Dutch. From this assumption it follows that OCP(onset, coda)/$\mu\mu$ rules out bimoraic /rVr/ but allows trimoraic /rVVr/.

There are, however, three problems involved. First, as mentioned above, not all consonants trigger the same haplological effects as does /r/. In terms of the model developed in this paper, this fact calls for a further parametrization of OCP (onset, coda) with respect to the kinds of consonants that fill onset and coda. Such parametrization is not at all unusual. In many languages constraints on possible structures of syllabic constituents must refer to sonority hierarchies or even to individual segments (e.g. Hammond 1997 on English syllables). Thus we can imagine that additional constraints such as OCP (onset, coda)/r and OCP (onset, coda)/n, in the appropriate ranking, regulate the differences between haplology effects when these consonants are involved.[14]

The second problem lies in the fact that *-aar* does not appear after non-coronal sonorants (cf. *bezem-er* vs. **bezem-aar* 'sweeper', Booij 1998). Neither in Booij's account nor in mine can this be derived in a straightforward manner from prosodic constraints, but must be stated as an idiosyncratic property.

Finally, the nature of the epenthetic consonant in Dutch is controversial. It is usually assumed that [n] is the default consonant in Dutch. The postulation of an epenthetic [d] runs counter to this assumption. However, putative epenthetic [d] does not only occur with the person noun forming suffix just discussed but also with the comparative suffix /ər/, the adjective-forming suffixes *-erig* (*zeur-d-erig* 'nagging') and the nominal suffix *-erij* (*boer-d-erij*). This can be interpreted in such a way that [d] has some kind of default status at least in certain morphological categories, if not in Dutch morpho-phonology in general. Under an allomorph selection approach, the generality of [d] is unaccounted for. Further research is necessary to substantiate arguments on the status of [d] in these derivatives.

Turning briefly to haplology in comparatives, an analysis similar to that proposed for person nouns is possible. The major difference between the person noun suffix and the comparative lies in the absence of [-aar] as a variant of the comparative suffix. I propose that this is the direct consequence of a different underlying representation of the comparative, namely /ər/ (as against /ar/ for person nouns). The two attested allomorphs have the distribution given in (`28a), examples are given in (28b):

(28) a. suffix allomorphs of comparatives
-der after stem-final /r/, *-er* elsewhere

b.

duister 'dark'	duisterder
groen 'green'	groener

The pertinent constraints are the same as above, with the interesting difference that LAPSE does not play a role, i.e. it is ranked below the constraints under discussion:

---

[14] A similar solution suggests itself for another peculiarity of Dutch. According to Booij (1995), Dutch does not allow sequences of /l/, long vowel and /l/ (i.e. */lVVl/), but readily admits /lVl/, i.e. a short vowel between two /l/s. This is exactly the reverse of what we observed with /r/. This fact could be accounted for by assuming that there is also an OCP (onset, coda) constraint that is parametrized for bimoraic syllables, OCP (onset, coda)/$\mu\mu$. Given the correct ranking of the two mora-sensitive OCP constraints and the consonant-sensitive OCP constraints, it should be possible to predict the correct optimal forms. The details of such an account remain to be worked out.

(29) Haplology and Dutch comparatives: underlying representation /ər/

Candidates	OCP (onset, coda) / $\mu\mu$	DEP
☞ gróener		
gróender		*!
☞ dúisterder		*
dúisterer	*!	

Therefore, the difference in allomorphy between person nouns on the one hand and the comparative on the other does not lie in the inexplicable absence of a third underlying allomorph, but in a different underlying representation.

To conclude the discussion of haplology with Dutch person nouns and comparatives, we have seen again that a small number of phonological constraints is responsible for haplology effects as well as for other kinds of allomorphy.

4. Conclusion

In this paper I have made a case for an output-oriented approach to morphological haplology. The proposed constrained-based model of haplology was illustrated by the (re-)analysis of a small number of well-known and less well-known phenomena in three Germanic languages. I have argued that, in general, the purely phonological constraints of the OCP family are responsible for morphological haplology effects. These constraints, which rule out adjacent identical phonological structures, are extended in the present model to syllabic contituents such as onset and coda, but not to morphological constituents such as affix or stem. The main advantage of the model lies in the motivation of seemingly contradictory properties of haplology, namely its universality and its variability.

It was shown that the similarities of haplology phenomena across and within languages can be explained by a set of universal phonological constraints against adjacent identical elements. At the same time, the observable variability of haplology among different morphological categories in one language and across languages turns out to be the consequence of affix-specific and language-specific rankings of the OCP constraints. The interaction of OCP constraints with other prosodic and morphological constraints on the other can also explain the variability of haplology among derivatives of the same morphological category (cf. *strychninize* vs. *feminize*).

According to the arguments presented above, the Repeated Morph Constraint and Stem-End Haplology both result from essentially the same mechanisms. Sometimes the phonologically identical elements happen to be exponents of morphemes, sometimes they do not. The former would traditionally be subsumed under the Repeated Morph Constraint, the latter under Stem-End Haplology. In my model this distinction becomes epiphenomenal.

If it is true that morphological haplology is triggered exclusively by OCP constraints, morphological haplology must be seen as a purely phonological phenomenon. It is only the affix-specific ranking of OCP constraints and other prosodic and morphological constraints that makes haplology appear to be a morphological or morpho-phonological phenomenon.

References

Anderson, Stephen R. (1992): *A-morphous Morphology*. Cambridge: CUP.

Aronoff, Mark (1976): *Word Formation in Generative Grammar*. Cambridge: MIT Press.

Booij, Geert E. (1977): *Dutch Morphology. A Study of Word Formation in Generative Grammar*. Lisse: de Ridder.

— (1983): Rezension von: Plank, Frans *Morphologische (Ir-)Regularitäten. Aspekte der Wortstrukturtheorie*, Tübingen: Narr, 1981. *Zeitschrift für Sprachwissenschaft* 2, 251-264.

— (1986): Form and Meaning in Morphology: The Case of Dutch 'Agent Nouns'. *Linguistics* 24, 503-517.

— (1995): *Dutch Phonology*. Oxford: Clarendon.

— (1998): Phonological Output Constraints in Morphology. In: Wolfgang Kehrein and Richard Wiese (eds.): *Phonology and Morphology of the Germanic Languages*. Tübingen: Niemeyer, 143-163.

Corbin, Danielle (1987): *Morphologie dérivationelle et structuration du lexique*. 2 Vols. Tübingen: Niemeyer.

Dressler, Wolfgang (1976): Phono-morphological Dissimilation. W. U. Dressler, O. E. Pfeiffer (eds.): *Phonologica 1976*, 41-48. Innsbruck: Institut für Sprachwissenschaft.

Fleischer, Wolfgang, and Irmhild Barz (1995): *Wortbildung in der deutschen Gegenwartssprache*. 2. Aufl. Tübingen: Niemeyer.

Grammont, Maurice (1895): *La dissimilation consonantique dans les langues indo-européennes et dans les langues romanes*. Dijon: Darrantière.

Hammond, Michael (1997): Vowel Quantity and Syllabification in English. *Language* 73, 1-17.

Hayes, Bruce (1989): Compensatory Lengthening and Moraic Phonology. *Linguistic Inquiry* 20, 253-306.

Hulst, Harry van der (1984): *Syllable Structure and Stress in Dutch*. Dordrecht: Foris.

Kager, René (1989): *A Metrical Theory of Stress and Destressing in English and Dutch*. Dordrecht: Foris.

Leben, William (1973): *Suprasegmental Phonology*. PhD thesis, MIT, Cambridge.

Menn, Lise, and Brian McWhinney (1984): The Repeated Morph Constraint: toward an Explanation. *Language* 60, 519-541.

Plag, Ingo (1999) *Morphological Productivity. Structural Constraints in English Derivation*. Berlin, New York: Mouton de Gruyter.

— (in press): The Polysemy of *-ize* Derivatives. The Role of Semantics in Word-formation. Geert Booij, Jaap van Marle (eds.): *Yearbook of Morphology 1997*. Dordrecht et al.: Kluwer.

Plank, Frans (1981): *Morphologische (Ir-)Regularitäten*. Tübingen: Narr.

Prince, Alan, and Paul Smolensky (1993): *Optimality Theory*. Ms., Rutgers University.

Raffelsiefen, Renate (1996): Gaps in Word-formation. In: Ursula Kleinhenz (ed.): *Interfaces in Phonology*. Berlin: Akademie-Verlag, 193-208.

Russell, Kevin (1997): Optimality Theory and Morphology. In: Diana Archangeli, Terence Langendoen (eds.): *Optimality Theory: An Overview*, 102-133. Oxford: Blackwell.

Stemberger, Joseph P. (1981): Morphological Haplology. *Language* 57, 791-817.

Wiese, Richard (1996): *The Phonology of German*. Oxford: Clarendon Press.

Yip, Moira (1998): Identity Avoidance in Phonology and Morphology. In: Stephen G. Lapointe, Diane K. Brentari, and Patrick M. Farrell (eds.): *Morphology and its Relation to Phonology and Syntax*. Stanford, CA: CLSI Publications, 216-246.

Section III: Morphology

Martin Neef

A case study in declarative morphology: German case inflection

German noun inflection is a complex topic. On the one hand, there are only eight inflectional categories to be considered, but, on the other hand, there are many ways in which nouns mark these morphological categories. Case inflection is illustrated by the following example of the neuter noun *Haus* 'house':

(1) Example for the nominal paradigm

singular nominative	das Haus
genitive	des Hauses
dative	dem Haus
accusative	das Haus
plural nominative	die Häuser
genitive	der Häuser
dative	den Häusern
accusative	die Häuser
gloss	house

Studies of German noun inflection differ in the number of different declension types they assume. Below I present some examples which illustrate this intriguing fact:

(2)

Carstairs (1987: 241, 243)	6 inflection paradigms
Duden (1995[5]: 220f.)	10 declension types + 5 sub-types[1]
Wegener (1995: 148)	11 inflection classes
Wahrig (1994[4]: 17ff.)	31 declension schemata + 9 sub-schemata
Mugdan (1977: 69)	32 declension patterns
Kunze/Rüdiger (1968: 254ff.)	77 declension types

The differences ensue mainly from the range of data taken into account and from the different assumptions concerning the relevance of phonological and/or orthographic representations. The central question arising from this overview is: How do we determine the membership of a specific noun to one of the inflection types assumed? To answer this question, most of the current analyses make use of arbitrary class features. This is not a desirable strategy, because it implies that the membership has to be learned for each individual noun.

---

[1] A criticism showing many inconsistencies of the Duden-system is given in Neef (1998a), where I show that according to the basic assumptions of Duden, at least 25 inflection types have to be estimated.

In the following sections, I will present an analysis of German case inflection that attempts to minimise the number of inflection types, as well as the number of arbitrary class features needed to determine the membership of nouns to the respective declension types. In particular, I will defend two theoretical assumptions:

1. Until recently, morphological analyses have been input-oriented. With respect to noun inflection, this means that one particular morphological form has been designed as the base form. The other categories of the nominal paradigm have been subjected to formal changes which had to be performed on the base form in order to get the correct inflected forms. Since the early 1990s, morphological theory has become more and more output-oriented. The focus of the analysis nowadays is on properties of the inflected forms themselves, without consideration of the steps assumed to transform a base form into a surface form. The specific output-oriented model of morphology that I will make use of is called *Word Design* (Neef 1996). Section 1 of this paper is devoted to an outline of this theory.
2. Another issue is whether case and number inflection have to be treated together or not. I will follow what I call the *Separation Hypothesis* which involves that case and number inflection are different areas of morphological knowledge. This hypothesis is discussed in section 3 which is concerned with case inflection in the plural. The main point of this section is whether the dative plural is related to the nominative singular or to the nominative plural (or to a singular stem or a plural stem, respectively). The advantage of relating the dative plural to a plural form is that case inflection in the plural is very simple and completely regular.

1. Word Design

The theoretical background of the following analysis is the model of morphology which I call *Word Design* (Neef 1996). This approach is output-oriented in that it describes properties of surface forms. It is also constraint-based, because it relies on the application of constraints on surface forms, rather than on rules deriving a surface form from an assumed deep structure form. Furthermore, this model presupposes constraints which are not ordered with respect to their application, but which are all available at the same time (as opposed to rules that are typically assumed to apply in an - even extrinsically - ordered fashion). Following Pollard & Sag (1987), this approach can thus be called declarative. Concerning the properties mentioned above, Word Design resembles two other theories concerned with morphology and/or phonology, namely, Optimality Theory (OT, Prince & Smolensky 1993), and Declarative Phonologie (DP, Scobbie & Coleman & Bird 1996), but in other respects, Word Design differs from both these models. In the following sketch of Word Design some of these differences will be elaborated on (cf. also Neef 1998b: ch. 1).

Within a declarative conception of grammar, I take linguistic knowledge to be spread out on different levels, rather than assuming that linguistic forms are separated onto different levels of representation. The lexicon specifies the knowledge that is related to lexemes.

Lexemes comprise knowledge of form, grammatical behaviour, and meaning that is not predictable from general regularities of the grammar. The formal part of a lexeme consists of an abstract stem which is traditionally called a 'stem morpheme'. Since I treat stem morphemes as part of the lexicon and affixes as part of the morphology, I refrain from using the term 'morpheme', which unifies phenomena that I do not find unifiable. In this a-morphous character (which has other proponents in, e.g., Becker 1990 and Anderson 1992), Word Design fundamentally differs from OT and DP. This assumption, however, is in line with a number of psycholinguistic and neurolinguistic studies which prove that the items in questions are to be treated differently (cf., e.g., Drews 1989, Cholewa & de Bleser 1995).

The first level of grammatical knowledge is phonology. Phonological constraints restrict the possible shape of phonological units like the syllable or the phonological word. In my declarative conception, I consider these constraints as unviolable and, consequently, as unordered (as opposed to assumptions in OT, but in accord with DP). I believe that phonological constraints can be language-specific, and, because they are surface-true generalisations, I assume that they can (and must) be learned from the surface information that language learners are exposed to. OT, on the other hand, adheres to the universal character of all constraints. In fact, there are no objective standards that determine what makes a constraint that has been found active in one language a universal one, and the mechanism that made the numerous and very specific constraints assumed in OT-analyses part of the human hereditary factors remains unexplained.

The level of grammatical knowledge Word Design is concerned with is morphology. Morphological conditions describe the well-formedness of morphological categories. Among these are inflectional as well as derivational categories that are traditionally conceived of as morphemes. Instead of stating properties of a derivational morpheme like *-er*, I analyse properties of lexeme formation patterns like the one represented by a word like *Lehrer* 'teacher'. The main difference is that I investigate properties of the whole word, instead of merely the so-called 'affix'. This enables me to take into account especially prosodic constellations that are treated equal to segmental specifications in Word Design. Morpheme-based approaches, on the other hand, focus on segmental specifications in the first place and take prosodic regularities as secondary phenomena of a principally different nature.

Conditions of morphological well-formedness, which I call *Design Conditions*, are relevant for specific morphological categories only. In language acquisition, semantic and formal properties of lexeme formation patterns, as of inflectional patterns, have to be learned. Among the formal properties are the relevant base and the design conditions that specify in which respect instances of a specific pattern have to differ from the base form. The following *Main Principle of Morphology* is based on this assumption:

(3) *Main Principle of Morphology*
A grammatical word is ideally identical with the phonological realisation of its base. Violations against this principle at the end of the base are less severe than violations at the beginning of the base.

This principle is violated whenever a grammatical word (in the sense of Aronoff 1994, viz. a surface form) is marked by specific phonological (segmental or prosodic) properties. Under this view, language users have to know the formal base of an inflectional or derivational form (which in its recourse to lexemes also contributes to the semantics of the words in question), and they have to know in which respects these forms differ from their base.

The *Main Principle of Morphology* furthermore states that a grammatical word must be as similar as possible to the base to which it is related. This guarantees a pragmatically relevant connection between a grammatical word and a lexeme (as an abstract unit of form and meaning). Design conditions, on the other hand, state which formal conditions a grammatical word must meet to be able to function as an instance of a particular morphological category. In many cases, design conditions lead to a formal difference between a base and a dependent grammatical word, thereby allowing to identify function via form which is also of pragmatic relevance. Obviously, design conditions typically lead to a violation of the *Main Principle*. Design conditions, which are at the heart of the Word Design model, describe what language users have to learn to handle the formal properties of a morphological category in an adequate way. The assumption is that every difference between a base and instances of morphological categories must be learned in an explicit way. It follows from the fact that design conditions are unviolable (except by forms which are considered to be lexically marked as irregular), that they are learnable.

In the following analysis of German case inflection, all categories of the nominal inflectional paradigm (e.g., the genitive singular or the dative plural) are analysed independently of each other by stating the specific design conditions that hold for each of these categories. As a result, the system of German case inflection is described with recourse to lexical specification. This means that nominal lexemes have specific lexical features that control their inflectional behaviour. Most nouns are only specified for gender. Other nouns have additional features that mark them as irregular with respect to their inflectional properties. Irregular nouns differ in their degree of irregularity, and I will show that this can be expressed adequately in the analysis presented below.

2. The singular paradigm

Before presenting the analysis of case inflection in the singular, it is necessary to introduce the relevant data. This is not an easy task, because it includes the definition of standard language as opposed to stylistic and dialectal variants. Furthermore, a structured presentation of data is always based on some kind of theory; no neutral or pretheoretic method exists to present data in a clear and enlightening way. With these problems in mind, I will present different types of singular inflection based on the outline given in Wahrig (1994[4]: 17ff.). The presentation of the data is morphemic or input-oriented in nature, i.e., an inflection type is characterised by the changes that have to be performed on the nominative singular form (which is taken to be the base form) in order to mark the three oblique case forms (genitive, dative, and accusative).

In three points I deviate from Wahrig (1994[4]): first, for a number of nouns, Wahrig takes into account two forms of the genitive and the dative, respectively (e.g., *Tags* and *Tages* 'day (gen.)', *Tag* and *Tage* 'day (dat.)'). To a large degree in accordance with Duden

(1995[5]: 221ff.), in most cases I take to be standard and regular the short forms, and regard the long forms as representing a higher or obsolete stylistic level. Second, I ignore the inflection of nominalised adjectives which retain their adjectival behaviour when they are used as nouns. Third, I disregard regularities that are purely orthographical.

The following list is derived from the presentation in Wahrig (1994[4]: 17ff.); the names of the types are mine:

(4) Summary of inflection types in the singular (morphematic)

	Type S1a	Type S1b	Type S2a	Type S2b	Type S2c	Type S3
sg. nom.	Brett (neut.)	Kreis (masc.)	Hase (masc.)	Bär (masc.)	Name (masc.)	Frau (fem.)
sg. gen.	Brett-s	Kreis-es	Hase-n	Bär-en	Name-	Frau
dat.	Brett	Kreis	Hase-n	Bär-en	ns	Frau
acc.	Brett	Kreis	Hase-n	Bär-en	Name-n	Frau
					Name-n	
gloss	board	circle	rabbit	bear	name	woman

In type S1a, the dative and the accusative form sound like the nominative form, but the genitive is characterised by an additional *-s*. Type S1b is similar to type S1a, except for the fact that the genitive is marked by *-es*. Types S2a and S2b have identical forms in the oblique cases which differ from the nominative case by an additional *-n* and *-en*, respectively. Type S2c is similar to type S2a, with the exception of the genitive which is marked by *-ns*. Finally, type S3 is characterised by identical forms in all four cases.

Type S2c is rare in modern German. According to Köpcke (1995), there are at most twelve nouns which are inflected according to this pattern. Furthermore, the number of nouns in this group is decreasing; their nominative form tends to be reanalysed as being nasal-final instead of schwa-final. The result is that they inflect according to type S1a (cf. *Funke* 'spark' → *Funken*). Therefore, I regard these nouns as being lexically marked and I refrain from discussing them in the following analysis.[2]

In the declarative analysis which I will present below, the focus of attention is on the distribution of schwa in types 1 and 2. The combination of the respective subtypes a. and b. into one type (which is also more or less explicitly assumed in all other studies of German case inflection) is justified only if the distribution of schwa is explainable in theoretical terms. Subsequently, I will show which features of nouns control the assignment of a noun into a particular singular type.

---

[2] There is one neuter noun that resembles this pattern, namely *Herz* 'heart' (differing only in the accusative which is *Herz*). Wahrig (1994[4]) does not include this item.

2.1. Type 1

Since the differences between types S1a and S1b are minimal, it is common practice to subsume them under one type. Assuming that the nominative singular is the base form of singular case inflection for all nouns, leaves only the genitive form to be accounted for. The following design condition is relevant for the morphological category of the genitive singular of type 1 nouns:

(5) *Design Condition of Segmental Ending*
The grammatical word must have a specific segmental ending.
Clause: The segmental ending must be [s].

This condition ensures that grammatical words that are subject to it (namely, instances of type 1 nouns in the genitive singular) are well-formed only if they end in [s]. Obviously, only the nouns of type 1a in (4) are described adequately by this design condition. Additional examples of nouns of type 1b are given in the following list which helps to reveal a further design condition relevant for type 1 nouns:

(6)

nom. sg.	gen. sg.	gen. sg.	gloss
das Glas	des *Glas	des Glases	'glass'
das Verständnis	des *Verständnis	des Verständnisses	'understanding'
der Überfluss	des *Überfluss	des Überflusses	'abundance'
der Strauß	des *Strauß	des Straußes	'bouquet'
der Reflex	des *Reflex	des Reflexes	'reflex'
das Gewürz	des *Gewürz	des Gewürzes	'spice'

The nouns in the second column satisfy design condition (5) in that they end in [s], but they are ungrammatical, nonetheless. I here propose that they are ungrammatical, because they are homophonous with the nominative singular form of their base. Homophony is allowed in the dative and accusative of type 1 nouns, but not in the genitive. Thus, the avoidance of homophony is a morphological restriction that has to be learned for specific morphological categories; it is not a general regularity of German grammar. The genitive forms in (6) are grammatical only if they differ from the nominative singular and still end in <s>. Therefore, the following condition (prohibiting homophony) is also relevant for singular type 1 nouns:

(7) *Design Condition of Difference to the Base*
The grammatical word must have a different phonological structure than the phonological realisation of its base.

All nouns of type 1 that do not end in [s] in the nominative singular satisfy the *Design Condition of Difference to the Base* simply by adding [s] which is required by the *Design Condition of Segmental Ending*. Only type 1 nouns that end in [s] in the nominative singular are forced to have a more complex phonological structure in order to differ from their base.

The *Design Condition of Difference to the Base* is rather unspecific as to the kind of difference that exists between the base and the dependent grammatical word. In what follows, I will discuss why the forms in the third column in (6) are grammatical and why other conceivable forms are ruled out. As an example, I look at the noun *Glas*. The simplest way to fulfil the requirements of both conditions relevant for type 1 nouns ending in [s] would be to add [s] to the base. The result would be *[glɑ:ss]. This form, however, is not well-formed phonologically. Tautosyllabic geminates are principally impossible in German. This is partly due to the sonority constraint which, among other things, demands that identical segments must not be adjacent within a syllable. However, in German, coronal obstruents are allowed as extrasyllabic elements at the edges of phonological words even if they violate the sonority constraint (cf., e.g., *stracks* 'straight' [ʃtʀaks]). This implies that the phonological ungrammaticality of a syllable like *[glɑ:ss] is not explainable in terms of sonority, but only by an explicit ban on geminates as a phonological constraint of German.

Another option to create a difference with the base is to organise the segmental material prosodically different, for instance, as *['glɑ:.s̩], or *['glɑ:s.s̩]. Structures like these are not exceptional in principle, as can be seen in the standard realisations of the infinitives *sehen* 'to see' and *rennen* 'to run', respectively, as ['ze:.n̩] and ['ʀɛn.n̩]. However, whereas nasals (or sonorants in general) are allowed as syllable peaks in German, obstruents may not be the most sonorous element of a syllable. This is a further independent phonological constraint of German which explains the ungrammaticality of the forms given immediately above.

Apparently, the required difference to the base cannot be achieved without adding or deleting segments.[3] Deletion is not an option in German (it is only allowed in a few morphological patterns), but addition is possible, namely, addition of the vowel schwa (which is traditionally characterised as an epenthetic vowel). The most natural way to create a difference to the base and still have [s] as the final element is to insert schwa into the base form with a result like #['glɑ:.əs]. This form, again, is ungrammatical. To explain this, no further phonological constraint or design condition has to be assumed, because the *Main Principle of Morphology* suffices in this respect. The principle as stated in (3) regulates that a difference between a base form and a dependent grammatical word is best achieved by the addition of segments outside the base (on the right side), rather than by the insertion of segments into the base. Therefore, a form like #['glɑ:.əs] with schwa inserted into the base *Glas* is ungrammatical. If schwa is added on the right side of the base, the resulting form would be #['glɑ:.zə], violating the *Design Condition of Segmental Ending*. Compliance with both design conditions plus the *Main Principle* results in the form ['glɑ:.zəs], which actually is the grammatical form.

With the example of genitive *Glases*, I have shown that the design conditions formulated in (5) and (7) allow us to combine the singular types S1a and S1b into one type. All nouns of this class strictly obey both design conditions, and their formal properties are described sufficiently by these morphological conditions. The question now is which nouns belong to this type 1? Obviously, gender is the decisive factor: all neuter nouns belong to type 1, as do a major part of the masculine nouns. The group of masculine nouns excluded from this

[3] Metathesis as in #[gɑ:ls] is impossible in German (although the given word form happens to be phonologically well-formed).

type will be identified and accounted for in the following section (they are the so-called 'weak masculines'). Following Wegener (1995:146) among others, I claim that the normal or default case for masculine nouns is that they belong to type 1.

The implication of my proposal is that knowledge of the gender of each noun is required in order to inflect nouns correctly in the singular. By and large, gender is an arbitrary feature of nouns (though there are some regularities that make gender predictable to a certain degree; cf., e.g., Köpcke & Zubin 1996). If a speaker knows the citation form of a noun, s/he also knows its gender, because the nominative singular definite article (which is part of the citation form) unambiguously determines gender. Moreover, gender can be inferred from agreement on the phrase level.[4]

2. Type 2

Nouns belonging to types 2a and 2b mark all oblique cases in the singular (and, incidentally, also all plural categories) by a final nasal. They are thus subject to the *Design Condition of Segmental Ending* below which demands a final nasal in the genitive, dative, or accusative singular. As nasal assimilation is found in at least some stylistic variants of German - as can be seen in the standard pronunciations of *Fragen* 'questions' as ['fʀɑː.gŋ̩] and *sieben* 'seven' as ['ziː.bm̩] - I suppose that the nasal consonant in question is underspecified for place of articulation. If there is no assimilation, the default case is a coronal nasal.

(8) *Design Condition of Segmental Ending*
The grammatical word must have a specific segmental ending.
Clause: The segmental ending must be [N].

Only nouns of subtype a. are adequately explained by this condition. For a more precise analysis we must consider those type 2 nouns that already end in a coronal nasal in the nominative singular (the list is presumably complete):

(9)		nom. sg.	gen. sg.	gen. sg.	gloss
	a.	der Titan	*des Titan	des Titanen	'Titan'
		der Tyrann	*des Tyrann	des Tyrannen	'tyrant'
		der Ulan	*des Ulan	des Ulanen	'ulan'
		der Veteran	*des Veteran	des Veteranen	'veteran'

4 Some foreign nouns that end in an unstressed full syllable (i.e. a syllable containing a full vowel) with a final [s] are irregular in that they leave the genitive unmarked (e.g. nom.sg. and gen.sg. *Chaos* 'chaos' with gen.sg. **Chaosses* being impossible). Since these data are somewhat obscure, I refrain from discussing them here (some relevant nouns allow both the unmarked and the long form of the genitive, e.g., *Atlas* 'atlas' and *Globus* 'globe', and, according to Wegener (1995: 144), even native nouns with the formal characteristics mentioned as *Untersuchungsausschuss* 'investigating committee' tend to allow an unmarked form of the genitive).

b.	der Ahn	*des Ahn	des Ahnen	'ancestor'
	der Diakon	*des Diakon	des Diakonen	'deacon'
	der Partisan	*des Partisan	des Partisanen	'partisan'
	der Senn	*des Senn	des Sennen	'dairyman'
	der Tribun	*des Tribun	des Tribunen	'tribune'
	der Untertan	*des Untertan	des Untertanen	'subject'
c.	der Hahn	*des Hahn	des Hahnen	'faucet'

The lists in 9a. and 9b. consist of animate nouns. The only inanimate noun occurs in 9c., a noun which occurs in Swiss dialects only as belonging to type 2. The nouns in 9a. always inflect according to type 2, the nouns in 9b. and 9c. may also pattern with type 1. These data seem to indicate that type 2 nouns are also subject to the *Design Condition of Difference to the Base*. However, among the data given by Marcus et al. (1995: 248f.), there are about 25 nouns (all animate) that are not described adequately by the two design conditions assumed so far:

(10)	nom. sg.	gen. sg. (explicit)	gen. sg. (colloquial)	gloss
a.	Narr	['naɐ̯.ʀən]	[naɐ̯n]	'fool'
	Rebell	[ʀe.'bɛl.lən]	[ʀe.'bɛln]	'rebel'
b.	Herr	['hɛɐ̯.ʀən]	[hɛɐ̯n]	'gentleman'
c.	Bär	['bæ:.ʀən]	[bæ:ɐ̯n]	'bear'
	Mohr	['mo:.ʀən]	[mo:ɐ̯n]	'moor'
	Zar	['tsɑ:.ʀən]	[tsɑ:ɐ̯n]	'tsar'
d.	Barbar	[baɐ̯.'bɑ:.ʀən]	[baɐ̯.'bɑ:ɐ̯n]	'barbarian'
	Husar	[hu.'zɑ:.ʀən]	[hu.'zɑ:ɐ̯n]	'hussar'
	Lakai	[lɑ.'kaɪ̯.ən]	[la.'kaɪ̯n]	'lackey'
e.	Nachfahr	['nɑ:x.fɑ:.ʀən]	['nɑ:x.fɑɐ̯n]	'descendant'

The nouns in (10) end in a liquid or in a diphthong, that is, in sounds that are more sonorous than the nasal which, according to the design condition in (8), is the obligatory final segment in the oblique cases. In explicit pronunciation, all the nouns in (10) end in a reduced syllable (i.e., a syllable containing schwa or a sonorant as its peak or most sonorous element). The reduced syllable is not required by the phonology and the colloquial pronunciations of these nouns end in full syllables instead.[5] The explicit as well as the colloquial pronunciations of these nouns obey the two design conditions found to be rele-

[5] In the examples that contain a stressed vowel as the last full vowel, the requirements of a maximal syllable are exceeded in the colloquial pronunciation. Regularly, only three phonotactic positions are available in the syllable rhyme, but here four positions are required under the assumption that tensed vowels occupy two such positions (cf. Neef 1996: 88ff.).

vant for the oblique cases. Therefore, a further design condition is needed which motivates the final reduced syllable:

(11) *Design Condition of Lower Limit for Reduced Syllables*
The grammatical word must end in at least one reduced syllable.

This condition is relevant for the oblique cases of type 2 nouns in explicit pronunciation, but not in colloquial pronunciation. This is the way in which differences between stylistic levels are analysed in Word Design: the design conditions relevant for a lower variant of a specific morphological category form a proper subset of those design conditions relevant for a higher variant of the same morphological category (cf. Neef 1997).

The *Design Condition of Lower Limit for Reduced Syllables* is able to motivate the behaviour of the nouns in (9) as well, indicating that, the *Design Condition of Difference to the Base* might not be necessary (although it is surface-true). In colloquial pronunciation, however, a noun like *Ahn* is not pronounced as monosyllabic [ʔaːn] in the oblique cases, but as disyllabic [ʔaː.n̩]. As the final reduced syllable cannot be attributed to the reduced syllable condition in (11) - which does not apply in colloquial pronunciation - the *Design Condition of Difference to the Base* proves to be relevant also for the oblique cases of type 2 nouns.

How can it be determined which nouns belong to type 2? This intricate matter has been illuminatingly dealt with in work by Bittner (1987) and Köpcke (1995). Gender is a necessary condition: all type 2 nouns are masculine. Traditionally, they are called the 'weak masculines' as opposed to strong masculines that belong to type 1. This indicates that gender is not sufficient to characterise type 2 nouns. The following picture emerges from the work cited: there are two principally different groups of nouns that constitute the weak masculines. First, all schwa-final masculines that denote an animate entity belong to this type. Only a few dialectal masculine nouns like *Piefke* 'pipsqueak' inflect according to type 1. The restriction to the semantic feature of animacy is somewhat redundant, because almost all schwa-final masculines are animate. The only exceptions are a few non-weak masculines like *Käse* 'cheese' and the 12 nouns of type S2c in (4).

Whereas the weak status of schwa-final masculines is almost completely predictable, the predictability of the second core group of weak masculines is more complicated. Many polysyllabic masculine nouns with final stress are weak. Typically, these nouns are representatives of certain lexeme formation patterns marked by specific segmental endings. For example, according to Köpcke (1995: 175)[6] all masculine nouns ending in *-graph*, e.g., *Telegraph* 'telegraph' are weak. All animate masculines ending in *-ist* like *Journalist* 'journalist' are weak, whereas all inanimate masculines of this pattern like *Aorist* 'aorist' are non-weak (it should be pointed out that there are only two nouns of the latter group). The regularities become less clear with nouns ending in *-ant*: all animate nouns of this pattern like *Spekulant* 'speculator' are weak, but among the inanimate nouns there are 16 weak ones, e.g., *Hydrant* 'hydrant' and 8 non-weak ones, for instance, *Krokant* 'cracknel'. Moreover, there are quite a lot of lexeme formation patterns with ultimate stress that have no weak members. Examples are the patterns represented by *Admiral* 'admiral', *Amateur*

---

6 The ratings Köpcke gives are based on the inverse dictionary by Mater (1970).

'amateur', or *Detektiv* 'detective'. Thus, the weak status of polysyllablic masculine nouns with final stress seems to be related to certain lexeme formation patterns plus the semantic feature of animacy, but there remain a lot of exceptions that have to be treated as lexically marked. Finally, a group of 35 monosyllabic animate masculine nouns like *Bär* 'bear' are weak. Since most nouns with these characteristics are not weak, e.g., *Hund* 'dog', this group also constitutes a lexically marked exception. Given this characterisation, the concept of weak masculines is quite complex and membership to this group is predictable only to a certain extent.

The traditional way to characterise a masculine noun as being weak is to look at the genitive singular: if this form ends in a nasal, the masculine noun is weak, otherwise (namely if it ends in [s]) it is strong or belongs to type 1. In the Word Design approach, however, this line of argumentation is not satisfactory, because the behaviour of nouns with respect to case inflection is intended to be made predictable from inherent properties of the base form. Moreover, Wegener (1995: 148) shows that the genitive case is acquired last in first language acquisition, indicating that knowledge of the formal properties of the other case forms cannot depend on the genitive form. Therefore, the unpredictable weak masculines are supposed to be lexically marked by a specific feature and they thus have to be learned one by one.

A further different way to predict the weak status of masculines is pursued by Carstairs (1987: 242ff.): weak masculines are those nouns that take the *n*-plural and have the semantic feature of animacy. As Carstairs (1987: 244) points out himself, this analysis is not completely successful, because there are a number of animate nouns with an *n*-plural which are not weak (e.g., *Professor* 'professor') and there are inanimate nouns with an *n*-plural which are weak (e.g., *Diamant* 'diamond'). Moreover, this approach is not sufficient to get rid of the arbitrary class feature 'weak' because it still has to be determined which masculines take the *-(e)n*-plural (which is not the default for masculines). Thus, the above-mentioned recourse to the phonological structure of the nominative singular and animacy seems to be more promising to determine whether or not a masculine noun is weak.

2.3. Type 3 and summary

The third class of nouns with a specific behaviour in singular case inflection is easy to describe: all case forms of nouns of this type are homophonous, or, to put it in Word Design terms, no design conditions are relevant to the oblique cases. In addition, type S3 is easy to characterise: all and only feminine nouns belong to this class.[7]

The following table summarises the formal properties of the three distinct noun classes with respect to singular case inflection. The table is restricted to the level of explicit articulation; the lower stylistic levels can be derived from this knowledge. I suppose that the information given in (12) as a description of the knowledge of a competent language user is part of the morphological component of grammar. In this way, the Word Design approach

[7] This statement is not completely faithful: some non-feminine foreign words ending in [s] show the same behaviour, e.g. *der Kasus* 'case' or *das Genus* 'gender'.

is fundamentally distinct from morphemic generative studies that focus on affixes and consider affixes part of the lexicon.

(12) Types of singular case inflection

	singular type 1 (non-weak non-feminines)	singular type 2 (weak masculines)	singular type 3 (feminines)
base	nominative singular	nominative singular	nominative singular
accusative	= nominative singular	Design Condition of Segmental Ending [N] Design Condition of Difference to the Base Design Condition of Lower Limit for Reduced Syllables	= nominative singular
dative	= nominative singular	= accusative singular	= nominative singular
genitive	Design Condition of Segmental Ending [s] Design Condition of Difference to the Base	= accusative singular	= nominative singular

The different cases are ordered with respect to salience in language acquisition (according to Wegener 1995).[8] Therefore, I take the accusative form to be the base of the two other oblique cases for the weak masculines, but this is of no further theoretical relevance. I take the nominative singular form as the base of singular case inflection, that is to say that the nominative singular has to be known in order to be able to inflect the nouns correctly. In fact, the nominative singular form is the citation form of nouns and this aspect is reflected in the analysis presented here. The nominative and the accusative singular are the only grammatical cases which make it possible to determine the gender of a noun unambiguously (given that the definite article is part of the citation form), but only from the nominative form, the other forms can be inferred. The accusative form would be a problematic citation form, because in the case of the weak masculines, the nominative form could not be inferred from the accusative form: the nominative form of the accusative *Bären* could equally well be *Bär*, *Bäre,* or *Bären.*

[8] Wurzel (1998) also prefers this order for different reasons.

3. The plural paradigm

Presentation of the data for plural case inflection involves more types than for singular case inflection. The following list relies on Wahrig (1994[4]: 17ff.):

(13) Summary of inflection types in the plural (morphematic)

	Type P1	Type P2	Type P3	Type P4	Type P5	Type P6
sg. nom.	Lappen (masc.)	Faden (masc.)	Messer (neut.)	Mutter (fem.)	Tag (masc.)	Hand (fem.)
pl. nom.	Lappen	Fäden	Messer	Mütter	Tag-e	Händ-e
pl. gen. dat. acc.	Lappen Lappen Lappen	Fäden Fäden Fäden	Messer Messer-n Messer	Mütter Mütter-n Mütter	Tag-e Tag-en Tag-e	Händ-e Händ-en Händ-e
gloss	cloth	thread	knife	mother	day	hand

	Type P7	Type P8	Type P9	Type P10	Type P11
sg. nom.	Gabe (fem.)	Bär (masc.)	Kind (neut.)	Dach (neut.)	Echo (neut.)
pl. nom.	Gabe-n	Bär-en	Kind-er	Däch-er	Echo-s
pl. gen. dat. acc.	Gabe-n Gabe-n Gabe-n	Bär-en Bär-en Bär-en	Kind-er Kind-ern Kind-er	Däch-er Däch-ern Däch-er	Echo-s Echo-s Echo-s
gloss	gift	bear	child	roof	echo

The estimate of 11 inflection types in the plural is a considerable challenge for any analysis. Compared to the numbers I cited in (2), this list appears to be relatively simple. It might seem contradictory, however, that in (2), I referred to Wahrig (1994[4]) as assuming 31 inflection types and 9 subtypes, whereas I derived only 6 singular types and 11 plural types from this source in my presentations in (4) and (13). The reason for this difference is that Wahrig treats the singular and the plural forms as creating only one paradigm, whereas I separate the singular forms from the plural forms. This separation allows me to reduce the number of different plural case inflection types to just 2, which I will demonstrate in the subsequent analysis. Before doing so, I will present some arguments in favour of this separation.

3.1. The separation hypothesis

Two types of analyses concerning German noun inflection can be distinguished: most authors take case inflection and number inflection to form an integral whole, whereas some regard each of these two subjects as topics in their own right. Among the former are the most important grammars of German (going back to the 16th century grammarians and spanning over Adelung 1782 and Grimm 1819 to the present day grammars like Heidolph et al. 1981, Engel 1988, Eisenberg 1994[3], and Duden 1995[5]), a number of studies in Natural Morphology by Wurzel (e.g. 1994, 1998) and Bittner (1994), and studies by Rettig (1972), Carstairs (1987), and Wunderlich (1997).[9] The *Separation Hypothesis*, on the other hand, claims that number inflection and case inflection are principally different areas of morphological knowledge. This approach has been introduced into German literature by Admoni (1966: 102), who refers to a tradition among a group of Russian Germanists founded by Sinder & Strojewa in the 1930s. This tradition is explicitly followed in pedagogical work by Darski (e.g. 1996) and implicitly in detailed studies by Mugdan (1977) and Wegener (1995). Finally, there are many studies that investigate regularities in number inflection only, as, e.g., Werner (1969) and Köpcke (1993) which more or less follow the *Separation Hypothesis*.

I will now present some theoretical reasons which support the *Separation Hypothesis*.[10] A number of nouns appears either in the singular or in the plural, but not in both (data taken from Köpcke (1993: 225); the list is far from being complete):

(14)	a.	singular nouns		b.	plural nouns	
		der Adel	'nobility'		die Einkünfte	'income'
		der Rauch	'smoke'		die Eltern	'parents'
		der Schmuck	'jewelry'		die Ferien	'holidays'
		der Schnee	'snow'		die Gebrüder	'brothers'
		die Jugend	'youth'		die Gezeiten	'tides'
		die Milch	'milk'		die Kosten	'costs'
		die Ruhe	'silence'		die Leute	'people'
		die Wolle	'wool'		die Masern	'measles'
		das Fleisch	'flesh'		die Naturalien	'natural produce'
		das Getreide	'grain'		die Passiva	'liabilities'
		das Gute	'good'		die Shorts	'shorts'
		das Stehen	'standing'		die Spesen	'expenses'

---

[9] For an extended review of this line of analysis see Pavlov (1995: Ch. 1).

[10] Booij (1996) gives similar arguments in favour of his distinction between inherent and contextual inflection. He mentiones number inflection for nouns as an example for inherent inflection and structural case marking on nouns as an example for contextual inflection, which shows that his terminology is closely connected with the *Separation Hypothesis*.

It could be argued that the information about the restricted use in number inflection is idiosyncratic and thus has to be encoded for every single lexical item. It could also be argued that the semantic information of the nouns under consideration is sufficient to restrict this range of use. The latter view is obviously true in many cases, but not in all. The plural noun *Eltern,* for example, denotes two specific persons, but it is also possible to refer to one of them. In German, the suppletive form *Elternteil* is used. Interestingly, in colloquial speech the back-formation *Elter* is sometimes used as the singular of the plural noun *Eltern* (with natural gender). Moreover, the children's disease *Windpocken* 'chickenpox' appears in the plural in German, but in the singular in English. Thus, restricted use in number inflection seems to be idiosyncratic in at least some cases.

In contrast, there is no noun in German that lacks a case form: any noun can appear in any grammatical case. This is even true for foreign words. Frequently, foreign words retain the form of the nominative plural of the source language, even if their the plural is not a standard form in German (cf., e.g., Italian *Gondoliere* 'gondolier', plural *Gondolieri,* or Latin *Genus* 'gender', plural *Genera*). With respect to case inflection, however, all these nouns behave as regular native nouns. There are no nouns that are inflected in the case paradigms according to their language of origin. This difference in the formal behaviour of case and number indicates that these are phenomena of a principally different quality. Whereas number is related to semantics or to the concept the noun stands for, case has no semantic influence on a noun, but serves to indicate a syntactic function.[11]

The main achievement of the *Separation Hypothesis* is the introduction of a second base form in the nominal paradigm: case inflection in the singular depends on the nominative singular, whereas case inflection in the plural depends on the nominative plural. This view does not deny the - at least partial - dependency of the nominative plural form on the nominative singular form, but it treats it as a different matter. The *Separation Hypothesis* has its most obvious advantages in the account of the dative plural which is considered to be related to the nominative plural. This makes the analysis of the dative plural much easier. The relationship between the nominative plural and the nominative singular has to be analysed independently any way. The main motivation for the combined analysis of case and number inflection lies in the aim to predict the inflectional behaviour of each noun. I will show that this aim (which is the most important one for each generative study) can also be achieved within an analysis following the *Separation Hypothesis*, and with even greater success.

3.2. The dative plural

Once the issue of number inflection is dealt with in a different way, the plural paradigm proves to be a simple system: the genitive and the accusative plural are always homophonous with the nominative plural. The only category that may be marked is the dative. The additional marking of the dative form is restricted to the plural types P3 - P6 and P9 -

[11] Based on observations like these, Wegener (1995: 150) pursues the idea that number and case are categories that (in first language acquisition) are acquired independently of each other.

P11 in (13). Nouns of the other plural types have forms of the dative which are identical to the nominative plural.

3.2.1 Some morpheme-based approaches

Before I present a Word Design analysis, I will look at some morpheme-based attempts to classify nouns with respect to their behaviour in the dative, and I will point out the problems these analyses run into. From a pedagogical starting point, Darski (1996: 4) formulates a rule of noun inflection according to which nouns that end in the graphemes <e>, <r>, or <l> in the nominative plural mark the dative plural by an additional <n>. This is an adequate description, as the following data show:

(15)	nom. sg.	nom. pl	dat. pl.	gloss
a.	Ball (masc.)	Bälle	Bällen	'ball'
	Jahr (neut.)	Jahre	Jahren	'year'
	Kraft (fem.)	Kräfte	Kräften	'force'
b.	Wald (masc.)	Wälder	Wäldern	'wood'
	Bild (neut.)	Bilder	Bildern	'picture'
	Mutter (fem.)	Mütter	Müttern	'mother'
c.	Henkel (masc.)	Henkel	Henkeln	'handle'
	Kabel (neut.)	Kabel	Kabeln	'cable'

Interestingly, Duden (1995[5]: 226) expresses this regularity in negative terms: all nouns mark the dative by an additional *-n* except those nouns that end in *-n* or *-s* in the nominative plural.[12] First, it should be noted that both of these analyses relate the behaviour of nouns in the plural to formal aspects of the nominative plural and not of the nominative singular. In this respect, they follow the *Separation Hypothesis*. Furthermore, the combination of these descriptions shows that the possible endings of nouns in the nominative plural are strongly restricted: only five different endings seem to be allowed here. However, a look at some marginal foreign words shows that there are two further endings possible for the nominative plural (there are more irregular nouns like these, but no more different endings than the ones listed):

(16)	nom. sg.	nom. pl	dat. pl.	gloss
a.	Genus (neut.)	Genera	Genera	'gender'
b.	Gondoliere (masc.)	Gondolieri	Gondolieri	'gondolier'
	Konto (neut.)	Konti	Konti	'account'

---

[12] This description is also given in Wurzel (1998). Wegener (1995: 147) formulates two different rules for the dative plural which depend on the morpheme-structure of the nominative plural. This structure, however, can only be obtained through recourse to the form of the nominative singular. In this sense, this analysis does not follow the *Separation Hypothesis*.

Darski's rule covers the data, whereas Duden falls short in these cases (but the rule could easily be augmented). The same shortcomings are found in Wunderlich (1997), who concentrates on the behaviour of affixes, rather than on formal aspects of nouns which only form one class in his view. According to his minimalist approach, the dative plural is always marked by the affix /n/, but this affix does not show up if it would add a syllable to the noun (due to a general constraint). Hence, words ending in [n] or [s] in the nominative plural do not get an additional [n] in the dative plural, because this would result in a word with one syllable added.[13] However, this approach fails for nouns as those in (16): *Genera* and *Konti* meet the conditions for the explicit affixation of dative-/n/, but the grammatical forms appear without a final nasal. A prerequisite of this analysis is that plural-*n* is treated differently from dative-*n*, because it typically adds a syllable (e.g., *Frau* 'woman' - *Frauen*). Correspondingly, Wunderlich (1997) treats all nouns that take a plural other than the *s*-plural as being irregular. This predicts an enormous learning effort for nearly the whole nominal core lexicon.[14]

Despite their descriptive adequacy, both the descriptions of Darski and Duden suffer from a central theoretical shortcoming: they define classes that are not natural in linguistic terms. Translated from orthography into phonology, Darski would claim that nouns ending in liquids or in schwa take a nasal as the marker of the dative plural. There is no phonological theory that would assume that these sounds - as opposed to other final segments that appear in the nominative plural (full vowels, nasals and obstruents) - form a natural class.

3.2.2. A declarative analysis

In the following Word Design analysis, I will show that there is a way to treat the distribution of the dative marker in terms of natural classes, even including the data in (16). I will proceed in two steps: first I will outline an analysis related to a prosodic category which leaves only some marginal data as irregular, and subsequently I will present an analysis related to a morphological concept that is able to explain all data adequately.

In contrast to an input-oriented approach which states which changes have to be made in order to transform an underlying representation into a surface form, an output-oriented approach states which conditions a surface form must meet. Under this point of view, plural nouns can be divided into two formally distinct sub-classes with regard to their behaviour in the dative, but this time with a different demarcation line. Except for plural type P11 as given in (13) (the *s*-plural) and those foreign nouns as given in (16), the dative plural of all other nouns ends in a nasal. This nasal is sometimes present in the nominative singular, as in the case of *Lappen* and *Faden* (types P1 and P2 in (13)), or it is present in the nominative

[13] Some studies like Carstairs (1987: 251) and Bittner (1994: 68) assume a phonological rule relevant for the non-addition of the dative plural-*n* for nouns ending in /s/ or /n/. The exact properties of this rule, however, remain unclear in both of these approaches.

[14] On the theoretical level, Wunderlich's approach is more complex than Word Design because he assumes rules as well as constraints, some of them being violable and some being specific for morphological categories.

plural as in the case of *Gabe* and *Bär* (types P7 and P8 in (13)),[15] or it is added, as in some other cases like *Tag*. The obvious regularity is that the dative plural has to end in a nasal. Hence, in the dative plural the sub-group of nouns under consideration (excluding the *s*-plural) is subject to the same *Design Condition of Segmental Ending* as given in (8), repeated here as (17):

(17) *Design Condition of Segmental Ending*
The grammatical word must have a specific segmental ending.
Clause: The segmental ending must be [N].

The *Design Condition of Segmental Ending* classifies all nouns ending in schwa or in a sonorant in the nominative plural into one group, and all nouns ending in a full vowel or in an obstruent (namely [s]) into another group. At first sight, this demarcation line is not more convincing than the one assumed by Darski or Duden. Looking at prosodic structure, however, makes this analysis more promising. All plural nouns that either end in schwa or in a sonorant in the nominative plural also end in a reduced syllable (although a sonorant-final syllable in German may well be a full syllable like [man] 'man'), whereas all nouns ending in a full vowel or in an obstruent in the nominative plural do not end in a reduced syllable but in a full syllable (although an obstruent-final syllable may well be a reduced syllable like in [ˈkɪn̥.məs] 'funfair'). Hence, nouns ending in a reduced syllable are subject to the *Design Condition of Segmental Ending* in the dative plural, but nouns ending in a full syllable are not. Obviously, these are prosodically defined natural classes.

A closer look at some colloquial plural forms gives rise to a slightly different analysis (data taken from Duden 1995⁵: 233):

(18)	nom. sg.	standard nom.pl.	colloquial nom.pl.	gloss
a.	Bengel	Bengel	Bengels	'lad'
	Kumpel	Kumpel	Kumpels	'pal'
	Mädchen	Mädchen	Mädchens	'girl'
b.	Junge	Jungen	Jungens	'boy'

These colloquial plural forms end in a reduced syllable. They do not, however, end in a nasal in the dative plural, but have identical forms in the whole plural paradigm. There are only a few other nouns ending in an obstruent-final reduced syllable in the nominative plural, like the dialectal nouns *Piefke* 'pipsqueak' (pl. *Piefkes*) and *Steppke* 'nipper' (pl. *Steppkes*), and they, too, leave the dative unmarked. Therefore, the class of plural nouns that are subject to the *Design Condition of Segmental Ending* in the dative has to be restricted to nouns that end in a reduced syllable, but not in an obstruent. Again, this is not a

---

15 In derivational terms, this regularity is sometimes described as a merging of the case marker with the number marker (cf. e.g. Wegener 1995: 143). This analysis, however, does not explain the circumstances under which merging is possible (it is, e.g., not possible for the genitive singular, see section 2), and it would have to be extended to the merging of case marking with stem segments.

natural class phonologically. It is, however, a morphological natural class. In Neef (1998a, c) I analysed the properties of the nominative plural and concluded that there are two principally distinct plural types: one type is called the *Reduced Syllable Plural*. It is subject to two formal conditions: first, any instance of this plural type has to end in at least one reduced syllable, and second, it must not end in an obstruent. The latter condition explains why *#Abend* 'evenings' is not a grammatical plural form, although it ends in a reduced syllable (the grammatical plural is *Abende*). The other plural type is the *s*-plural. Its instances are characterised by a final [s] and they must not be identical to the nominative singular. This condition explains why the plural of the Christian name *Jonas* is not *#Jonas*.

The assignment of nouns to one of the plural types is quite straightforward: core nouns take the *Reduced Syllable Plural*, peripheral nouns take the *s*-plural (or the strictly irregular patterns in (16)). The peripheral nominal vocabulary is constituted by, e.g., proper names, unassimilated borrowings, onomatopoetic words, nominalised function words, and truncations (cf. Marcus et al. 1995: 229). There are two general qualifications: peripheral nouns that end in [s] take the *Reduced Syllable Plural* (the plural of *Jonas* is *Jonasse*), and core nouns that end in an unstressed full vowel predominantly take the *s*-plural, because taking the *Reduced Syllable Plural* would lead to a phonologically ungrammatical form (the plural of *Auto* 'car' can not be **Auto*[ə] because this form is phonologically not well-formed).[16] This model has some problems. For instance, it remains unclear why some assimilated borrowings still take the *s*-plural (*Schal* 'shawl', *Deck* 'deck', *Chef* 'boss'). The *Reduced Syllable Plural* has three sub-types. The membership of a core noun to one of these sub-types is to a great extent explainable, but not completely. This issue - which is not relevant to the topic of case inflection - is extensively dealt with in Neef (1998a, c).

The notion of the *Reduced Syllable Plural* makes the properties of the dative plural explainable in terms of natural classes: all nouns that have the shape of the *Reduced Syllable Plural* in the nominative plural are subject to the *Design Condition of Segmental Ending* [N] in the dative form, whereas all other nouns are not subject to it (and are subject to no other design condition). This analysis results in the finding that there is no single noun that is irregular with respect to plural case inflection. The phonological form of the nominative plural is sufficient to adequately determine the behaviour in plural case inflection.

4. Summary

The declarative analysis of German case inflection within the theory of Word Design leads to the following picture which is supposed to mirror the grammatical knowledge of competent language users. The formal properties of the inflectional behaviour of nouns are captured within the morphological component of linguistic knowledge. A nominal

[16] This phonological constraint which I call the *Syllable Peak Adjacency Constraint* is dealt with in detail in Neef (1998b).

paradigm consists of one base form (the nominative) and three dependent categories that are related to the base form in terms of design conditions.

In singular case inflection, three different types have to be distinguished. These types are called type 1, type 2, and type 3, respectively, and their formal properties are given in table (9) above. In order to assign a noun to one of these types, gender has to be known. With respect to masculine nouns, it also has to be known whether these nouns are weak or not. Gender is given once the citation form (i.e., the nominative singular including the definite article) is known. The weak status of masculine nouns is to a certain extent predictable from the feature of animacy plus the phonological structure of the nominative singular. The number of irregular nouns in singular case inflection is small. It is made up of at most twelve masculine nouns of type S2c in (4) plus the neuter noun *Herz* 'heart'.

(19) Defaults of German case inflection

a. singular case inflection

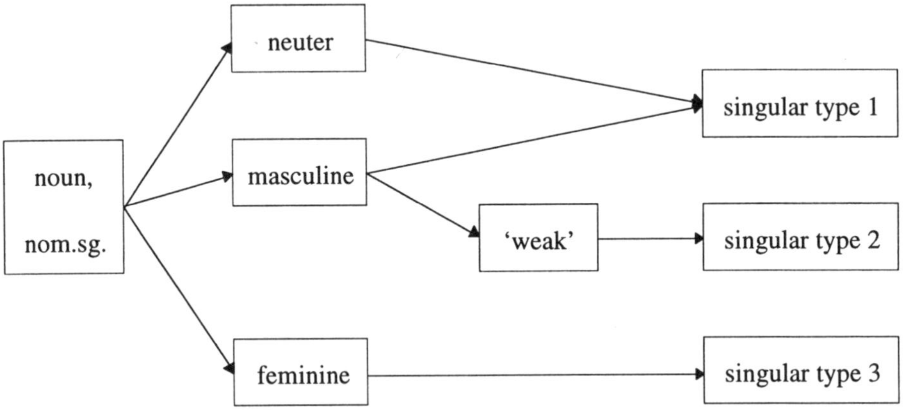

b. plural case inflection

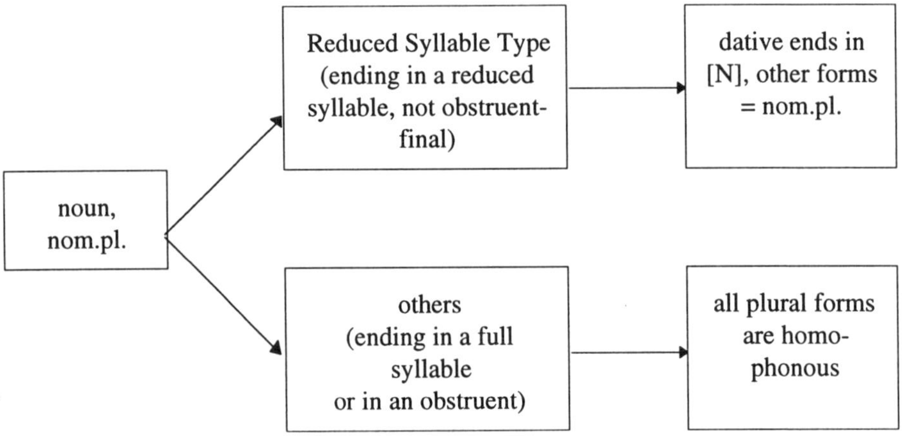

The analysis of plural case inflection presented in this paper differs from many other studies in that the regularities of the nominative plural are put aside as a different matter. The result is, that concerning case inflection, only two distinct types have to be assumed which is similar to assumptions in other studies adopting the *Separation Hypothesis*. Contrary to these studies, the Word Design analysis manages to capture the division line in terms of natural classes: all nouns that have the shape of the *Reduced Syllable Plural* in the nominative plural behave as one group (namely in that the dative form has to end in a nasal), and all other nouns behave differently (namely in that all plural categories are homophonous). As a consequence, there is no single noun that has to be marked as irregular in the lexicon with respect to plural case inflection. This means that there is very little to know in order to master plural case inflection.[17]

References

Adelung, Johann Christoph (1782): *Umständliches Lehrgebäude der Deutschen Sprache, zur Erläuterung der deutschen Sprachlehre für Schulen, Band 1.* Leipzig.

Admoni, Wladimir (1966²): *Der deutsche Sprachbau.* Moskau, Leningrad: Proswešcenie.

Anderson, Stephen R. (1992): *A-Morphous Morphology.* Cambridge: Cambridge University Press.

Aronoff, Mark (1994): *Morphology by Itself. Stems and Inflectional Classes.* Cambridge/Mass., London: MIT Press.

Becker, Thomas (1990): *Analogie und morphologische Theorie.* München: Fink.

Bittner, Dagmar (1987): Die sogenannten schwachen Maskulina des Deutschen - ihre besondere Stellung im nhd. Deklinationssystem. *Linguistische Studien,* Reihe A, 156: 33-53.

— (1994): Die Bedeutung der Genusklassifikation für die Organisation der deutschen Substantivflexion. In: Klaus-Michael Köpcke (ed.): *Funktionale Untersuchungen zur deutschen Nominal- und Verbalmorphologie.* Tübingen: Niemeyer, 65-80.

Booij, Geert (1996): Inherent Versus Contextual Inflection and the Split Morphology Hypothesis. *Yearbook of Morphology* 1995, 1-16.

Carstairs, Andrew (1987): *Allomorphy in Inflexion.* London, New York, Sydney: Croom Helm.

Cholewa, Jürgen &Ria de Bleser (1995): Neurolinguistische Evidenz für die Unterscheidung morphologischer Wortbildungsprozesse: Dissoziation zwischen Flexion, Derivation und Komposition. *Linguistische Berichte* 158, 259-297.

Darski, Jósef (1996): Die deutsche Substantivflexion in pädagogischer Aufbereitung. Ms.

Drews, Etta (1989): *Die Bedeutung von Morphemen für die Sprachanalyse.* Opladen: Westdeutscher Verlag.

Duden (1995⁵): *Grammatik der deutschen Gegenwartssprache.* Mannheim, Leipzig, Wien, Zürich: Bibliographisches Institut (= Duden 4).

Eisenberg, Peter (1994³): *Grundriß der deutschen Grammatik.* Stuttgart, Weimar: Metzler.

Engel, Ulrich (1988): *Deutsche Grammatik.* Heidelberg: Groos.

Grimm, Jacob (1819): *Deutsche Sprache, Teil 1.* Göttingen.

Heidolph, Karl Erich et al. (1981): *Grundzüge einer deutschen Grammatik.* Berlin: Akademie Verlag.

Köpcke, Klaus-Michael (1993): *Schemata bei der Pluralbildung im Deutschen. Versuch einer kognitiven Morphologie.* Tübingen: Narr.

[17] I would like to thank Janet Grijzenhout, Wolfgang Kehrein, Kirsten Raulf, Carsten Steins, Richard Wiese, and Dieter Wunderlich who helped to improve the present text. Thanks are also due to the SFB 282 'Theorie des Lexikons' for financial support.

— (1995): Die Klassifikation der schwachen Maskulina in der deutschen Gegenwartssprache. *Zeitschrift für Sprachwissenschaft* 14: 159-180.

Köpcke, Klaus-Michael & David Zubin (1996): Prinzipien für die Genuszuweisung im Deutschen. In: Ewald Lang & Gisela Zifonun (eds.): *Deutsch - typologisch*. Berlin, New York: de Gruyter, 473-491.

Kunze, Jürgen & Barbara Rüdiger (1968): Algorithmische Synthese der Flexionsformen des Deutschen. *Zeitschrift für Phonetik, Sprachwissenschaft und Kommunikationsforschung* 21: 245-303.

Marcus, Gary F. & Ursula Brinkmann & Harald Clahsen & Richard Wiese & Steven Pinker (1995): German Inflection: The Exception That Proves the Rule. *Cognitive Psychology* 29: 189-256.

Mater, Erich (1970): *Rückläufiges Wörterbuch der deutschen Gegenwartssprache*. Leipzig: VEB Verlag Enzyklopädie.

Mugdan, Joachim (1977): *Flexionsmorphologie und Psycholinguistik*. Tübingen: Narr.

Neef, Martin (1996): *Wortdesign. Eine deklarative Analyse der deutschen Verbflexion*. Tübingen: Stauffenburg.

— (1997): Die Alternationsbedingung: Eine deklarative Neubetrachtung. In: Dürscheid, Christa & Monika Schwarz & Karl Heinz Ramers (eds.). *Sprache im Fokus. Festschrift für Heinz Vater*. Tübingen: Niemeyer, 17-31.

— (1998a): A Declarative Path through the Jungle of German Noun Inflection. Düsseldorf, Wuppertal: Universität (= *Theorie des Lexikons 102*).

— (1998b): *Elemente einer deklarativen Wortgrammatik*. Hürth: Gabel.

— (1998c): The Reduced Syllable Plural in German. To appear in: Ray Fabri &Albert Ortmann & Teresa Parodi (eds.) (1998): *Models of Inflection*. Tübingen: Niemeyer.

Pavlov, Vladimir (1995): *Die Deklination der Substantive im Deutschen. Synchronie und Diachronie*. Frankfurt/Main: Peter Lang.

Pollard, Carl & Ivan A. Sag (1987): *Information-Based Syntax and Semantics. Vol. 1: Fundamentals*. Stanford: Center for the Study of Language and Information.

Prince, Alan & Paul Smolensky (1993): *Optimality Theory. Constraint Interaction in Generative Grammar*. Ms., Rutgers University (= *Rutgers University Center for Cognitive Science Technical Report #2*).

Rettig, Wolfgang (1972): *Sprachsystem und Sprachnorm in der deutschen Substantivflexion*. Tübingen.

Scobbie, James M. & John S. Coleman & Steven Bird (1996): Key Aspects of Declarative Phonology. In: Jacques Durand & Bernard Laks (eds.): *Current Trends in Phonology: Models and Methods. Volume II*. Salford: European Studies Research Institute, 685-709.

Wahrig, Gerhard (1994[4]): *Deutsches Wörterbuch*. Gütersloh: Bertelsmann.

Wegener, Heide (1995): *Die Nominalflexion des Deutschen - verstanden als Lerngegenstand*. Tübingen: Niemeyer.

Werner, Otmar (1969): Das deutsche Pluralsystem. Strukturelle Diachronie. In: Hugo Moser (ed.) (1969): *Sprache - Gegenwart und Geschichte*. Düsseldorf: Schwann, 92-128.

Wunderlich, Dieter (1997): Towards a Constraint-Based Minimal Representation of German Noun Inflection, a First Improvement. Ms. Universität Düsseldorf.

Wurzel, Wolfgang Ullrich (1994): Gibt es im Deutschen noch eine einheitliche Substantivflexion? oder: Auf welche Weise ist die deutsche Substantivflexion möglichst angemessen zu erfassen? In: Klaus-Michael Köpcke (ed): *Funktionale Untersuchungen zur deutschen Nominal- und Verbalmorphologie*. Tübingen: Niemeyer, 29-44.

— (1998): Drei Ebenen der Struktur von Flexionsparadigmen. To appear in: Ray Fabri & Albert Ortmann & Teresa Parodi (eds.): *Models of Inflection*. Tübingen: Niemeyer.

Carsten Steins

Against arbitrary features in inflection: Old English declension classes

1. Introduction

1.1 Inflectional class features: Indispensable or impossible?

The analysis of rich inflectional paradigms containing a number of inflectional classes has always been a testing ground for morphological analyses.[1] Every major morphological theory has taken up the challenge to analyze inflectional systems with at least several classes.

The main task consists of the problem to uniquely assign the inflectional affixes of class X with the noun stems of class X, ensuring (a) that no class X affix will combine with stems of class Y and that (b) no affix of class Y can combine with noun stems of class X. This is normally done by assigning features to the noun stems, which can then be used by the respective affixes (or spell-out rules) as context. Thus, a combination of the right stems with the right allomorphs is ensured.

While it is largely uncontroversial that such features be used, it is however much less clear how these features might be interpreted. Most modern morphological theories incorporate the notion of 'inflectional class feature', referring to a set of nouns defined by some abstract label such as 'Class I', 'A' or the like.[2] The use of such a notion is not unproblematic, however: Inflectional class labels like 'Class I', 'A' etc. do not refer to any contentful feature within the morphological system and are thus being abstract features with arbitrary content.

A different view is maintained by Wunderlich and Fabri (1995),[3] who have outlined a theory (which they term *Minimalist Morphology*) which —in contrast to many current theories— imposes rather rigid restrictions on the inflectional system of morphology, designing an account of morphology as minimalist and restricted as possible. Thus, besides other restrictions they require the theory to refrain from the use of inflectional features if they are not already used for independent reasons elsewhere, thus being arbitrary in nature. (*cf.* W&F 1995: 242) Their objection against these arbitrary inflectional features is explained with both theory-internal and theory-external shortcomings. Firstly, the stipulation of such additional features which are not independently needed constitutes an unnecessary

[1] This study was carried out in the research project SFB 232 'Theorie des Lexikons', which is supported by the Deutsche Forschungsgemeinschaft. I would like to thank Albert Ortmann, Curt Rice, Richard Wiese and Wolfgang Kehrein for their insightful comments.

[2] A more explicit example is Corbett & Fraser 1993, a less explicit one is Halle & Marantz 1993.

[3] In the following abbreviated as 'W&F'.

and undesirable complication. Secondly, regarding language acquisition, it is unclear how children will be able to learn features with arbitrary content.

This objection against inflectional features which are only based on arbitrary reference, however, does not imply that inflectional classes as such are considered a morphological *persona non grata*. It is a well-known linguistic fact that lexical categories do not always pattern in the same way, but in many languages form classes according to their inflectional behaviour. Likewise, in Minimalist Morphology it is possible to group lexical categories into inflectional classes, as long as their class feature uses inherent categories. Thus, possible inflectional features for nouns may refer to the semantic gender or gestalt or shape properties of the referent, as these are categories inherent to the noun. Alternatively, phonological characteristics of the noun can be used to differentiate various sets of noun stems, e.g. the difference between vocalic and consonantal noun stems, the syllable count of the stems or specific phonemes at the right or left edge of the stem.

My goal in this study is to show that arbitrary features are not needed in the analysis of inflectional systems of natural languages. While I can not speak for each and every language here, this present case study will clearly show that arbitrary features are unnecessary if one chooses to make effective use of (a) the phonological and (b) the semantic features of lexical entries and (c) various constraints and principles of a morpheme-based theory of inflection.

In fact, traditional descriptions of inflectional classes have been referring to such features to some extent. However, because their approach was historically oriented and motivated, the actual practice of using labels for inflectional classes in a specific language had only little reality in a specific language under synchronic considerations. Thus, the traditional practice of distinguishing inflectional classes somehow started out by referring to information inherent to the respective lexical categories[4], but soon diverted from this practice so that synchronically the inflectional class labels referred to arbitrary features.

1.2 The case of the Old English declension

The rejection of arbitrary inflectional classes is a strong claim which seems to conflict with the observation that numerous languages exist which distinguish a great number of different inflectional classes, so that it seems impossible —at least at first sight— to differentiate the classes on the basis of inherent features. Because it is not W&F's claim to ban inflectional classes altogether, but rather only those distinguished by arbitrary features, it is only possible to verify the validity of this claim through a detailed case study of a language with a great number of inflectional classes.

My aim is to present a detailed case study of a moderately complex inflectional system in order to assess the validity of W&F's claim. The language which will serve as the basis for this case study, Old English (OE), has a moderately complex noun declension. Traditionally, descriptive analyses have distinguished at least five major noun classes (going back to the Indo-European noun stems), if one neglects several minor classes for

---

4 The restriction to inherent categories was probably more unconscious and intuitive rather than a motivated theoretical restriction.

which only a handful of nouns exist.[5] For each of the major noun classes a number of subclasses exist, originally determined by differences of the stems, such as light/heavy stems and theme vowels.

Apart from the traditional analyses in the handbooks (such as Brunner 1962, also Hogg 1992), a number of previous analyses exist in the literature, among them a discussion between S.J. Keyser, P. Kiparsky and W. O'Neil, as well as treatments by Dresher and Lahiri.[6] However, all of these analyses are more concerned with the diachronic aspects of the OE noun morphology, i.e. how to derive the OE surface forms from the corresponding etymological origin. For that purpose, these analyses take inflectional classes as given, being an etymological heritage from Germanic (or Indo-European). Therefore, they do not shed any light on the question whether we need to employ arbitrary features in order to differentiate the OE declension classes or not. They are therefore not to be discussed in detail, instead, they will be referred to where necessary.

After enlarging on the traditional view of OE declension classes, I am going to examine each declension in detail, trying to avoid the use of any arbitrary features. The result will give some more insight on the discussion whether arbitrary features are needed or not. In closing, I will comment on the insights on the OE declension system which have been gained through this case study.

2. Old English declension: The traditional view

The OE declension classes derive directly from the Germanic and indirectly from the Indo-European declension classes. Consequently, the handbooks distinguish three main types of noun stems, according to their stem extension: stems with a vocalic extension ('vocalic'), stems with a consonantal extension ('consonantal'), and those with no extension ('athematic nouns'). The respective stem extensions are given in (1.a-c), which differ for the vocalic stems on account of sound change from Indo-European to Germanic.

(1)	a.	Vocalic Stems				
		-o,	*-i,*	*-ā*	*-u*	declensions (IE)
		-a,	*-i,*	*-ō,*	*-u*	declensions (Germanic)[7]
	b.	Consonantal Stems				
		-n	*-r*	minor declensions: *-es/-os; -et/-ot; -nd*		
	c.	Athematic Stems				
		no extension				

5 E.g. Brunner (1962).

6 A discussion between Keyser and Kiparsky & O'Neil in Linguistic Inquiry was concerned to a large extent with the OE declension: Keyser (1975), Kiparsky & O'Neil (1976). Keyser & O'Neil (1985a-b), too, deal with this subject; Lahiri (1982) is a PhD Dissertion containing a chapter which deals with the OE declension; Dresher & Lahiri (1991) is a more recent treatment, based on metrical considerations.

7 Throughout this paper, I will be using the Germanic terminology to refer to OE vocalic stems.

In OE, the *a*- and *i*-stems were by far the most common nouns, accounting together for approx. 60% of all nouns in the OE lexicon.[8] Second to these are the *ō*-stems with approx. 25% of all OE nouns. The *u*-stems had become nearly obsolete in OE: Most nouns of this class had fused with the *a*-, *i*-, or *ō*-stems (according to their gender), so that only a handful of nouns remained in this class.

Among the consonantal nouns, *n*-stems were quite numerous with approx. 15% of all OE nouns. *r*-stems, however, were very infrequent, containing only some kinship terms (*broðor*, *sweostor*, *moðor*, *fæder*, etc.). The other consonantal declinations are only marginally attested in OE.

The athematic noun stems were also rather infrequent, but among them were a few common nouns, such as *mann* – 'man'.

The distribution of the major OE declension classes is represented graphically in (2), distinguished by gender and stem extension.[9] An overview over the affixes for all OE declension classes is given in (3).

(2) The distribution of OE declension classes (% of all OE nouns)

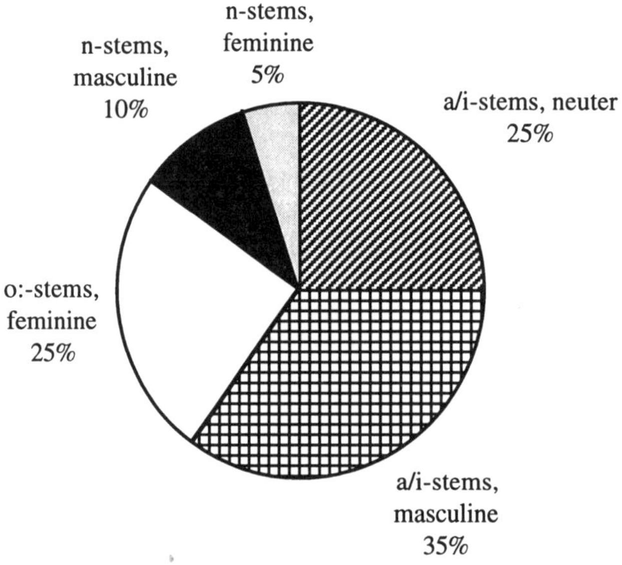

8 The statistics of OE noun classes are taken from Hogg 1992.

9 As will be shown later on, *a*- and *i*-stems can not be distinguished in a strictly synchronic analysis and have been grouped together here.

(3) Overview: The main OE declensions

		a/*i*-stems	*ō*-stems	*u*-stems	*n*-stems	athm.-stems
sg	nom	— / *-u*	— / *-u*	— / *-u*	*-a* / *-e*	—
	acc	— / *-u*	*-e*	— / *-u*	*-an*	—
	gen	*-es*	*-e*	*-a*	*-an*	*-es*
	dat	*-e*	*-e*	*-a*	*-an*	[Umlaut]
pl	nom	*-as* / *-u*	*-a*	*-a*	*-an*	[Umlaut]
	acc	*-as*	*-a*	*-a*	*-an*	[Umlaut]
	gen	*-a*	*-a*	*-a*	*-ena*	*-a*
	dat	*-um*	*-um*	*-um*	*-um*	*-um*

In the following section, I will go through each declension class, attempting to give an analysis for each class without relying on arbitrary features, but still assigning each affix unequivocally to its respective noun stem.

3. An analysis of the OE declension classes

3.1 *a*-stems (IE *o*-stems)

As already mentioned, this class was the most numerous noun class in OE: More than half of all OE nouns belonged to this class. Unsurprisingly, it was also the productive declension class in OE: Loan words patterned according to this declension,[10] nouns from other classes tended to migrate into this declension and *a*-stem nouns usually never moved to other declension classes. Nouns belonging to the *a*-declension were only masculine or neuter, so that feminine nouns cannot be found in this class.

The *a*-stems were not only the productive declension class, but also the most complex. Several subclasses can be distinguished according to the gender and phonological shape of

---

[10] If compatible with its gender.

the stem: Firstly, originally these nouns could have a glide (/j/ or /w/) between stem and vocalic extension, resulting in *a*-, *ja*- and *wa*-stems.

Besides this basic three-way subdivision, light and heavy noun stems display a different inflectional pattern. This distinction between light and heavy stems in OE is a consequence of *High Vowel Deletion*, which had great impacts on OE morphology, affecting all final high vowels after a heavy syllable. The primary target of this rule are, of course, inflectional affixes: Thus, as a result of *High Vowel Deletion*, all heavy stem nouns lost their inflection in those forms where the affix consisted out of a single high vowel, leaving behind only the bare stem.

Lastly, the inflectional pattern for *a*-stems differed according to the gender of the noun, so that there is a total of twelve possible subclasses: three theme vowels × two syllabic distinctions × two genders. Out of these twelve subclasses, only nine classes can actually be distinguished, the rest being homophonous to other subclasses. (4) lists all subclasses which can be clearly distinguished, together with examples for each class.

(4) *a*-stems: Subclasses

		masculine			neuter					
		a *stān*[11] *dæġ*	*ja* *here* *ende*	*wa* *snāw* *bearu*	*a* light *scip*	*a* heavy *word*	*ja*[12] 'light' *cynn*	*ja* heavy *wīte*	*wa* light *searu*	*wa* heavy *ʒād*
sg	nom	—	*-e*	*-u*	—	—	—	*-e*	*-u*	—
	acc	—	*-e*	*-u*	—	—	—	*-e*	*-u*	—
	gen	*-es*	*-es*	*-wes*	*-es*	*-es*	*-es*	*-es*	*-wes*	*-wes*
	dat	*-e*	*-e*	*-we*	*-e*	*-e*	*-e*	*-e*	*-we*	*-we*
pl	nom	*-as*	*-as*	*-was*	*-u*	—	—	*-u*	*-u*	—
	acc	*-as*	*-as*	*-was*	*-u*	—	—	*-u*	*-u*	—
	gen	*-a*	*-a*	*-wa*	*-a*	*-a*	*-a*	*-a*	*-wa*	*-wa*
	dat	*-um*	*-um*	*-wum*	*-um*	*-um*	*-um*	*-um*	*-wum*	*-wum*

[11] Translations: *stān* – 'stone', *dæg* – 'day', *here* – 'army', *ende* – 'end', *snāw* – 'snow', *bearu* – 'forest', *scip* – 'ship', *word* – 'word', *cynn* – 'kind', 'species', *wīte* – 'punishment', *scearu* – 'scissors', *ʒād* – 'need', 'lack of'.

[12] As will become clear later on, etymologically light *ja*-stems were not light in OE any more.

From the paradigm in (4) it is immediately obvious that the genitive and dative forms are similar throughout all subclasses: gen.sg is signalled by *–es/–wes*, dat.sg by *–e/–we*, gen.pl by *–a/–wa* and dat.pl by *–um/–wum*, with only the *wa*-stems differing by the presence of a glide. More heterogeneous are the nominative and accusative forms. In nom/acc.pl, the allomorphs are selected according to the gender of the noun stem: masculine forms always mark nom/acc.pl with *–as/–was*, whereas the neuter forms use *–u* or the bare stem. In singular, nom/acc forms vary between *–e/–u* and Ø. In general, though, nominative and accusative forms are always syncretistic for the *a*-stems.

The differences in the nom/acc.pl forms seem to be related to *High Vowel Deletion*, assuming that neuter forms are marked by the affix *–u* for nom/acc.pl. At this point, a closer look at *High Vowel Deletion* is needed. *High Vowel Deletion* (or also Apocopy) intuitively deletes a word-final high vowel after a heavy syllable or two light syllables.[13] Only high vowels after a single light syllable remain unaffected. Various proposals have been given in the literature to account for this phonological rule.[14] A reasonable analysis has been proposed by Dresher & Lahiri (1991), generalizing over the fact that the context of the deleted vowel is always the weak position of a foot, as shown in (5).

(5) High Vowel Deletion (Dresher & Lahiri 1991:255)

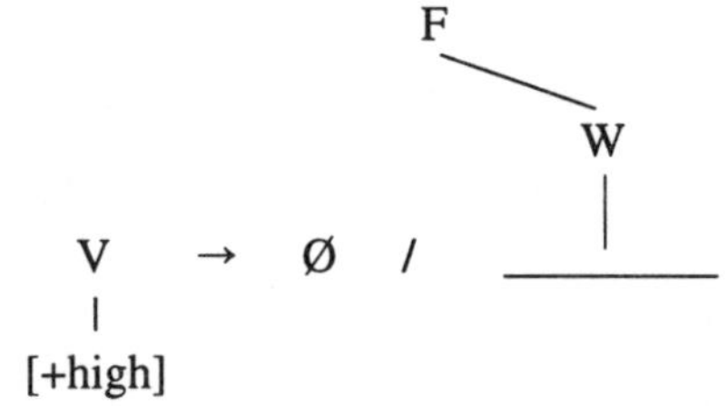

While it does not matter for present purposes which format is chosen to represent *High Vowel Deletion*, it is clear that it was a very common rule in OE and not a matter of dispute. A brief look at (4) will suggest that the empty cells in the nom/acc.pl forms for neuter stems might be explained as a consequence of *High Vowel Deletion*: The exponent for nom/acc.pl for neuter stems, *-u*, would be deleted after heavy stems, resulting in an empty cell.

Neuter *a*- and *wa*-stems behave exactly in the expected way: While the light stem form *scip-u* surfaces with a final *–u*, the underlying heavy stem form **word-u* surfaces as *word* after the deletion of the final *–u*. Likewise, in *sear-u* the final *–u* is not deleted, while the final *–u* of **cneaw-u* is deleted, so that the surface form is *cneaw*.

While *a*- and *wa*-stems confirm our expectations, *ja*-stems are much more problematic. Here, the exact reversal applies: stems which originally belonged to the Germanic light stems delete the final *–u* affix, whereas originally heavy stems retain it. From a synchronic perspective, though, the picture is less puzzling: *ja*-stems classified here as light are only 'etymologically' light. In Germanic, a combination of C + /j/ geminated to CC after short vowels, so that in all light OE *ja*-stems all final consonants had geminated, inevitably

[13] In OE, syllables with two short vowels in the orthography behave as light syllables.
[14] Cf. the references in fn. 6.

turning into heavy stems. Thus, with all originally 'light' *ja*-stems becoming heavy, they became a potential target for *High Vowel Deletion*. Consequently, the absence of the *–u* affix is expected and confirmed by the data.

But what still remains a puzzle is why heavy *ja*-stems do not delete the *–u* in nom/acc.pl. These stems (such as *wīte*) were originally heavy and of course remained so in OE. They would be expected to delete their nom/acc.pl inflection and their failure to do so is the only case where *High Vowel Deletion* is violated in OE and has not been explained convincingly in the literature.[15] This present study is not the place to offer such an explanation. It is obvious that the correct derivation of the form *wītu* is a matter of phonology proper and does not affect the present discussion whether arbitrary features are needed to establish inflectional classes.

Lahiri (1982) offers a solution which technically derives the correct forms, though not very satisfactorily. She maintains an underlying /j/-stem extension in the underlying form for *wīte*. A series of ordered rules apply to derive the correct singular and plural forms from the underlying form /w i i t j/, as shown in (6).

(6) Derivation of *wīte* and *wītu* (Lahiri 1982: 134-135)

	nom/acc.sg	nom/acc.pl
	/ w i i t j /	/ w i i t j u /
syllabification	w i i.t j	w i i.t j u
High Vowel Deletion	—	—
Glide Deletion	—	Ø
Word Final Vocalization	i	—
Lowering	e	—
	[w i i. t e]	[w i i. t u]

The desired effect (preventing *High Vowel Deletion* from applying) is achieved by the underlying glide /j/ which shelters the final *–u* from being deleted by *High Vowel Deletion*. This can only be achieved by extrinsic rule ordering, placing *High Vowel Deletion* before *Glide Deletion*.

All nom/acc.pl forms can be derived correctly by having two nom/acc.pl affixes distinguished by gender: *–u* applies only to neuter stems, *–as* to masculine stems.

***wa*-stems**

Another idiosyncrasy in paradigm (4) is due to the glide /w/ which surfaces in some forms of the *wa*-stems. This idiosyncrasy can easily be explained as a characteristic of the stem, if the glide /w/ is taken to be part of the stem. This final /w/ will be linked to a vowel position

[15] Most of the analyses cited in fn. 6 deal with this problem to a large extent.

and surface as /u/ if syllabification makes it necessary. E.g. a *wa*-stem noun like *bearu* will have an underlying form /b e a r w/, which will surface as /b e a r u/ if no affix follows (e.g. in nom/acc.sg). If, however, an affix follows which allows the glide /w/ to be parsed into the onset position, it will surface as /w/, exemplified by e.g. the gen.sg form /b e a r w e s/.

Now, because *wa*-stems have the in-built potential to realize their final /w/ as /u/, we would expect this /u/ to be subject to *High Vowel Deletion*, thus being deleted after heavy stems. This assumption is borne out by heavy *wa*-stems such as *ʒǣd*. From the affixed forms it can be seen that *ʒǣd* is a *wa*-stem, and consequently a final /u/ would be expected in nom/acc.sg. Being subject to *High Vowel Deletion*, this /u/ is deleted and the surface form /j a a d/ results.[16]

On the other hand, heavy *wa*-stems which are able to parse their final /w/ into their syllable structure should not delete it, as glides are not affected by *High Vowel Deletion*. Exactly this scenario obtains with the heavy *wa*-stems such as *sǣaw* – 'juice'. Here the final /w/ can be parsed into a syllable for lack of another coda-consonant. Consequently, it is not affected by *High Vowel Deletion* and remains even if not followed by an affix.

ja-*stems*

The last subclass of this declination to be analyzed, *ja*-stems, displays some similarity to the *wa*-stems in that *ja*-stems have a final vowel in their nom/acc.sg forms. It differs from the *wa*-stems, though, in those forms where an affix follows: Here, the original glide does not surface, in contrast to the /w/ of the *wa*-stems.

This idiosyncrasy of the *ja*-stems can easily be explained if one assumes that the final /e/ is realized in a 'floating position', e.g. as a vowel melody not linked to a timing slot on the CV-Tier, as shown in (7).

```
(7)   e   n   d   e
      |   |   |
      X   X   X
```

Now, if a V-initial affix follows, at the point of syllabification, the stem-final /e/ cannot be linked to a V-position and will remain unrealized. If, however, no affix follows, as in the nom/acc.sg forms, a V position can be inserted and the /e/ will be realized.

Generalization of all a-stem affixes

After a close inspection of all affixes of the *a*-declination, it turns out that the idiosyncrasies of *wa*- and *ja*-stems are due to special properties of the stem. Also, the different nom/acc.pl affixes clearly depend on the gender information of the stem: masculine *a*-stems form their nom/acc.pl with *–as*, neuter with *–u*. Forms where a bare noun stems occurs instead of an affixed form are the results of a general phonological rule *High Vowel Deletion*. There is no need to revert to arbitrary features in order to assign the *a*-stem affixes to their respective stems in order to derive the correct forms.

---

[16] Note that the /w/ is also lost when followed by a /u/ affix: *searw* + *u* → *searu*.

All *a*-stem affixes can be organized in an inheritance tree, as in (8).[17] The interpretation is monotonic for morphological information: Each leaf inherits the information of its mother node; new information is added via monotonic unification: values can only be added, they are never deleted or overridden. The organization of the phonological information is of course non-monotonic, each leaf introducing a new lexical entry: a new affix for the present purpose. The base node is only marked with the respective lexical categories, to ensure that the affixes organized in this inheritance tree concatenate only with noun stems.

(8) Affixes of the *a*-stems: Inheritance tree

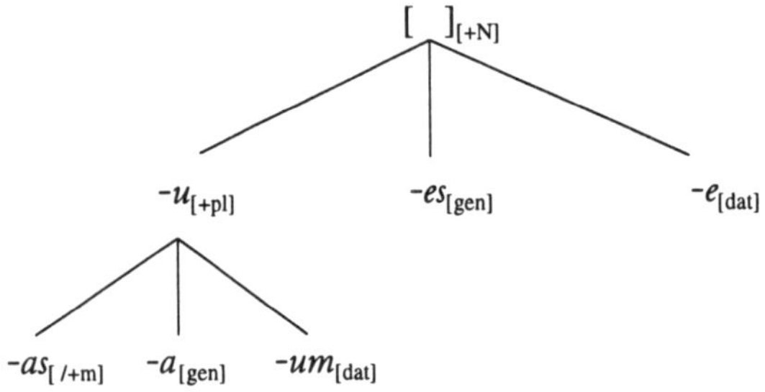

The representation of affixes in such an inheritance tree has some advantages which cannot be achieved by simply listing them separately. Firstly, some redundancies can be eliminated by the inheritance structure: Number information [+pl] need not be repeated in the information of the affixes *–as*, *–a* and *–um*. Likewise, category information has to be only represented once in the top node, rather than repeating it for each affix. Secondly, the inheritance tree (8) directly encodes a markedness relation of the affixes involved. Thus, the affix *–a* is more marked than the affix *–es* because it inherits information from two nodes, whereas *–es* inherits information only from the top node (which inherits from no other node, thus being the default node).

Since gender information is inherent to the noun, it only needs to be specified on the affix as context information, being represented on the right side of a slash, in the fashion of Categorial Grammar. Note that I take neuter to be the default gender in OE,[18] so that only the plural affix for the masculine stems (*–as*) has to be marked for gender. The neuter plural affix (*–u*) is underspecified and has no context information, being the default affix for plural.

Underspecification applies also to the case information used in (8): Since nominative and accusative forms are not distinguished for *a*-stem nouns, it would be an unnecessary complication to assume an additional accusative besides the nominative form. There is simply no accusative case *a*-stem form, but only a single *Elsewhere* case form which applies whenever the more specific genitive and dative case forms can not be used. Being an *Elsewhere* case form, it is underspecified and no case information is provided.

[17] A similar inheritance tree is used by W&F (1995), though only for the representation of irregular inflectional elements, e.g. auxiliaries, determiners and irregular verbs.

[18] This is supported by independent evidence, neuter being the case of expletives, impersonals and as subject of 'psych' verbs see also Steins (1997).

3.2 *i*-stems

The next declination to be analyzed, the *i*-stems, had either masculine or neuter gender. There were no subclasses besides the general OE split between heavy and neuter stems and the gender distinction. Paradigm (9) lists all forms of the *i*-stems.

(9) *i*-stems: Subclasses

		masculine		neuter	
		light *wine*[19]	heavy *enȝle*	light *spere*	heavy[20] *hǣl*
sg	nom	*-e*	—	*-e*	—
	acc	*-e*	—	*-e*	—
	gen	*-es*	*-es*	*-es*	*-es*
	dat	*-e*	*-e*	*-e*	*-e*
pl	nom	*-as*	*-as*	*-u*	—
	acc	*-as*	*-as*	*-u*	—
	gen	*-a*	*-a*	*-a*	*-a*
	dat	*-um*	*-um*	*-um*	*-um*

A short glance at (9) reveals that the inflection of the *i*-stems is parallel to that of the *ja*-stems. In fact, some grammars describe *i*-stems as having been absorbed completely by the *a*-declination. In fact, the analysis given for *a*-stems can be transferred directly to the *i*-declination: If the light *i*-stems are represented with a final floating *–e* like the *ja*-stems, no additional assumptions have to be made: Being the default declination, the affixes of the *a*-stems are directly available to *i*-stems as well. The gender-specific plural forms, too, result directly from the context conditions assigned to the plural *a*-stem affixes. Masculine *i*-stems receive the affix *–as*, which is marked with a [+m] context condition, and neuter *i*-stems inflect with the default plural affix *–u*, which is being deleted in the case of heavy neuter *i*-stems as a result of *High Vowel Deletion.*

Thus, light/heavy masculine *i*-stems resemble light/heavy masculine *ja*-stems and light/heavy neuter *i*-stems resemble how light/heavy neuter *ja*-stems should have patterned

---

19 Translations: *wine* – 'friend', *engle* – 'angel', *spere* – 'spear', *hǣl* – 'salvation'.

20 Note that etymologically pure heavy neuter *i*-stems are not recorded, but nouns shifting from other declinations (here: originally heavy *jō*-stems) have filled this slot, so that in OE they pattern exactly like heavy neuter *i*-stems would be expected to inflect.

without the complication achieved by Germanic gemination and non-application of *High Vowel Deletion*.

With the *i*-stems patterning exactly parallel to *a*-stems, there is no need to establish a separate inflectional class from a synchronic perspective. If *a*-stems and *i*-stems share exactly the same affixes and if the lexical entries for their stems do not show any differences, they can in fact not be distinguished and consequently do not constitute separate classes. It is therefore redundant to refer to *a*-stems and *i*-stems separately. Instead, in the following I am going to refer to both declinations simply as *a*-stems, which will include those noun stems etymologically belonging to the *i*-declination.

3.3 *ō*-stems (IE *ā*)

Having established an analysis of the *a*-stem (and *i*-stem) nouns, the productive (default) declination in OE, it is now necessary to turn to the other declinations to find out whether these declinations can also be analyzed without the use of arbitrary features. Where the investigation of the *a*-stems only needed to be concerned with deriving the right forms for each subclass, the task at hand now is more complex: Besides deriving each subclass correctly, there is a twofold need to unequivocally assign affixes to stems. On the one hand, affixes should not be able to concatenate with noun stems from other declinations; on the other hand noun stems should only be inflected with affixes from their respective declination. The latter part is not trivial since there is a default declination with no context condition (*a*-stems) whose affixes can in principle be affixed to nouns of any declination.

The next major declination besides the *a*-stems is the *ō*-declination. *ō*-stems consisted exclusively of feminine noun stems. Accordingly, if nouns from minor ('irregular') declinations shifted to one of the main declinations (i.e. 'became regular'), they patterned with the *a*-stems if they were masculine or neuter and with the *ō*-stems if they had feminine gender. Just like *a*-stems, *ō*-stems could also have a glide (/j/ or /w/) between the stem and the vocalic extension, resulting in *jō*- and *wō*-stems as subclasses.

As can be seen from the nom.sg forms in (10), *ō*-stems are also affected by *High Vowel Deletion*, but without the irregularities observed with the *a*-stems. If *–u* is assumed to mark nom.sg for *ō*-stems, the right forms will automatically be derived by *High Vowel Deletion*. Light *ō*-stems have the expected final *–u*, whereas heavy stems delete it (e.g. *ār*: /a: r u/ → /a: r/). The same holds true for heavy and light *wō*-stems, but *jō*-stems need some more explanation. Just like *ja*-stems, *jō*-stems were also subject to the rule of *Gemination* before the OE period. This resulted in the light *jō*-stems geminating their final consonant, so that synchronically light OE *jō*-stems had actually become heavy. Thus we would expect light *jō*-stems, just like heavy *jō*-stems, to undergo *High Vowel Deletion*, deleting the nom.sg affix *–u*. The data clearly confirms this expectation: Both *jō*-stems, heavy and light, have no *–u* in nom.sg. For *wō*-stems, the glide /w/ can be taken as part of the stems and the same analysis which derived the correct forms for *wa*-stems will give the right results.

(10) *ō*-stems: Subclasses

		feminine		
		ō-stems heavy/light *ār* / *ʒiefu*[21]	*jō*-stems heavy/'light' *ʒierd* / *sibb*	*wō*-stems heavy/light *mǣd* / *beadu*
sg	nom	— / *-u*	— / —	— / *-u*
	acc	*-e*	*-e*	*-we*
	gen	*-e*	*-e*	*-we*
	dat	*-e*	*-e*	*-we*
pl	nom	*-a*	*-a*	*-wa*
	acc	*-a*	*-a*	*-wa*
	gen	*-a*	*-a*	*-wa*
	dat	*-um*	*-um*	*-wum*

Having eliminated the idiosyncrasies of the *ō*-stem subclasses, four affixes can be segmented out of the forms in paradigm (10): *–u* for nom.sg, *–e* as a general affix for governed case in the singular, *–um* for dat.pl and *–a* as a general plural case. Because *ō*-stems are exclusively feminine in gender and *a*-stems never feminine, the context condition [+f] will suffice to prevent the *ō*-stem affixes from combining with *a*-stem nouns. The four *ō*-stem affixes can be represented using the inheritance tree (11). The context condition [/+f] is encoded on the top node, together with the categorial information +N, thus being inherited by all other nodes.

(11) Affixes of the *ō*-stems: Inheritance tree

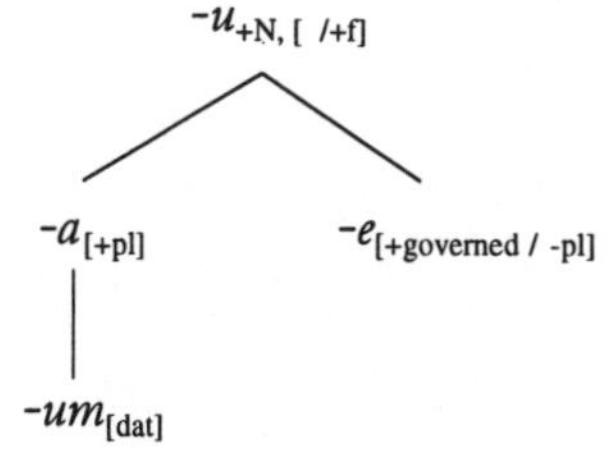

[21] Translations: *ār* – 'honour', *giefu* – 'gift', *gierd* – 'switch', 'crop', *sibb* – 'peace', *mǣd* – 'meadow', *beadu* – 'battle'.

In (11) uses the somewhat intuitive case specification [+governed], referring to any case besides the subject case. So far, the case features used in the analyses have been somewhat dissatisfying. Firstly, they are not binary like all other features used in the analyses. Secondly they do not constitute a coherent system with specific features being used such as dat, gen, as well as general features such as [+governed]; and lastly, most of the features employed do not make use of underspecification.

Therefore, I would like to introduce the system of case features developed in Wunderlich's (1997) *Lexical Decomposition Grammar* (LDG)[22] at this point. This system has a clear advantage over the system used so far in that it is a coherent system of case features being underspecified and using only binary values.

The core of the LDG case system is the decomposition of verbs into complex predicates, which yields a hierarchy of all arguments of the verb. This hierarchy can be used to link each argument to its specific case by aligning cases to positions in this hierarchy. These positions can be encoded in terms of the binary features [±hr] ('there is a higher role') and [±lr] ('there is a lower role'). If the different cases are represented with the features listed in (12), they can be linked to their respective slots in the argument hierarchy, the most specified case having priority over underspecified cases: Dative will be linked to any position having a higher as well as a lower role (typically the recipient in 3-place verbs, cf. 12.b.iii). Accusative will be linked to the argument which is dominated by another higher role (the remaining lowest argument in 3-place verbs (cf. 12.b.iii) or the lowest argument in 2-place verbs, cf. 12.b.ii). The *Elsewhere* case is Nominative; being unspecified, it can be linked to the remaining argument positions, which is in each case the highest argument slot (cf. 12.b.i-iii). Genitive is the case occupying an argument slot with a higher role, but which is governed by a nominal element ([+N]), cf. 12.b.iv.[23]

(12) The case system of Lexical Decomposition Grammar (Wunderlich 1997)

a. Case linkers

nom	[ ]
acc	[+hr]
dat	[+hr,+lr]
gen	[+hr,+N]

b. Sample derivations (German)

(i.)	*schlafen*	λx	λs	SLEEP(x) (s)
		-hr		
		-lr		
		$[\ ]_{NOM}$		

[22] A similar system has been proposed by Kiparsky (1992).

[23] Note that this system can easily be extended to various other case systems. See Wunderlich (1997) for details.

(ii.) *küssen*	λy	λx		λs	KISS(x,y) (s)
	+hr	-hr			
	-lr	+lr			
	$[+hr]_{ACC}$	$[\ ]_{NOM}$			

(iii.) *geben*	λz	λy	λx	λs	CAUSE(x, BEC(POSS(y, z)))(s)
	+hr	+hr	-hr		
	-lr	+lr	+lr		
	$[+hr]_{ACC}$	$[+hr,+lr]_{DAT}$	$[\ ]_{NOM}$		

(iv.) *Vater*	λy	λx	FATHER(x,y)
	+hr	-hr	
	-lr	+lr	
	$[+hr,+N]_{GEN}$		

The advantages of this system for our present analysis are obvious: The system consists out of a minimal amount of three features (±hr, ±lr, ±N) with a coherent interpretation for all cases. All features are strictly binary, which allows a direct encoding of markedness, and makes it possible for them to be treated in the same way as the other features employed so far (such as ±pl, ±m, ±f). Finally, the case system in (12) makes use of underspecification, avoiding any redundancies.

Going back to the analysis of the OE *ō*-stems, it is now possible to rewrite the inheritance tree (11) with the features proposed in (12.a). As can be seen from (13), the scope of the affix *–e*, which had earlier been described with [+governed], is now easily accounted for with the case specification [+hr]. The input [/ -pl] is necessary for this affix in order to prevent a 'double' affixation $-a_{[+pl]}-e_{[+hr]}$ for acc/gen.pl.

(13) Affixes of the *ō*-stems: LDG case features

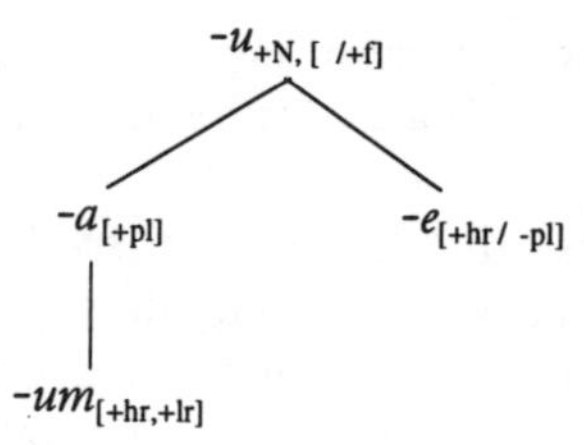

It turns out then, that not only the *a*-stems, but also the *ō*-stems, the second most important declension in OE in terms of quantity, can also be analyzed without the need to refer to arbitrary features: The gender feature [+f] suffices to distinguish them from *a*-stem nouns.

3.4 *n*-stems

The weak OE declension, the *n*-stems, were the third largest group of noun stems in the OE lexicon. Originally, the *n*-declination contained nouns of all three genders, but in OE this variability had (almost) been levelled out, so that only two neuter nouns still belonged to this group: *eage* – 'eye' and *eare* – 'ear'. Apart from these two exceptions, all other *n*-stem nouns were either masculine or feminine. Furthermore, both genders were distinguished phonologically: masculine forms always had a final *–a* in nom.sg, feminine nouns a final *–e*. Apart from this gender distinction, no subclasses can be distinguished within the *n*-stems, as can been seen in (14).

(14) *n*-stems: Inflectional affixes

		masculine/feminine *ȝuma / tunge*[24]
sg	nom	*-a / -e*
	acc	*-an*
	gen	*-an*
	dat	*-an*
pl	nom	*-an*
	acc	*-an*
	gen	*-ena*
	dat	*-um*

The inflections of the *n*-stems are not very differentiated, most forms containing only the suffix *–an*. Besides the nom.sg form, only in plural there is a distinction for case: gen.pl and dat.pl.

The gender specifications of *n*-stems cut across the declensions, so that here, the phonological information inherent to *n*-stems has to be used to specify the right context for the *n*-stem affixes. Because *a*-stems have a closed final syllable, masculine *n*-stems can be singled out by referring to their final /a/ and their [+m] gender together. The other feminine nouns, the *ō*-stems in the present analysis also have a consonantal stem, their final /u/ being a nom.sg affix. Consequently, feminine *n*-stems can also be clearly separated from all other stems by referring to gender ([+f]) and phonological features (final /e/) at the same time. These conditions combined together disjunctively will ensure that all *n*-stems can be identified uniquely.

As can be seen from (15), the disjunctive context condition [(/a/,+m) ∨ (/e/,+f)] is specified on the top node, thus being inherited to all other nodes. There are two specific plural case affixes: *–ena* and *–um* with the specifications [+pl,+hr,+N] and [+pl,+hr,+lr] for

[24] Translations: *ȝuma* – 'man', *tunge* – 'tongue'.

gen.pl and dat.pl. The affix *–an* is the elsewhere affix which covers the remaining paradigm cells. This affix is nevertheless specified for case in order to prevent if from attaching to nom.sg forms. The disjunctive specification [+hr ∨ +pl] includes all governed cases as well as default plural forms.

This analysis presumes that the final vowel in nom.sg of the *n*-stems is part of the stem, unlike the final nom.sg *–u* of the *ō*-stems. This is needed so that these vowels can be referred to in the context condition. Note that these final vowels are realized in a floating position, in the same way as the final /e/ of *ja-* and *jō*-stems. If a vowel-initial affix follows the stem, these floating vowels cannot be linked to a V-position and do not surface, as the examples (16) show.

(15) Affixes of the *n*-stems: Inheritance tree

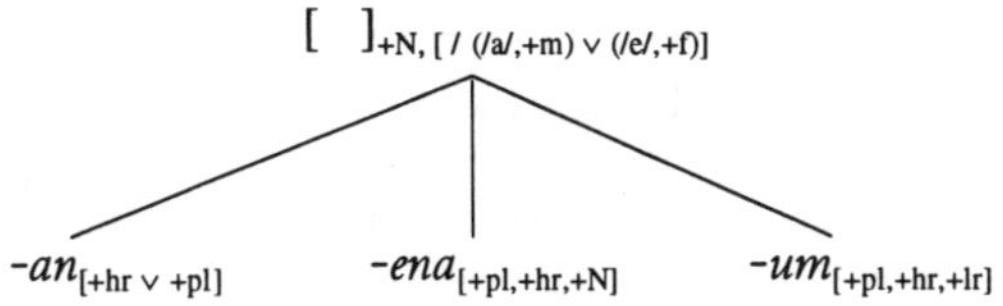

(16) a. *ʒuma + an* → *ʒuman*
b. *tunge + an* → *tungan*
c. *tunge + um* → *tungum*

3.5 Athematic noun stems

Athematic nouns exhibit i-umlaut of the stem vowel in the dat.sg and nom/acc.pl forms, a fact which distinguishes them from all other OE nouns. This is a consequence of the interplay of the absence of a stem vowel extension and productive i-umlaut in Germanic: In forms where the inflection had an initial high front vowel (in Germanic dat.sg and nom.pl), the stem vowel became a potential target for i-umlaut. In OE, i-umlaut ceased to be a productive phonological process; nevertheless the umlauted stem vowel was grammaticalized and even extended by analogy to the acc.pl of athematic stems. Therefore, in OE, athematic nouns had two stems: one general default stem and one stem for dat.sg and nom/acc.pl with umlauted stem vowel, cf. (17). A number of these umlauted stems have remained irregular plural stems to this day.

(17) Athematic noun stems: Inflectional affixes

		masculine *fōt – fēt*[25]	feminine *hnutu – hnyte*
sg	nom	—	—
	acc	—	—
	gen	*-es*	*-e*
	dat	[Umlaut]	[Umlaut]*-e*
pl	nom	[Umlaut]	[Umlaut]*-e*
	acc	[Umlaut]	[Umlaut]*-e*
	gen	*-a*	*-a*
	dat	*-um*	*-um*

Athematic nouns were not very common, numbering approx. 25 nouns, most of the nouns being feminine.[26] The inflections of the non-umlauted forms are parallel to the *a*- and *ō*-stems, according to the gender of the noun. Because i-umlaut was not a productive rule in OE anymore and because the number of athematic noun stems is very limited, these nouns belonged to the irregular inflection and should therefore be listed in the lexicon. (18) is an example for a listing of two of these stems. Here, too, the forms can be listed in the form of an inheritance tree, as has been done for affixes throughout this analysis. The default ('citation') stem occupies the top node and the umlauted stem is listed on a lower node, inheriting all information from the top node (e.g. lexical category, semantic representation, etc.), but being supplied with a case/number specification: [+hr,+lr ∨ +pl] (dat.sg or default plural). The representation of feminine athematic stems is roughly like in (18), but will be revised later on.

(18)

fōt	$hnut^{u}$
|	|
$fēt_{[+hr,+lr \vee +pl]}$	$hnyte_{[+hr,+lr \vee +pl]}$

The other inflected forms can be generated automatically with the affixes already available from other declensions, i.e. no specific affixes have to be given for the athematic nouns. (19) lists all possible combinations of masculine athematic nouns with compatible *a*-stem

[25] Translations: *fōt* – 'foot', *hnutu* – 'nut'.

[26] Feminine: *hnutu, studu, hnitu, bōc, āc, gāt, brōc, gōs, burg, furh, sulh, turf, grūt, lūs, mūs, þrūh, cū, ēa, neaht*; masculine: *fōt, tōþ, mann*; neuter: *scrūd*. The inflectional forms of the neuter form *scrūd* are not all attested and are therefore not included in the paradigm.

affixes. Not compatible are *ō*-stem affixes (gender mismatch) and *n*-stems (no masculine athematic noun stems has a final /a/).

(19) Masculine athematic noun stems + *a*-stem affixes

a. Correct forms

fōt + -*es*$_{[+hr,+N]}$ → *fōtes*$_{[+hr,+N]}$ (gen.sg)
fōt + -*a*$_{[+pl,+hr,+N]}$ → *fōta*$_{[+pl,+hr,+N]}$ (gen.pl)
fōt + -*um*$_{[+pl,+hr,+lr]}$ → *fōtum*$_{[+pl,+hr,+lr]}$ (dat.pl)

b. Impossible combinations

fōt / *fēt*$_{[+hr,+lr \vee +pl]}$ + -*as*$_{[+pl/+m]}$ → **fōtas*$_{[+pl]}$ / **fētas*$_{[+pl]}$ (pl)
fēt$_{[+hr,+lr \vee +pl]}$ + -*a*$_{[+pl,+hr,+N]}$ → **fēta*$_{[+pl,+hr,+N]}$ (gen.pl)
fēt$_{[+hr,+lr \vee +pl]}$ + -*um*$_{[+pl,+hr,+lr]}$ → **fētum*$_{[+pl,+hr,+lr]}$ (dat.pl)
fēt$_{[+hr,+lr \vee +pl]}$ + -*es*$_{[+hr,+N]}$ → **fētes*$_{[+pl,+hr,+N]}$ (gen.pl)
fēt$_{[+hr,+lr \vee +pl]}$ + -*e*$_{[+hr,+lr]}$ → **fēte*$_{[+pl,+hr,+lr]}$ (dat.pl)

The correct forms *fōt-es*$_{[+hr,N]}$, *fōt-a*$_{[+pl,+hr,N]}$ and *fōt-um*$_{[+pl,+hr,+lr]}$ are derived correctly (19.a), whereas the incorrect forms (19.b) are excluded: **fōt-as*$_{[+pl]}$ is blocked by the umlauted stem *fēt*$_{[+pl]}$; **fēt-as*$_{[+pl]}$ is formed by redundant affixation; **fēt-a*$_{[+pl,+hr,+N]}$ and **fēt-um*$_{[+pl,+hr,+lr]}$ are blocked because the simpler forms *fōta*$_{[+pl,+hr,+N]}$ and *fōtum*$_{[+pl,+hr,+lr]}$ are available; **fēt-es*$_{[+pl,+hr,+N]}$ is less specific than the preferred *fōta*$_{[+pl,+hr,+N]}$ and similarly **fēt-e*$_{[+pl,+hr,+lr]}$ is also less specific than *fōtum*$_{[+pl,+hr,+lr]}$.[27]

A close inspection of the forms of feminine athematic nouns reveals a puzzle. Generally it seems that —like masculine athematic nouns— feminine atematic nouns also share their inflectional affixes with the prominent feminine declension (*ō*-stems). This is true apart from one form: acc.sg is not the expected *hnut-e* (like e.g. the *ō*-stem *ʒief-e*), but instead a form homophonous with the nom.sg *hnutu*. This can be redeemed by enlarging the specification of the default stem of feminine athematic nouns with an optional specification [+hr/-N] ('having a higher role, dominated by a non-nominal (=verbal) category), referring to accusative or dative cases. Because dative case is already specified fully by the second stem *hnyte* it blocks *hnutu* for dative. What remains for *hnutu*$_{[+hr/-N]}$ is only the correct cell: acc.sg. A revised representation of the feminine athematic stems given in (20).

(20) *hnut*$^{u}_{[(+hr/-N)]}$
|
hnyte$_{[+hr,+lr \vee +pl]}$

Having established the correct specifications of the feminine athematic noun stems, (21) – (22) list the possible combinations of stems and affixes. Feminine athematic nouns can combine with either *a*-stem (default) or *ō*-stem affixes (feminine context), with the most specific affixes being preferred. The affixes of *n*-stems cannot apply since there are no feminine athematic nouns with a final /e/, which is the context of these affixes.

---

27 Disjunctive specifications (e.g. [+hr,+lr ∨ +pl]) are less specific than a specification without disjunction (e.g. [+pl]). Therefore the combination of *fēt*$_{[+hr,+N \vee +pl]}$ with the affix -*es*$_{[+hr,+N]}$ is less specific than the combination *fōt*$_{[\ ]}$ + -*a*$_{[+pl,+hr,+N]}$.

(21) Feminine athematic noun stems + *a*-stem affixes

a. Correct forms

$hnut^{u}_{[\,(+hr\,/\text{-}N)\,]} + \text{-}a_{[+pl,+hr,+N]}$	→	$hnuta_{[+pl,+hr,+N]}$	(gen.pl)
$hnut^{u}_{[\,(+hr\,/\text{-}N)\,]} + \text{-}um_{[+pl,+hr,+lr]}$	→	$hnutum_{[+pl,+hr,+lr]}$	(dat.pl)

b. Impossible combinations

$hnut^{u}_{[\,(+hr\,/\text{-}N)\,]} + \text{-}es_{[+hr,+N]}$	→	$*hnutes_{[+hr,+N]}$	(gen.sg)
$hnut^{u}_{[\,(+hr\,/\text{-}N)\,]}\,/\,hnyte_{[+hr,+lr\,\vee\,+pl]} + \text{-}u_{[+pl]}$	→	$*hnut^{u}\text{-}e_{[+pl]}\,/\,*hnyte\text{-}e_{[+pl]}$	(pl)
$hnyte_{[+hr,+lr\,\vee\,+pl]} + \text{-}a_{[+pl,+hr,+N]}$	→	$*hnyte\text{-}a_{[+pl,+hr,+N]}$	(gen.pl)
$hnyte_{[+hr,+lr\,\vee\,+pl]} + \text{-}um_{[+pl,+hr,+lr]}$	→	$*hnyte\text{-}um_{[+pl,+hr,+lr]}$	(dat.pl)
$hnyte_{[+hr,+lr\,\vee\,+pl]} + \text{-}es_{[+hr,+N]}$	→	$*hnyte\text{-}es_{[+pl,+hr,+N]}$	(gen.pl)
$hnyte_{[+hr,+lr\,\vee\,+pl]} + \text{-}e_{[+hr,+lr]}$	→	$*hnyte\text{-}e_{[+pl,+hr,+lr]}$	(dat.pl)

(22) Feminine athematic noun stems + *ō*-stem affixes (context [+f])

a. Correct forms

$hnut^{u}_{[\,(+hr\,/\text{-}N)\,]} + \text{-}e_{[+hr\,/\text{-}pl]}$	→	$hnute_{[+hr]}$	(gen.sg)

b. Impossible combinations

$hnut^{u}_{[\,(+hr\,/\text{-}N)\,]}\,/\,hnyte_{[+hr,+lr\,\vee\,+pl]} + \text{-}a_{[+pl]}$	→	$*hnut^{u}\text{-}a_{[+pl]}\,/\,hnyte\text{-}a_{[+pl]}$	(pl)

The forms in (21.b) are mostly incorrect for the same reasons why the same combinations with masculine stems were incorrect (19.b). Additionally, the form $*hnutes_{[+hr,+N]}$ (gen.sg) is blocked because the affix $\text{-}e_{[+hr/\,\text{-}pl]}$ is available and is to be preferred because of its specific input condition [+f]. The combination of the default feminine stem $hnut^{u}_{[\,(+hr\,/\text{-}N)\,]}$ with the *ō*-stem affix $\text{-}e_{[+hr\,/\text{-}pl]}$ is possible and results in $hnute_{[+hr]}$ (22.a), yet in paradigmatic contrast with the available simple stem form $hnut^{u}_{[\,(+hr\,/\text{-}N)\,]}$, the form $hnute_{[+hr]}$ can only be used in [+N] contexts (gen.sg), because the more specific $hnut^{u}_{[\,(+hr\,/\text{-}N)\,]}$ blocks it for [-N] contexts (acc.sg). Concerning (22.b) a combination of both stem forms with the *ō*-stem plural affix $a_{[+pl]}$ is possible, but is blocked by the presence of the available simple stem form $hnyte_{[+hr,+lr\,\vee\,+pl]}$, which already covers [+pl] contexts.

The athematic declension can be analyzed be listing two separate stems in the lexicon. It is not necessary to list all inflectional forms of this declension, — instead, the default affixes available from the two major declensions suffice to derive all forms correctly. It is not necessary to postulate separate affixes with an arbitrary class feature as context condition.

3.6 *u*-stems

One of the minor OE declensions is the *u*-declension. It comprised 10 OE nouns, the majority being masculine, two feminine and none neuter.[28] The forms are given in paradigm (23).

[28] Originally, *u*-stems also contained neuter nouns, but in OE these had already migrated to other declension. In OE, the *u*-declensions consisted of the following nouns: masculine: *sunu*, *wudu*, *feld*,

(23) *n*-stems: Inflectional affixes

		heavy/light *feld* / *sunu*[29]
sg	nom	— / *-u*
	acc	— / *-u*
	gen	*-a*
	dat	*-a*
pl	nom	*-a*
	acc	*-a*
	gen	*-a*
	dat	*-um*

With only a handful of nouns belonging to this inflectional class, it is obvious that this was not a productive declination. Therefore it can safely be assumed that the nouns belonging to the *u*-declination are listed in the lexicon as irregular items. However, not all forms have to be listed, as default inflectional affixes (those of the *a*-stems) are available. Therefore, the form *sunum* (dat.pl) does not have to be listed, but instead is automatically generated by concatenating the dat.pl *–um* of *a*-stems with the stem *sunu*. Only two different forms have to be listed: *sunu* and *sunum*.

(24) $sun^{u}{}_{+N}$
|
$suna_{[+hr(+N,+lr) \vee +pl]}$

The nom.sg sun^{u} is –as always– the default top node, whereas *suna* occupies the lower node, accounting for the other case forms. The case forms of *suna* could easily be accounted for by the specification [+hr ∨ +pl] (dat.pl being provided by the more specific sun^{u} + *um*). This however would not prevent a further affixation with the dative and genitive affixes of the *a*-stems, $-e_{[+hr,+N]}$ and $-es_{[+hr,+N]}$, which as default affixes are potential candidates also for *u*-stems. This would result in the non-attested **sune* (dat.sg) and **sunes* (gen.sg). If

ford, *sumor*, *winter*, *æppel*; feminine: *duru*, *hand*. Note that none of these nouns contains a final /a/ or /e/, so that it could potentially conflict with the context condition of the *n*-stems.

29 Translations: *sunu* – 'son', *feld* – 'field'.

however, the less general specification [+hr (+N,+lr) ∨ +pl][30] is chosen for *suna*, the problem is solved because affixation of further dative or genitive affixes is blocked.[31]

3.6 Miscellaneous declensions

There are a number of other minor declensions (*r*-, *es-/os*-, *et/ot*-, *nd*-declensions). These, however, contain even less nouns than the *u*-stems and can be regarded as fully irregular. Their forms are listed in the lexicon, in a similar fashion as athematic noun stems and *u*-stems are listed in the lexicon, sharing some of the affixes of other declensions. A detailed analysis of these nouns, though, is clearly beyond the scope of this paper.

3.7 Representation of all affixes together

While in the present analysis the affixes of each declension class have been treated independently with a separate representation for each class, it is unlikely that these affixes will be stored in the lexicon separately. Instead, a representation which groups all these affixes together seems to be much closer to the reality.

Again, an inheritance tree is a suitable tool to form a single unit out of all affixes of the OE noun inflection. By combining all affixes into a general inheritance tree, more redundancy can be avoided: Thus, the dat.pl affix *–um* has been included for each declension class. If however it is placed on a higher node in a general inheritance tree for all classes, it is available for all noun stems and need not be listed for each class separately. Such a general inheritance tree is given in (25).

(25)

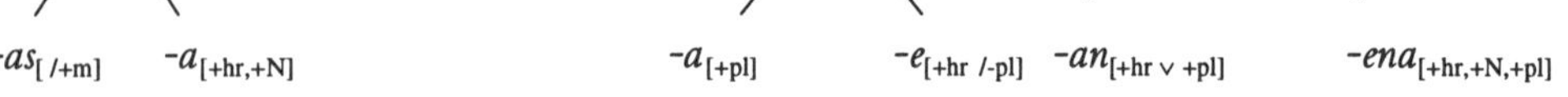

Like before, the top node displays information about the lexical category. On the second level nodes, there are on the one hand the default affixes of the *a*-stems and on the other hand the former top nodes of the *ō*-stem and *n*-stem affixes. Note that even though the output of the second level node [ ]$_{[/ (/a/,+m) \vee (/e/,+f)]}$ is empty, it nevertheless adds new in-

---

[30] The specification [+hr(+N,+lr)] is the short version for [+hr,+N ∨ +hr,+lr].

[31] Note that the affixation of the *a*-stem gen.pl affix $-a_{[+pl,+hr,+N]}$ to *u*-stems is not blocked but vacuous: *sun*^{u} + *a* → *suna*.

formation by virtue of its context condition. Now, the dat.pl affix *–um* can apply to all declensions and need not be listed separately.

4. Conclusions

The analysis presented above is able to assign all affixes of the OE noun inflection uniquely to their respective noun stems, while avoiding the use of any features which are not needed for independent reasons. Only the gender features [±m] and [±f] are needed with neuter being the unspecified default gender. In some cases phonological information of the stems is needed as a context condition for affixes. Unproductive declension classes have some of their forms listed in the lexicon, the other forms are generated automatically through combination with affixes available from other declensions.

Coming back to the question whether arbitrary features are needed in the analysis of inflectional classes, this case study of the OE declension supports the view that arbitrary features are unnecessary. Obviously, since this is only a case study of a single language, it can not be any proof for the hypothesis that arbitrary features are unnecessary in all languages. Further case studies are needed to bring substantial support for this hypothesis.

At this point, it is worth considering if it would be conceivable that inflectional classes might surface as an interim phenomenon in the development of a language. A phonologically delimited class could become opaque to the learner by phonological change, but still remain active as a class or pattern for some time until those lexical items have merged with a more transparent class or formed a new one. Some reflexes of this can be found e.g. in the different subregularities observed within the German irregular verbs. Thus, it has often been observed that speakers produce irregular preterite forms for artificially construed verbs such as *kringen* (produced preterite form: *krang*) in analogy to the pattern of *singen – sang*, *stinken – stank*, *trinken – trank*, even though perfectly regular forms such as *winken – winkte* and *schminken – schminkte* exist. In how far these phenomena occur only as interim stages in the diachrony of a language and if arbitrary features are needed to explain this behaviour is here left to further research.

Apart from contributing to the discussion about arbitrary inflectional features, this case study has also shed more light on the OE declension. It has shown that there are three major productive declension classes: *a/i*-, *ō*- and *n*-stems. The other declension classes do not display productive patterns. However, not all of their forms are 'irregular' in the sense of being listed in the lexicon. Both the athematic declension and the *u*-stem nouns have two stems which are listed in the lexicon; the remaining inflectional forms are still generated productively. They can therefore be called 'semi-productive'.

Among the three fully productive declension classes in OE there is a clear markedness hierarchy: *a/i*-stems are the default, unmarked class with no context restriction; *ō*-stems in contrast are marked with the context condition [+f]; most marked are the *n*-stems, having a complex input condition referring to both gender and phonological information.

The effects of this markedness can be seen in quantity and diachronic robustness. Thus, the most unmarked declension class (*a/i*-stems) comprises more than half of all OE nouns.

Diachronically, this class has persisted to this day: the Modern English *–s* plural can be traced back to the *a*-stem plural affix *–as*. The more marked *ō*-stems are less common, constituting 25% of all OE nouns. Remnants of the *ō*-stem plurals can still be found in Late Middle English (e.g. plural *–e*). *n*-stems are highly marked, not very common (15% of all OE nouns) and have not been very stable diachronically: Apart from a few exceptions[32] the *n*-stem inflection has only remained until the Middle English period.

(26) Markedness of the OE declension classes

	% of all OE nouns	*diachronic stability*
a/i-stems	60 %	Modern English
ō-stems	25%	Late Middle English
n-stems	15%	Middle English

The ranking of the OE declension classes with regard to quantity and diachronic stability thus directly corresponds to their morphological markedness as evidenced by the complexity of context conditions. Inflectional classes with a more complex input are morphologically more marked and less preferred: they tend to be confined to less items and speakers are inclined to abandon them in favour of less marked classes.[33]

Note that it is only possible to establish such a correspondence when not making use of arbitrary inflectional features. Because arbitrary features are not ordered in an intrinsic hierarchy, it is not possible to establish a scale of morphological markedness with arbitrary features. Thus implications regarding quantity and diachronic stability are not possible.

References

Brunner, Karl (1962): *Die englische Sprache: Ihre geschichtliche Entwicklung.* Zweiter Band: Die Flexionsformen und ihre Verwendung, Tübingen: Niemeyer.

— (1965): *Altenglische Grammatik: Nach der Angelsächsischen Grammatik von Eduard Sievers,* third edition, Tübingen: Niemeyer.

Corbett, Greville & Norman Fraser (1993): Network Morphology: A DATR account of Russian inflectional morphology, *Journal of Linguistics* 29, 113-142.

Dresher, B. Elan & Aditi Lahiri (1991): The Germanic foot: Metrical coherence in Old English, *Linguistic Inquiry* 22, 251-286.

[32] An exception which exists to this day is ModE *ox-en*. The word *kine* – 'cows', which apparently still had been used by some speakers at the beginning of this century, also contains the *n*-stem plural /n/ but originally belonged to the athematic declension.

[33] Note that I am not claiming here that markedness and quantity always coincide. Interesting asymmetries in this respect might be found throughout natural language.

Halle, Morris & Alec Marantz (1993): Distributed Morphology and the pieces of inflectionin: K. Hale & S.J. Keyser (eds.), *The view from building 20: Essays in linguistics in honor of Sylvain Bromberger*. Cambridge, MA: MIT Press, 111-176.

Hogg, Richard M. (1992): Phonology and morphologyin. In: R.M. Hogg (ed.): *The Cambridge history of the English language*, vol. I: The beginnings to 1066, Cambridge: Cambridge University Press, 67-167.

Keyser, Samuel Jay (1975): Metathesis and Old English phonology, *Linguistic Inquiry* 6, 377-411.

Keyser, Samuel Jay & Wayne O'Neil (1985a): The simplification of the Old English strong nominal paradigms. In: R. Eaton, O. Fischer, W. Koopman & F. van der Leek (eds.): *Papers from the 4th International Conference on English Historical Linguistics, Amsterdam:* Benjamins, 85-107.

— (1985b): *Rule generalization and optionality in language change*, Dordrecht: Foris.

Kiparsky, Paul (1992): *Structural case*, Ms., Institute for Advanced Study, Berlin.

Kiparsky, Paul & Wayne O'Neil (1976): The phonology of Old English inflections, *Linguistic Inquiry* 7, 527-557.

Lahiri, Aditi (1982): *Theoretical implications of analogical change: Evidence from Germanic linguistics,* PhD Diss., Brown University.

Luick, Karl (1921-1940): *Historische Grammatik der englischen Sprache*, Band I-II, Leipzig: Tauchnitz.

Steins, Carsten (1997): *Disjunctive information in affixes: A study of syncretism in English*, Ms., Heinrich-Heine-Universität.

Wunderlich, Dieter (1997), Cause and the structure of verbs, *Linguistic Inquiry* 28, 27-68.

Wunderlich, Dieter & Ray Fabri (1995): Minimalist Morphology: An approach to inflection, *Zeitschrift für Sprachwissenschaft* 14, 236-294.

Susi Wurmbrand

Heads or phrases? Particles in particular*

1. Introduction

Complex verbs in languages like German can be formed with two kinds of preverbal elements (PEs): (separable) *particles* and (inseparable) *prefixes*. Particles are generally described as phonologically and syntactically autonomous items - they show an independent stress pattern, can be separated from the verb stem by certain inflectional prefixes and are obligatorily stranded in a verb-second (V2) context. Prefixes, on the other hand behave more like affixes - they form an inseparable unit with the verb stem and are part of the stress pattern of the verb. PEs in German are given in (1):

(1)	prefixes:	*be-, ent-, er-, ge-, miß-, ver-, zer-*					
	prefixes or particles:	*durch-*	*hinter-*	*über-*	*um-*	*unter-*	*wider-*
		through	behind	over	around	under	against
	only particles:	*ab-*	*an-*	*auf-*	*ein-*	*weg-*	etc.
		down	on	up	in	away	etc.

The following descriptive generalizations can be made about PEs in German. First, particles consist of at least one heavy syllable and hence constitute possible prosodic words (assuming that words must be at least bimoraic in German). Prefixes, on the other hand, can be formed by a single light syllable (most clear when the vowel is schwa), hence they are not necessarily possible prosodic words. Second, in prefix-verb combinations, the most prominent stress falls on the root, while particle-verb combinations exhibit compound stress (i.e., the most prominent stress falls on the particle). Third, all PEs that are ambiguous between a prefix and a particle can also function as prepositions that assign accusative case to their objects. However, not all ACC assigning prepositions can function as particles and prefixes (e.g., *auf* 'up/on' which can only function as a particle) and not all particles are

* This paper originated as my generals paper *Prefixes and Particles in German.* I would like to thank my committee members Alec Marantz, Noam Chomsky and Kai von Fintel for their guidance throughout various stages of this paper. Special thanks also to Morris Halle for many invaluable meetings and lectures on various aspects of German phonology and morphology, as well as to Jonathan Bobaljik for numerous encouraging discussions. Furthermore, I profited from discussions with Ken Hale, Michel deGraff, David Pesetsky, Cheryl Zoll and the participants of the Postgenerals Workshop at MIT in March 1998. Thanks also to the audience of the conference *Phonology and Morphology of the Germanic Languages* in Marburg and to Birgit Alber, Wolfgang Kehrein und Richard Wiese for very helpful comments. Needless to say that all errors are mine.

prepositions that assign ACC case. Fourth, prefixes (except the PEs that have two lives) are bound morphemes that cannot appear without their host. Particles, on the other hand, are independent lexical items - most particles also function as prepositions, however, not all prepositions can function as particles (e.g., *neben* 'beside, next to').

The main aim of this paper is to investigate the status of prefixes and particles from a global point of view. Although PEs in German have received extensive attention in the literature, most approaches suffer from the fact that the issue is approached exclusively from a syntactic, semantic or morphophonological point of view, thus ignoring and relegating peculiarities of PEs to other components. I will give an overview of various aspects of the syntax, semantics and phonology of PEs, and show that a comparison of the main properties of PEs reveals certain patterns in the behavior of prefixes and particles that all seem to indicate that particles are phrasal complements of the verb, whereas prefixes are verbal elements on their own. Obviously, detailed analyses for all phenomena under consideration cannot be provided. In section 2.1, I will discuss the main syntactic difference between prefixes and particles, namely separabilty. In section 2.2, interpretive effects like focus and modification will be investigated. Section 2.3, gives an overview of the argument structure of complex PE-verbs. Finally section 3. investigates the prosodic structure of prefixes and particles.

2. Prefixes vs. particles - heads vs. phrases

2.1. Separability without excorporation

The main syntactic difference - separability - is illustrated in (2) with the PE *um-* which can function as either a particle or a prefix:

(2) a. Frederik *umfuhr* das Verkehrsschild
Frederik around-drove the traffic-sign
'Frederik drove around the traffic sign' *prefix*
'*Frederik knocked down the traffic sign' **particle*

b. Frederik *fuhr* das Verkehrsschild *um*
Frederik drove the traffic-sign around
'*Frederik drove around the traffic sign' *prefix
'Frederik knocked down the traffic sign' particle

Particles are left behind in a V2 context (2)b; prefixes are pied-piped (2)a. This contrast leads to two basic questions: what is the difference between prefixes and particles; and where and how is the difference represented? Assuming V2 is syntactic movement of the verb to the complementizer position, there are two basic ways to derive the contrast in (2): first (and as most authors assume), prefix-verbs and particle-verbs have the same syntactic structure (i.e., both are represented as a complex V°s in syntax) and additional syntactic and/or phonological constraints force excorporation of the verb in a particle-verb combination but block excorporation in a prefix-verb combination (Koopman 1995, Neeleman 1994, Roberts 1991). Alternatively, one could assume that prefix-verbs and particle-verbs have different syntactic structures: prefixes form a complex V° with the verbal stem, but particles are not part of the V° node at the level where V2 applies (Booij 1990, Zeller 1997). I will argue in this section that the second approach is preferable since it does not have to invoke a notion of excorporation and it allows us to derive various syntactic differences between prefixes and particles in a less ad hoc way. Moreover, we will see that the structural difference I will propose for prefixes and particles correlates with other syntactic and semantic properties.

The analysis in this paper is based on the following assumptions about the internal architecture of the verbal projection(s): external (agent) arguments are generated outside the VP in the specifier of a light verb projection *v*P (cf. Chomsky 1995, Kratzer 1994, Marantz 1993), and the VP consists of one or more VP-layers (cf. Larson (1988)) that host the internal arguments of the verb (see section 2.3 for some discussion of how arguments are thematically licensed):

(3)

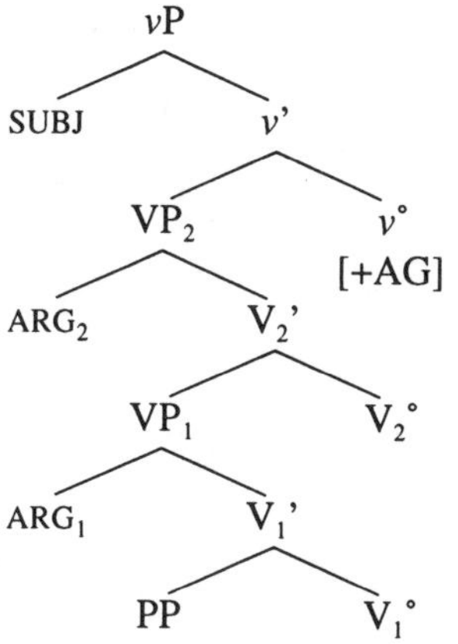

The idea that I will pursue here is that prefixes (PRFXs) and particles (PARTs) enter into different relations with the verb: particles are *arguments* of the verb - i.e., generated as a sister to the verb (cf. Zeller 1997); whereas prefixes are *heads* that combine with a VP-complement (cf. (4)a vs. (4)b). More specifically, I propose that prefixes are the overt instantiation of the V_2° head in the structure in (3).[1]

Following standard assumptions about verb-movement (Travis 1984, Baker 1988), the verb raises to its designated host in a successive cyclic fashion; i.e., it attaches to every

[1] One might object that some of the prefixes are (homophonous with) prepositions and therefore should not appear as the head of verbal projections. However, the preposition-like character of certain 'verbal' elements is not only found with prefixes. Consider for instance the infinitival marker *zu* 'to' that is homophonous with a preposition in a number of languages but nevertheless is considered as some kind of inflectional element. Furthermore, as we will see below, prefixes behave like verbs since they license an argument position.

intervening head and picks up the relevant features on the way to INFL or COMP.[2] Under these assumptions, an account for the separability of particles vs. the inseparability of prefixes is straightforward. In a structure like (4)a, verb-raising - i.e., movement of $V_1°$ to $V_2°$ - leaves behind the particle since the particle is not part of the verbal head $V_1°$ that undgoes head-movement. In a structure like (4)b, the verbal head that raises is also $V_1°$ (cf. (5)). However, incorporation of the verb into $V_2°$ where the prefix is located combines the prefix with the verb, and the newly formed *V°* - i.e., the prefix + the verb - raises further to I° and C°. Prefixes are thus carried along with the verb just as other inflectional elements are.

(4) a.

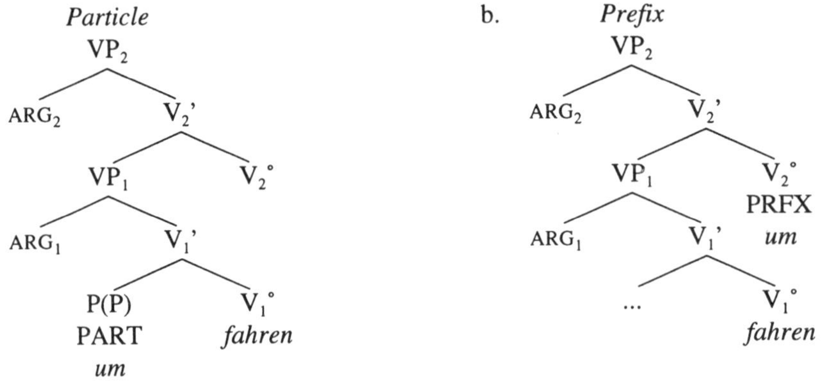

(5)

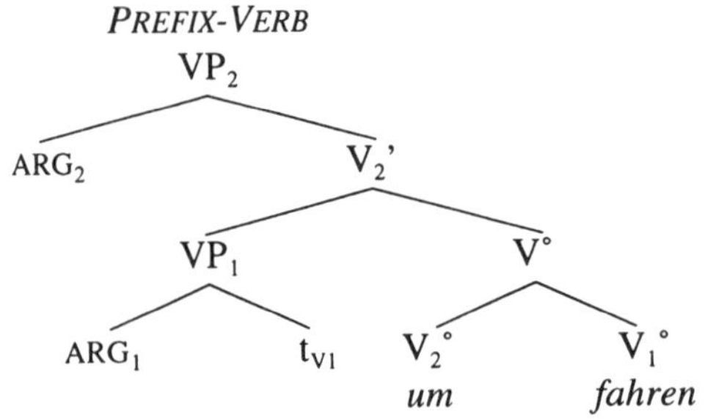

As can be seen in (4)a vs. (5), 'particle-verbs' and 'prefix-verbs' have very different structures: the combination of a particle and a verb yields a phrasal category (cf. (4)a); the combination of a prefix and a verb yields a head (cf. (5)).[3]

---

2 I assume here for convenience that overt V°-to-I° rasing (i.e., to a head-final I°) takes place in embedded clauses in German; this assumption is by no means obvious and quite controversial. However, it does not bear on the analysis proposed here.

3 Throughout this paper, I will assume for convenience that the direct object in a particle-verb construction is the object of the verb rather than the subject of a small-clause headed by the particle. The question whether particles involve a small-clause structure or are simple complements of the verb has been a longstanding issue (proponents of a small-clause approach include den Dikken 1995, Hoekstra 1988, Kayne 1985; proponents of a simple complement approach include Booij 1990, Neeleman 1994, Stiebels & Wunderlich 1994). It seems that there are

Summarizing, the advantage of the approach taken here is that stranding of particles does not receive a special treatment and no additional principles or constraints are necessary beyond the restriction that head-movement applies only to heads.[4] The structures in (4) allow us to get rid of the unattractive and powerful notion of 'excorporation' and to reduce the difference in separability between prefixes and particles to a structural difference that - as I will show in the next sections - is independently motivated.

2.2. Some semantic aspects of prefixes and particles

Building on the structure for particles in (4)a, I would like to propose that particles do not form a complex head with the verb at any level of representation. This is different from most syntactic approaches that involve some sort of overt or covert incorporation of the particle into the verb (cf. Koopman 1995 and Zeller 1997). The main reason for the assumption that particles undergo some form of overt or covert incorporation is that particle-verbs can receive a (semi-)idiomatic interpretation that cannot be determined by the meanings of their parts. To account for the idiomatic character of certain particle-verbs, many authors assume that the particle and the verb have to get together at LF and form a complex head to which the special meaning can be assigned. Similarly, it has been argued that the (semi-)idiomatic character of particle-verbs provides evidence for the lexical status of particle-verbs (cf. Stiebels and Wunderlich 1994, Zeller 1997).

In contrast to both, the lexical approach as well as the LF-incorporation approach, I argue here following Marantz (1997) that the availability of idiomatic readings does not imply that the particle and the verb have to form a complex head. Note that particle-verbs do not differ from many other verb-complement constructions w.r.t. the possibility of (semi-)idiomatic interpretations. The verb-phrases in (6) all have some kind of (semi-)idiomatic reading that cannot be determined compositionally without additional assumptions (cf. Marantz 1984, 1997):

(6) take a break, take a nap, take advantage of, take five, take two aspirins, take many notes, take revenge, take the 5 o'clock bus, take offense etc.

It is uncontroversial that phrasal idioms of this sort receive a 'special' interpretation that has to be assigned or listed somewhere. However, it is hardly arguable that phrasal idioms are actually formed in the lexicon *and* inserted as heads in the syntax (which is exactly what is proposed for particle-verbs). Phrasal idioms show that the semantic component of grammar has to include a mechanism that assigns idiomatic interpretations to certain verb-complement constructions (see also Travis forth. for the assumption that there is an overlap between syntactic and lexical structure). It therefore seems unnecessary to postulate additional lexical rules for the interpretation of particle-verbs (especially since - as I claim here - particle-verbs and verb-complement configurations have the same syntactic structure).

---

arguments for both positions; I will therefore leave the issue as an unresolved question here (see Wurmbrand in prep. for a comparison of the two approaches).

4 I concentrate here on verb-movement of the form V-to-I-to-C; verb-raising in modal or restructuring contexts is ignored (see Wurmbrand in prep.)

Rather, I assume that (semi-)idiomatic interpretations are assigned to particle-verbs in whatever way they are assigned to phrasal idioms - i.e., neither phrasal idioms nor verb-particle constructions are formed in the lexicon and they do not involve LF-incorporation.

The assumption that particles appear in complement position to the verb makes the predictions i) that they should share properties with arguments of the verb (or "arguments" within phrasal idioms as in (6)) and ii) that we should find some evidence for an independent phrasal status of particles. Prefixes, on the other hand, which are verbal heads, should share properties with inflectional affixes and should not exhibit independent phrasal properties. Let us start with the phrasal status of prefixes and particles; the argument structure of PE-verbs will be discussed in section 2.3.

A common test for phrasality in German is topicalization; i.e., only maximal projections can move to SpecCP. As expected, prefixes cannot be topicalized without the verb (cf. (7)).

(7) a. **Ver* hat Peter den Brief (ge)schickt
PRFX has Peter the letter sent
'Peter mailed the letter'

b. **UM* hat Hans das Verkehrsschild (ge)fahren
around has Hans the traffic-sign driven
'John drove around the traffic sign'

With particles, the situation is more complex: unfocused particles cannot be topicalized ((8)a). If, however, the particle is contrastively focused ((8)b) or modified ((8)c), topicalization becomes possible (no such difference is found for prefixes):[5]

(8) a. **Auf* hat Peter die Tür gemacht
open has Peter the door made
'Peter has opened the door'

b. *AUF* hat Peter die Tür gemacht (nicht zu)
open has Peter the door made (not closed)
'Peter has opened the door'

c. Ganz weit *auf* hat Peter die Tür gemacht
completely wide open has Peter the door made
'Peter opened the door completely'

A similar phenomenon is found with degree particles and negation. Simple degree particles or negation cannot undergo topicalization ((9)a,c). But as with particles, topicalization is fine when the degree word or negation is modified ((9)b,d):

[5] A similar contrast seems to hold for phrasal idioms in English; i.e., topicalization tends to be improved as phrasal idioms are enriched. Though interesting for a more general approach to complex predicates, I cannot discuss phrasal idioms here.

(9) a. **Sehr* hat Hans seine Frau verehrt
very has John his wife revered
'John revered his wife very much'

b. So *sehr* hat Hans seine Frau verehrt (daß ...)
so much has John his wife revered(that ...)
'John revered his wife so much that ...'

c. **Nicht* hat Hans seine Frau verehrt
not has John his wife revered
'John didn't revere his wife'

d. *Überhaupt nicht* hat Hans seine Frau verehrt
absolutely not has John his wife revered
'John absolutely did not revere his wife'

It has to be noted at this point that the possibility of adding modifiers or focus to particles is not available for all particles. Certain particles appear to allow modifiers (cf. (10)a) but they can nevertheless not be topicalized and focused (cf. (10)b,c; see also Stiebels & Wunderlich 1994).

(10) a. Moel hat die Suppe ganz *auf*gegessen
Moel has the soup completely up-eaten
'Moel completely ate up the soup'

Hans hat das Verkehrsschild halb *um*gefahren
Hans has the traffic-sign half down-driven
'John partially knocked down the traffic sign'

b. *Ganz *auf* hat Moel die Suppe gegessen
Completely up has Moel the soup eaten
'Moel completely ate up the soup'

*Halb *um* hat er das Verkehrsschild gefahren
Partially down has he the traffic-sign driven
'John partially knocked down the traffic sign'

c. **UM* hat Hans das Verkehrsschild gefahren
DOWN has John the traffic-sign driven
'*John knocked DOWN the traffic sign'

**AUF* hat Moel die Suppe gegessen
up has Moel the soup eaten
'*Moel completely ate UP the soup'

To account for contrasts as in (8) and (10), Stiebels & Wunderlich (1994) propose that there are two kinds of particles: 'true' particles as in (10) and resultative particles as in (8)b,c. Resultative particles are the heads of independent predicative phrases and hence can be modified syntactically and undergo topicalization. True particles, on the other hand, combine with verbs in the lexicon, yielding a complex verb that is inserted as a single head in the syntax (separability is guaranteed by the stipulation that particles have to be visible in the syntax). The modifiers in (10)a are thus attached to the complex particle-verb rather than to the particle itself.

There are several shortcomings with a lexical approach to particles. First, it is not obvious how the approach could be extended to degree words and negation that clearly do not involve a resultative meaning. Since degree words, negation and particles are subject to the same restriction - i.e., topicalization of these elements is only possible when they are focused of modified - it seems desirable to give a unified account for these phenomena. Second and more importantly, as I pointed out above, only focused or modified particles display phrasal properties in the sense that they can appear in topic position. Since the meaning of the complex verb *weg-schicken* 'send away' is the same in all of (8)a-c (i.e., resultative), one would expect that the particle should function as a predicative XP in all three examples. However, since topicalization is prohibited in (8)a, it has to be assumed in a lexical approach that resultative particles have to combine with the verb in the lexicon as 'true' particles in cases where they are not focused or modified later on in the syntax. It is not clear how this kind of 'look-ahead' property of lexical composition can be implemented in a lexical approach to particles.

The assumption that resultative particles are predicative XPs and 'true' particles are part of the lexical verb thus does not seem to be sufficient to account for the facts in (8) through (10). What then is the correct generalization for the (im)possibility of topicalization of particles in German? What I will propose here is that the crucial property that licenses topicalization is indeed an interpretive property, but contra Stiebels & Wunderlich (1994), I argue that this property cannot be reduced to the difference between a resultative vs. non-resultative interpretation of particles. Rather, I will make the simple claim that topicalization is restricted to phrases that are contrastively focused. In other words, particles can only be topicalized when the particle itself (to be distinguished from the particle-verb combination) is contrastively focused. This assumption immediately accounts for the contrast between (8)a and (8)b: in the former example, the particle is not focused and therefore topicalization is blocked.

As a consequence of the assumption that focus is a necessary condition for topicalization, particles that for independent reasons do not permit contrastive focus can never undergo topicalization. I will now show that the resistance to focus in fact plays a crucial role in the examples in (8) through (10). Consider first how contrastive focus is instantiated with particles. A resultative particle as in *auf-machen* 'open-make' can easily be contrasted with a particle expressing a possible counterpart (cf. (11)a). Particles in combinations like *auf-essen* 'eat up', or *um-fahren* 'knock down', on the other hand, do not seem to have any counterpart (cf. (11)b,c; note again that what has to be contrasted here is the particle *auf* in *auf-essen* and not the whole particle-verb).

(11) a. *auf*machen und *zu*machen
open-make and closed-make
'open and close'

b. *auf*essen und ??essen
up-eat and ??eat
'eat up and eat ??'

c. *um*fahren und ??fahren
down-drive and ??drive
'knock down and knock ??'

The reason for the lack of a focus counterpart for the particles in (11)b,c has to do with the way meaning is assigned to these particle-verb combinations. Particle-verbs like *eat up* or *knock down* receive an idiomatic interpretation; that is, a reading that is not assigned compositionally (see the discussion at the beginning of this section). Particle-verbs with an idiomatic reading are thus not transparent semantically but constitute an opaque domain for interpretation. Suppose now that interpretational effects like focus or modification cannot 'see' into semantically opaque domains. As a consequence, particles in (semi-)idiomatic particle-verb combinations are not accessible for contrastive focus or modification.

The impossibility of topicalization in the examples in (10)b,c can be accounted for as follows: the particles in (10) are part of idiomatic particle-verbs and hence are not accessible for modification. Thus, the modifiers cannot appear inside the particle PP but can only be attached to the particle-verb; i.e., the structure of (10)a,b is (12)b, rather than (12)a (which is the structure of (8)c). In other words, while the modifier and the particle form a constituent in (12)a (=(8)c), they do not form an independent constituent in (12)b (=(10)a,b). Since topicalization cannot affect discontinuous constituents in German, the structures in (10)b are ill-formed.[6]

(12) a. *transparent PART-verb*

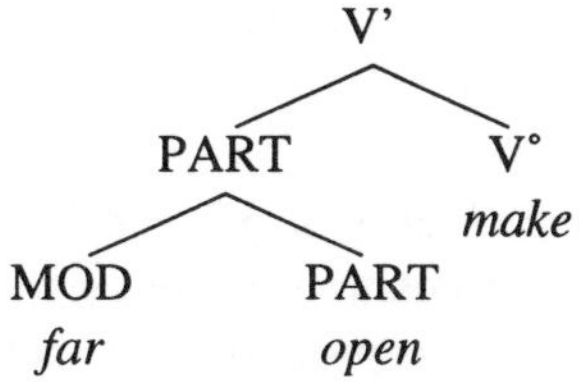

b. *non-transparent PART-verb*

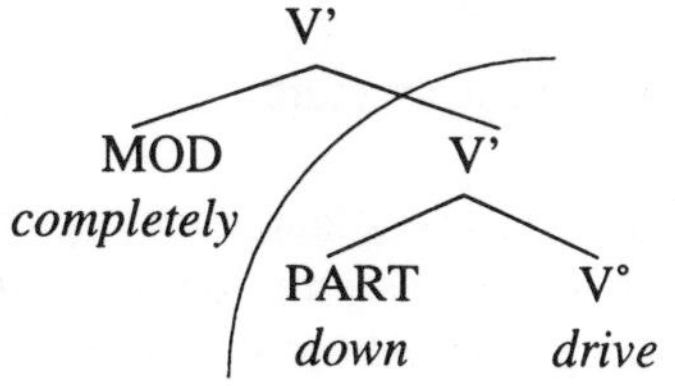

In (8)c, on the other hand, nothing blocks a modifier inside the particle PP - i.e., the particle forms a constituent with the modifier and topicalization is fine (as for the focus require-

---

6 It was pointed out to me by Uli Sauerland that there is a possible structure for (10)c,d under which the examples should be well-formed. One might think that (10)c,d involve remnant topicalization (i.e., movement of the VP including the modifier and the particle after the verb has raised to a higher head). I will simply assume here that topicalization of a VP-layer is only possible if it contains the lexical verb (see Wurmbrand in prep. for details).

ment, I will simply assume that adding a modifier puts the modified phrase automatically in focus).

To summarize, the examples in (8) to (10) are accounted for as follows: (8)a, (9)a,c are impossible because the particles are not focused; (8)b,c, (9)b,d involve focused (or modified) particles and hence are licit topicalization structures; and finally (10)b,c are blocked because the particles are in a semantically opaque domain which renders the particle inaccessible for modification or focus, and hence a necessary precondition for topicalization cannot be met. Note again that while particle-verbs represent an opaque semantic domain (i.e., modification or focus cannot affect parts of the particle-verb combination), they do not constitute an opaque syntactic domain. This becomes clear when we recall syntactic processes like verb-raising that crucially affect only the verb and cannot apply to the particle-verb combination.

Returning now to the difference between prefixes and particles, one might speculate that prefix-verbs are like idiomatic particle-verbs in that they do not allow modification or focus due to the fact that they form an opaque semantic domain. This assumption, however, has to be rejected for various reasons. First, it is empirically wrong, since most prefix-verb combinations show a transparent rather than an idiomatic interpretation (but nevertheless prohibit modification and focus). Second, the syntactic difference between prefixes and particles still has to be accounted for (i.e., prefixes are never stranded in a V2 context, particles always have to be stranded - independent of whether they have an idiomatic or compositional meaning). And third, it would miss the generalization that all prefixes generally disallow modification or focus (whereas particles only in certain circumstances do).

To conclude, we have seen that the impossibility of focus or modification for prefixes can be taken as support for the assumption that prefixes are functional heads whereas particles act more like XP-complements of the verb. If prefixes and particles had the same structure, one would lose the generalization that only particles show phrasal behavior. Furthermore, the analysis proposed here allows us to give a unified account for 'true' and resultative particles that does not involve a syntactic condition on lexical composition.

2.3. Argument structure

This section investigates the argument-structure of PE-verbs which will provide further support for the assumption that particles appear in complement position of the verb and prefixes are verbal heads. The first piece of evidence for the analysis proposed here is that particles but not prefixes can saturate an argument of the verb. Stiebels & Wunderlich (1994:953) note that an underlying prepositional object can only be left unexpressed if the PE ends up as a particle (cf. (13)a,b); if the PE is incorporated into the verb, object drop is impossible (cf. the prefix in (13)c):

(13) a. Sie setzt den Hut auf (den Kopf) *particle*
she puts the hat on (the head)
'She is putting the hat on (her head)'

b. Sie läuft durch (den Park) *particle*
she runs through (the park)
'She is running through (the park)

c. Sie durchläuft *(den Park) *prefix*
she through-runs (the park)
'She is running through the park'

Another argument for different syntactic structures of prefixes and particles is provided by the argument structure alternations encountered only with prefix-verbs but not with particle-verbs (cf. van Hout 1996, Olsen 1995a,b, Stiebels & Wunderlich 1994). Prefix-verbs behave like applicative constructions (cf. Baker 1988) - i.e., ACC is assigned to the underlying prepositional argument and the underlying theme argument ends up as an (optional) oblique instrumental PP. This is illustrated in (14): in (14)a, the PE *über* functions as a preposition, and the theme argument is assigned ACC. In the prefix-verb constructions in (14)b,c, theme arguments show up as instrumental PPs, and underlying locatives get ACC.

(14)	a.	weil	der Hans	die Zettel	*über* das Loch	klebte		*prep.*
		since	the John	[the notes]-ACC	over [the hole]-ACC	stuck		
		'since John stuck the notes over the hole'						
	b.	weil	der Hans	das Loch	(mit den Zetteln)	*über*	klebte	*prefix*[7]
		since	the John	[the hole]-ACC	(with the notes)	over	stuck	
		'since John covered the hole with the notes'						
	c.	weil	der Hans	die Tür	(mit den Zetteln)	*be*	klebte	*prefix*
		since	the John	[the door]-ACC	(with the notes)	PRFX	stuck	
		'since John stuck the notes on the door'						

Particle-verbs, on the other hand, do not allow this argument structure and case pattern (cf. (15)a,b) but always assign ACC to the underlying theme argument (cf. (15)c):[8]

(15)	a.	*weil	der Hans	das Loch	mit den Zetteln	*über*	klebte	*particle*
		since	the John	[the hole]-ACC	with the notes	over	stuck	
		'since John stuck the notes over the hole'						

[7] Underlining indicates the most prominent stress. As will be shown in section 3.1, particle-verbs and prefix-verbs crucially differ w.r.t. their stress properties - particle-verbs receive compound stress, prefix-verbs receive word stress. Stress can thus be taken as a way to differentiate between prefixes and particles.

[8] In examples like (15)c, the preferred position for the ACC argument is to the left of the PP (i.e., it has to undergo scrambling). For the discussion here, this fact does not matter. Furthermore, for most speakers, the particle *über* has to show up with the pronominal element *d(a)r*. Although ultimately important for a characterization of the particle *über*, it can be ingored here since *d(a)r* is not obligatory with all particles (e.g., *Hans hat den Zettel an den Kühlschrank angeklebt* 'John stuck-on the note on the fridge')

b. *weil	der Hans	die Tür	mit den Zetteln	<u>*auf*</u>	klebte	*particle*
since	the John	[the door]-ACC	with the notes	on	stuck	

'since John stuck the notes on the door'

c. weil	der Hans	(über das Loch)	die Zettel	dr<u>*über*</u>	klebte	*particle*
since	the John	(over the hole)	[the notes]-acc	dr-over	stuck	

'since John stuck the notes over the hole'

The pattern is schematized in (16); optional arguments are in brackets:

(16) a.	SUBJ	THEME-ACC	PP-LOC	VERB	= (14)a
b.	SUBJ	(THEME-INSTR)	LOC-ACC	PRFX-VERB	= (14)b,c
c.	*SUBJ	THEME-INSTR	LOC-ACC	PART-VERB	= (15)a,b
d.	SUBJ	THEME-ACC	(PP-LOC)	PART-VERB	= (15)c

ACC = holistic interpretation

Furthermore, as has been noted in the literature (cf. Anderson 1971, Tenny 1994, van Hout 1996 and references therein), the argument that ends up with ACC case receives a so-called holistic interpretation. In examples like in (14)a and (15)c, a holistic interpretation applies to the underlying theme argument; i.e., *the notes* have to be used up completely. In (14)b,c, on the other hand, the holistic interpretation applies to the underlying locative arguments; i.e., *the hole* or *the door* have to be covered completely.

To account for the pattern in (16), I will make the following assumptions about case and thematic licensing:[9] i) an argument has to be in a local relation with its licenser (following Bobaljik 1995, I assume that head-complement as well as head-specifier are local relations), and ii) ACC is assigned in Spec*v*P to which the closest argument raises. Let us see how these assumptions together with the structures for prefixes and particles as proposed in (4) account for the case and argument alternations.

The structure in (17) is the basic structure of a transitive verb with a prepositional object. The direct theme argument is generated in SpecVP where it is in a local relation with the theta licensing verb (theta relations are indicated by indices). The locative argument appears as the complement of the preposition, hence it is in a local relation with the licensing P-head which also assigns case to the prepositional complement. As for ACC case, ACC is assigned to the closest argument to Spec*v*P, i.e., the theme argument in SpecVP.[10]

[9] The analysis proposed here is intended to present an outline of an account of the case and argument structure properties of PE-verbs. In many places, I will refrain from specific mechanical implementations that seem to be orthogonal to the issues discussed in this paper. However, for a more thorough theoretical account see Wurmbrand (in prep.).

[10] This of course raises various questions about issues like equidistance, multiple specifiers etc. that seem to be irrelevant for the discussion here. For the sake of this paper, I will simply assume that the subject in its base position does not interfer with ACC case checking of the object.

(17) <u>*Prepositional über*</u> = (14)a

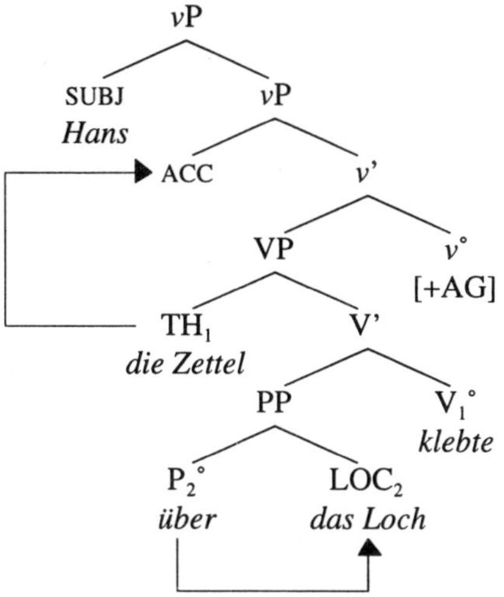

Turning to the prefix-variant of the PE *über* as in (14)b, recall that prefixes are the head of a VP-layer above the VP headed by the main verb. The crucial idea is that the presence of a prefix extends the argument structure of the main verb - i.e., prefixes open an additional thematic position. As in (17), the underlying theme argument is in specifier or complement position of V_1 where it is theta-licensed by the main verb. The locative argument, however, cannot be generated inside VP_1 since it is thematically associated with the prefix rather than with the main verb, and hence it would fail to be licensed thematically in VP_1. However, since prefixes open an additional argument position ($SpecVP_2$), there is a position where the locative argument can be generated and licensed thematically - in $SpecVP_2$, LOC is in a local relation with its theta licenser, the prefix *über* in V_2.

Assuming that the specifier of VP_2 is the base position of the underlying locative argument, we have now an explanation for the case pattern of prefix-verbs: since the locative is closer to Specv*P* than the theme, it is the one that gets assigned ACC case. Since ACC case is only assigned once in German,[11] the theme argument in $SpecVP_1$ is left without case and shows up as an oblique instrumental PP.[12]

[11] It is claimed in descriptive grammars that there are a few verbs that apparently allow two ACCs. However, in spoken language, one of the two ACC is always replaced by a DAT.

[12] I don't have an explanation why theme arguments end up as instrumental PPs (the same pattern is found for the class of *spray/load* verbs in e.g., English).

(18) Prefix *über* = (14)b

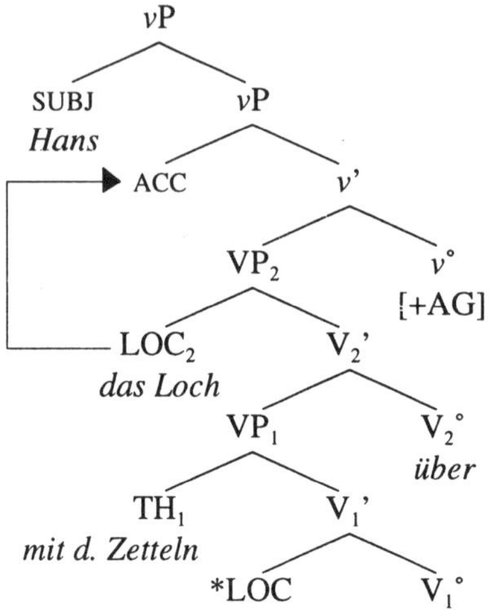

Finally, consider the case where *über* is a particle, i.e., when it merges with a verb. In order to be thematically licensed, the theme argument shows up in SpecVP_1 again where it is in an appropriate relation with the licensing verb (and also the closest argument for ACC assignment). In contrast to the prefix-construction above, there is no VP-layer headed by *über* where the underlying locative could be licensed.[13] The only position where a locative DP would be licensed would be as a sister to the particle. However, this would then result in a prepositional structure as in (17) again rather than in a particle construction.

(19) Particle *über* = (15)c

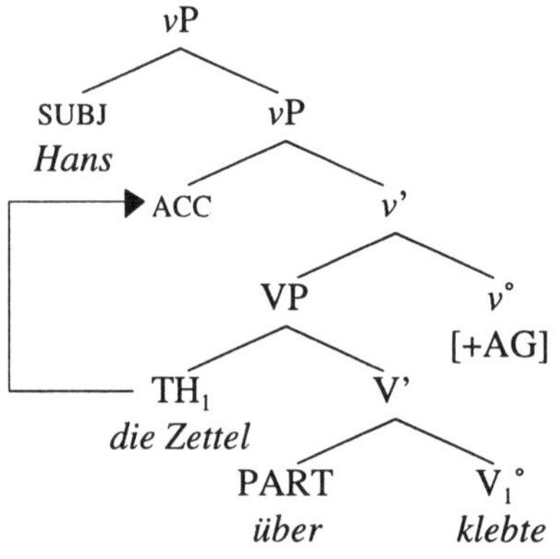

[13] Note that I do not assume that there is a ban against empty headed VP-projections (e.g., double object constructions). Rather, the implicit assumption here is that, in the absence of a prefix, the number of VP-layers is determined by the argument structure of the main verb. If the main verb (like *stick* in the examples), does not give rise to an additional VP-layer, no additional VP is available.

The impossibility of examples like (15)a,b in contrast to (14)b,c is thus be accounted for by the lack of the additional thematic position that is created by prefixes but not by particles. Since the locative argument - by failure of being in a local relation with a licensing head - cannot be licensed thematically, it has to remain unrealized (cf. (19)). If, however, an additional preposition is available, the locative argument can show up us the object of this preposition. This analysis then provides an account for the PE-doubling effect in particle-verb constructions in German (example (15)c repeated here as (20)a):

(20)	a.	weil	der Hans	*über* das Loch	einen Zettel	dr*über*	klebte	*particle*
		since	the John	over the hole	[a note]-ACC	*dr*-over	stuck	
		'since John stuck a note over the hole'						
	b.	weil	der Hans	*auf* der Tür	einen Zettel	*auf*	klebte	*particle*
		since	the John	on the door	[a note]-ACC	on	stuck	
		'since John stuck a note on the door'						

Before turning to the prosodic properties of PE-constructions, I will first address an apparent counterexample to the theory proposed so far.

2.4. An apparent counterexample

Stiebels & Wunderlich (1994) claim that argument inheritance (i.e., when the locative argument becomes the direct argument of the PE-verb) is not only attested with certain prefix-verbs, but apparently also possible with particle-verb combinations. Examples of the following sort would constitute a problem for the analysis proposed here since the PE-combination in (21) is a particle-verb which seems to display the case pattern described for prefix-verbs:

(21)	a.	weil	Hans	Farbe	an den Schrank	malte	
		since	John	color-ACC	on the cupboard	painted	
		'since John painted color on the cupboard'					
	b.	weil	Hans	den Schrank	mit Farbe	*an*	malte
		since	John	[the cupboard]-ACC	with color	on	painted
		'since John painted the cupboard with color'					

ACC assignment to the locative argument as in (21)b is unexpected since the locative argument should not be licensed thematically in a particle-verb construction (cf. (21)b vs. (15)).

Let us look at these examples in more detail: note first that the case properties change when the surface object *color* is replaced with a DP like *a face*:

(22)	a.	weil	Hans	ein Gesicht	an den Schrank	malte
		since	John	[a face]-ACC	on the cupboard	painted
		'since John painted a face on the cupboard'				

b.

#weil	Hans	den Schrank	mit einem Gesicht	*an*	malte
since	John	[the cupboard]-acc	with a face	on	painted

'*since John painted a face on the cupboard'
'#since John painted the cupboard with a face'

c.

weil	Hans	den Schrank	mit einem Gesicht	*be*	malte
since	John	[the cupboard]-ACC	with a face	PRFX	painted

'since John painted a face on the cupboard'

Comparing (21)b with (22)b, we see that an instrumental PP is only possible in a particle-verb construction when the PP is interpreted as a semantic instrumental PP rather than an underlying theme argument. Thus, a sentence like (22)b is pragmatically bizarre, since faces are usually not used as painting utensils. In contrast, no requirement of a 'real' instrumental interpretation has to be fulfilled for *with*-PPs in prefix-constructions like in (22)c. The contrasts in (21) and (22) follow, if it is assumed that *with*-PPs in particle-verb constructions are real adjunct PPs that are not generated in the specifier position of any VP. Examples like (21)b, thus lack an underlying theme argument which 'frees' the Spec-VP position. Under these circumstances, a locative argument can be realized in Spec-VP since it ends up in a local relation with the particle.

(23) *Particle-verb with no underlying direct object*

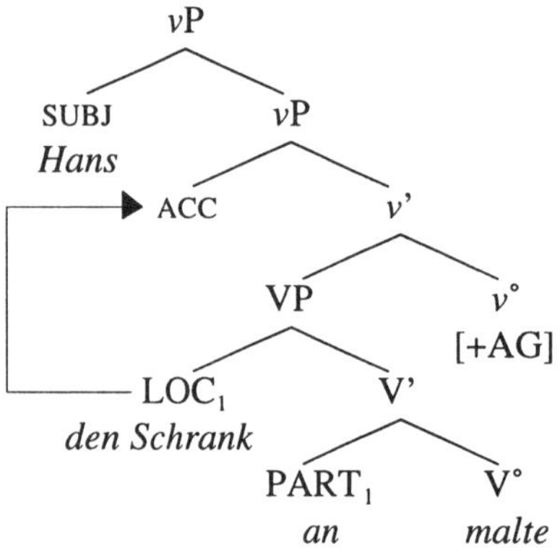

2.5. Conclusion

I have proposed that the difference between prefixes and particles - i.e., the assumption that particles are complements of the verb but that prefixes are verbal heads that open a new thematic position - together with basic assumptions about case assignment and thematic licensing provide an account for the case and argument structure properties of prefix- and particle-verbs. Syntactic separability, the behavior of particles w.r.t. topicalization, and the similarity between particle-verbs and phrasal idioms have shown that a lexical approach to particle-verbs is inadequate: a stipulative account of syntactic head movement seems unavoidable, and the lexicon has to be extended as to include syntactic information like modification of focus.

For prefix-verbs, the situation is more complex and it seems that a decision between various approaches can only be made at a theoretical level rather than on empirical grounds. To illustrate this point, compare the approach taken here with the standard analysis of applicative constructions (i.e. P-incorporation à la Baker 1988) which has also been extended to prefix-verbs (cf. Büring 1991, Zeller 1997). The main difference between the analysis proposed here and the P-incorporation approach is the relative ordering of the prefix and the verb: while the verb starts out higher than the prefix in a P-incorporation analysis (hence the prefix incorporates into the verb), I have proposed that the verb starts out in a lower position than the prefix (hence the verb incorporates into the prefix). Both approaches explain why prefixes behave like heads and why they cannot be separated from the verb. The distribution of ACC case is usually accounted for by means of a notion of 'government' in a P-incorporation approach: case is assigned by the verb under government; and incorporation of the prefix renders the PP transparent for government (cf. Baker 1988). To account for the distribution of ACC case in the approach taken here, a notion of 'being closer' has been adopted (Chomsky's 1995 *Attract Closest*). Thus, at this point, a V-incorporation approach and a P-incorporation approach seem to be empirically indistinguishable and to reduce to the question which approach is more appropriate in a given theoretical background. Since it is assumed here that structural case is not assigned under government by the verb but is rather instantiated as a checking relation between a noun phrase and a functional head, I have chosen the V-incorporation approach which does not require any notion of government, barrierhood, or special mechanism of case assignment.

To sum up, I have shown that different structures for prefixes and particles correlate with different syntactic, semantic, and argument structure properties of prefixes vs. particles. While each property could of course be seen as an independent phenomenon, I consider it an advantage that the theory proposed here allows us to tie various facts together and give a unified account that is based on one major assumption: particles are arguments, prefixes are verbal heads.

3. Prosodic structure of prefixes and particles

Besides the syntactic differences between prefixes and particles discussed in the previous section, prefixes and particles also differ in their phonological properties. In this section, I will show that the head vs. complement distinction I have proposed for prefixes vs. particles carries over to phonology. We will see that prefix-verbs behave like simple words w.r.t stress assignment and deletion under identity (a deletion process to be discussed in detail below), whereas particle-verbs behave like phrases. Assuming that different syntactic structures translate into different prosodic structures, it is correctly predicted that particle-verbs are syntactically *and* prosodically phrases - therefore carry phrasal stress, whereas prefix-verbs are syntactically *and* prosodically heads - therefore bear word stress.

Under the syntactic structure I have proposed for PE-verbs, prefix-verbs are heads and particle-verbs are phrases. I will assume that syntactic structures are mapped into prosodic structure as follows: minimal categories (X°s) correspond to prosodic words (PWds); non-minimal categories (X'/XP) correspond to phonological phrases (PhPs; cf. Selkirk 1972, 1995).[14] This yields the following prosodic structures for PE-verbs:

(24) a. *Prefix-Verb*

V° ⇒ PWd

PRFX V°
be stellen

b. *Particle-Verb*

V' ⇒ PhP

PART V°
auf stellen

Thus, a prefix-verb is a PWd, whereas a particle-verb is a PhP. In the following sections, I will discuss how this prosodic difference accounts for the stress (section 3.1) and deletion under identity properties (section 3.2) of PE-verbs.

3.1 Stress properties of PE-verbs

The major phonological difference between prefixes and particles is illustrated by the PE-verb *umfahren* which has two stress patterns. If the PE bears the most prominent stress, it can only be a particle, if the verb bears the most prominent stress, the PE is a prefix (the most prominent stress is indicated by underlining):

(25) a. weil er das Verkehrsschild *um*fuhr *prefix*
'since he drove around the traffic sign'

b. weil er das Verkehrsschild *um*fuhr *particle*
'since he knocked down the traffic sign'

More specifically, particles carry compound stress (which is initial in German); prefixes are unstressed or carry at most secondary word stress.

(26) a. *Particle*
áuf-gèben
PART-give
'give up'

párticle-vèrb
*pàrticle-vérb

b. *Prefix*
ver-gében
PRFX-give
'forgive'

prèfix-vérb
*préfix-vèrb

[14] Although it does not seem to bear directly on the discussion in this paper, I will assume (following Selkirk (1993) among others) that there are two kinds of phonological phrases: Major Phrases and Minor Phrases, and that particle-verbs form Minor Phrases.

c. *Compound*
Schréib-maschìne
'typewriter'

d. *Derived Word*
gràmmatikálisch
'grammatical'

One way to approach this difference is to assume that the domain for assignment of word stress is the PWd, whereas the domain for compound stress is the PhP.[15] Prefix-verbs are PWds, hence they are subject to the rules for word stress. Particle-verbs, on the other hand, are PhPs and are therefore subject to the stress rules for compound stress.

As I will discuss in more detail in section 3.2.2, the analysis proposed here implies that compounds in general are phrasal categories rather than words. Note that the assumption that compounds are prosodically different from simple words has the advantage that the domain for compound stress - which in many languages is different from the domain of word stress - can be defined prosodically. If compounds and simple words were both of the category PWd, additional assumptions would be necessary to prevent the application of word stress rules to compounds. In the next subsection, I will show that the structural difference between prefixes and particles also plays a crucial role for certain deletion properties of PE-verbs.

3.2 Deletion under Identity

In this section, I will investigate the so-called *Deletion under Identity* or *Coordination Reduction* construction. We will see that the deletion facts provide some further insight into the prosodic structure of prefixes and particles. Before investigating the behavior of prefixes and particles w.r.t. deletion under identity, I will first discuss when deletion under identity is possible and what the relevant constraints are.

3.2.1 First approach: particles are words, prefixes are smaller than words

Deletion under identity refers to the following quite common deletion process in German (unpronounced material is indicated by strike-out):

(27) a. weil Maria Gurken~~salat~~ und Tomatensalat verabscheut
since Maria cucumber ~~salad~~ and tomato salad detests
'since Maria detests cucumber salad and tomato salad'

---

15 I will not commit myself here to a specific theory of stress assignment. An analysis of stress in German would run the risk of diverting the attention from the main topic of this paper to the quite complex and controversial issue of stress in German. For extensive discussions of stress in German and/or Dutch see for instance Giegerich (1985), Kager (1989), Booij (1995), Lechner (1995), or Wiese (1996). What is important for the discussion in this paper is that particle-verbs pattern with compounds whereas prefix-verbs pattern with simple or affixed words. Every theory of stress has to involve the difference between compound stress and word stress in some or the other form. The reader is therefore asked to chose his favorite approach to stress assignment in German and apply it to the examples in the text.

b. weil Maria Gurkensalat und ~~Gurken~~gemüse verabscheut
'since Maria detests cucumber salad and ~~cucumber~~ vegetables'

Typically, identical material that appears in both parts of a conjunction can be deleted under certain conditions. That the structure involves some kind of deletion rather than simply coordination of the left part of the compound is discernible from the meaning of a the utterance: what is detested in (27)a is not salad consisting of cucumbers and tomatoes, but cucumber salad and tomato salad. Booij (1985) defines the conditions for deletion under identity in Dutch as follows (the constraints can be applied to German as well):

(28) *Coordination reduction* (optional) Booij (1985:151)

Delete Y. Conditions:
a. $Y = \omega^m$ $m \geq 0$
b. Y is adjacent to a conjunction
c. There is a remnant that, like its counterpart, can function as a focus constituent

The first condition states that deletion can only apply to phonological words or bigger prosodic units. For bound morphemes, this implies that only affixes that have the status of a phonological word can be deleted. Evidence for this claim is provided by suffixes like *-ig* '-y' vs. suffixes like *-artig* '-like' that derive adjectives from nouns. The former class of affixes undergo syllabification with the stem whereas the latter represent an independent domain for syllabification. The suffix *-artig*, when attached to a noun, does not resyllabify with the noun: the *-s* in the coda of the noun *eis* 'ice' cannot be syllabified as the onset of the suffix (cf. (29)a); instead insertion of the glottal stop takes place in onset position. The suffix *-ig*, on the other hand, shows the opposite distribution: it cannot be preceded by a glottal stop but it has to syllabify with the noun (cf. (29)b).

(29) a. eis + artig ⇒ eis.ʔartig, *ei.sartig
ice-like

b. eis + ig ⇒ *eis.ʔig, ei.sig
ice + y

Assuming that the syllabification facts and the distribution of glottal stop indicate that -*artig* constitutes an independent PWd, wheras *-ig* is of a smaller prosodic category, the first condition in (28) predicts that *-artig*, but not *-ig* can be deleted under coordination:

(30) a. eis~~artig~~ oder wasserartig
icelike or waterlike

b. *eis~~ig~~ oder rutschig
icy or slippery

As the contrast in (30) shows, deletion is possible in the case of *-artig* but blocked in the case of *-ig* which follows from a difference in the prosodic structure of the two suffixes: the former projects to a PWd, while the latter doesn't.

The second condition on coordination reduction requires that the deleted material is adjacent to a conjunction. This assumption seems to be too strict since there are for instance cases where deletion can apply between two arguments in the absence of a conjunction.[16] In order to capture this observation, Wiese (1996) reformulates the conditions on deletion as follows:

(31) *Word Deletion* Wiese (1996:70)

Delete a phonological word,
a. if it occurs adjacent to a phrase boundary, and
b. if a phonologically identical phonological word exists in an adjacent sister phrase

Wiese's formulation of deletion has two advantages: i) it involves a more accurate characterization of the environment where deletion can apply (condition a.); and ii) it includes a notion of parallelism which is a necessary precondition for deletion (condition b.). However, it does not involve a restriction on the remnant structure - i.e., Booij's third condition. I will now show that a condition on the remnant is indeed necessary and cannot be reduced to constraints on the deleted material.

The third condition on coordination reduction requires that the *remnant* has to form a *(focus) constituent*. This constraint is crucial for examples with a more complex structure. As is shown in (32), deletion of one noun in a compound consisting of three parts is not always possible: while it is fine in examples like (32)d, it is impossible in examples like (32)c:

(32) a. Reiseschreibmaschinen und Büroschreibmaschinen
travel-typewriters and office-typewriters
'portable typewriters and office-typewriters'

[16] Consider the following examples:

i. weil der Hans die Erst- den Zweitjahresstudenten vorgestellt hat
since the John the first- the second year students introduced has
ii. *weil der Hans die Erst- gestern den Zweitjahresstudenten vorgestellt hat
since the John the first- yesterday the second year students introduced has
iii. ?die Erst- hat Hans gestern den Zweitjahresstudenten vorgestellt
the first has John yesterday the second year students introduced
'since John introduced the first year students to the second year students yesterday'

The example in i. illustrates that 'deletion under identity' can apply in the absence of a conjunction. However, what is interesting is that this form of deletion also requires some form of adjacency: if the two arguments involved are separated by an adverb, deletion is blocked (cf. ii.). On the other hand, the adjacency restriction is loosened if one of the arguments is topicalized. We will not draw any conclusion from these facts w.r.t scrambling or topicalization here but leave the issue for future research.

b. Reise~~schreibmaschinen~~ und Büroschreibmaschinen
travel and office-typewriters

c. *Reiseschreib~~maschinen~~ und Büro(schreib)maschinen
travel-type and office-typewriters

d. Schreibmaschinen~~vertreter~~ und Büromaschinenvertreter
type-writers-salesman and office-machines-salesman
'salesman for typewriters and office machines'

To see what the difference between these two constructions is, consider the structure of the compounds in (32):

(33)

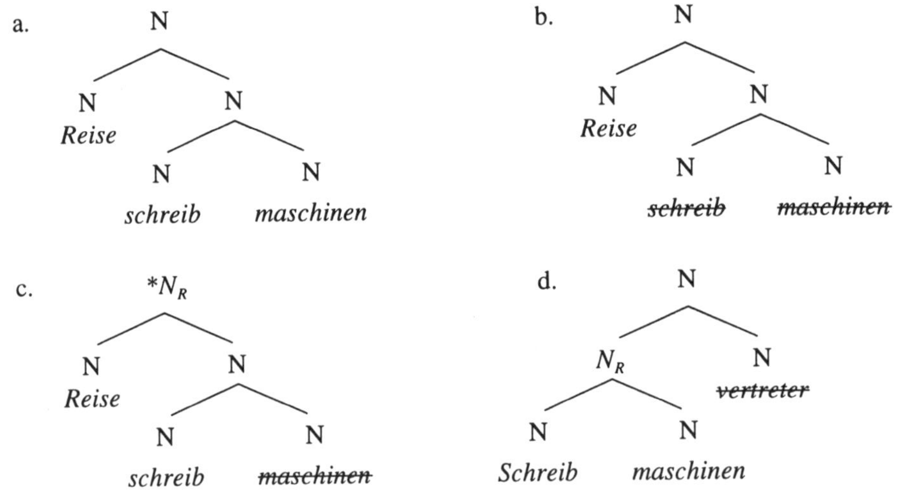

Booij's insight is that the remnant parts have to be part of a single constituent that does not include the 'trace' of the deleted material. If only the rightmost part of the compound in (32)a is deleted as in (32)c/(33)c, the remaining parts (i.e., N_R) do not form a constituent that excludes the deleted material; therefore deletion is ruled out. If, on the other hand, the compound has a left branching structure as in (32)d/(33)d, deletion of the rightmost part is fine since the remnant N_R forms a constituent excluding the trace. Assuming Wiese's conditions on deletion, however, it would not be clear how this contrast could be accounted for: the deleted material in (32)c/(33)c is clearly a PWd; the deleted noun is adjacent to a phrase boundary (condition a. is met); and a phonologically identical phonological word - i.e., *Maschinen* - exists in an adjacent sister phrase in the coordinative structure. It would thus be falsely predicted that (32)c/(33)c should be a possible deletion configuration. I conclude that the third of Booij's original conditions has to be kept in order to give an adequate description of deletion under identity.[17] The considerations above, lead to the following reformulation of Booij's and Wiese's conditions on deletion under identity:

(34) *Deletion under Identity* (Booij 1985 & Wiese 1996)

Delete a phonological word,

a. if it occurs adjacent to a phrase boundary
b. if a phonologically identical phonological word exists in an adjacent sister phrase
c. there is a remnant that, like its counterpart, can function as a focus constituent

Let us now look at the behavior of particles and prefixes w.r.t deletion under identity. If the assumptions about deletion under identity (Booij 1985 & Wiese 1996) are correct, deletion provides a test to determine whether prefixes and particles are PWds. Provided that conditions a., b. and c. are met, a PE would constitute a PWd if deletion is possible. If deletion is prohibited, the PE is not a PWd. Starting with particle-verbs, (35)b shows that deletion of the particle is possible. One thus concludes that particles have the status of PWds.

(35) a. weil altes Bier gewöhnlich *über*schäumt oder *über*sprudelt *particle*
since old beer usually PART-froths or PART-bubbles
'since old beer usually froths or bubbles over'

b. weil altes Bier gewöhnlich *über*schäumt oder *~~über~~*sprudelt *particle*
since old beer usually PART-froths or ~~PART~~-bubbles
'since old beer usually froths or bubbles over'

Turning now to prefix-verbs, we see that in contrast to the particle in (35)b, deletion of the prefix is prohibited in (36)b:

(36) a. weil sie ständig mit Arbeit *über*häuft und *über*fordert wird *prefix*
since she always with work PRFX-heaped and PRFX-loaded becomes
'since she gets always inundated and overloaded with work'

b. *weil sie ständig mit Arbeit *über*häuft und *~~über~~*fordert wird *prefix*
since she always with work PRFX-heaped and ~~PRFX~~-loaded becomes

Wiese (1996) concludes from the ungrammaticality of (36)b that prefixes are smaller units than PWds. The remnant (i.e., the verb) clearly forms a constituent (hence condition c. is met). The deleted material is adjacent to a phrase boundary (hence condition a. is met). However, assuming that prefixes are not PWds, neither the requirement that the deleted item has to be a PWd nor condition b. can be met: by parallelism the non-deleted prefix would not be a PWd either and hence condition b. - which requires that an identical phonological word exists in an adjacent sister phrase - is violated.

[17] Richard Wiese pointed out to me that examples like (32)c show some variation among speakers; some speakers do not find (32)c ungrammatical, which would mean that the third condition on deletion is in fact not active for those speakers.

3.2.2 Second approach: particle-verbs are phrases, prefix-verbs are heads

At this point the question arises what constitutes a 'PWd'. Since phonologically the same string of sounds and phonological properties is involved in the particle *über* and the prefix *über* it is not clear why the two elements should be assigned different prosodic values. Furthermore, prefixes like *über* show properties typically associated with PWds: *über* is disyllabic and carries secondary stress, hence clearly has to be considered as a foot (Ft). Moreover, *über* can appear independently without being attached to a host. What is different, however, is the character of the category that is *created* by combining the particle *über* and a verb vs. the prefix *über* and a verb: a prefix-verb is a head or a PWd, whereas a particle-verb is a phrase or a PhP. The aim of this subsection is to provide an analysis that does not require different prosodic structures for phonologically identical elements, but makes use of the structural difference between prefix-verbs and particle-verbs as argued for throughout this paper.

I would like to suggest that what determines whether an element is a PWd or not depends solely on the phonological shape of the item. Items like the prefix *über* that project to a foot (cf. stress) also project to a PWd. Syllables containing schwa do not project to a foot, and therefore also cannot project to a PWd (following the assumption that prosodic units cannot be skipped in the prosodic hierarchy; cf. Selkirk 1995).

Under these considerations, the conditions on deletion under identity (cf. (Booij 1985 & Wiese 1996) yield the wrong results. To see why this is the case, consider (36)b again. If prefixes like *über* are PWds, it would be predicted that they should be able to undergo deletion (provided that the other conditions are met). However, since (36)b is ungrammatical (and condition a.-c. in (34) are met), it is impossible to keep both the assumption that prefixes like *über* are PWds and the condition that PWds (or bigger categories) can be deleted freely. Since for the reasons mentioned above I believe that elements like *über* should be characterized as PWds, a reformulation of the condition on the prosodic nature of items that can undergo deletion is necessary. To do so, let us consider the structure of a prefix-verb vs. a particle-verb again:

(37) a. *Prefix-Verb*

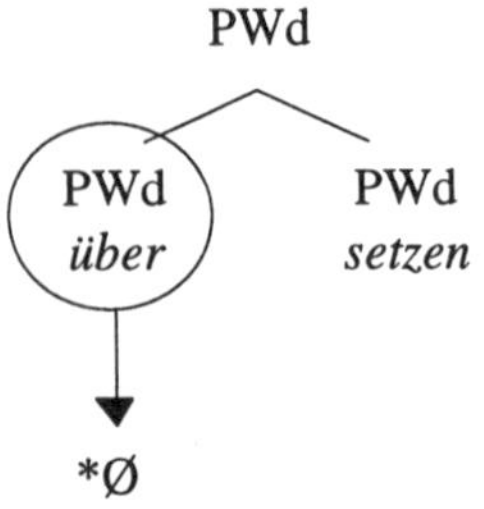

b. *Particle-Verb*

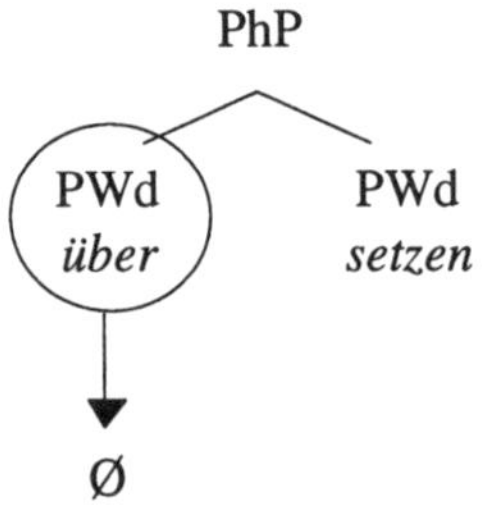

The comparison of the structure of a prefix-verb with the structure of a particle-verb shows that while particles are dominated by a PhP, prefixes are dominated by a PWd. I will assume that this kind of recursive structure is what blocks deletion of prefixes. The idea is that in a recursive structure (setting aside compounds for the moment; see below), only the highest recursive PWd can be deleted. I will therefore suggest the following modification for the conditions on deletion under identity:

(38) a. *Deletion under identity* (final version)

X may be deleted if
- X is not dominated by a PWd
- X occurs adjacent to a phrase boundary and an identical X exists in an adjacent sister phrase
- the remnant Y is a constituent that is contrastively focused with a counterpart of Y

The first condition in (38) also explains why deletion of affixes as in (30)b (repeated as (39)a) and deletion of prefixes as in (39)b is impossible: in both cases, the deleted item is part of a PWd - the PWd dominating the affix and the host, and therefore the first condition in (38) is not met. Note that under this definition of deletion under identity, the status of the deleted item is irrelevant (in contrast to Booij 1985 and Wiese 1996).

(39) a. *eis~~ig~~ oder rutschig
*ice~~y~~ or slippery

b. *überhäufen und ~~über~~fordern
*PRFX-heap and ~~PRFX~~-load

Let us now see how these assumptions could account for the deletion facts of compounds, particles, and examples which involve affixes that have PWd status as in (30) (repeated as (40)a). Since deletion is possible in all of (40), the deleted items cannot be dominated by a PWd.

(40) a. eis~~artig~~ oder wasserartig
ice~~like~~ or waterlike

b. überschäumen oder ~~über~~sprudeln
PART-froth or ~~PART~~-bubble

c. Gurken~~salat~~ und Tomatensalat
cucumber ~~salad~~ and tomato salad

Building upon the idea proposed in the discussion of stress in section 3.1, I would like to claim that expressions like those in (40)a and the compounds in (40)c have the same prosodic structure as particle-verbs (40)b - i.e., are PhPs rather than PWd (see also Wiese 1996 for similar speculations). This claim is supported by the stress pattern: all of the examples in (40) have compound stress and not - as would be expected if they were words - word stress. The assumption that compounds are phrases, of course, raises many questions about how compounds are formed, whether they are phrases throughout the derivation etc., which I cannot address here. Answers to these questions are highly dependent on specific theoretical backgrounds and general assumptions about the organization of grammar. For this paper, it is sufficient to assume that (at least) at the level where deletion or stress assignment applies, the expressions in (40) are phrases rather than words.

The deletion properties from (39) through (40) are schematized as follows:

(41) a. PhP

PWd	~~PWd~~	*compound*
~~PWd~~	PWd	*particle*

b. *PWd

PWd	~~PWd~~	*suffix*
~~PWd~~	PWd	*prefix*

Furthermore, the analysis proposed here makes the (correct) prediction that deletion of the verb should be possible in a particle-verb construction (i.e., a PhP), but not in a prefix-verb construction (i.e., a PWd). This is illustrated in (42)a vs. (42)b:

(42) a. weil er die Torte gerecht *ein*~~teilte~~ und *auf*teilte *particle/particle*
since he the cake fairly PART-~~divided~~ and PART-divided
'since he divided and split/distributed the cake fairly'

b. ??weil er die Torte gerecht *zer*~~teilte~~ und *ver*teilte *prefix/prefix*
since he the cake fairly PRFX-divided and PRFX-divided
'since he split and distributed the cake fairly'

Examples like (42)b are slightly better for some speakers when the prefix is stressed (i.e., contrastive stress overrules the regular stress pattern). I will assume here that in the latter case, prefixe-verbs are reanalyzed phonologically as phrases.

Turning finally to the last condition for deletion under identity in (38), I adopt to a large extent Booij's (1985) third condition on the structure of the remnant. First, the remnant has to form a constituent (cf. the contrast between (32)c and (32)d). Second, I assume (elaborating on Booij's condition) that deletion can only apply if the following semantic prerequisite is met: the remnant has to be contrastively focused with a counterpart. The examples in (43) illustrate that - apart from the prosodic constraint as discussed above - certain semantic criteria have to be met as well in order for deletion to be acceptable. The particle-verb *an-stellen* 'turn on' can be contrasted with the particle-verb *ab-stellen* 'turn off', and deletion of the verb in the first conjunct is possible (cf. (43)a).[18] The examples in (43)b and (43)c, however, show that if either of the two particle-verbs is replaced by the particle-verb *ein-stellen* 'adjust', deletion becomes impossible. This pattern is not surprising (given the third condition on deletion under identity), since the particle-verb *ein-stellen* 'adjust' gets a semi-idiomatic interpretation and therefore the particle is not accessible for contrastive focus in a coordination structure (see also the discussion in section 2.1).

---

[18] Note that reversing the two particle-verbs would be pragmatically odd. I assume that, as a general property of coordination, temporal relations have to correspond to linear order; e.g.,'#turn off and on' is only felicitous in a world where things are switched off before they are switched on. Similar considerations apply to binomials (cf. Müller 1997).

(43) a. Der Mechaniker hat den Motor *an~~gestellt~~* und *ab*gestellt
the mechanic has the engine on-~~turned~~ and off-turned
'The mechanic turned the engine on and off'

b. *Der Mechaniker hat den Motor *ein~~gestellt~~* und *ab*gestellt
the mechanic has the engine PART-~~turned~~ and off-turned
'The mechanic adjusted the engine and turned it off'

c. *Der Mechaniker hat den Motor *an~~gestellt~~* und *ein*gestellt
the mechanic has the engine on-~~turned~~ and PART-turned
'The mechanic turned on the engine and adjusted it'

d. Der Mechaniker hat den Motor *ein~~geschaltet~~* und *ab*geschaltet
the mechanic has the engine on-~~turned~~ and off-turned
'The mechanic turned the engine on and off'

That nothing in principle blocks coordination with the particles *ein* 'on' and *ab* 'off', is illustrated in (43)d where the same particles allow a contrastive interpretation again and deletion becomes therefore licit.

A final note on the nature of deletion under identity: the semantic prerequisite as well as the second condition on deletion under identity - i.e., that the deleted item has to be adjacent to a phrase boundary - seem to challenge the status of this deletion process as a phonological operation. At this point, I will merely raise the speculation that deletion under identity might have to be considered as a syntactic rather than a pure phonological operation. Adopting a syntactic approach to deletion under identity would have various implications for the syntax/phonology interface and open many interesting questions (like for instance the *syntactic* structure of compounds) that I cannot address here. Since this paper is mainly concerned with the structure of particles and prefixes, I will leave a deeper investigation of deletion under identity for future research.

Summary

In this paper I have discussed a range of characteristics of prefixes and particles that can all be explained by different functions and structures of prefixes and particles. The properties discussed are summarized in the following table:

Table 1: Properties of Prefixes and Particles

PROPERTIES	*PARTICLES*	*PREFIXES*
separable from verb stem	yes	no
can be modified or focused	yes	no
can saturate an argument of the verb	yes	no
deep object is surface object	yes	no
receive most prominent stress	yes	no
can delete under identity	yes	no
hosting verb can be deleted under identity	yes	no

The main proposal is that particles are arguments, hence complements of the verb, and prefixes are verbal heads that trigger incorporation of the verb. The properties that particles (but not prefixes) can be modified and are able to saturate an argument of the verb follow immediately from this basic difference. Furthermore, obligatory stranding of particles and obligatory pied-piping of prefixes reduces to standard assumptions about head-movement. The different stress patterns of prefix-verbs vs. particle-verbs are accounted for by the different structures resulting from combining a particle and a verb vs. a prefix and a verb: the former yields a phrase, the latter yields a head - a difference that is also represented in the prosodic structure. Finally, the discussion of the last section has shown that the prosodic difference proposed for prefixes and particles allows us to also account for various deletion properties without stipulating different prosodic structures for phonologically identical items.

References

Anderson, Stephen (1971): On the role of deep structure in semantic interpretation. *Foundations of Language* 7, 387-396.

Baker, Mark (1988): *Incorporation. A Theory of Grammatical Function Changing*. Chicago: The University of Chicago Press.

Bobaljik, Jonathan David (1995): *Morphosyntax: the syntax of verbal inflection.* Cambridge, Mass: Ph.D. Dissertation, MIT.

Booij, Geert (1985): Coordination Reduction in Complex Words: a Case for Prosodic Phonology. Harry van der Hulst, Norval Smith (eds.): *Non-linear Phonology*, 143-160. Dordrecht: Foris.

— (1990): The Boundary between Morphology and Syntax: Separable Complex Verbs in Dutch. *Yearbook of Morphology* 3, 45-63.

— (1995): *The Phonology of Dutch.* Oxford: Clarendon Press.

Büring, Daniel (1991): Semantische Transparenz und Linking. *Linguistische Berichte* 135, 346-374.

Chomsky, Noam (1995): *The Minimalist Program.* Cambridge, Mass: MIT Press.

Dikken, Marcel den (1995). *Particles. On the Syntax of Verb-Particle, Triadic, and Causative Constructions.* New York/Oxford: Oxford University Press.

Giegerich, Heinz (1985): *Metrical Phonology and Phonological Structure: German and English.* Cambridge: Cambridge University Press.
Halle, Morris & Alec Marantz (1993): Distributed Morphology and the pieces of inflection. In: Ken Hale, S. J. Keyser (eds.): *The View from Building 20. Essays in Linguistics in Honor of Sylvain Bromberger*, 111-176. Cambridge, Mass: MIT Press.
Hoekstra, Teun (1988). Small Clause Results. *Lingua* 74, 101-139.
Holmberg, Märta Åsdahl (1976): *Studien zu den verbalen Pseudokomposita im Deutschen.* Göteborger Germanistische Forschungen 14. Acta Universitatis Gothoburgensis.
Hout, Angeliek van (1996): *Event Semantics of Verb Frame Alternations. A case study of Dutch and its acquisition.* Tilburg: Ph.D. dissertation, University of Tilburg.
Kager, René (1989): *A Metrical Theory of Stress and Destressing in English and Dutch.* Dordrecht: Foris.
Kayne, Richard (1985): Principles of Particle Constructions. J. Guéron, H. Obenauer, J.-Y. Pollock (eds.): *Grammatical Representation*, 101-140. Dordrecht: Foris.
Keyser, Samual Jay & Thomas Roeper (1992): Re: The Abstract Clitic Hypothesis. *Linguistic Inquiry* 23, 89-125.
Koopman, Hilda (1995): On Verbs That Fail to Undergo V-Second. *Linguistic Inquiry* 26, 139-163.
Kratzer, Angelika (1994): On External Arguments. In: E. Benedicto, J. Runner (eds.): *Functional Projections, University of Massachusetts (Amherst) Occasional Papers*, 103-130. Amherst, Mass: University of Massachusetts.
Larson, Richard K. (1988): On the Double Object Construction. *Linguistic Inquiry* 19, 335-391.
Lechner, Winfried (1995): Stress in German. Ms., Amherst, Mass: University of Massachusetts.
Marantz, Alec (1984): *On the Nature of Grammatical Relations.* Cambridge, Mass: MIT Press.
— (1993): Implications of Asymmetries in Double Object Constructions. In: Sam A. Mchombo (ed.): *Theoretical Aspects of Bantu Grammar,* 113-150. Stanford, California: CSLI Publications.
— (1997): No Escape from Syntax: Don't Try Morphological Analysis in the Privacy of Your Own Lexicon. *UPenn Working Papers in Linguistics* 4.2, 201-225.
Müller, Gereon (1997): Phonological Constraints on Binomial Formation in German. Paper presented at the conference *Phonology and Morphology of the Germanic Languages,* August 1997, Marburg, Germany.
Neeleman, Ad (1994): *Complex Predicates.* Utrecht University: OTS Dissertation Series.
Olsen, Susan (1995a): Über Präfix- und Partikelverbsysteme. *FAS Papers in Linguistics* 3, 86-112.
— (1995b): Zum Status der Kategorie Verbpartikel. *FAS Papers in Linguistics* 3, 113-134.
Roberts, Ian (1991): Excorporation and minimality. *Linguistic Inquiry* 22, 209-218.
Selkirk, Elisabeth (1972): *The phrase phonology of English and French.* Cambridge, Mass: Ph.D. Dissertation, MIT.
— (1993): Constraints on prosodic structure - A modular approach. *Paper presented at the ESCA Workshop on Prosody*, September 1993, Lund University.
— (1995): The Prosodic Structure of Function Words. In: J. Beckman, S. Urbanczyk, L. Walsh (eds.): *Optimality Theory. University of Massachusetts (Amherst) Occasional Papers.* Amherst, Mass: University of Massachusetts.
Stiebels, Barbara (1996): *Lexikalische Argumente und Adjunkte.* Berlin: Akademie Verlag.
Stiebels, Barbara & Dieter Wunderlich (1994): Morphology feeds syntax: the case of particle verbs. *Linguistics* 32, 913-968.
Tenny, Carol (1994): *Aspectual roles and the syntax-semantics interface.* Dordrecht: Kluwer Academic Publishers.
Travis, Lisa (1984): *Parameters and Effects of Word Order Variation.* Cambridge, Mass: Ph.D. Dissertation, MIT.
— (forthcoming): The L-syntax/S-syntax boundary: evidence from Austronesian. To appear in: I. Paul, V. Phillips, L. Travis (ed.): *Formal Issues in Austronesian Syntax.* Dordrecht: Kluwer.
Wiese, Richard (1996): *The phonology of German.* Oxford: Clarendon Press.
Wurmbrand, Susi (1997): Minimal and Maximal Heads. Ms., Cambridge, Mass: MIT.
— (in prep.): *When Verbs do and don't move*. Cambridge, Mass: Ph.D. Dissertation, MIT.
Zeller, Jochen (1997): Against Overt Particle Incorporation. *UPenn Working Papers in Linguistics* 4.2, 291-307.

Addresses of contributors

Alber, Birgit
Institut für Germanistische Sprachwissenschaft
Philipps-Universität Marburg
Wilhelm-Röpke-Str. 6A
D-35032 Marburg
alber@mailer.uni-marburg.de

Árnason, Kristján
Department of Icelandic
University of Iceland
Árnagarði v. Suðurgötu
101 Reykjavík, Iceland
kristarn@rhi.hi.is

Booij, Geert
Faculteit der Letteren
Vrije Universiteit Amsterdam
De Boelelaan 1105
NL-1081 HV Amsterdam
booij@let.vu.nl

Golston, Chris
Department of Linguistics, M/S 92
California State University Fresno
USA-Fresno, CA 93740
chrisg@zimmer.csfresno.edu

Grijzenhout, Janet
Seminar für Allgem. Sprachwissenschaft
Heinrich-Heine-Universität Düsseldorf
Universitätsstr. 1
D-40225 Düsseldorf
grijzenhout@phil-fak.uni-duesseldorf.de

van der Hulst, Harry
HIL, RU Leiden
PO Box 9515
NL-2300 RA Leiden
hulst@rullet.leidenuniv.nl

Kehrein, Wolfgang
Institut für Germanistische Sprachwissenschaft
Philipps-Universität Marburg
Wilhelm-Röpke-Str. 6A
D-35032 Marburg
kehrein@mailer.uni-marburg.de

Kooij, Jan G.
HIL, RU Leiden
PO Box 9515
NL-2300 RA Leiden
kooij@rullet.leidenuniv.nl

Neef, Martin
Institut für Deutsche Sprache und Literatur
Universität zu Köln
Albertus-Magnus-Platz
D-50923 Köln
neef@uni-koeln.de

Ortmann, Albert
Seminar für Allgem. Sprachwissenschaft
Heinrich-Heine-Universität Düsseldorf
Universitätsstr. 1
D-40225 Düsseldorf
ortmann@phil-fak.uni-duesseldorf.de

Plag, Ingo
Institut für Anglistik und Amerikanistik
Philipps-Universität Marburg
Wilhelm-Röpke-Str. 6D
D-35032 Marburg
plag@mailer.uni-marburg.de

Riad, Tomas
Nordiska språk
Stockholm University
S-10691 Stockholm
tomas.riad@nordiska.su.se

Steins, Carsten
Seminar für Allgem. Sprachwissenschaft
Heinrich-Heine-Universität Düsseldorf
Universitätsstr. 1
D-40225 Düsseldorf
steins@ling.uni-duesseldorf.de

Wiese, Richard
Institut für Germanistische Sprachwissenschaft
Philipps-Universität Marburg
Wilhelm-Röpke-Str. 6A
D-35032 Marburg
wiese@mailer.uni-marburg.de

Wurmbrand, Susi
Department of Linguistics
MIT, E39-245
USA-Cambridge, MA 02139
susi@mit.edu